THE FIRST BRITISH EMPIRE

THE FIRST BRITISH EMPIRE

GLOBAL EXPANSION IN THE EARLY MODERN AGE

JOHN OLIPHANT

AMBERLEY

For Zoya and Maya, Dougie and Maggie, future readers and beneficiaries of good History

First published 2023

Amberley Publishing
The Hill, Stroud
Gloucestershire, GL5 4EP

www.amberley-books.com

Copyright © John Oliphant, 2023

The right of John Oliphant to be identified as the Author of this work has been asserted in accordance with the Copyright, Designs and Patents Act 1988.

All rights reserved. No part of this book may be reprinted or reproduced or utilised in any form or by any electronic, mechanical or other means, now known or hereafter invented, including photocopying and recording, or in any information storage or retrieval system, without the permission in writing from the Publishers.

British Library Cataloguing in Publication Data.
A catalogue record for this book is available from the British Library.

ISBN 978 1 4456 9680 5 (hardback)
ISBN 978 1 4456 9681 2 (ebook)

1 2 3 4 5 6 7 8 9 10

Typesetting by SJmagic DESIGN SERVICES, India.
Printed in the UK.

Contents

Preface	7
Introduction	10

Part I: Origins

1. Turbulent Frontiers: The British Isles, 1558-1603	19
2. Piracy, Mines and Abortive Plantations, 1558-1604	26

Part II: Toeholds, 1603-1651

3. Empire and the British Revolutions	39
4. Mainland North America: The Conquest of the Chesapeake	45
5. New England: Pequots, Puritans, Fish and Furs	53
6. The Caribbean, 1604-*c.*1651: Privateers, Pirates and Plantations	62
7. Eastern Enterprise	69

Part III: Expansion, 1651-1713

8. Republic, Restoration and War	77
9. Mainland North America: The South and the Middle Colonies	88
10. New England, Hudson's Bay and the Clash with New France	94
11. The Caribbean: Sugar, Slaves and Conquest	102
12. West Africa and the Growth of the Atlantic Slave Trade	110
13. Asian Enclaves	117

Part IV: Global Power? 1713-1763

14. From Utrecht to Paris	125
15. Mainland North America: from Salutary Neglect to Imperial Intervention, 1713-1754	134

16. Mainland North America: The French and
    Indian War, 1754-1763   145
17. The Caribbean: Slave Economies and Great Power Contests 153
18. The Indian Bridgeheads, *c.* 1713-*c.* 1765   164
19. West Africa, 1713-1763: Slaves, Guns and Wars   173

Part V: Crisis, 1756-1783

20. From Triumph to Defeat, 1763-1783   181
21. The Origins of the American Revolution, 1755-1775   192
22. The Global War of American Independence, 1775-1783   202
23. Canada and Florida: Colonies of Conquest   214
24. West Indies, 1763-1783   220
25. India: from Clive to Hastings   228
26. West Africa, 1763-1783   234
27. Reconnaissance: British Penetration of the Pacific   238

Part VI: Recovery and Survival, 1783-1815

28. From Crisis to Triumph   247
29. India: The Rise to Dominance   257
30. Australasia: Settlement, Invasion, Resistance   264
31. The Atlantic Empire Reconstructed   273

Epilogue: A New British Empire?   284
Endnotes   289
Suggested Further Reading   302
Index   309

Preface

Historians have a duty to disclose their methodology and deliberations to their readers. In an age of excited discussion of aspects of imperial history, that duty is particularly pressing. This book is intended to offer a comprehensive, non-partisan, single-volume introduction to the early modern British empire between *c.* 1558 and *c.* 1815.

I have chosen a narrative approach divided by period. The period sections are subdivided into regional chapters for those with a particular geographical interest. Within that structure I have tried to explain some of the themes and debates exercising the minds of professional historians.

The term 'first British empire', for example, comes from the notion that British imperialism changed fundamentally after the disaster of the American Revolution, and indeed was lucky to survive at all. Yet it did survive, substituted an Asian for an Atlantic focus and expanded dramatically. Whether that transformation was really so dramatic is one of the many unsettled questions the reader will encounter here.

'Doing history' is a little like trying to solve a dynamic jigsaw puzzle with many pieces missing and a box lid either lost or defaced. Diligent research and luck might uncover some lost pieces of knowledge, supposing we search in the right places; but we will never have them all, so that it's often unclear where a particular piece should fit. Therefore, historical understanding advances through evidence-based debate; and such debate depends upon a willingness to consider all the evidence, weigh every viewpoint, and to modify one's position in the face of stronger interpretations.

Sound historical knowledge and understanding matter more than ever in an age of 'culture wars' and 'cancel culture' where, as Professor David Olusoga puts it, history is treated as a repository of handy myths to be 'raided and deployed for political usage'. Nine decades after W. C. Sellar and R. J. Yeatman's *1066 and All That* pilloried nationalist myths (Britain

The First British Empire

as 'top nation') and ill-informed moral absolutism (Good Kings and Bad Kings) the targets of their satire are with us in intensified form. This book is written in the belief that there is still a popular appetite for accuracy, nuance, balance and the fruits of scholarship.

Three themes run throughout this work: collaboration and resistance, the vulnerability of most early modern British colonies, and the strategic role of the empire in balancing Britain's weakness in Europe. In each case I have tried to introduce the reader to the relevant debates and to offer a tentative direction of travel.

British expansion cannot be accounted for in largely Anglocentric terms, nor even in terms of core and periphery, metropole and colonies of settlement. Historians must consider the societies being invaded and conquered and analyse the experience of empire from a 'subaltern' perspective. This is a complex undertaking; especially as imperial opportunity was determined by variable local conditions. In India, collaborators were far more important than firearms. Biological and ecological factors – imported diseases, animals and ways of farming – devastated indigenous North American and Australian societies. Everywhere, armed resistance to invasion was prolonged and formidable – conquest was never inevitable.

Indeed, the early British empire was very fragile and vulnerable. The first North American settlements failed in the face of hunger, disease and Native American strength. Caribbean settlement was only possible in zones beyond the immediate reach of Spanish power and on islands already cleared of formidable native populations; and by 1700 slave resistance was an unrelenting reality and slave revolution a constant possibility. Until the mid-eighteenth century the East India Company was confined to tiny enclaves at the mercy of the Mughal empire and its successor states. West African factories were hemmed in by, and dependent upon, powerful coastal kingdoms. And there was always the danger of overwhelming rival European descents.

For the empire's underlying function was strategic, a means of compensating for the fundamental weakness of the British kingdoms, even after the Anglo-Scottish Union of 1707. Great Britain and Ireland were not a great power until 1763, and even then were far less powerful than France, and terrifyingly weaker than a combination of Bourbon France and Spain, a nightmare that became reality during the War of American Independence.

I am indebted to all those who in my long apprenticeship to the historian's trade have offered their guidance and insights, and others who have influenced my work as a qualified craftsman. Juliane Horn, Jane Sanderson. Jane McMahon and Lucy Wintle gave me confidence that I could write for the non-specialist reader. Of the many former students who refined my teaching and understanding of imperial history, I must

Preface

mention Barbara Bielecka and Nhi Kieu, whose keen intelligence and continuing friendship keeps my own mind alert and even young. Connor Stait at Amberley exercised immense patience in what proved to be the very long gestation of this book. Finally, as ever, I have to thank my wife for her forbearance, encouragement and occasional proof-reading.

Last, but crucially, I am grateful for the numerous scholars whose expertise ranges far beyond my own research field of the Native American frontier and the British Army, and upon whose work I have so copiously drawn. While I hope that this volume will provide a newcomer's gateway to their specialist work, any shortcomings it may contain are mine and not theirs.

Introduction

The British Isles entered the oceanic empire business rather late. The English colonial empire that was conceived after 1558 and grew up in the long seventeenth century was part of the great European expansion that J. H. Parry called the Age of Reconnaissance,[1] and which began two hundred years earlier. That transformative expansion marks the watershed between the medieval and modern worlds.

European expansion began with the completion of the centuries-long Christian reconquest of the Iberian Peninsula by the Crowns of Portugal, Castile and Aragon. The Aragonese kingdoms carried their crusading, commerce and empire building east into the Mediterranean, but Portugal and Castile possessed long Atlantic coastlines. Their deeply ingrained crusading traditions carried over into attacks upon the North African Islamic states and efforts to reach their West African sources of gold, ivory, slaves and pepper. In the very long run, these religious, economic and geopolitical goals were expressed in attempts to outflank the Ottoman Empire and its dominance of the overland trades with Asia.

Beginning in 1415, the Portuguese had invaded Morocco, colonised Madeira, the Cape Verde Islands and the Azores, explored the coast of West Africa, tapped into its gold and slave exports and found the Cape route to Asia around the tip of Africa. In the early sixteenth century they built a network of Indian Ocean bases and commercial enclaves sustained by naval force and diverted a significant portion of the trades in spices from the Red Sea and Gulf to their Cape route. In the early sixteenth century they acquired an American colony in Brazil. From 1492, Spain, or rather the Castilians, completed the conquest of the Canary Islands, begun as early as 1402, and began to explore the westward transatlantic route to Asia, only to find their way barred by the gigantic double land mass of the Americas. By 1540 they had occupied the larger Caribbean Islands, conquered the fantastic wealth of Mexico and Peru, and made

Introduction

Spain the dominant land and naval power of Europe. While there were sporadic attempts to find an alternative route to Asia through the Arctic, the English hunt for colonies did not begin until well into the reign of Elizabeth I (1558-1603) and the first permanent colony was not founded until 1609, in the time of her successor James I.

That is not to say that there were no English seaborne ventures, but they were intermittent and tiny in scale. In the 1490s Henry VII sponsored several westward voyages in hopes of finding an Arctic passage to Asia well away from the claims of his Spanish allies. The first three expeditions were undertaken by an Italian navigator based in Bristol, John Cabot. The earliest voyage was abortive and the second involved only one small ship, the *Matthew*, and a crew of perhaps twenty seamen. Cabot made landfall somewhere on the North American coast, most likely on Newfoundland or Cape Breton Island, and claimed it for Henry VII – almost certainly without contact with any Native Americans. The third voyage was made by a flotilla of five ships, one of which turned back and the other four were once supposed to have been lost at sea. The Cabot Project team at the University of Bristol has now assembled evidence suggesting that at least part of the expedition may have returned safely, leaving a settlement behind in North America. If so, it was short-lived and never followed up. In 1508-1509 John's son Sebastian seems to have reached the mouth of Hudson Bay, which he thought might be the beginning of a passage to Asia and explored southwards as far as Chesapeake Bay. The attempt to find a north-western passage to Asia well away from Spanish claims having failed, and Henry VII having been succeeded by Eurocentric Henry VIII, both the Crown and private enterprise lost interest.

The only significant enterprise in this period was an attempt by Sir Hugh Willoughby and Richard Chancellor to find a north-east passage to Asia. Willoughby and his companions were killed by the Arctic winter while Chancellor entered the White Sea, landed near present-day Murmansk, and travelled overland to the court of Ivan the Terrible at Moscow. The result was the Muscovy Company, formed to trade English woollens and weapons for Muscovy's furs, but no settlements and no colonial frontier.

The English, Scots and Irish were therefore almost two centuries behind the imperial game. Why was this so?

Geography and technology

Part of the answer lies in geography. Whereas the Iberian states were well-placed to exploit the clockwise Atlantic wind systems, the English were on its north-western fringes. Possession of the right combinations of technology and skills was once thought to be crucial, and it is true that until the mid-sixteenth century very few deep sea navigators were English. But that begs the question as to why, if the need was there, these skills were not acquired. Conversely, one may wonder why the Chinese, possessed of maritime technologies at least as sophisticated as those available to Europeans, did not set about building a global seaborne empire.

The Iberian caravel was an ideal vessel for long-range reconnaissance, but it seems to have evolved as a result of the great fifteenth-century voyages, not before them. The *caravela latina* carried a single lateen (triangular) sail on each of up to three masts, giving it great agility and remarkable ability to work into a foul wind, making it a much more satisfactory vessel for West African coasts than the square rigged *barca*. By 1487, as voyages grew ever longer, the *caravela redonda* (round caravel) appeared. Combining manoeuvrability with power when sailing before the wind, and capable of carrying heavier artillery, she was the ideal vessel to take small crews into dangerous and possibly hostile waters. The answer, then, is that the technologies evolved in response to the economic, religious and geopolitical needs of Europeans.

If the Portuguese and Spanish could make such innovations in response to need, why not the British nations? What was lacking was adequate motivation and available resources. For in the fifteenth century England was in the process of losing a European empire.

The Hundred Years War

Since 1066 English kings had had possessions on both sides of the Channel, and although most of these provinces had been lost by 1259, they retained Gascony in Aquitaine. From 1337 to 1453 they fought a series of wars against France, later labelled 'The Hundred Years War', partly to defend Gascony but also to make good English claims to the French throne. Fortunes swayed to and fro – a series of spectacular English victories was followed after 1360 by a strong French resurgence. In October 1415, three months after the Portuguese seized the Moroccan port of Ceuta, the first European colony overseas, King Henry V's English army shattered a much larger French host at Agincourt. In 1420 the Treaty of Troyes made him heir to the French throne and after the Battle of Verneuil (1424) he controlled Normandy, Paris, and Aquitaine. Every available man, horse, ship and penny was absorbed by this titanic struggle, leaving no resources or motivation for oceanic expansion. There followed another French revival, which ended in 1453 with the expulsion of the English from the whole of France except for a small coastal enclave, the Pale of Calais. Yet the lost French lands continued to exercise a powerful fascination. Henry VIII (1509-1547) fought three wars against France in 1512-1514, 1522-1526 and 1543-1546, gaining no more than the port of Boulogne and that only for a short time. His daughter Mary I (1553-1558) went to war in alliance with her husband Philip II of Spain with, as we shall see, tragic results.

Introduction

Internal turbulence
The decline and final defeat of the English in France was rapidly followed the period of internal dynastic strife known as the Wars of The Roses. The first conflict saw feeble and incompetent Henry VI overthrown and murdered; in the second, Edward IV was defeated and exiled before returning to destroy his enemies by 1471; and the third (1483-1487) saw Edward's brother Richard III defeated and killed at the battle of Bosworth in 1485. The victor, Henry Tudor, was enthroned as King Henry VII and crushed a rebellion at Stoke in 1487. When Columbus first sailed westward in 1492 Henry was still not secure on his throne. and in 1497 he faced three revolts and a potential Scottish invasion.

Under his successor Henry VIII, there was an East Anglian rising in resistance to a forced loan and a major upheaval, the Pilgrimage of Grace, in response to the dissolution of the smaller monasteries in 1536. 1549 saw a series of major risings in the West Country, Buckinghamshire and Oxfordshire and East Anglia. In 1554 a rebellion against Mary I's proposed marriage to Philip of Spain swept through Kent and penetrated to the Ludgate in London.

While many of these rebellions were dangerous and distracting, they cannot wholly explain the lack of serious English oceanic enterprise before 1558. None were successful, none evolved into prolonged civil war and in between there were long periods of relative stability. A much stronger factor was opportunity for colonisation within the British Isles.

British frontiers
The end of the *reconquistas*, and the consequent dearth of conquerable lands where a down-at-heel noble might carve out a fief, drove the Portuguese and Spaniards to the frontiers of Asia, Africa and America. Within the British Isles – the future 'core' of the British empire - there were still two turbulent frontiers and still room for internal conquest and settlement. Opportunities for expansion were particularly extensive in a land that most English people thought particularly wild, barbaric and frightening: the island of Ireland.

Ireland had been a lordship of the English king, at least in name, since 1171, and in 1541 Henry VIII had erected it into a kingdom. A Lord Deputy exercised the king's authority and under a statute known as Poynings' Law meetings and laws of the Irish parliament had to be approved in England. In reality, the Lord Deputy controlled only the Irish Pale, a small area around Dublin about thirty miles long and fifty deep. Larger territories in the south and west were held by the great Anglo-Irish feudal lords and their retainers, notably the warring Fitzgeralds and Ormondes, but most of the island was still in the hands of the native Irish chiefs. The more powerful chieftains exerted almost independent control of their own territories, maintained substantial armies, and demanded the submission of weaker neighbours by extorting tribute known as 'black rent' or 'black mail', often in the form of cattle. In the north-east, Scots mercenaries and settlers had established a deep bridgehead. For both kingdoms, Ireland was indeed a turbulent frontier.[2]

After a rebellion led in 1534 by 'Silken Thomas', the Earl of Desmond, Henry VIII not only broke Geraldine power but initiated a policy of Anglicisation intended to tame the unruly Hibernians. From 1537 the Irish were legally required to speak English and wear English clothes, and the chiefs were encouraged to adopt English farming and English houses. In the 1540s he set about taming the Irish nobility with a system historians call surrender and regrant. Gaelic chiefs were persuaded to give up their lands and the custom of succession by election; in exchange they would have English titles, hold their lands from the crown and accept inheritance by primogeniture. In theory this should have produced dynasties dependent upon the English crown for their lands and status. In practice, discontented younger sons often challenged the claims of their elder brothers in the name of Gaelic tradition, and the Pale came under attack.

Under Edward VI (1547-1553) and Mary I (1553-1558) there was a real danger of French intervention in support of rebellious nobles and chieftains, prompting English governments to maintain their Irish army at about 1,500 men, and to consider planting English settlers there. The idea was to impose English 'civility' upon a culture of 'fighting and feasting'. Under Mary I an attempt to colonise Laois and Offaly, thirty miles or so west of Dublin, was an early failure, but the direction of travel was clear. By 1558 the English Crown was committed to the conquest and colonisation of this threateningly turbulent island.

There was no prospect of colonising Scotland, at least not in the short term, but it presented complex problems which made it an object of military intervention and potential conquest. While the Anglo-Scottish border was the scene of frequent cattle raids and military incursions in both directions, Scotland itself had an untamed frontier in the Western Isles and in north Ireland, a frontier which successive Scottish kings strained to subdue. Henry VII tackled the problem of the border – where French-inspired invasion was a constant possibility – by marrying his daughter Margaret to James IV of Scotland in 1503. That did not prevent her husband, under pressure from France, to respond to Henry's declaration of war by attacking England. He and 10,000 Scots died at the Battle of Flodden but the threat - and cross-border raiding – remained. French influence was strengthened in 1538 when his son James V married Mary of Guise. James invaded England in 1542, only to be heavily defeated at Solway Moss in November. James's daughter Mary, born days before his death in December 1542, was now an infant queen.

Introduction

By the 1543 Treaty of Greenwich, she was to have an English guardian until she was ten years old, after which she would be taken to live in England until her marriage to Henry's son and heir, Edward. Henry's intention was that Edward and his children would eventually rule both kingdoms – a union in which England would inevitably be the senior partner. That, combined with attachment to the French alliance and the Roman Catholic Church, is why the Scottish parliament rejected the treaty, initiating eight years of warfare known as the Rough Wooing. The English sack of Edinburgh in 1544 failed to bring the Scots to obedience, and a fresh invasion in 1547 became pointless when Mary was shipped off to France and betrothed to the Dauphin Francis, later Francis II. The English occupation of the lowlands dragged on ingloriously until 1550 and in 1554 Mary of Guise became regent. All the Rough Wooing had achieved was to bring Scotland and France close to a dynastic union which would permanently threaten England.

Religion
Whereas the Catholic crusading zeal of the *conquistadores* helped to drive the Iberians around the globe, English Catholicism lacked such a deep-rooted holy war tradition. There was no overwhelming English desire to outflank the North African states and the Ottoman empire as the Portuguese had done, or to find lands to Christianize by persuasion and force like the Spaniards. The Reformation, however, changed everything.

Early English Protestantism was a blend of a number of reformed faiths: Lutheran, Anabaptism, Zwinglianism and, from mid-century, Calvinism. The English Reformation, once regarded as a 'bottom-up' revolution, was largely a 'top-down' transformation driven by the monarchies of Henry VIII, his son Edward VI and, after a five-year reversion to Catholicism under Mary I, his younger daughter Elizabeth I. Mid-twentieth century interpretations, by relying heavily upon Church court records, made too much of clerical scandals, popular protests, and underground reform movements. Henry, who had been a violent critic and persecutor of Protestants, broke with Rome in 1533-1534 for largely dynastic and personal reasons. That is, he wanted to change wives, and with the Tudor regime still not entirely secure, he needed a male heir.

The 1534 Act of Supremacy replaced papal supremacy with that of the monarch, but otherwise did not officially change doctrine. His more radical successor, Edward VI (1547-1553) inclined to Calvinism and under him two successive Acts of Supremacy imposed two Books of Common Prayer, prescribing English-language services with a strong reformed doctrinal element. By the time of his early death English Protestants were a minority but too strong to be rooted out. His Catholic half-sister Mary I (1553-1558) burned three bishops and over three hundred lay people, but many more survived. Those able to emigrate went to Geneva and other Calvinist centres where they imbibed that uncompromising faith and brought it back to England in 1558.

Calvinism, with its doctrine of double predestination, gave its adherents a sense of being the elect, God's chosen people, and a duty to fight against the anti-Christ, the papacy. Among others, it attracted piratically minded West Country gentry and seamen, for whom anti-Spanish privateering became a religious as well as a profitable duty. Out of their predations arose the idea of establishing English bases in the Americas. In Scotland, in the form of John Knox's Presbyterian reformation, it was even more divisive, pitting a largely militantly Calvinist lowlands against a largely Catholic highland region.

Piratical patriots
That is not to say that there was no crusading zeal among English Protestants, but that zeal was directed primarily not at Islam but Catholic Spain and Catholic Ireland. In the early 1550s, under the ultra-Protestant Edward VI and Lord Protector Northumberland, predatory seamen (often West Countrymen like William Hawkins, Robert Reneger and Thomas Wyndham) preyed on shipping in the eastern Atlantic and began to challenge Portugal's West African trade monopoly.

While Mary I was in alliance with Spain, these religious pirates were constrained by fear of royal displeasure, but when Spain later evolved into the national and religious enemy, activities like theirs became associated with patriotism. It was not a big step from launching plundering raids on the Spanish empire to planning operational bases in the Americas. Oceanic expansion became a means of compensation for England's weakness in a war-torn Europe.

PART I
Origins

Ireland, c. 1603.

1

Turbulent Frontiers: The British Isles, 1558-1603

On 31 December 1557, 20,000 French troops crossed the frozen marshes into the Pale of Calais, the last remnant of what had once been a great continental English empire. English preparations had been sluggish and inadequate, and the garrison was woefully under strength. The invaders quickly occupied the Risbank Tower, a strongpoint lying between the town of Calais and the harbour entrance, effectively cutting off any hope of reinforcement. Massive batteries opened fire on the defences and on the night of 5-6 January the French stormed the castle. By the following evening the attackers were forcing their way into the town itself, and at 6 am on 7 January the governor surrendered the town with all its arms, munitions and supplies. Fifty English officers were held for ransom and 4,200 citizens were allowed to leave. Six days later the French moved against the Pale's stoutest remaining fortress at Guînes. The commander there, Lord Grey of Wilton, resisted valiantly until 20 January when the French captured the castle's outworks. Next day, with his garrison refusing to fight on, Grey surrendered and on the night of 22 January the English garrison at Hammes, the third and last Pale fortress, fled to Spanish-held St. Omer. After just a year as the active ally of her husband Philip II of Spain, Queen Mary I had lost the last fragment of a once formidable European empire and England's continental frontier was closed.[3]

It is no longer possible to assert, as traditional patriotic English histories once did, that England was now free immediately to fulfil her destiny as a maritime and imperial power. Yet the loss of Calais was a deliverance, and not merely from the enormous expense of its defence. Since 1453, the enclave had been tantalisingly reminiscent of past glories and liable to draw English monarchs into wars of recovery which, in the face of an increasingly powerful France, she was now ill-equipped to wage. Wool, which was England's major export, had passed through the Calais exchange or Staple, but most of the trade was with Philip's

Netherlands dominions. In the long run the disaster turned men's minds to the Atlantic opportunities being tentatively exploited by piratical West Country gentry, and by London-based venturers seeking a north-east passage to Asia.

That, however, was not Mary's view and she carried on with the war in hopes that Philip would regain Calais for her at the peace conference. That goal was still unachieved at her death in November, but the new queen, her half-sister Elizabeth, was no less entranced by the Calais chimera. Philip, however, appalled at the weak English war-effort, was determined to sacrifice Calais to secure more valuable Spanish goals in Italy and elsewhere. The Peace of Câteau-Cambrésis (2 April 1559) provided for the return of the Pale after eight years, failing which France would pay an indemnity of 500,000 crowns in lieu, providing England kept the peace. France would also pacify Elizabeth's frontier with France's ally Scotland. This face-saving formula did not diminish the queen's desire to reconquer Calais or at least to obtain another continental port.[4] In 1559, however, Elizabeth was on the defensive at home and abroad.

Domestically, she had to find a Protestant settlement acceptable to her subjects, two thirds of whom were conservative or Catholic in their religion. A new Act of Supremacy marked a new break with Rome, establishing the monarch as Supreme Governor of the Church of England without formally claiming the Pope's role of spiritual head. The Act of Uniformity imposed a revised Book of Common Prayer, containing a liturgy with both Catholic and Protestant elements. The sentences to be read at the giving of Communion, for example, hinted simultaneously at a Catholic 'Real Presence' of Christ in the bread and the wine, a Calvinist spiritual presence, and a Zwinglian remembrance service. Clergy were to wear vestments in the Catholic tradition and clerical marriage was tolerated. Her aim was to secure her throne by uniting as many of her people as possible behind her Church. Mandatory Sunday attendance was more important than the precise details of private belief. But most of the Marian bishops refused to accept the new order and, with a number of lesser clergy, were deprived of their livings.

Externally she was worried about the Franco-Scottish threat to her own realm in the person of her Catholic cousin, Mary, Queen of Scots. Mary, with a claim to the English throne at least as strong as Elizabeth's, was newly married to Francis, son and heir to King Henry II of France. Already Francis and Mary were displaying the intertwined arms of England and France, a calculated political statement. When in April Henry II was killed in a tournament held to celebrate the Peace of Câteau-Cambrésis, and Francis succeeded him as Francis II, the danger became even more explicit. Mary's French mother, Mary of Guise, was her regent in Scotland where she posed a constant threat to England's only land frontier. Although neither Philip II nor the Pope would yet support Mary's claim, from London the combined French, Scottish and internal threats were terrifying.[5]

Fortunately for Elizabeth, the French position in Scotland was weakened by an uprising of Calvinist nobles calling themselves the Lords of the Congregation, who appealed to Elizabeth for aid against the regent's French professionals. A militant Calvinist faction on her Privy Council urged Elizabeth to intervene openly, but the queen was not to be drawn into an open-ended ideological conflict. At first, she consented only to send a naval expedition to blockade Leith, the port of Edinburgh, where the bulk of the French troops were concentrated. Only in February 1560, when an Anglo-Scots alliance was at last formalised at Berwick, did she commit an army and then for a strictly limited objective: the capture of Leith. The attack on Leith failed, but the destruction of the French fleet in a storm, a Huguenot uprising in France itself, and the death on 10 June of Mary of Guise, brought the French to the conference table. The Treaty of Edinburgh (July 1560) provided for the evacuation of foreign troops, recognition of Elizabeth as the lawful ruler of England, for Mary to cease using English royal insignia, for the pacification of the Anglo-Scottish border, and for England to intervene in Scotland whenever its interests were threatened. Mary, unwilling to give up her claim to the English throne, refused to ratify the agreement, but the sudden death of Francis II effectively severed her from the French court and in August 1561 she returned to a Scotland partly dominated by a Calvinist reformation led by John Knox.

This weakening of the Franco-Scots connection tempted Elizabeth to try to recover a continental colonial enclave. When the Huguenots approached her for military help, she agreed to provide 6,000 troops and a loan of £30,000 in return for occupation of Le Havre and Dieppe, both already in Protestant hands, as security for the ultimate reconquest of Calais. Le Havre was duly taken over by a garrison under Ambrose Dudley, Earl of Warwick, in October 1562. Her apparent subsequent actions were, however, sadly misjudged. She refused to send her troops to the relief of nearby Caen and the town duly fell. Catholic forces were unable, however, to achieve outright victory. In December the Huguenot army was defeated at Dreux but retreated in good order; and in February-March the Catholic siege of the Protestant's base at Orleans made slow progress. With the more intransigent leaders on both sides now either killed or captured, a compromise peace was agreed in March 1563, freeing the combined French forces to turn on the English intruders. Le Havre was quickly besieged: artillery was massed against its walls and soon its fortifications were crumbling. On 28 July a badly wounded Warwick agreed to surrender. The subsequent Treaty of Troyes (April 1564) cancelled both the promised eventual return of Calais and the indemnity in lieu. Elizabeth had had her fingers badly burned and forever thereafter avoided becoming entangled in wars of religion. The episode was her last serious attempt to recover a continental enclave.[6]

The international situation was transformed by a revolt against Spanish rule in the Netherlands, and then by the arrival there in 1567 of a powerful Spanish army under the Duke of Alva. The presence of a tough Spanish army so close to England was a shock in itself, but it also raised the spectre of direct Spanish support for Catholic rebels and Mary Stuart's claim to the English throne. Mary Queen of Scots, overthrown in Scotland, fled to England where she was detained by Elizabeth and became the focus of a series of plots to place her on the English throne. An abortive Northern Rebellion in 1569 was followed by Elizabeth's formal excommunication in 1570, which in theory freed her Catholic subjects from their allegiance, and then by a Spanish-sponsored scheme to dethrone her. France and England moved from simmering hostility into uneasy alliance. In Scotland the new infant king, James VI, was raised as a Protestant and, as the unmarried queen aged, emerged as her only plausibly legitimate and non-Catholic heir. Scotland, far from being tamed by England or providing a foreign base against her, was about to absorb her more powerful neighbour.[7]

In Ireland the Lord Deputy, the earl of Sussex, was struggling with the ambition of Shane O'Neill to become 'the O'Neill', Irish ruler of Ulster. Under the surrender and regrant arrangement with Shane's father Conn, now earl of Tyrone, the succession should have passed by primogeniture to Shane's elder brother Matthew. Conn preferred Shane and the result was all-out dynastic war. Having survived a clumsy military intervention by Sussex in 1557, in 1558 Shane had Matthew murdered by his allies the Scots Macdonnells and drove his father into exile in the Pale. When Conn died in 1559, Shane immediately sued for recognition as earl of Tyrone. Sussex responded with a second fruitless campaign and a third in 1561, during which his rear guard was ambushed. After each campaign, Sussex submitted a plan for the systematic colonisation and military subjugation of Ireland – but he was no nearer that goal in 1561 than in 1557.

Sussex's failure to defeat Shane caused Elizabeth to summon him to London, where the two sides negotiated from January to May 1562. Shane insisted that the surrender and regrant of 1542 was not an act of grace by the Crown, but a treaty between the Crown and the elected head of the O'Neills. Consequently, he was earl of Tyrone by right. That would have undermined the whole purpose of the surrender and regrant system, which was to remove the Gaelic succession custom and place the Irish lords more firmly under English control. The talks reached an impasse which could only be resolved by war. Shane was allowed to depart under safe conduct but both sides prepared for armed conflict.[8]

Shane set about violently asserting his authority over the subordinate Ulster clans and attacked the Macdonnells, who were alarmed at his wooing of the English crown. Sussex now tried (and failed) to have Shane poisoned and a belated attempt at appeasement foundered when the O'Neill pitched his demands too high. A fourth invasion of Ulster in 1563 was no more successful than the others, and soon Shane was plotting with Mary, Queen of Scots and trying to obtain French military support. In 1567 Sidney's Irish ally Hugh O'Donnell surprised and defeated Shane, who fled to the Macdonnells. They cut his throat and send his pickled head to Dublin. Even that did not end O'Neill intransigence: through alliances with both O'Donnells and Macdonnells, Shane's successor Turlough recruited vast numbers of Scots mercenaries and gradually established his authority across Ulster.

Clearly, until Ireland was pacified the Pale could not be secure and foreign intervention would always be likely – all the more so now that Alva was in the Netherlands. Sussex responded with yet another plan for the conquest and colonisation of Ireland, possibly inspired by Spanish practice in the Americas, which was taken up and modified by the next Lord Deputy, Sir Henry Sidney. Sidney wanted to establish small colonies across Ireland, using lands confiscated from rebels or still in the hands of surviving monasteries. For north-eastern Ulster, with its Scottish incursions and potential for resistance, he planned something much larger and disruptive: a plantation of 2,000 settlers on the Ards peninsula east of the River Bann. It attracted not the hoped-for aristocratic supporters but land-hungry, predatory West Country expansionists such as Sir Peter Carew, Humphrey Gilbert and Sir Richard Grenville – all of them survivors of Kett's rebellion against Mary Tudor and veterans of Warwick's occupation of Le Havre – and who were in turn connected to Francis Drake and his Hawkins cousins. A neighbouring enterprise under Walter Devereux, first earl of Essex, had significant West Country support. Drake made a devastating raid on a Scots base, Rathlin Island, that ended in a massacre of civilians. Grenville and other West Country men backed an attempted plantation in Munster.[9] In short, these ventures appealed to those violent Calvinists who were already, or were to become, involved in Atlantic piracy and plans for American bases.

Underfunded, poorly managed and without permanent English garrisons, these plantations were all disasters. The Ards peninsula enterprise, chaotically organised by Sir Thomas Smith and incompetently led by his son, failed quickly and both Smiths were killed. Essex persevered until 1576, demonstrating once again that while English armies could raid through Ulster they could not hold it down. In Munster, already devastated by a private war between Gerald, Earl of Desmond and Thomas Butler, Earl of Ormond, ran headlong into a revolt by Desmond's cousin, James Fitzmaurice Fitzgerald. In June 1568, after Desmond was imprisoned, Fitzmaurice appealed for Catholic and foreign backing. and his cause spread rapidly across the whole south-west, aided by resentment at the arrival of the English Protestant settlers in February 1569. In any case, each of these projects threatened to replace one set of overmighty subjects with another.

The Munster settlement projectors, including Grenville and one of Sidney's clients, wanted Elizabeth to finance the venture and give them letters patent granting them all the native Irish lands in Munster, including the entire south-west coast, the right to trade with any country not at war with England, and complete powers of governance over their plantation. In other words, they wanted independence and the Queen's licence to plunder at will. Elizabeth was not about to sanction such a state within a state, and she thought that compromise with the Gaelic chiefs would involve less expense and fewer commitments. When Fitzmaurice finally surrendered in 1572, he was pardoned and Desmond released from his English prison and returned to Ireland.[10] The queen had chosen collaboration over conquest. Nevertheless, she was about to be sucked deeper than ever into the Irish bogs.

For Desmond and Fitzmaurice, submission was merely a ruse. Desmond began openly to prepare for another rebellion while Fitzmaurice left Ireland to seek French and Spanish assistance. Their activities, together with the Atlantic depredations of English pirates and interlopers (see Chapter 3) and Elizabeth's support for a new Dutch revolt, made Spanish intervention in Ireland all too likely. In 1579 Ireland was invaded by Fitzmaurice and an English papal nuncio, supported by papal money and Spanish and Italian troops, and joined by Desmond himself. Munster and Leinster rose and there were further upheavals as far away as Ulster. It took 6,500 English troops and a new and brutally ruthless Lord Deputy, Lord Grey of Wilton, to break the rebellion. Summary executions, burned crops and slaughtered cattle spread famine far and wide, and cleared the way for the systematic colonisation of Munster and Connaught. Begun in 1586 on Desmond's forfeited Munster estates, grants of 4,000 to 12,000 acres were awarded to thirty-four English landlords, who were obliged to bring in English tenants. Although only 775 out of a projected 1,760 tenancies had been taken up by 1589, so that the new gentry had to recruit Irish tenants and labourers after all, the plantation was already a viable economic entity. The Connaught plantation based on the 'composition' method was more successful, but both were disrupted by another massive upheaval in Ulster.

Hugh O'Neill's rebellion of 1593-1603, the Nine Years' War as it is known in Ireland,[11] was the most dangerous challenge to English authority, the one that finally convinced a reluctant and parsimonious Elizabeth that a complete and final conquest was essential. Fearing for his position in Ulster, he turned to arms in 1593, quickly raising a formidable force of 1,000 pikemen, 4,000 musketeers and 1,000 horse. Elizabeth, as usual, hesitated: raising an army of her own but fearing the expense of an

Turbulent Frontiers: The British Isles, 1558-1603

actual campaign she made a truce with O'Neill, thus giving him time to seek foreign support. The Armada sent against both England and Ireland in 1596 failed to arrive but O'Neill was able to widen his Ulster revolt into an Irish war of independence. In 1598 he destroyed an English army at the battle of the Yellow Ford, the Munster plantation was obliterated and rebels took control of Connaught. More than one historian has noted the parallel between the English position in Ireland in 1599 and that confronting Spain in the Netherlands.

Elizabeth was forced to recognize that Ireland must finally be conquered, but her first choice of military commander was unfortunate. Robert Devereaux, second Earl of Essex, was essentially a flashy and ambitious courtier whose star was already on the wane. Given over 17,000 troops, he preferred a march through Leinster and Munster to an invasion of Ulster, made a truce with O'Neill and raced uninvited back to London to justify his actions. While he was gone – to disgrace, rebellion and execution – O'Neill swept south to the port of Kinsale.

The new English commander, Charles Blount, Lord Mountjoy, was a different proposition. His armies reconquered the south, pushed O'Neill back into Ulster and devastated rebel crops and farms. The sudden appearance at Kinsale of 3,400 Spanish veterans seemed to turn the tide yet again, forcing Mountjoy to hurry south to besiege the port. O'Neill followed and by 21 December 1602 he had the disease-ridden English army caught between his own force and the Spanish garrison. Tactically, however, Mountjoy was more than a match for him. Attacking as O'Neill's army deployed, he routed the Irishmen while the Spaniards sat tight behind their fortifications. Tyrone had to retire to Ulster leaving the Spanish no option but to surrender on 2 January. O'Neill sustained a guerrilla resistance for a few months before submitting on 30 March 1603 (just six days after Elizabeth died). Mountjoy gave him generous terms: recognition as sole lord of Ulster under the Crown and a pledge that the Crown would henceforth rule through trusted nobles.

The conquest of Ireland may be seen as a precursor of colonisation in the Americas. It involved many of those already involved in privateering and in scheming to seize or found naval bases sited to prey on Spanish colonies and shipping. It was brought about through military force, by exploiting divisions within Ireland, and by the recruitment of collaborators. In terms of religion and culture it remained separate from England, yet also part of the British Isles core that would establish dependencies around the world.

2

Piracy, Mines and Abortive Plantations, 1558–1604

Queen Elizabeth I (1558-1603) was not naturally predisposed to anti-Spanish marauding. With her fixation upon recovering Calais, and the threatened combination of a Franco-Scottish pincer offensive with a Catholic uprising in favour of Mary, her real enemy was France. Spain was therefore more valuable as a friend than as an enemy. Elizabeth's problem was to keep the two Catholic powers apart whilst ensuring the loyalty of her own people – two thirds of whom were either Catholic or conservative in their religion. Thus ambition, security, and her own spiritual leanings, led to her moderate Protestant religious settlement of 1559,[12] which might be acceptable to her Catholic subjects and to Spain.

Unfortunately for her, as touched upon earlier, only one of the Marian bishops accepted the new dispensation, so the rest had to be deprived of their livings. About two hundred lesser clergy were deprived or resigned for their Catholicism and as many again went for other reasons. Elizabeth had now to fall back upon returned Calvinist exiles for whom the new settlement was too popish. Their resistance began with a massive iconoclasm - vestments, rood lofts and crucifixes were incinerated by her own parish visitors – and continued with a bitter dispute over clerical dress.[13] These internal pressures combined with a growing threat from Spain in Europe and with the provocative actions of Calvinist seamen, to push her external policy in a more radically Protestant direction. That in turn led to the idea of securing naval bases in North America and even to the prospect of an English empire well clear of Spanish interference. By the late 1570s there was even an emerging theory of empire.

The idea of a powerful and extensive maritime reach was promoted at Court by John Dee, astronomer, astrologer, scientist, geographer and adviser to Elizabeth I. Dee's influence mattered because although hordes of pirates took to the seas, the Crown's support proved essential for long-distance expeditions, for colonising ventures and for exploration.

Piracy, Mines and Abortive Plantations, 1558-1604

Dee's *General and Rare Memorials pertayning to the Perfect Arte of Navigation* (1577) called for naval dominance around the British Isles, as far north as Shetland and as far west as the coasts of North America. Though his vision of a 'British Impire' did not embrace the need for self-supporting bases in America, Richard Hakluyt 'the Elder' (*c*. 1530-1591) made that connection and became an enthusiast for colonisation. So was Hakluyt's cousin Richard 'the Younger' (*c*. 1552 -1616) – cleric, geographer, prolific author and editor – who was close to Francis Walsingham and later to Robert Cecil, son and successor to Elizabeth's chief minister.

Interlopers
In 1562 John Hawkins undertook a slaving expedition to West Africa with the idea of selling his captives in Spanish America and loading his ships with colonial exports such as leather. He used a show of force to persuade the Spanish colonial authorities to accept his illicit cargoes of much-needed labour and to allow him to load exports, for which existing Spanish shipping was inadequate. Elizabeth could see advantages in this approach: for his second voyage in 1564 she lent him an ageing ship, *Jesus of Lubeck*, in return for a large share of the expected profits. Though she did not give Hawkins a royal commission, she effectively licensed him to breach the Portuguese and Spanish commercial monopolies. Yet she was not about to risk a naval conflict with Spain. In 1566, reacting to Spanish objections, her privy council forbade Hawkins to lead a third voyage. That venture was commanded by one Richard Lovell, who found the Portuguese and Spanish authorities now very reluctant to do business. In 1566 the suppression of a serious Dutch revolt against Spanish rule by local forces seemed to prove the wisdom of treating Spain with extreme caution.[14]

But Philip II had already dispatched the Duke of Alva with a veteran force by way of Italy, Switzerland and the Rhine – the 'Spanish Road'. Alva's arrival in 1567 changed everything. Acting as if as if he were a vice-regal consul, he set up a special court, the Council of Troubles, and proceeded to hunt down and execute rebels and Protestants. William of Orange, the exiled principal Dutch leader, could do no more than issue letters of marque, licences to prey on Spanish shipping, to multi-national bands of pirates and to Dutch freebooters – the *Watergeuzen* or Sea Beggars – based on the French Huguenot port of La Rochelle. From London the situation looked terrifying. The greatest naval power in Europe had massed 8,000 crack troops, rapidly reinforced to about 40,000, within a hundred and forty miles of London in an apparent anti-Protestant crusade. In 1568 the danger was compounded by the arrival in England of the fugitive Queen of Scots. From then until her execution in 1587, Mary was to be the focus of Catholic-Spanish plots to unseat Elizabeth.

The First British Empire

Elizabeth's reaction, or rather that of her adviser Robert Cecil, was of provocation short of confrontation. While eschewing direct intervention, she allowed the Beggars to sell plunder and refit ships in English ports. When Alva's pay ships sought refuge in Cornish harbours, she 'borrowed' the money – after all, it really belonged to Philip II's bankers. A northern rising in favour of Mary, her own excommunication by the Pope in 1570, and even an ill-conceived plot involving English Catholics, Spain, and the Papacy, failed to move her. Instead, in 1572 she yielded to Spanish pressure and expelled the Beggars from English ports. The Beggars' subsequent seizure of the port of Brill and the immediate outbreak of a fresh Dutch revolt attracted only her covert support. Nevertheless, much against her will, she was becoming locked into the European ideological struggle – and that in turn led her to sanction private naval operations against Spain.

As early as 1568 she and the privy council had not only decided to allow Hawkins to sail, but to lend him the old *Jesus* and another royal ship, the *Minion*. The queen was prompted by a tale of a rich gold mine south of the Portuguese enclave of El Mina on the Guinea coast. Could not the English establish their own gold-yielding colony there? No-one else took the story seriously, and the mine project became a blind for yet another interloping venture. Spain saw through it: just as Hawkins was preparing to sail, seven Spanish ships entered Plymouth Sound and bore down on his anchored squadron. They withdrew when the English vessels opened fire, but the attempt at intimidation was plain to see. Elizabeth reprimanded Hawkins for firing first, but she did not withdraw her support, and did not forbid him to proceed.[15]

Against stiffening resistance by Portuguese and Spanish officials, Hawkins managed to gather a cargo of slaves on the Guinea coast and to sell them in the West Indies. He then retired to San Juan d' Ulloa on the Gulf of Mexico for repairs, only to be interrupted by the appearance of the annual outward-bound convoy from Spain. On board was the Viceroy of Mexico himself who – unlike the local functionaries – had both the will and the means to enforce the Spanish monopoly. A truce allowed the thirteen Spanish ships to enter the harbour unmolested, but after two days they launched a fierce assault on the English flotilla. Hawkins and his cousin Francis Drake were lucky to escape and Drake, a militant Calvinist, was bent on revenge.[16] Thereafter Elizabeth began to issue letters of reprisal – licences to seek redress from a foreign power by force – and more general warrants to prey on Spanish shipping. The raids that followed aimed at plunder, seizing the key nodal points of the silver and gold traffic, and at establishing bases close to Spanish territory. They demonstrated that while English marauders could often surprise ports and seize eye-watering quantities of silver and gold, they could not hold key enclaves in the face of Spanish counter-measures.

Piracy, Mines and Abortive Plantations, 1558–1604

Raiders

A favourite target was the overland route between Panama City on the Pacific and Nombre de Dios on the Gulf of Mexico. In 1572 Francis Drake attacked Nombre de Dios, too late to intercept that year's silver, and was driven off. He remained on the coast, however, and in 1573 met a noted French Protestant explorer, mapmaker and privateer, Guillaume Le Testu, who commanded an 80-ton ship and brought news of the 1572 St Bartholomew's Day massacre of Huguenots in Paris. Drake and Le Testu joined forces and with the support of *cimarrones*, escaped black slaves fighting a guerrilla war against the Spanish, set out for a second attempt on the Isthmus. For the first time, local collaborators were playing a key role.[17]

This time they bypassed Nombre de Dios. In February 1573 a raiding party led by Drake and Le Testu landed eighteen miles away and pushed inland over mountains and through jungle to the Panama road. There, on I April, they ambushed a gold- and silver-laden mule train and drove off the escort. The haul was prodigious, about twenty tons of precious metal, far more than the tiny expedition could carry. Burying what they could not remove, Drake and Le Testu made for the coast and their boats. The Spanish pursuit was hot – the wounded Le Testu was captured and beheaded – and in the end most of the booty had to be abandoned. Drake reached home with just five per cent of the silver. But it was enough to make him rich and famous and to obscure the facts that Nombre de Dios had not been taken and the mule train raid had been a near-disaster.[18]

Later attacks on the Isthmus proved far less successful from the outset. Fearing that a fresh English assault might cost them Nombre de Dios or even Panama City, the Spaniards strengthened their defences. In 1576 John Oxenham, one of Drake's former comrades, tested their preparations with an expedition against Panama City. Marching overland he wintered with the *cimarrones*, constructed a large cedar boat and sailed down-river into the Pacific. Here, in 1577, he surprised and captured two small treasure-bearing ships, but was later tracked down by local Spanish forces. Wounded and with most of his men dead, Oxenham fled inland, only to be captured the following year and executed in Lima in 1580. There was no further serious attempt on the Isthmus until after the terminal at Nombre de Dios had been moved to nearby Porto Bello. In 1601 William Parker attacked and took the place but was unable to hold it for more than a day. He withdrew with substantial booty – enough to make him Mayor of Plymouth and subsequently a founder member of the Virginia Company – but that was the extent of his achievement.[19] Clearly, while the English could sometimes launch damaging raids, they could not permanently seize the bases that would have given them control of the silver traffic.

The most spectacular voyage of all had nothing to do with empire-building. Conceived in Drake's brain or among the hard-line Calvinist crusaders at Court, it was nothing less than a raid against the relatively undefended settlements and shipping on the Pacific coast of South and Central America. The most tempting targets were the seaborne silver traffic between Peru and Panama, and the annual Manila galleon that sailed from Acapulco to the Philippines laden with silver and returned laden with Asian goods. Another goal, perhaps originally even more important than plunder, was to gather geographical information. Elizabeth herself secretly approved and invested her own money in the expedition. To confuse the enemy, she granted Drake a patent for settlement in any lands not already claimed by Spain, but colonisation was never part of the scheme. Drake sailed from Plymouth in December 1577 with five ships. His own galleon was named *Pelican* on Elizabeth's instruction, in honour of her favourite religious symbol, a calculated mark of her approval.

The late start led to early losses and severe delays. In September 1578, now with only three ships, he entered Magellan Strait where violent storms destroyed one vessel and forced another to return home. He seems to have coasted the western side of Tierra del Fuego and may possibly have sighted Cape Horn. Pressing on in the *Pelican*, now renamed *Golden Hind*, Drake began to attack settlements and shipping along the Chilean coast. Valparaiso was sacked. Off Lima he seized a vessel laden with Peruvian gold and a little later intercepted the Manila galleon with its twenty-six tons of silver. Cruising north along the coast of California he finally turned west towards the East Indies. After loading a cargo of spices in the Moluccas he sailed for home via the Cape of Good hope, reaching Plymouth in September 1580 – an apparently miraculous resurrection long after he had been presumed dead.[20]

Drake's reappearance coincided with a frightening intensification of the threat from Spain. Parma, the new Spanish commander in the Netherlands, was making serious gains; Phillip was funding the Catholic League in the French Wars of Religion; in 1579 a Spanish force had landed in Ireland; and in 1580 Philip enforced his claim to Portugal by arms. Invasion might not be very far away. Elizabeth's own galleons may have been at the cutting edge of naval technology, but there were not many of them, and it was by no means certain that they could win a fleet action. In a risky demonstration of defiance, she knighted Drake on the deck of the *Golden Hind* at Deptford. Her message was clear: England's naval reach and ambition were greatly extended. Should the Spanish threaten England, she would attack their empire in every quarter.

Yet Drake's astonishing feat of navigation and seamanship had neither added much to geographical knowledge nor founded a colony. In later years the circumnavigation became encrusted with various imperial myths, which are still matters of dispute. Drake did not, as we have seen, find and exploit the passage to the south of Cape Horn which now bears his name. Nor did he discover and claim Elizabeth Island in Magellan Strait. He probably did not claim northern California for England as 'New Albion', and the suggestion that he left a garrison there – so far from home and without hope of relief – is bizarre in the extreme. Nor did he attempt to return by the north-west passage, the so-called 'Straits of Anian', for he turned westward well south of the limits of earlier Spanish explorations.[21]

However, Drake's next adventure did appear to aim at establishing a permanent English base in the West Indies. As usual, the queen put money into the voyage but this time she gave Drake her commission, so this was an official, public offensive. Elizabeth was looking for plunder to pay for her military intervention in the Netherlands (she concluded a formal treaty with the Dutch in 1585), and Drake's proposal to cross the Isthmus and sack Panama must have looked attractive. But Drake also wanted to take and hold Havana, the strongest and most important Spanish fortress in the New World. Havana guarded the Florida Strait, the vital homeward channel for the combined annual convoy.

This was to promote hope over experience. It is probably true that, as N. A. M. Rodger argues, the English could have taken almost any Spanish city they chose. The Spanish were on the horns of their usual strategic dilemma: they could not be strong everywhere at once, nor with any certainty anticipate the marauders' target. However, the defences of Havana were powerful. Even if it could be seized, the climate, distance and limited English resources would have made it impossible to hold against the inevitable Spanish counter-offensive. Indeed, at this point Drake may have been misled by his own vanity and by poor strategic perception. If so, once he was at sea, old habits and old realities took over. Vigo on the Spanish mainland was assaulted. The Cape Verde Islands were raided but not occupied. Santo Domingo and Cartagena were taken but not held, and disease so reduced his striking force that Havana was never attacked.[22]

Only then, indirectly and by chance, did Drake become involved in a genuine attempt at settlement. He picked up intelligence that the Spanish were planning an expedition from Florida to find and root out a small English colony established recently on Roanoke Island, a potential privateering base on the coast of modern North Carolina. Determined to disrupt the attack, he stormed and burned St Augustine, but failed to catch the garrison, his main objective. He then sailed on to warn, rearm and reinforce the Roanoke settlers. As we shall see, he found a community on the brink of internal collapse.

A Virginian venture[23]
The idea of a settlement colony well away from the centres of the Spaniards' power, yet near enough to harass them, was not new. In

1575-1576 Sir Richard Grenville proposed a new colony, probably near the Rio de la Plata on the Argentinian coast, with the dual aims of finding gold and silver mines and raiding the Spanish colonies to the north. He may also have wanted to reconnoitre Magellan Strait preparatory to penetration of the Pacific. The plan lapsed when the queen refused to back it. In 1578 Humphrey Gilbert obtained a commission to seek sites for a settlement far to the north of Spanish possessions, but he was unable to find financial backing until 1583. Sailing in June, Gilbert reached the international summer fishing settlement of St John's in Newfoundland and formally claimed the island for Elizabeth, along with all lands within 200 leagues to north and south. He then probed south along the Labrador coast and turned for home before finding land hospitable enough for settlement. His own vessel, the tiny *Squirrel,* was lost in a tempest, leaving the only surviving ship to bring the news home.

That was not the end of the matter. Walter Raleigh, another associate of Walsingham and a Court favourite since about 1581, believed that Gilbert had searched too far north. In his estimation, a settlement should be nearer Spanish targets and in a friendlier climate. He, the younger Richard Hakluyt and other backers of a new venture were thinking of the coast of 'Virginia', the coast between Florida and Chesapeake Bay, already known to Spanish and English explorers. A reconnaissance in 1584 identified Roanoke Island, tucked behind the Outer Banks, the long chain of islands off what is now North Carolina, well away from prying Spanish eyes and approached by narrow, easily defended waterways. Two Croatan Indians brought back to England may have picked up enough English to convey basic geographical, economic and even political intelligence about the region. The expedition, commanded at sea by Richard Grenville, sailed in April 1585 and reached the Outer Banks in June.

From the first there were unexpected problems. The entrances to the Sounds behind the Banks were extremely shallow, even at high tide, and vital supplies were ruined when Grenville's flagship, the *Tyger,* ran aground in one of them. The amount of cultivable land was very limited, and the season late for clearing fields and sowing crops. Much would now depend upon the willingness and ability of the indigenes to feed the settlers in the first year, and that was far from assured – in his reconnaissance of the Sounds, Grenville destroyed the town of Aquascogoc over a missing silver cup. Grenville then sailed for England and further supplies, leaving the governor, Ralph Lane, and his 107 men facing an uncertain future.

John White, the expedition's gifted artist, has given us a meticulous visual record of the native culture the settlers encountered. He shows this Iroquoian people living in well-organised towns, at least one open and with groves of trees, another tightly enclosed inside a palisade. They practised agriculture, growing maize, squash, potatoes and beans, and fished from dug-out canoes in ponds formed by weirs. Those on Roanoke were initially welcoming, perhaps because after the destruction of rival Aquascogoc the English appeared as useful allies. Such food as the islanders could afford was sold to the incomers, no doubt in return for desirable metal goods.

Some general histories of empire still assert that there was no attempt to farm and make the settlement self-supporting, that they tried to buy food from the Indians who had little surplus themselves, and so quickly wore out whatever welcome they originally had had. According to this view, the settlers were overwhelmingly gentlemen bent on plunder and gold mines, or artisans unused to husbandry and unwilling to till the soil. David Quinn's earlier, more specialised and nuanced examination demonstrates that this was not so. They do seem to have successfully bought corn to make up for stocks damaged or lost on the voyage, and this tided them over the winter adequately, if not comfortably. In the spring of 1586 the Indians gave them some seed corn, which they planted, using techniques learned or copied from the natives, in three fields each of an acre or more. The sowings were made successively to ensure a long harvest period, a method clearly illustrated in John White's annotated drawing of the town of Secotan. A progressive harvest of Indian corn from up to six acres – a crop far more heavy-yielding than wheat – could have marked an important step towards self-sufficiency. The gentlemen adventurers who had come purely for gold and refused to do other work were in a decided minority.

On the other hand, relations with the Indians did indeed turn sour. While the corn grew both settlers and Indians were short of food, so the spring and summer of 1586 was a hungry time, with the English reduced to scouring beaches for shellfish. Lane's daily demands for food drove the Indians first into abandoning the island and then into a plan concerted with neighbouring towns to wipe the settlement out. A bloody pre-emptive strike by Lane averted immediate disaster but at the cost of permanent native hostility. The promised re-supply from England failed to appear, and the search for gold, silver and copper – any of which would have created a prosperous export trade – yielded nothing substantial.

When Drake arrived, he found a settlement weaker than he had been led to believe: hungry, demoralised, barely a hundred men rather than three hundred. The defence he had hoped to establish was clearly unviable. After conferring with Lane, he agreed to provide a ship to take the weak and sickly (and perhaps the discontented) directly home, and to lend the governor a small vessel, the *Francis*, with which to explore Chesapeake Bay for a better site. The plan was frustrated by a gigantic three-day storm accompanied by huge hailstones. Anchors were lost, cables were snapped or cut, and four of Drake's largest ships had to run out to sea to avoid destruction. The *Francis* vanished, leaving the settlement without a craft suited to inshore exploration. Lane gave up his Chesapeake expedition and went home with Drake and all the remaining colonists.

A second attempt, launched in 1577 under John White, was intended for Chesapeake Bay, but in the event the settlers were landed at Roanoke, with all its problems. The Roanoke Indians were at best uncommunicative, at worst hostile. Towards the end of the year the situation was so desperate that White sailed for England to find relief. However, the Armada emergency prevented a resupply mission in 1588 and it was not until 1590 that White was able to hitch a ride with one of Raleigh's privateering expeditions. He found a deserted settlement. The houses were intact but empty and stripped of everything, such as window frames and door locks, that might be useful elsewhere. There was no sign of fire or violence, suggesting that all or most of the settlers might have made a planned departure for the Chesapeake. The only other clue, the word 'Croatoan' carved into a gatepost in the palisade, pointed to a different destination: Croatoan Island some fifty miles to the south, where White himself had restored amicable relations with the natives. Plans to investigate both Croatoan and the Chesapeake were frustrated by foul weather and after several attempts the flotilla decamped on its privateering mission. The lost colonists were never seen again.

Perhaps the Roanoke settlers were driven away by Spaniards, hunger, native hostility, or disease. It may be that some deliberately set out for the Chesapeake, but a later Spanish expedition found no sign of English activity there. Possibly a small party stayed on Roanoke, only to be expelled by some unexpected event, and then absorbed into a native community such as the Croatoans. The archaeological evidence is still thin and inconclusive, so all such explanations are speculative. What is certain is that both in 1585-86 and in 1587-90 war and plunder took precedence over settlement. The very conditions that had prompted settlement prevented its success.

The lure of the East

While some dreamed of establishing piratical American bases, other looked for a northern passage to Asia, one that might be dominated by English outposts and fleets. By the 1560s it was fairly clear that a north-east passage was impracticable; consequently, attention shifted to the possibility of a route around the north of America. John Davis, a West Country neighbour of Walter Raleigh and a friend of John Dee, had proposed a new voyage to probe for the north-west passage, only to have his enterprise vetoed by the Muscovy Company, which held theoretical monopoly rights over all Arctic navigation. Another key enthusiast was Martin Frobisher[24] – slaver, privateer, mercenary, secret agent – who in 1574 approached Michael Lok, merchant and London agent of the Muscovy company, with a scheme he had been nursing since around 1561.

Piracy, Mines and Abortive Plantations, 1558–1604

Between them, these two concocted a petition to the privy council for a patent and fiscal support for a voyage of exploration, and then an appeal to the Muscovy Company for permission to invade their monopoly. Lok put together a consortium of investors, including privy councillors, some members of the Muscovy Company, and the Court geographer John Dee. Lok himself lent the enterprise £800. Thus in 1576 Frobisher sailed with two small three-masted ships, *Michael* and *Gabriel*, and a pinnace.

The pinnace was lost soon after rounding the south of Greenland and storms forced the *Michael* to turn for home; but Frobisher in *Gabriel* entered what he thought was the eastern entrance to the north-west passage. It was in fact a deep bay in the south-eastern tip of Baffin Island. On a small nearby island his sailing master came across a black rock, which his men took to be sea coal, and which Frobisher himself brought home as a token of English possession of these newly found lands. Indeed, that was its whole significance: in London three different metallurgists assayed it for precious content and found it to be worthless.

This was not good enough for Lok who, needing to protect his investment, set out to persuade his partners and the queen that a second voyage could return great profits. He took the ore to an Italian alchemist who, keen to produce the answer his client required, declared it gold-bearing and produced some gold dust as proof. Lok then suppressed the negative reports and used the new findings to obtain backing for a fresh expedition. Elizabeth herself invested £1,000 in the venture, chartered Lok's consortium as the Cathay Company, and allowed it to buy or rent one of her ships. The Company ordered Frobisher to defer the search for a passage to Asia in favour of founding a mining settlement, and thirty Cornish miners sailed with the expedition. Subject to the quality of the ore, the Cathay Company intended to establish a permanent North American settlement, almost a decade before the first attempt to colonise Virginia and almost forty years before the first successful settlement there.

Some two hundred tons of black ore came home to England, but no-one was prepared to wait for a proper assessment of its value. Such was the gold fever among the Cathay Company men and at Court that a third expedition was prepared immediately, with the intention of establishing a permanent mining settlement of 100 men. Once again, Frobisher returned to Baffin Island where he did indeed attempt to found a settlement and extracted a large quantity of ore; but the weather was cold, the Inuit intermittently hostile and the problem of food supply unresolved. Thus, the first attempt to establish a permanent English settlement on the North American continent came to an end in 1577. The black ore turned out to be worthless iron pyrites, which was eventually used to repair roads. Frobisher was disgraced, his services at Court no longer required, and he sought employment in the suppression of the Desmond rebellion in Ireland.

The search for a north-west passage was far from over. From 1583 John Davis began to lobby for royal support through Francis Walsingham. A first reconnaissance was followed up in 1586, when Davis probed what is now Davis Strait, between Baffin Island and the west coast of Greenland. Pressing on into the wider expanse now called Baffin Bay, he reached as far as 67° North, where his way was barred by polar ice. An attempt to find a way around the north of Greenland from the west was similarly frustrated. A third voyage in 1587 reached Disko Island at 72° N – a place previously seen only by the Inuit and long-departed Viking fishermen and traders – before being again blocked by impenetrable ice. If this was the north-west passage, it was unnavigable.

Yet there remained the possibility of a passage further south. The chartering of the East India Company on 31 December 1600, though primarily aimed at exploiting the Cape route to Asia, fuelled further interest in seeking a shorter, more secure northern route. In 1602 George Weymouth, another Devon man, sailed 300 miles into Hudson Strait, opening the possibility of a less ice-bound passage there. In the next reign this led to the exploration of Hudson Bay and the growth of large-scale fur trade with Native Americans. Already there were substantial, if mostly seasonal, fishing settlements on Newfoundland and from about 1597 along the northern coast of New England – although Davis's claim of sovereignty was difficult to make good in practice. One might argue that these settlements were a far more substantial embryo of empire than the much better documented failures further south.

Thus, by the end of Elizabeth's reign the aim of establishing self-supporting English bases in the New World was well-established. Such bases were unlikely to be wrested from the Spaniards, but they might be combined with fishing, trade with Native Americans and with the continuing search for a north-west passage to Asia. However, until 1604, when James VI and I made peace with Spain in the Treaty of London, English energies were largely absorbed with the war. There were two further Spanish attempts on England after 1588; and the harrying of Spanish naval bases, the interception of Spanish shipping, and plundering in the Spanish Caribbean were far more attractive than the tedious business of supporting developing colonies. Hawkins had been right: the way ahead was to penetrate the Spanish commercial monopoly, and that could not be done in wartime. War, the inspiration for the imperial idea, was also the doom of its earliest expressions.

PART II
Toeholds
1603-1651

3

Empire and the British Revolutions

It has often been argued that the development of 'empire' in the early seventeenth century was conducted almost wholly through private enterprise and therefore, to some, cannot be properly regarded as 'empire' at all. There is a lot to be said for this thesis if we define an empire as a state-controlled entity. Even so, from a very early period the state began to seek ways and means to intervene in and exercise tighter control over the English settlements in mainland North America and the Caribbean. As early as 1622, James VI and I established a committee of the Privy Council to advise upon trade and colonial problems. Twelve years later, Charles I created a new body to build both royal authority and the power of the Church of England in America, and especially in the New England settlements. In Ireland, a vigorous policy of plantation and Anglicisation was tightening English control. This process was cut short by the outbreak of civil war in all three kingdoms, the king's execution and the creation of a republic embracing England, Scotland and Ireland. But by 1651 that republic was about to turn its attention to tighter control of colonies and colonial trade, and towards aggressive colonial expansion.

While James I was unenthusiastic about transatlantic expansion, which might cause conflict with Catholic Spain, he saw Ireland as a strategic defensive problem. Tyrone had surrendered just in time to preserve some shreds of his power and even after the Treaty of London he continued to hope for more Spanish aid. His flight to the continent in 1607, and a short-lived rebellion the following year, highlighted the continuing fragility of England's position in Ulster and in Ireland generally. Following the private initiatives of three Scots landlords in Counties Down and Antrim, James appointed commissioners to prepare a plan to clear the supposedly barbaric and sub-human Ulster Irish out to the west of Ireland. The vacated lands were granted, in lots of 1,000 to 2,000 acres, to some 1,050 English and Scots Protestants, who were obliged to build fortifications and to offer sub-grants and non-traditional leasehold tenancies exclusively to non-Irish settlers. Twenty-three towns – including Londonderry, Enniskillen and Belfast – were created and from 1615 they were linked by a network of military roads. In the same spirit he set about demilitarising and taming the remaining Irish chiefs by challenging their land titles and seizing and reallocating the territories of those who could not, a process continued from 1633 by Charles I's Deputy, Thomas Wentworth, Earl of Strafford.

All this was supposed to produce a stable and loyal Protestant society, but the reality was rather different. The Scots and English immigrants – 100,000 by 1641, far more than settled in the New World – were too few to replace the native Irish tenantry. At an early stage the rules had to be changed to allow grants to three hundred Irishmen and the return of some Irish tenants, usually under exploitative leases. Irish chiefs, even those outwardly anxious to Anglicize, continued to uphold traditional values and to keep retinues of swordsmen. Discriminated against as Catholics, responses to their petitions for toleration repeatedly deferred and their land titles often challenged, they were often mired in debt by the costs of conspicuous Anglicization, building up a dangerous head of religious, cultural and economic resentment. Though the process was largely peaceful, under the surface they were building towards a massive Catholic eruption in 1641.[1]

James long resisted pressure from a Puritan network for a new predatory war against Catholic Spain. The Elizabethan tensions between those who accepted the Book of Common Prayer and those who wanted a purely Calvinist Church of England had not gone away, and Calvinist proponents of oceanic aggression were prominent in colonising ventures. James gave a charter to the Virginia and Somers Island (Bermuda) Companies because their commercial and prospecting activities and relatively remote locations were unlikely to mortally offend the Spaniards. Though he licensed Raleigh (imprisoned and under suspended sentence of death for plotting against James's succession) to look for gold mines on the coast of Venezuela, he specifically forbade contact with Spanish settlements – and executed him when he disobeyed. The king's position became particularly awkward after the outbreak of the Thirty Years' War in 1618, pitting the Union of German Protestant States against the Catholic League, the Holy Roman Emperor and Spain. The rapid defeat and dethronement of his Protestant son-in-law Frederick, Elector Palatine and briefly elective King of Bohemia, obliged James to appear to be ready to use force. For that he needed money, which parliament was ready to provide in return for an aggressive and profitable naval war against Spanish colonies. The English navy was not strong enough for such a role, and in any case could not help Frederick to recover the Rhineland. Besides, war would mean alliance with the ominously strengthening powers of France and the Dutch Republic. Therefore, James preferred negotiation to conflict, but by 1624 he had been forced into the maritime war Calvinist MPS had been demanding.

The war went badly: an attempt to emulate the Elizabethan raids on Cadiz was a fiasco, the Spanish colonies and silver fleets were untouched, and in Europe the Catholic powers made dramatic progress against both the League and its ally, Denmark. When James died in March 1625 he bequeathed to his son Charles an expensive war, a divided national church and political nation wary of royal ambitions and demands for money.

Charles I was far less politically adroit than his father, who balanced competing factions and knew when to yield to opposition. A convinced follower of the Anglo-Catholic doctrine known as 'Arminianism', and rigidly insistent upon his prerogatives as head of church and state, Charles appointed to office only those who shared his views, alienating both Calvinists and those who sought to limit the powers of the Crown. Marriage to a French Catholic princess, Henrietta Maria, and a spate of high-profile conversions at Court did not help matters. Three obstreperous parliaments insisted upon anti-Catholic crusading – by 1627 he was at war with both Catholic Spain and her great rival Catholic France – yet they denied him the finances needed to fight either effectively. In 1629 he made peace with both countries, dismissed his third parliament and began eleven years of (perfectly legal) personal rule.

Parliamentary subsidies were replaced by revenues from prerogative taxes, such as Ship Money for the navy, which, while just about defensible in royal courts of law, stoked up significant resentment. Free now to impose Arminian doctrines on the Church and to enforce discipline through prerogative courts, Charles stirred up even more suspicion of his religious orientation. When the Archbishop of Canterbury died, Charles chose William Laud, a staunchly Arminian bishop to fill the vacancy. In his dual role as Charles's most important Privy Councillor, Laud enforced Church discipline through the prerogative Court of High Commission. Strict adherence to the Book of Common Prayer and the wearing of full clerical vestments were required across the country. Communion tables were moved from church naves to become Catholic-looking railed-off altars at the east ends of parish churches. The 1632 grant of Maryland to Lord Baltimore as a refuge for English Catholics also looked suspicious.

The Puritan leaders, now denied a parliamentary platform for their opposition, were kept together through their creation of the Providence Island Company, which colonised the remote Caribbean island later known as Tortuga. Founder members included the earl of Warwick (later to lead the navy against Charles I), Lord Saye and Sele, Oliver St John (soon to defend John Hampden in the test case challenging Charles's Ship Money tax) and John Pym (later opposition leader in the early years of the Long Parliament). Granted the power to issue letters of marque, the place became a privateering base until destroyed by the Spaniards in

1641.[2] The Massachusetts Bay Company, founded in 1629 by Separatists who rejected the state church altogether, secured virtual independence by taking their charter with them to New England.

By 1634, Charles and his Privy Council, realising that they had very little control of their American possessions, made Laud head of a new Commission to Regulate Plantations, intended to claw back some royal authority and strengthen the Church of England. But while Maryland and Virginia were happy to accept the Crown officials, Massachusetts – now virtually an independent republic – would not. When Charles's government used a legal device called *quo warranto* to call in the Massachusetts charter for examination, it was simply ignored. The Privy Council condemned the charter and Charles began, somewhat fancifully, to consider using force against the Bay colony.[3] Meanwhile a much deeper crisis was developing in Ireland, in some ways England's first colony but also part of the imperial core.

Anglicisation, plantation and rebellion in Ireland
Just as in England and in New England, in Ireland Charles was determined to assert royal authority and to impose his Arminianism. His instrument was Thomas Wentworth, whose vigorous administration capped, for the time being, an underlying volcano of resentment.

Unlike previous Deputies, Wentworth stood outside Dublin political factions and played them off against one another. He obtained subsidies from the Irish parliament with promises which he then refused to keep and began to apply the plantation programme to the Old English nobility. This further reduction of overmighty subjects was perhaps necessary, but it added dangerously to the tensions within the kingdom. Yet at the same time he began the resumption of former church lands already granted to planters and offended their Presbyterianism by enforcing Arminian doctrines and the authority of the Church of Ireland. By 1641 he had expanded royal power and removed some abuses in the Church, but at the expense of creating an unnatural, if not unholy, alliance of native Irish, Old English landlords and New English settlers.[4]

The eruption was triggered by events on the British mainland, where James and Charles both attempted to tame their other turbulent kingdom, Scotland. Though his proposal for a united kingdom was rejected on both sides of the border, James had made limited progress towards pacifying the lawless border and highland regions, and even persuaded the Presbyterian lowlands to accept church government by bishops. Charles and Laud went further, trying to impose an Anglican liturgy upon the Kirk and to recover lands seized during the Reformation. Their policy provoked a military confrontation known as the First and Second Bishops' Wars of 1638-1640, the first of the 'Wars of the Three Kingdoms' (1638-1652). In the first war Scottish military superiority obliged Charles to accept a truce, requiring the disbanding of both armies and the summoning of parliament. His military and financial weakness cruelly exposed, Charles recalled Wentworth, now Earl of Strafford, who advised him to call the English parliament. The so-called 'Short Parliament' demanded redress of grievances before it would vote taxes. True to form, Charles chose inflexibility over compromise and in May 1640 disbanded parliament only weeks after it had first met. The Scots 'Covenanters' had not disbanded their army and in August they poured across the River Tweed, brushed aside a feeble royal force at Newburn and occupied Northumberland and Durham. At Ripon, the king's representatives were forced to agree to pay the Scots £850 a day while they occupied English soil and Charles was forced to summon the parliament that eventually brought down the monarchy. Meanwhile, with Strafford gone, the unnatural alliance of Old and New English collapsed and in October 1641 Ireland exploded into bloody civil war.

From October 1641 until the spring of 1642, small bands of Catholics, supported by larger forces raised by the Anglo-Irish lords, attacked English garrisons and Protestant plantations in the name of Charles I. In 1642 Parliament's threat to extirpate Irish Catholicism and to seize more lands drove the lords together in the Confederation of Kilkenny, which controlled two-thirds of Ireland including the important ports of Waterford and Wexford and access to foreign aid. The confederates were not pursuing independence but autonomy under the Crown with security for their lands and religion, aims they claimed had been ordered by Charles. Consequently, they fought in the name of the king, terrifying the English, strengthening the king's opponents and making an English civil war all but inevitable.[5]

Wars in three kingdoms
The Irish revolt in turn triggered rebellion in England. Tales of Catholic atrocities against hapless Protestants lost nothing in the telling – 4,000 deaths quickly became 40,000 – while Protestant massacres of Catholics fell from view. Even in Yorkshire, rumours of an Irish invasion spread panic. Unwilling to trust their king with the army needed from Ireland and fearing that Charles would use the confederate army against themselves, parliamentary radicals tried to seize control of England's armed forces. Fatally, they also published a 'Grand Remonstrance' detailing the king's misdeeds, in effect appealing to the people against the Crown and shocking the moderates into support for the king. Having already been forced to give up his prerogative taxes and courts, and obliged to execute Strafford and imprison Laud, sensing that moderate opinion was swinging his way in January 1642 Charles made a botched attempt to arrest the opposition leaders and lost London as a result. By the autumn he was sucked into open civil war. His armies came close to victory in 1642-1643 but Parliament had superior financial resources, control of the Navy and

major ports, and from 1644 the support of the Scots. Charles's attempt to redress the balance by coalition with the Irish confederates brought no military advantages and propaganda damage in England and Scotland. Despite trapping a major parliamentary army in the West Country, he lost the North in 1644 and suffered catastrophic defeat at Naseby in 1645. In May 1646 he surrendered to the Scots.[6]

Four years of fighting now gave way to over two years of futile negotiation for a settlement. Charles's supposition that, as only legitimate king, he was indispensable, led him to reject quite generous offers, hoping to divide the alliance of Parliament, its army (which by now had its own grievances and a radical religious agenda) and the Scots (who wanted to impose Presbyterianism on England). In 1648, he managed to start a second civil war in collusion with English royalists and the Scots, only to be rapidly defeated by the army. The army radicals, now bent on execution, purged the parliament of moderates and obliged the remaining MPs, the so-called 'Rump', to charge Charles with treason. Convicted by a specially created court, he was beheaded in January 1649, leading to the establishment of Britain's first and only republic.

Scotland immediately recognised the Prince of Wales as King Charles II, subject to his (wholly insincere) acceptance of Presbyterianism. Ireland was still in revolt and although some New England settlers had come home to fight for Parliament, Virginia and Barbados were controlled by Royalists. Henrietta Maria, the new king's mother, was busy trying to rouse her French relatives to intervene and his cousin the Dutch Prince of Orange was sympathetic to the royal cause. Fortunately, though the Thirty Years' War had ended in 1648, France and Spain were still at war, so it was important to subdue Ireland and Scotland as quickly as possible. For the Irish command, the Rump chose Oliver Cromwell, formerly the New Model Army's cavalry commander, a reluctant republican and regicide, and now its most prominent remaining general. Cromwell broke the back of the Irish revolt rapidly and brutally in 1649, massacring the garrisons of Wexford and Drogheda, before his recall to deal with Charles II and the Scots. His seaborne invasion struck determined opposition. After a fortuitous victory at Dunbar, followed by a winter of strategic stalemate in the lowlands. he had to strike south to counter Charles Stuart's west coast invasion of England. His final victory at Worcester in 1651 drove Charles into exile and brought Scotland along with Ireland into a united British republic.

The new republic, the 'Commonwealth', was keen to eliminate the Dutch threat and bring the royalist colonies to heel. To this end, in 1650 the Rump banned foreign shipping from the colonies and despatched Sir George Ayscue to the Caribbean to reduce Barbados. More significant in the long run was the passage of the Navigation Ordinance in 1651. With the British Isles now under tighter control than ever, the republic was about to embark on a campaign of imperial centralisation and aggressive expansion.

4

Mainland North America: The Conquest of the Chesapeake

Colonising projects before 1604 had failed partly because England possessed too few maritime resources to support a distant infant colony in time of war. However, when in that year the Treaty of London 1604 secured peace with Spain, the nature and prospects of any such plantation were transformed. Although privateering diminished rather than vanished, investors, ships and seamen were now available for the expansion of trade and overseas settlement. Instead of creating a pirate base, a settlement in mainland North America would thrive by trading with Spanish colonies for tobacco and sugar, and with luck might turn out to have its own sources of gold and silver. And then there was the prospect of 'improvement': in the minds of those interested, a Virginian settlement's resources could be exploited to produce glass, iron, timber boards and other products. Raleigh was now in prison for plotting to prevent the accession of James I, but merchants from Plymouth and London were interested.

As ever, nothing could be done without a Crown patent, so the first step was to get in touch with courtiers who appreciated the opportunities. Londoners and Plymouth men formed themselves into a Virginia Company and approached courtiers such as Sir Thomas Roe, soon to be James VI and I's ambassador to the Mughal empire in India. In April 1606 their lobbying produced a royal charter licensing both groups to establish settlements between 34° and 45° N, the Londoners in the south, the Plymouth men in the fishing areas to the north. In 1607 both groups sent expeditions, the Plymouth group to Sagadahoc in Maine and the Londoners to Chesapeake Bay. The Maine venture collapsed within a year for lack of financial resources, fresh settlers and leadership and in the teeth of Indian hostility. The better-funded London Chesapeake colony came close to sharing a like fate.

The Company's instructions to its colonists reveal that lessons had been learned from the Roanoke fiasco, and at the same time demonstrate an extraordinary detachment from Virginian reality. A third of the men were to farm so that the colony could be fed, but the other two-thirds were to be engaged in military duties or a search for a north-west passage to Asia. A fortified settlement was to be far enough up some major river to be safe from Spanish detection and to tap inland trade opportunities; yet the native Amerindians were to be cleared out of the land between settlement and sea, a task far beyond the strength of the 144 intended first settlers.

> [Y]ou must in no case suffer any of the native people of the country to inhabit between you and the sea coast; for ... they will grow discontented with your habitation, and be ready to guide and assist any nation that shall come to invade you.[7]

Food was to be bought from the Indians before they realised that the English had come to stay, and they must never be allowed to handle muskets or to see Englishmen ill or dying.

In the spring of 1607 the Company's four ships, carrying 144 male settlers, penetrated some forty miles up the James River, which discharges into the western side of Chesapeake Bay. In May they landed upon an uninhabited island separated from the mainland by a narrow creek, where the river ran six fathoms deep by the shore and a bend in the river facilitated concealment and defence. About 105 of the men elected to remain and constructed a triangular stockade, which they named after King James. Despite the apparent strength of the fort, the new colony was a fragile thing. The very commerce the settlement was supposed to thrive on was already disappearing as, colony by colony, the Spaniards clamped down on illegal trade. New Granada was closed in 1607 and the trade with Trinidad did not survive 1612. Jamestown island was swamp-ridden and harboured malaria and other maladies. The soil was poor, the water brackish and, despite the lessons of Roanoke, little thought had gone into the problems of self-sufficiency. Most of the settlers were gentlemen or their servants – not farmers or agricultural labourers – and they tended to focus upon disorganised searches for gold. Three relief expeditions from England brought fresh supplies but also more mouths to feed, as the Company strove to build up the population. Disease and hunger combined to kill more people than survived – despite the efforts of a new governor, Captain John Smith, to impose discipline and make every man work. But the very greatest peril was not starvation: it came from the powerful Algonquian confederacy among whom they had landed.[8]

For this, of course, was not empty country. The territory around the York and James Rivers and extending southward almost to Roanoke was dominated by the *Tsenacommacah*, or Powhatan confederacy, an Algonquian native empire built over the previous twenty years by a Panunkey chief called Wahunsenacawh. Wahunsenacawh, known to the English as Powhatan, created his expanded dominion partly to fend off

Mainland North America: The Conquest of the Chesapeake

raids by Siouan and Iroquoian enemies, partly to gain control of the important copper trade, and perhaps also to relieve growing population pressures. As *mamanatowick*, or 'great king', Powhatan sat at the apex of a hierarchical governance structure, embracing perhaps 15,000 people and some thirty subject tribes. Below him were the weroances, leaders of the subject tribes and sworn to loyalty to the paramount ruler. Lesser weroances governed the towns within each kingdom.

This was not a stable empire: to keep it together Powhatan took vigorous and often ruthless action against Algonquian groups outside or only nominally attached to his dominion. Around 1597 he attacked his too-powerful neighbours, the Kecoughtans, at the tip of the peninsula between the York and James Rivers. A decade later he wiped out the Chesapeakes in the land south and east of the James and the following year he crushed the Piankatunks, another Algonquian group who lived on the York River. But not every disobedient group could be thus disciplined. The Patawomecks of the Potomac River to the north, the Chickahomonies along a tributary of the James, and the Algonquian groups on the eastern shore of Chesapeake Bay were too powerful and too distant to be cowed. Their adherence was either nominal or as allies rather than as subjects.[9]

On the other hand, these awkward allies needed the support of the Powhatan confederacy against outside attack. The confederacy was essentially a tidewater polity, lying between the sea and the fall-line, a zone of rapids and waterfalls where the soft coastal sediments meet hard bedrock. Above the fall-line, several apparently quite powerful Siouan and Iroquoian confederations presented an ever-constant military threat. The Siouan Monacans and Mannahoacs who controlled much of the piedmont between the fall- line and the mountains frequently clashed with the Powhatan tribes. The Massawomecks, who inhabited some thirty fortified towns and maintained a war fleet of 300 canoes on Lake Erie, presented an even more alarming threat, frequently launching devastating long-distance raids into Powhatan's territory. The Patawomecks, lying directly in the southward path of these marauders, were particularly hard hit. Effective defence and retributory raids could only be sustained collectively. Thus the Powhatan confederacy was created in the context of native frictions and rivalries, not in response to a European threat yet to fully manifest itself. The occasional visits of small ships with tiny crews and the fiasco at Roanoke did not suggest an imminent invasion. Powhatan was far more concerned with dangers already on his doorstep.

When the Jamestown settlers arrived, therefore, he had to assess whether these few strangers were a threat, could become useful allies, or were merely transient visitors. At first, he seems to have assumed that like earlier Europeans they would soon leave. When they began to build Fort James, it became obvious that they intended to remain permanently, so he had to test their strength. And that could only be done in actual combat. Powhatan co-ordinated – but did not take part in – an attack which killed two Englishmen and wounded twelve before musketry and the ships' artillery drove off the assailants. Impressed with the whites' defensive firepower but noting their numerical and dietary vulnerability, he then dissociated himself from the violence and set about turning them into subordinate allies. He fed the colony through the winter of 1607-08 and far into the following year, demonstrating that he held the key to their survival.

Nevertheless, the settlement would probably have collapsed for want of direction, had not Captain John Smith, the most dynamic of the leaders, imposed military-style discipline. Henceforth, all settlers had to work, and farming took priority over prospecting. Smith also led expeditions up the James River to buy food. At the town of Kecoughtan, when the Indians insisted on being paid in muskets and swords, he used force to seize what was needed and left only hatchets in exchange. He repeated the process at other towns until Powhatan decided to tame him once and for all. In December, Powhatan's powerful half-brother ambushed Smith's party on the Chickahominy River and dragged him a prisoner to Powhatan's chief town of Wahunsanacock. Contrary to Smith's later account – and to enduring popular legend – his life was not saved by Powhatan's daughter Pocahontas (at least not in the way described), but by her father's shrewd decision to make use of the English Smith as a 'son', or at least as a subsidiary chief. Thus, the settlers were fed and the Indians gained steel hatchets and additional supplies of copper – but not the guns and powder the paramount chief so much desired. However, the Indians found another way. The sailors from the ships very quickly established a black market in stolen weapons, which they exchanged for food. That undermined Smith's authority and his ability to bargain, so while he had bought time for the settlement, the long-term military potential of the Powhatans was overwhelming.

This uneasy peace endured until August 1609 when the arrival of a fleet with more settler mouths to feed – and too few supplies – moved Smith to disperse the newcomers along the James and to redouble his food raids. Within weeks about two hundred of the new settlers were dead and James Fort was closely invested. This was the 'starving time' when half of the beleaguered English died. The survivors were in the process of abandoning Jamestown when a new relief fleet arrived carrying a hundred seasoned soldiers with armour capable of resisting Powhatan arrows. The siege collapsed, the English sallied out, and the fighting became a matter of vicious raid and counter raid, in one of which Pocahontas was captured. In 1614, the first Anglo-Powhatan War ended in a stalemate and the peace was sealed by the marriage of Pocahontas to a prominent settler. For the time being the enlarged settlement was militarily secure. There followed by a short period of relative amity. Some Powhatans moved into the English settlements, trade thrived and a policy of cultural integration was begun. Opechancanough,

Mainland North America: The Conquest of the Chesapeake

who succeeded Powhatan in 1618, was even able to obtain musketry instruction for his warriors in return for allowing Christian education.[10]

Even so, the settlement was saved from economic collapse only by the discovery that tobacco could be a lucrative cash crop, valuable enough to turn a profit after a transatlantic voyage. Experiments with the local plant had begun as early as 1611, but the real breakthrough came with the arrival of a Caribbean variety, *Nicotiana tabacum*. In 1617 the first cargo turned an encouraging profit. In 1619 James I's privy council obligingly issued a proclamation banning tobacco growing in England, ostensibly on the grounds that College of Physicians certification that tobacco 'grown in England and Ireland is much more unwholesome than that imported from countries where it grows naturally'.[11] Like all bans on addictive drugs, it was widely ignored, but enforcement eventually became effective enough to give Virginian planters a guaranteed market and, at 100% duty, to give the Crown and its tax farmers access to a lucrative and easily collected revenue. Between 1617 and 1621 exports from Virginia rose from 20,000 to 350,000 pounds. Though disease slowed population growth, immigrants arrived in large numbers, and in 1619 - partly to encourage independent settlers – the Company allowed Virginia an elected assembly called the House of Burgesses.

It was this rapid expansion that induced the second Powhatan War of 1622. As the tobacco plantations spread, they destroyed forest and displaced game vital for the Indians' existence, undermining the viability of town after town. English occupation of most of waterfront lands cut Powhatans off from the river, its reedbeds and from some of their fields. Close contact with the whites also fostered disease. The Powhatans, who may have acquired some immunity after sixteenth-century ship-borne epidemics, began to die at the hands of the invaders' insidious biological allies, measles and smallpox prominent among them. Immigration and disease had brought the able-bodied white male population to rough parity with the Powhatans' warrior numbers, and in 1619 the sale of muskets to Indians became a capital offence. By 1622, as he watched the demographic and military balance shift, Opechancanough was convinced that a war was inevitable. It was also clear that the Indians would need surprise to counteract the whites' superior firepower. The nation's very survival could depend upon a sudden, brief and devastating onslaught.[12]

On 22 March 1622 the Powhatans struck suddenly at over thirty English settlements. Unarmed Indians pretending to bring gifts of fruit and other food seized whatever tools lay at hand – spades, axes – and slaughtered their would-be hosts. Between 300 and 400 whites – about a third of Virginia's population - died on that first day. But there was no follow-up action, either because Opechancanough had not thought his strategy through, or because he expected the colonists either to leave or submit. It was a fatal error. The English withdrew from their outlying settlements, concentrated their forces in eight fortified towns and launched bloody counter attacks, burning villages and corn and pursuing fugitives with dogs. In the only major battle of the war a combination of steel armour and snaphaunces, flintlock muskets, proved invincible. Far from eradicating the colony, in settlers' minds the conflict of 1622-1624 justified the further aggressive seizure of Indian land and their entire expulsion from the tidewater. Only in 1632 was a fragile and unstable peace achieved, by which time the natives had been driven off all the land between the James and the York Rivers. By 1643 the settlements had reached the Potomac and in 1644 near-centenarian Opechancanough made his last bid to save the Powhatan empire.

As in 1622, he relied on surprise. On 18 April Indians struck at outlying settlements, killing some five hundred people. But whereas in 1622 he had wiped out a third of the settlers and almost driven the invaders into the sea, he was now struggling against a predominantly adult male population of over 14,000, and the core settlements could not be assailed. The heavily armed and armoured English retaliated by raiding and burning corn fields, though they made few actual contacts with the enemy. The conflict ended with Opechancanough's capture and murder in spring 1645, followed in 1646 by a treaty agreed by his successor Necotowance. By 1650, the once-powerful Virginian Indians had been reduced to a reservation calculated at fifty acres per warrior, pathetically small for a semi-agricultural society of hunters.

The forces of tobacco cultivation and land seizure were crucial to the development of Virginian society, but the wars also brought about a radical change in the colony's legal status. In 1624 the Virginia Company, which had been pouring money and people into the province since 1607, collapsed. With the seaborne tobacco trade too valuable to be lost, James I stepped in and Virginia became the first royal colony. In the same stroke he took over Virginia's remote offshoot colony, Bermuda, founded after a shipwreck in in 1609. The war also marks the emergence of the governor's council – not the elected Burgesses – as the voice of the land-hungry Indian-hating settler interests against the restraint of royal government. In 1635, apparently with militia support, the council arrested and expelled a royal governor for concluding the 1632 truce, trying to regulate tobacco planting, and for challenging settler land claims.[13] The pattern was to be repeated later in the seventeenth century and established a mindset which was to have enormous repercussions in the eighteenth century.

Maryland

Although In terms of Indian conflicts and social development, Virginia set the pattern for the entire region, if not for all the future southern colonies, the next Chesapeake colony had rather different origins. In 1632 Charles I granted a charter to George Calvert, a courtier and Catholic convert who intended to found a refuge for his co-religionists. To evade the 1624 Monopolies Act, a large tract to the north of Virginia was granted not to a chartered company but as a feudal tenure, to be held by the

Mainland North America: The Conquest of the Chesapeake

Calvert family on similar terms to those on which the Bishop of Durham held his palatinate. Calvert died before he could act, but the grant and project was taken up by his son, Cecilius. In March 1634 the first settlers landed on an island at the mouth of the Potomac River. To balance the Calverts' authority, the charter required all laws made in the colony to be approved by the inhabitants, so within a year the colony had an elected assembly. Although the first party of colonists comprised seventeen Catholic gentlemen and about two hundred of their retainers, subsequent immigration attracted more Protestants than Catholics, and in 1644 the Calverts were temporarily overthrown by a Protestant revolt. Although over time the Protestant majority were to become resentful of Catholic dominance, Maryland would remain a place where Catholics could live and worship in relative security.

As in Virginia, the economy, and the whole structure of society, rested on the cultivation and export of tobacco. Of the 400,000 seventeenth-century migrants to the colonies, about 120,000 immigrants arrived in Chesapeake, and most of those between 1630 and 1660. The vast majority came as indentured servants, essential labour for the big tobacco estates – in Virginia a 'headright' system guaranteed acres to every man who imported at least one servant obliged to repay his passage by being bound to his master's service for a period of years. As the Indian populations were pushed back and more land became available, even men of modest means were able to acquire the space and hire the couple of servants needed to start a plantation. As a result, labourers were almost impossible to retain beyond the terms of their indentures and landless adult males were rare. A few black slaves were filtering into these tobacco economies, Virginia having only 405 as against a white population of 18,376. In Maryland the ratio was higher, 300 blacks to 4,204 whites,[14] but slave labour was still the exception rather than the rule. That demographic profile was to be radically altered over the next half-century.

By 1650 the tiny toehold at James Fort had been widened into two populous provinces and was still expanding at the expense of Amerindians. Hostility towards natives and a now less justified fear, combined with suspicion of imperial interference to produce what might be termed a frontier mentality. At the same time, tobacco planters were aware of their dependence upon the English market, and of the colony's perilous isolation and vulnerability to seaborne attack from Spanish Florida to the south, Dutch New Netherland to the north, and direct from Europe. These tensions were soon to escalate as imperial governments sought to gain further control over their colonies and colonial trade.

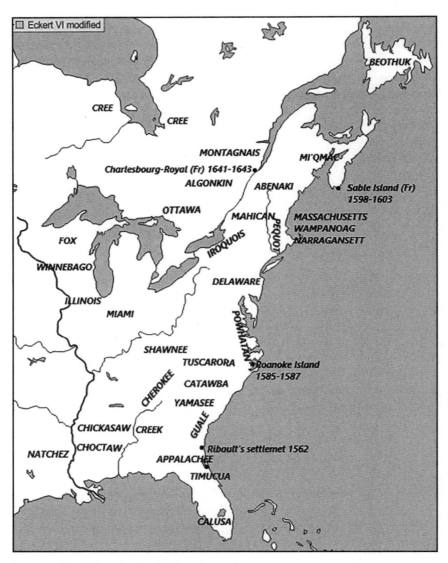

Eastern North America in the late sixteenth century.

5

New England: Pequots, Puritans, Fish and Furs

To the east and north of the Chesapeake, beyond the Delaware and Hudson rivers where the Dutch and Swedes were busy establishing colonies, and south of the French settlements in the St. Lawrence Valley, dwelt the Algonquian speakers of the New England forests. Here was no powerful Amerindian empire but a bewildering array of Algonquian-speaking tribes and clans. To the east of the Hudson lived the Mohegan, Pequot, Pocumtuc, Podunk, Tunxis, and Narragansett; and in the wide Connecticut River Valley were eight or so groups collectively known as River Indians. To their north around Massachusetts Bay lived the Wampanoag, Massachusett, Nipmuc, Pennacook, Penobscot, Passamaquoddy, and Quinnipiac peoples. Abenaki-groups stretched through northern New England and Nova Scotia to beyond the St. Lawrence. Like the Powhatan, these peoples cultivated crops such as maize and hunted in the winter. Their dwellings were 'wigwams' framed with bent saplings, interwoven with bark strips and domed to withstand the worst New England winters. These were the peoples whose lands were invaded by seventeenth century Puritans and disease.

The 1607 attempt to settle Sagadahoc in Maine was succeeded by the summer camps of fishermen and fur traders, who brought with them European diseases. In 1617-1619 an epidemic killed ninety per cent of the coast-dwelling Native Americans but stopped short on the eastern side of Narragansett Bay. The resultant power vacuum, combined with rivalry for control of the fur trade, provided the surviving Pequot and Narragansett people opportunity and motive for violent expansion at the expense of their Narragansett, Mohegan, Wampanoag and Lenape neighbours. By the early 1620s, Pequots were acting as middlemen, buying furs from northern Indians and selling them on to the New Netherland Dutch. In 1626 they defeated the River Indians and reduced them to subordinates, thus gaining control of the Connecticut River and its trade.

By 1630 they had extended the empire to eastern Long Island, the source of the wampum that was used a medium of exchange.[15] The aggressive expansion brought them into confrontation with the Narrangansetts.

The same power vacuum coincided with the arrival of English religious migrants, Calvinists leaving Laudian England to found godly communities in the American wilderness. This was the beginning of what has been labelled the 'Great Migration' to America of small family groups of decent but modest means - some 10,000 people were to reach New England within a decade – with the physical and mental toughness to endure the pioneering of a wilderness. On the shores of Massachusetts Bay, they found the natives were diminished and divided, their slash-and burn fields empty and their abandoned food stores available to incomers. Providence, it seemed to them, had made the region ripe for white invasion.

Plymouth Colony
As ever, the authority for English individuals and companies to attempt colonisation had to come from the Crown. As early as 1610 a Newfoundland Company was licensed to promote and protect English fishing on the Grand Banks, but for many years its settlement remained a tiny village. So did later settlements on the island, including a Welsh expedition and an Irish one sent out by Lord Falkland. In 1621, a West Country gentleman, Sir Ferdinando Gorges, obtained a charter for his Council for New England to colonise lands between 40 and 48 degrees north, but as at first it did little apart from selling leases to other colonising enterprises. Interested parties included Catholics harassed by the penal laws passed during Elizabeth's war with Spain, Puritan churchmen who wished to build a model for the future reform of the Church of England, and Puritan separatists who thought the Church of England beyond redemption. The first successful colony in the region, however, began with no charter at all.

Like the failed Maine plantation, Plymouth was founded by West Country gentry seeking both profit and a land where Puritans could impose a religious regime more to their liking than the Church of England. Unlike most Calvinists, these so-called 'Pilgrim Fathers' were Separatists, men who rejected not only Catholic survivals within the Church of England but also the concept of a centralised national church. Mostly Brownists, followers of a gentleman cleric called Thomas Browne, they were a tiny minority and generally tried to avoid notice. One of their congregations, from Scrooby in Nottinghamshire, departed for the supposedly friendlier environment of Leyden in the Dutch Republic. Godly exile, however, led to poverty, alarm at their children losing their English identity and – as they saw it – their corruption by Dutch worldliness. Leaping at the Virginia Company's offer of privileges for emigrants to America, many returned to England and joined forces with some London separatists

New England: Pequots, Puritans, Fish and Furs

(and with some more secular strangers') with a view to founding a godly settlement in northern Virginia. The expedition sailed in 1620 aboard the *Speedwell* and the *Mayflower*. Ironically, it was the *Speedwell* that proved unseaworthy, leaking so badly that she had to turn back. The *Mayflower*'s navigation miscarried and she made landfall in Massachusetts Bay, some 200 miles north of her intended destination.

Here was a dilemma. The Massachusetts Bay coast was attractive in a number of ways: it had fresh water and – thanks to the recent devastating epidemic – cleared Indian fields and abandoned stores of recently gathered Indian corn. Because Indians had regularly burned off undergrowth to encourage game, the woods had an open, parklike appearance. It was also well away from the existing Virginian settlements and so a happier prospect for a community anxious to keep itself separate and pure. On the other hand, the colonists were well outside the limits of the Virginia Company's charter, and some argued that the Company's patent had no force so far north – that the settlement would be illegal. Even after the leaders responded with their own instrument of government, the Mayflower Compact of November 1620, the settlers then took a month to choose a suitable site and to begin a village they called Plymouth.

It was now December 1620, with the North American winter already gripping a company weakened by scurvy and other maladies. Freezing temperatures and inadequate housing killed almost half of the original 102 emigrants before the spring. The survivors owed their lives to the abandoned Indian corn. Nevertheless, the community endured, partly because of intelligent leadership by the governor, William Bradford, but also because of a commonality of purpose engendered by a shared religion.

The Founding of Massachusetts

The next colony began with a West Country clergyman. John White (not to be confused with the Roanoke artist) was Rector of Holy Trinity and St Peter's churches in Dorchester, the county town of Dorset. Unlike the Separatists, and belonging to the Calvinist, or Puritan, wing of the Church of England, he believed that the Church could be reformed from within. A colony developed on Calvinist lines would be both a model for a reformed Church and also a refuge for those moderate Puritans driven out of Plymouth. He persuaded Richard Bushrod, a Dorchester merchant deeply involved in the Newfoundland fishing and fur trades, that a settlement somewhere in New England could be an economic success as well as a holy one. It took about half as many hands to sail to America as it took to fish once there, meaning that Bushrod had to cover the expense of double-manning. However, a self-sustaining colony would cut costs and supply the fleet with local hands and food for the fishing season. He also secured the support of Sir Walter Earle, a substantial Dorset landowner, magistrate and member of the Virginia Company. Earle, Bushrod and 117 other backers subscribed to a new enterprise, the Dorchester Company, which received a licence from the Council for New England in February 1623. Between 1623 and 1625 the Company sent three expeditions to establish and sustain a settlement at Cape Ann, at the very northern tip of Massachusetts Bay. By 1625 the fifty men established there had been joined by some refugees from Plymouth. White's plan seemed to be working.

However, the enterprise did not flourish. Cape Ann was too far from the best fishing grounds and the land was poor for farming. On the advice of one of the Plymouth exiles, Roger Conant, the settlers decamped southwards to the place known as Naumkeag. When the woefully undercapitalised Dorchester Company became bankrupt in 1626, White found backers for another joint-stock venture. This New England Company took over the Dorchester's debts and assets and obtained the necessary patent from the Council for New England in March 1628. The Dorchester men were now marginalised by London investors but at least a viable rescue plan was in place. The following month two small vessels laden with 1,000 new settlers sailed for Naumkeag, soon to be renamed Salem. (John White thought it a pity the name was changed. He believed the Indian name was Hebrew and was really Nahum Keike, which he translated as 'the bosom of consolation', thus indicating a link between the natives and the lost tribes of Israel.) In June a third ship departed with a new governor, John Endecott, on board. Within two years the colony's future capital, Boston was founded.

The arrival of the 'new planters' waving their legal claims caused some initial friction with Conant's 'old planters', to whom the settlement owed its survival. The problem was overcome by negotiation and compromise on the spot, but another issue needed reference to London. The new patent overlapped with other grants made by the Council for New England as long ago as 1623. Though these grants had never been exploited, they belonged to some very influential figures, including the Earl of Warwick and to Gorges himself, who accused the New England Company of fraud. To secure its title the Company needed a grant from an overriding authority and that could only be the Crown. White threw himself into the business of attracting further investment and lobbying for a royal charter. In 1629, the charter was granted to the enlarged enterprise under its new name – the Massachusetts Bay Company.

There was now very little West Country influence left. The first seven hundred settlers were recruited from East Anglia and Lincolnshire by John Winthrop, an indigent East Anglian gentleman and lawyer. Their geographical origin was reflected in the naming in 1630 of Boston, the future capital of Massachusetts. Though not Separatists, Winthrop's people were decidedly more radical in religion than the likes of John White, who may have envisaged a Presbyterian style of church government.

New England: Pequots, Puritans, Fish and Furs

The Boston and Salem settlers were akin to those later called Independents (or Congregationalists), who wanted an extremely decentralised national church in which every parish managed its own affairs, a position close to that later adopted by Oliver Cromwell. Massachusetts Independents, however, did not share Cromwell's feeling for religious toleration, even when it came to fellow radicals. In a famous dispute in the 1630s, Antinomianism (Greek anti, 'against', nomos, 'law') – belief in personal direct revelation – was punished by exile. The Massachusetts ministers looked less to religious liberty than to religious dominance.

Within months of obtaining their charter, eight proprietors meeting at Cambridge took advantage of the document's failure to specify a location for the Company's annual meeting. This group decided to emigrate with the charter to Massachusetts, and meanwhile to work to buy out others who wished to remain in England. The removal of the Charter and the governing body to the colony gave the settlement virtual independence. The governing structure of the Company became identified with the governance of the colony: the Governor of the Company became the head of the colony's executive, and the General Council of the Company was the General Court or legislature. The Crown could now apply little pressure. As we have seen, in 1638 Charles I's attempt to revoke the charter was simply ignored and he was contemplating the use of force when the outbreak of the First Bishops' War turned his attention closer to home.

A key feature of Massachusetts government was decentralisation, the delegation of most powers to the towns. Each town was required to have a church (which all inhabitants had to attend) and was allocated an area land to manage – 200 square miles in one case – and the vote was granted to 'freemen', male freeholders. However, the requirement that they must also be full church members, and the rule that to become a full member one had to prove a conversion experience – that is, promotion by God's grace into the elect – limited the franchise to about than 20 per cent of adult males, or less than 10 per cent of the whole population. Annual elections chose the Governor, Deputy Governor and the two houses of the legislature, the Court of Assistants and General Court. The Old Testament-based legal code, the Body of Liberties – which specified the death penalty for twelve crimes, including blasphemy and idolatry – applied everywhere. Apart from these broad brushstrokes, there was little interference from Boston. In most towns, the freemen elected their own councils (the 'selectmen'), to manage finances, allocate land to families and to maintain law and order.

Breakaway provinces
Religious dissent partly explains why other settlements – Connecticut, Rhode Island, New Hampshire and New Haven - broke away from

Massachusetts, and why the first three became separate colonies. Economic factors also played a role. By the mid-thirties the Plymouth and Massachusetts settlements had little pasture left for increasing numbers of livestock, driving some families to move outwards. In 1634 the town of Windsor was founded in Connecticut River valley, and the following year the first religious refugees appeared. Thomas Hooker and his followers were Independents but preferred to extend the franchise to all professed Christians. When in 1636 John Winthrop's son appeared at the mouth of the Connecticut with a sub-lease from the Earl of Warwick and founded a settlement called Saybrook, Hooker and the town leaders set about negotiating a compromise constitution which recognised the rights of 'inhabitants', not merely the godly. 'Inhabitants' of course meant propertied males, but even so –and allowing for the strict Independency of the prevailing church – government in Connecticut was far more representative than in Massachusetts.

Two fishing settlements had been established by the Council for New England in New Hampshire as early as 1622, but the population only began to grow significantly in the 1630s, with the arrival of religious and political exiles from Massachusetts. Rhode Island, on the other hand, was first settled in 1636 by Separatists led by Roger Williams, who found Bay independency not too stringent but too lax. Williams and his followers stood for total rejection of the Church of England, for stricter criteria for church membership, for denial of the King's right to grant lands in America, and for clerical enforcement of the first four Commandments. They founded the town of Providence in 1635 and were soon joined by other radicals, including Anne Hutchinson, an Antinomian leader expelled from Massachusetts for blasphemy, who arrived in 1637. Such a congeries of outcasts worked against coherent government and the towns combined only when threatened from the outside – by Indians or by other colonial claimants. The Bay colony so pressed its claim that Williams sailed for England in 1644, hoping to obtain a charter from the Puritan parliament at war with Charles I.

New Haven, on Long Island Sound, arose from the 1643 confederation of four towns recently settled by Puritan immigrants from Yorkshire and Surrey. Here, access to church membership was stricter even than in Massachusetts, Bible-based laws rejected in the Bay colony were implemented, and trial by jury was not allowed. But the new settlement was itself riven with dissent and its mercantile ambitions were frustrated by a poor harbour and competition from its neighbours, including the Dutch in New Netherland. It also lacked a charter and was therefore vulnerable to those possessing a formal title to the region. By 1651 Massachusetts was clearly preparing to take control, but Connecticut already had ambitions there too.

New England: Pequots, Puritans, Fish and Furs

The Pequot War of 1636-1638

By 1633 the Pequot ascendency was under threat. Already the Dutch had established their own treading post, the House of Good Hope at the future site of Hartford on the Connecticut River. When a smallpox epidemic reduced their numbers from around 13,000 to 3,000, the Pequots of course saw their dominance gravely weakened, and in 1634 they responded by killing a party of fur traders, probably Narragansetts, on their way to trade at Good Hope. That provoked the Dutch to kidnap and murder the principal Pequot sachem, despite accepting a ransom. As their tributaries and allies deserted to the Narragansetts, the Pequot approached Massachusetts for help, but their price was enormous: essentially, sovereignty over the Connecticut River Valley. The agreement was followed by the influx of settlers noted above and the construction of Fort Saybrook. Then the Pequots helped to bring ruin on themselves by attacking an anchored ship they believed to be Dutch, slaughtering the crew, looting the cargo and burning the vessel to the waterline.[16]

Unfortunately for them, neither the vessel nor its crew were Dutch. The commander, John Stone, was a violent and disreputable English pirate and trader, whose demise might well have been overlooked or even celebrated. Why then did Massachusetts provoke war by demanding the surrender of the killers? Part of the answer lies in the machinations of a Mohegan sachem called Uncas, who told the English that the Pequot were going to attack them. Another part lies in territorial ambition: if the squatters in the Connecticut Valley struck first, they might be able to assert their independence, so it was important for the Bay colony to pre-empt them. However, it is also important to consider the role of the Puritan mindset, which saw the world divided into God's chosen people and the legions of the Devil. Indians, primitive inhabitants of a threatening wilderness, were clearly in the Devil's camp. Besides, had not Providence given them this opportunity to seize land and wealth? Economic ambition and religion formed an explosively aggressive cocktail.

As long as the Pequots could exploit their superior mobility and use stealth and surprise they remained formidable foes. They had few muskets but some of these may have been flintlocks – lighter, more reliable and more likely to hit a moving target than the colonial forces' matchlocks. The war began with a blundering Massachusetts offensive that burned a Pequot town and cornfield but was otherwise evaded. The Pequots encircled Fort Saybrook, its foraging parties ambushed, and Connecticut towns were raided. Their Achilles heels were the two heavily fortified villages of Weinshauks and Mystic, on the river of the same name – solid fixed targets for a European counter-offensive.

In 1637 a joint Massachusetts and Connecticut expedition evaded the main Pequot forces by landing in Narragansett Bay and, accompanied by Narragansett and other Indian allies, marched overland to Mystic.

The village was surrounded and attacked early in the morning of Friday 26 May. The Pequots quickly recovered from their surprise and fought hard, killing two soldiers and wounding twenty others, and the attackers made slow progress through the maze of alleys and wigwams. The English then fired the village, razing it even as the Pequots fought on to the death. Those few who fought clear of the flames were cut down by troops encircling the fort. Between 600 and 700 Pequots died that morning, seven were taken prisoner and seven escaped. Though afterwards officers were divided as to Pequot bravery and the necessity of the massacre, most held that it was a just punishment for those guilty of treachery against the Elect.[17]

Weinshauks was still intact and many Pequot warriors dogged the English retreat, but the nation's morale was fatally broken. Villages broke up as their inhabitants sought safety in flight to neighbouring tribes. A band of forty hid in a swamp north of Weinshauks and several hundred were overtaken at another swamp called the Sadque where they made a last stand. Prisoners were caught and either killed or enslaved, and those who fled to the Mohawks were killed by their hosts. At Hartford, the Mohegan and Narragansett sachems agreed to summit all disputes to English arbitration and the Pequots were declared forever expelled from their homeland. When a Pequot village reappeared late in 1638 it was immediately attacked and destroyed.[18] Throughout New England the destruction of the Pequots was seen as God's will and confirmed the whites' title to Indian lands.

Moreover, victory in the Pequot war did not relieve the settlers' fear of Indian conspiracies, and in 1643 the colonies formed a defensive federation, the United Colonies of New England. Although they dared not yet tackle the 30,000-strong Narragansetts, divine favour and a rapidly expanding population were bound to produce further conflict. The United Colonies' first action was to procure the assassination of their former ally, the Narragansett sachem Miantonomi.[19]

The war also confirmed Connecticut's status as a separate colony. The shortcomings of the Massachusetts commission appointed to manage the conflict led the settlers to act more independently and in 1639 they adopted their own constitution, the Fundamental Orders. The new constitution was almost identical to that of Massachusetts, with the significant difference that the franchise did not depend upon church membership. As in Massachusetts, the towns had considerable autonomy and the prevailing culture remained Congregationalist.

New England at mid-century
As in the Chesapeake, the outbreak of the Wars of the Three Kingdoms weakened England's grip on her colonies. Rhode Island was able to obtain its charter in 1644 and all the colonies carried on with their local

parochial concerns. Civil war also reversed the flow of emigrants, far more so than in the Chesapeake, as men hurried home to serve in what they thought to be the cause of godly reformation.

Compared with the Chesapeake colonies, New England had few noble and gentry immigrants. Many of its people were yeoman farmers or craftsmen who arrived in family groups and literacy and educational ambitions (with a sharp religious focus) were high. Ordinary people had to be literate to read the Bible, so in Massachusetts every large town had to have a school, and Harvard College was founded in 1636 less from a love of learning than from a desire to train ministers. Congregationalist ministers had very significant influence in every colony, even where the franchise did not depend upon church membership. In 1646 an intercolonial synod laid down a Platform of Church Discipline, published in 1648-1649, which established common principles for Massachusetts, Connecticut, Plymouth and New Haven.[20] Religion and shared experience was bringing about a strong sense of regional cohesion.

Economically, the New England colonies lacked an export staple like tobacco or sugar, and for a while only a steady stream of emigrants and capital kept them going. When both dried up in 1641, casualties of the developing conflicts in the British Isles, there was a prolonged economic crisis. In the long run, however, colonists learned to exploit the resources on their doorsteps and constructed an economy far more stable than those of the Chesapeake and West Indies. Maize rapidly replaced wheat, which was susceptible to a local disease, and was grown on mixed farms alongside large numbers or cattle and other livestock. Though most properties produced a modest living – subsistence plus a small surplus for local markets – the colonies as a whole produced much more than they needed for themselves. More profitable was fishing: by 1645, when the value of fish exports reached £10,000, New Englanders were the principal participants in the Atlantic cod fisheries. The vast forests were exploited for shipbuilding. The result was a thriving trade in timber and food to the Chesapeake and to the West Indies. These exports paid for resaleable imports, such as wine from the Portuguese and Spanish Atlantic islands and sugar products from the Caribbean.

By mid-century this collection of minister-dominated, vehemently Calvinist communities had found an important role in inter-colonial trade and in the support of shipping, the key to the security of the British Isles and the empire as a whole. At the same time, self-sufficient isolation, ideological and physical, was producing intense versions of the usual settler identification with local interests and resistance to imperial controls. The communities were also still rapidly expanding at the expense of Native Americans and new and devastating frontier conflicts were soon to erupt.

6

The Caribbean, 1604-*c*.1651: Privateers, Pirates and Plantations

The real core of early seventeenth-century English expansion was neither the Chesapeake, nor New England. In terms of capital invested, settlers attracted, and wealth produced, this was the Leeward Isles, the northern end chain of tiny islands in the eastern Caribbean known as the Lesser Antilles. Perhaps sixty per cent of all seventeenth-century English emigrants to the Americas went to the West Indies. St Christopher (St Kitts) was settled in 1624 (at the same time as the French) and Barbados three years later. Nevis was settled from its near-neighbour St Kitts in 1628, followed by Montserrat and Antigua (with its valuable harbour) in 1632 and the Bahamas in 1646.

The appeal of the Leeward Isles
What made the West Indies – and these peripheral isles in particular – so attractive? They were certainly more appealing than the steamy and disease-ridden Guiana coast, where a series of early ventures foundered between 1604 and 1621 and dispirited settlers made abortive attempts on St Lucia and Granada. In 1622, a returning settler called Thomas Warner chanced to land on St Kitts and went on home to get a royal patent and financial backing for a colony. He returned with about forty fellow adventurers in 1624, his arrival coinciding with the appearance of a French expedition with whom they divided the island, the French taking the north and south, Warner's people the coasts in between. At about the same time, one John Powell landed on Barbados, and finding it lovely, fertile and apparently deserted, went on to England to find backing for a colony. In 1625 an Anglo-Dutch venture landed at St Croix in the Virgin Islands, to the east of Puerto Rico. In 1627 Powell, having gained the support of Sir William Courteen, a London merchant, returned to settle Barbados.

In London Warner gained the support of the Earl of Carlisle, who saw at once that a territorial grant from the Crown would, at the very

The Caribbean, 1604-c. 1651: Privateers, Pirates and Plantations

least, keep his numerous creditors at bay, while Powell's ambitions were financed by Courteen, who in turn had the ear of the Earl of Pembroke. In the same way as in mainland North America, both peers obtained overlapping quasi-feudal grants before Pembroke's was revoked and Carlisle was confirmed as 'Lord of the Caribbee Isles'. Carlisle kept Warner as governor in St Kitts but imposed his own man in Barbados, and Courteen and his followers lost their investments. The St Kitts settlers, pointing out that Carlisle had done exactly nothing for them, refused to pay the taxes and dues to which his patent entitled him. In Barbados there were factional clashes between those who owed their property to Courteen and those who held their plantations from Carlisle.

There was more to the islands' appeal than tropical beauty or relief at escaping the misery of Guiana. They were ideal for the cultivation of tobacco, and like Virginia, Bermuda and the Bahamas, were too insignificant, too lacking in precious metals, and too far to windward of the Greater Antilles to warrant much attention from an already overstretched Spanish empire. They could therefore be settled without immediately violating the peace of 1604, while from 1619 the Dutch West India Company distracted Spain with its attacks on shipping, Brazil, and the islands of Curacao, Saba, St Martin and St Eustatius.

The outbreak of the Thirty Years' War, which pitted the Hapsburg emperor and Spain against the Protestant powers of Germany and the Dutch, led to Hapsburg clashes, direct and indirect, with France, Denmark and Sweden. Even though there was no open conflict with the Ottomans, these wars were ultimately beyond Spanish strength, leaving little to spare for the Caribbean. That did not make the Leewards completely invulnerable. England was at war with Spain from 1625 until 1630, and in 1629 the Spaniards managed to mount a successful expedition against St Kitts and Nevis, but when Charles I made peace in 1630 they gratefully handed them back.

Spain was for some time unable to deal even with the nests of pirates established on the islands of Providence, Henrietta and Association (later Tortuga) off Nicaragua. These settlements were born of another Puritan enterprise designed to establish a godly commonwealth, supported by cotton, tobacco and privateering. Its twenty original backers were prominent members of the Puritan network opposed to Charles I's Arminianism, his personal rule and his allegedly pro-Spanish foreign policy. They included the Earl of Warwick, Lord Saye and Sele, Warwick's brother Lord Holland, Oliver St John (later to defend John Hampden in the Ship Money case), and the future parliamentary leader John Pym. Their Calvinist ideals did not survive the realities of West Indian colonisation. In the words of one historian, 'the culture of piracy and smuggling, as well as the cruel exploitation of unfree labour, transcended considerations of building a religious utopia and rendered their community indistinguishable from those of other European settlers in neighbouring islands'.[21] The settlement on Association was destroyed in 1635, but the others were not wiped out until 1641. Even then, Warwick, Parliament's admiral during the Civil Wars of 1642-1651, mounted large scale raids, using his own ships and manpower recruited from Barbados and St Kitts.[22]

The Leewards also offered relatively less formidable indigenous resistance than the Windward Isles to the south. The inhabitants were the Kalinago (Carib) peoples – once thought to be invaders from the mainland, but now recognised as a congeries of ethnicities and cultures displaced by Spanish conquest – were formidable archers and seafarers. By the early seventeenth century they had created a 'poison arrow curtain' between the Greater and Lesser Antilles, and their canoe-borne raids challenged English and French attempts at settlement in the Windwards and Leewards. As early as 1605 they wiped out an English party on St Lucia and in 1609 repelled an attempt to colonise Grenada. As late as 1641 they defeated a second, more serious, attempt on St Lucia. By 1630, however, weakened by conflict and disease, the Kalinago had concentrated their numbers on a few carefully chosen islands and abandoned the rest. Barbados, now totally uninhabited, became the most prosperous and attractive of all the early seventeenth-century English acquisitions. Elsewhere, English and French invaders sought to settle places where the Kalinago were relatively weak.[23]

Even so, resistance was fierce. On St Kitts both French and English faced three years of persistent opposition, before a series of Anglo-French alliances – and a brutal surprise massacre – drove most of the Kalinago from the island. A 1628 settlement on Barbuda was almost instantly expelled. Meanwhile the French successfully overcame resistance on Martinique and Guadeloupe but were checked on Grenada, Marie Galante and La Desirada. In 1640 the Kalinago counter-attacked, storming a settlement on Antigua, and in 1641 they erased a second settlement on St Lucia. Even by 1650 the English were still struggling to secure their footholds in the Leeward Islands and the Kalinago still controlled many of the Windwards.[24]

Tobacco, sugar and slaves

In none of the islands was there a native population adequate for slave labour on tobacco plantations. Indigenous captives rapidly died from overwork and exposure to imported pestilence. As in the Chesapeake, the answer was not yet black slaves but white indentured labourers. Over the century, almost half of the 220,000 West Indian settlers were indentured, just a little lower than the Chesapeake in percentage terms, and far higher in terms of numbers. These people were brought

The Caribbean, 1604-c. 1651: Privateers, Pirates and Plantations

out to the Indies by prospective employers, whom they repaid with labour for a fixed term of, usually, seven years. There was of course an element of deceit, exploitation and coercion in these arrangements; but on the other hand they gave poor people entry to a land which promised far brighter prospects than rural labouring in England. At the end of his indentures a man was free to set up a farm on his own, and many did so. When land prices rose in the islands many decamped for Virginia and other mainland colonies where the supply of land seemed endless. Indenture was an unequal system but one which had mutual benefits.

By 1640, however, tobacco prices were falling and planters were tempted to turn to sugar. In 1630 the Dutch had conquered Pernambuco in north-eastern Brazil, then the world's greatest sugar producer, and the knowledge they had gained there, along with Dutch capital to finance the necessary crushing and boiling mills, was available to enterprising English settlers. Moreover, Dutch shipping provided the cheapest and most efficient means of exporting the finished product. The final incentive emerged in In June 1645, when the Dutch West India Company's religious mismanagement and continued aggression in Portuguese Brazil provoked a major uprising in Pernambuco, disrupting sugar production and driving up prices. Aided by Portuguese troops and ships, the rebels gradually gained ground until, in 1654, the last Dutch surrendered.[25] In those fifteen years, with Pernambuco's plantations more or less out of action, English planters seized their opportunity.[26]

The Sugar Revolution, as historians call it, was not for the poor or the timid. The expense of installing the necessary works was too high for smaller farmers, and even big plantations could not show a profit for at least two years. More substantial and daring men, however, made fortunes. Others followed their lead and the smaller, less viable plantations were bought up by those who could better bear the initial investment. Thomas Modyford arrived in Barbados in 1645 with enough capital to buy 500 acres and employ white servants and black slaves to work it. Two years later he was one of the largest planters and a very rich man. By about 1651 Barbados had overtaken both Brazil and Hispaniola, and raced far ahead of French rivals, to export £3,000,000 worth of sugar every year. Now a net importer of food and barrel staves, the island was a profitable market for the New England colonies and was more valuable than all the other English possessions put together

The transformation of the islands into predominantly sugar producers was well under way. Not only was the Barbadian economy transformed by this 'Sugar Revolution' but the island's whole social structure as well. The year-round hard labour needed to grow sugar – clearing, planting, tending, harvesting, boiling and crushing – was very unattractive to white workers, indentured or free. Many men freshly out of indentures, finding land in short supply and very expensive, tended to decamp for Virginia. During and after the British Civil Wars some relief was supplied by the transportation of royalist prisoners whose sentences were open-ended. Between 1649 and 1655 some 10,000 such captives, largely Scots and Irish victims of the campaigns of 1649-1651, arrived in Barbados. However, this supply soon dried up, partly because of opposition in Interregnum parliaments to sending Englishmen into a servitude akin to slavery.[27]

The solution, as earlier in Hispaniola and Brazil, was the employment of black African slaves. Indentured labour did not immediately disappear, but servants were increasingly worked alongside, and increasingly treated as, slaves. The result was resistance by white and black. As early as 1634 the Barbadian authorities had uncovered a planned servants' revolt, and another plot was detected in 1647. More dangerous were the bands of runaway slaves that plagued the island in the 1650s. Barbados was becoming a land with a white elite of planters, managers and overseers, and a mass of enslaved and resentful black workers.

Sugar made slower progress in the Leewards, partly because the land was less suitable, but largely because they were more exposed to foreign attack and therefore less attractive targets for heavy capital investment. These islands continued with mixed economies producing tobacco, cotton and indigo as well as fish and cattle. In this context the expression 'Sugar Revolution' is less appropriate. Nevertheless, there, too, black slave labour was replacing white indentured servants.

The West Indies had become the principal English market for West African slaves, so stimulating English trade with West Africa. Until mid-century most of this trade was not in slaves but in items such as gum arabic and redwood (for the English cloth industry), hides, wax and gold. Before then, such slaves as did reach the West Indies came mainly in Portuguese or Dutch vessels. By 1650 about 23% of the populations of the British islands was black, much higher than elsewhere in the French and English North America, but a long way short of the 88% reached by 1710. The Sugar Revolution therefore virtually created the English slave trade.

Settler parochialism and the British Civil Wars

The islands quickly asserted their right to local self-government. Carlisle's patent required him to govern in accordance with the advice of the settlers and by 1639 Barbados had an assembly elected on a freeholder franchise, a model which by mid-century had spread to the other English islands. These assemblies fell quickly into the hands of the planter elites determined to protect their interests against interference from proprietor or Crown; to preserve their right to trade freely, especially with the Dutch; and to ensure that servants and slaves were kept in order. These fundamental aims tended to override the often bitter internal factional disputes. In terms of English

The Caribbean, 1604-c. 1651: Privateers, Pirates and Plantations

politics and the Wars of the Three Kingdoms, the 'plantocracy' refused to compromise their independence by taking sides. In Barbados there was at first a friendly truce between Royalists and Parliamentarians. The execution of Charles I in January 1649 drew more Barbadian and Antiguan planters to the Royalist side, less in support of divine right than out of fear that the new Commonwealth would adopt protectionist policies. These fears were soon to be confirmed by the 1650 exclusion of foreign merchants from the Caribbean trades and by the Navigation Ordinance of 1651. In April 1650, the Royalist-dominated Barbados militia seized control and on 7 May the assembly voted to accept Charles II's appointee, Lord Francis Willoughby, as governor. Parliamentarian planters were expelled from the colony and their plantations were confiscated.[28]

The Rump's response was to dispatch a fleet under Sir George Asycue to crush the insurrection. Asycue, who arrived off Barbados in October 1651, had only 860 soldiers on board, too few to confront the 5,000 Barbadian militia, but he possessed the vital weapon of blockade. He also set about sapping morale by launching hit-and-run coastal raids, releasing the news of Charles II's defeat at Worcester, attempting to divide the defenders, subduing royalist Antigua and obtaining the submissions of St Kitts, Nevis and Montserrat. After three months of psychological and economic pressure the Barbadians reluctantly agreed to negotiate. The subsequent agreement, the Charter of Barbados, saw them recognise parliamentary sovereignty and Parliament's right to appoint the governor; in return they were granted indemnity, retaining their assembly and their right to trade as before 'with all nations that do trade and are in amity with England'. Willoughby's personal settlement on the Surinam River in Guiana was allowed to remain in the hands of a royalist governor. The Rump, many saw at the time, would abrogate the Charter if ever it found itself able to fully enforce the Navigation Ordinance – but for the time being that was beyond its power.[29] The plantocracy had achieved, if only temporarily, its real objectives.

Submission did not necessarily mean quiescence. Daniel Searle, the new governor of Barbados, found a discontented population, dislike of the English republic and even a desire for independence. Nevertheless, there was no appetite for renewed active resistance. The appearance of Prince Rupert's royalist squadron in May 1652 did not provoke uprisings in the islands. None of the governors would let him buy supplies, so he had to rely on French and Dutch colonies. Though he captured many prizes and raided the island coasts, he did not attempt to reconquer any of the English colonies and indeed was not strong enough to do so. After a hurricane damaged his ships, drowned his brother Prince Maurice and forced a major refit in the Virgin Islands, he left the Caribbean with just five battered men of war.[30]

Within three years of Rupert's departure the island governments were to provide large numbers of recruits to the Interregnum's most ambitious military project - Cromwell's Western Design.

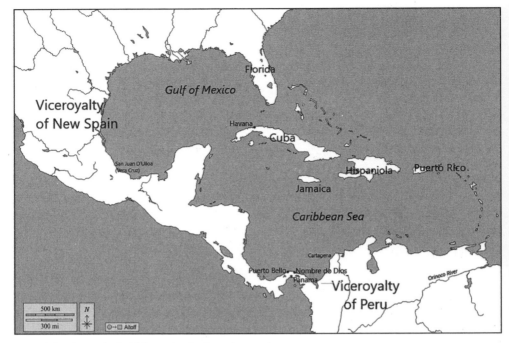

The Spanish Caribbean in the late sixteenth century.

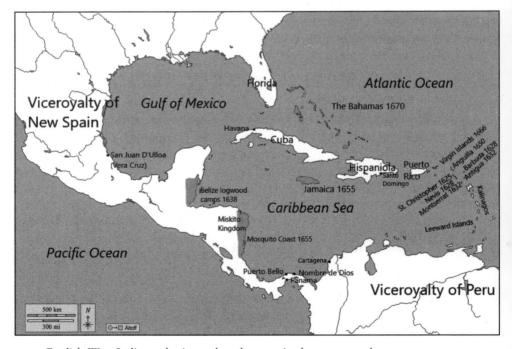

English West Indian colonies and settlements in the seventeenth century.

7

Eastern Enterprise

By the end of the sixteenth century it was evident that the only viable seaborne commercial route from Europe to Asia was by way of the Cape of Good Hope. That meant voyages of thousands of miles in large ships with all the hazards of storms – especially south of the Cape – accident, enemy action and piracy. The ships had to be crewed, equipped and supplied, and saleable cargoes, usually silver bullion, had to be found for the outward leg. Homeward cargoes valuable enough to pay for the whole round voyage – usually pepper, cinnamon, cloves and nutmeg – had to be found to pay for the whole. Reliable agents had to be recruited to negotiate with foreign states and to honestly manage the trade. Moreover, there was intense competition from the established and shorter overland routes by way of the Red Sea, Persian Gulf and the Levant, which would have to be undercut or suppressed. Such demands could be managed only by the state or by a wealthy consortium of merchants and financiers.

The Portuguese met the problem by creating a department of state, the *Estada da India*, charged with forcibly diverting the spice traffic from the overland route via the Red Sea and Persian Gulf. They established a network of enclaves around the northern Indian Ocean, with headquarters at Goa, and with outposts at the entrance to the Red Sea and Persian Gulf, on the Straits of Malacca and on the East African coast. For a while they were spectacularly successful, but the system failed to permanently check the overland trade. Profits dwindled, but the system was still in place in 1580, when Philip II enforced his claim to the Portuguese empire by entering Lisbon with an army. That union brought the Dutch, already in revolt against Spain, and the English, openly at war with Spain from 1585, into direct competition with the *Estada*. In the 1590s merchant groups of both countries sent fleets to Asia and encouraged by the profits they formed joint-stock companies to exploit the opportunities more efficiently. The English East India Company was given its royal charter in 1601 and the Dutch East India Company followed two years later.

Recent work has stressed that the East India Company functioned more like an early modern state than a simple trading organisation, and therefore its emergence as the dominant power in India by 1815 was not the result of a mid-eighteenth-century transformation.[31] Nor were its military and political endeavours always defensive. Ideologically, organisationally and in terms of its economic ambition, the Company was from the beginning a player in South Asian power politics. However, it is still fair to argue that in the early seventeenth century it was a very minor player, vulnerable to the vagaries of upheavals on the subcontinent and the Indonesian archipelago, and dependent upon the goodwill of powerful local states, particularly the aggressively expanding Mughal empire. It certainly did not possess the network of fortified enclaves that emerged by 1713.

Spice islands

The principal target of the Dutch and English companies was the Indonesian archipelago. Although pepper was grown in southern India, and right through the East Indies, only the smaller Molucca group – the 'Spice Islands' - produced cinnamon, mace, nutmeg and cloves. These treasures could be loaded at the many ports outside Portuguese control, and by tapping the Moluccan production at source, the Dutch and English hoped to weaken competition from the overland commerce which had so damaged the Portuguese. Not surprisingly, they clashed violently with the Portuguese and with each other.

In this contest the Dutch company, with more abundant long-term investment, was able to defeat its English rival. From 1609 the Dutch began to intercept English ships and in 1618-19 the two companies fought a short, fierce maritime war. A peace agreement in 1619 stipulated that in return for a fiscal contribution, the English could take one-third of the crop collected by the Dutch. The Dutch never fully honoured their part of the bargain and the Moluccan trade rapidly became unprofitable for the English. In 1622 they decided to withdraw from the Moluccas (though not from Indonesia) in favour of India and the inter-Asian 'country' trades. The Dutch murder of ten English merchants at Amboina in 1623 merely confirmed this change of policy. While they were not driven out of the islands altogether, henceforth their principal field of operations was the subcontinent.[32]

The English maintained valuable footholds in the archipelago long after 1622, however. The Dutch never quite made good their monopoly over production in the islands, so that Asian vessels continued to take cloves to English ports, especially to Macassar in Celebes. Indeed, in the 1630s Macassar received more cloves from Amboina than the Dutch were able to export for themselves. Bantam continued to be a valuable Sumatran base.

India: the Mughal Empire [33]

The Mughal empire had emerged in the late sixteenth century, successor to a chain of unstable Muslim states established by waves of invaders from Afghanistan and Central Asia. Whereas the earlier north Indian polities had been vulnerable to succession disputes, Afghan-Turkic conflict, rebellious nobles and over-mighty ministers, the great Mughal leader Akbar had managed to ameliorate these problems and to establish substantial stability and a measure of legitimacy. He tamed the Sunni Turkic nobility and the fundamentalist religious establishment by recruiting Persian Shias who were more amenable to authoritarian rule. He also drew in mainly Rajput Hindus as imperial servants, thus attaching conquered peoples to the regime as well as building the religious balance. To systemise the ranks in this heterogenous restructured nobility, he introduced a system of numbered ranks corresponding to status, income and duties.

In military terms a noble *mansabdar* might be required to provide up to 10,000 troops, and from the 1590s the number of heavy cavalrymen (*sawars*) was also specified. The *mansabdar* units were part of the paid standing army but were organized to imperial standards of training and equipment. Additionally, there was a central military organisation presided over by a powerful official, the chief Bakhsi. This man managed the household troops, including the weekly rotation of guard commanders, as well as all troops directly employed by the emperor across the empire.

The Mughal army relied heavily on massed cavalry to dominate the Gangetic plain and the valleys of the more mountainous districts. However, the horsemen were supplemented by large numbers of infantry, many of them armed with matchlocks and supported by a powerful field and siege artillery corps.

Moreover, Akbar was able to introduce such an efficient fiscal system that despite his numerous campaigns and huge military establishment, the imperial budget was consistently in surplus. There was little if any gap between Indian and European military technology and on land the empire possessed vastly superior numbers and an elaborate command structure. It was at sea that Europeans had an advantage, with their formidable combination of ship design, sailing rig and shipboard artillery. In Asian waters that power belonged to the Portuguese and the monarch they shared with Spain.

This was the empire that the English encountered when in 1608 their first ship, the *Hector*, arrived at the busy Gujurati port of Surat. Its captain was one William Hawkins, possibly a nephew of John Hawkins, who carried with him letters of introduction from James I to the deceased Moghul emperor, Akbar. Hawkins and the Company's agent, William Fitch, were quick to recognise that spices could be purchased with local products, especially Indian cottons and silks, thus reducing the need to import silver from Europe. This diversification into 'country' trades would have the added advantage of reducing the risk of relying upon the sale of spices in Europe: static demand and Dutch competition tended to drive prices downwards.

Surat was, however, under the direct authority of the new Mughal emperor, Akbar's son Jahangir (1605-1627). Without Jahangir's permission they could not do business at all. He was not interested in a commercial treaty with a minor European king, and he already had business arrangements with the Portuguese.

The chief Moghul official in Surat, Mukarrab Khan, an ally of the Portuguese, seized the *Hector*'s cargo. A little later two of her boats were taken by the Portuguese and their crews sent as prisoners to Goa. When the *Hector* sailed for Bantam, Hawkins and Finch were left alone. Hawkins set out for the Mughal court at Agra, while Finch stayed to arrange the recovery of the *Hector*'s cargo and a survey of the commercial possibilities of Surat: cloths, mercury, ivory, coral and even sword blades. In 1610 he followed Hawkins to Agra.

Fortunately for the Company, Jahangir was curious about European culture and goods and, more practically, was determined to prevent Portuguese naval interference with the trade and pilgrim routes from Surat to the Red Sea and Persian Gulf. In 1609 he received William Hawkins at his court at Agra, warning the Portuguese Jesuits there against trying to poison him. For his part, Hawkins accepted a bride, an Armenian Christian woman pressed upon him by Jahangir as a symbol of friendship, and he became a nightly participant in the emperor's opium sessions. However, Jahangir was cautious: he was not about to offend the region's dominant seaborne power in favour of an untried rival. Moreover, Hawkins' position was undermined when Finch foolishly outbid a member of Jahangir's family for a quantity of indigo. It was further damaged by Mukarrab Khan's return to royal favour, Hawkins's own stubbornness over the valuation of the *Hector*'s goods, and by the arrival in Agra of drunken survivors of an English shipwreck. Portuguese intrigues and promises did little to help the Englishman and In 1611 Hawkins left Agra never to return. If the Company were to make any progress at all in north India, it would have to prove its naval credentials.

In 1612 its opportunity came. A larger Portuguese squadron unsuccessfully engaged four English galleons in the Suvali estuary north of Surat. Though little damage was done by either side, three of the Portuguese vessels ran aground, so the skirmish could be presented as an English victory. It may have persuaded Jahangir of the potential of an English alliance. In 1613 he formally offered the Company his protection and the right to trade at Surat. This was very far from a wide-ranging commercial treaty, let alone a naval pact, but for the Company it was at least a start.

Eastern Enterprise

In 1615 the Portuguese again attacked English ships off Surat and when English trading activities extended into the Persian Gulf, their opposition intensified. The Company retaliated by making common cause with the Persians and supported their successful assault upon Hormuz in 1622. In return, the English received valuable privileges in Persian ports. An Anglo-Dutch attack on Bombay in 1629 miscarried, but when peace was made in 1635, the English were well established in the Gulf and permanently entrenched at Surat. The breaking of the Portuguese grip on the Gulf and Red Sea routes made the Company's naval power indispensable to the Mughals and in 1634 it was allowed to trade in Bengal, valued for its silk and saltpetre, a component of gunpowder.

From 1615 to 1618 the English ambassador Sir Thomas Roe lived at and travelled with the Mughal court based at Ajmer, in north-western India. He liked and respected Jahangir, who was delighted with his principal present, an English carriage, which he had copied and used. Roe was especially welcome because he shared Jahangir's passion for wine and opium. Significantly, he also won over the emperor's prospective successor, Khurram, who would reign as Shah Jahan, and who had previously favoured the established Portuguese over the newcomer English. Roe, indeed, was the most sophisticated and intelligent of all early English travellers to South Asia. For a very long time Western scholars, without access to the relevant Moghul documents, assumed that Roe's account of the Mughal court and its politics was the most complete and trustworthy text available. In terms of solid diplomatic gains, however, Roe was far less successful.

By its nature, his mission – to obtain exclusive trading rights for the English East India Company – conflated diplomatic and commercial goals, a connection unacceptable at the Mughal court, and made all the more confusing because of his dual accreditation by the East India Company and James I. In official, as opposed to personal business, Roe's tendency to stand on his dignity as an ambassador of a sovereign king did not help matters. Moreover, the coach apart, Jahangir was unimpressed by the quality of the presents Roe had to offer, and Roe failed appreciate the Moghul habit of evaluating the importance of an embassy by the value of the gifts it brought. More fundamentally, the emperor had nothing to gain from granting exclusive trading rights to anyone: it was in his interest to play English, Dutch and Portuguese off against each other. Roe had to leave without the concessions he wanted.[34]

The Hindu states of the south

As early as 1611 an English ship was sent to the Coromandel Coast, on the south-eastern flank of the subcontinent, to open a trade with Bantam in cotton cloth. A factory was established at Masuliputam, the port of the Deccan sultanate of Golconda. From there the English moved into the

Vijayanagar empire, a Hindu polity created in reaction to Muslim raids into the Deccan.

Until a disastrous war with the five Deccan Sultanates in 1565, the empire had been very successful, but thereafter it was much weaker and vulnerable to secessionism. By 1613 Mysore had ceased to send tribute and imperial revenue to the emperor. The states of Ginjee, Nayaka, Madurai and Chitradurga also achieved independence and in 1613 the empire was reduced to a rump. It was perhaps out of desperations as much as weakness that in 1639 the Vijayanagar emperor sold to the East India Company a three-mile strip of land at Madras (modern Chennai) on the Coromandel coast and allowed it to build a fort there. Fort St George was constructed in 1640 and when Vijayanagar fell to the Moghuls six years later, the English were allowed to continue in possession.

Madras was hardly a glittering prize. The village supported only a few fishermen so there was no established commercial centre. It did not even have a decent harbour. Ships would anchor two miles offshore in the roadstead and cargoes would be loaded and unloaded from the beach by boats braving the surf. It was even suggested, somewhat fancifully, that the Company's representative could only have chosen the site to be near his mistress. A more plausible explanation that it was the one place that was offered, and did at least provide a reasonably secure base, with access to Indian weavers and brokers, and over which the Company could gradually assert greater control. For the time being, however, it was less a triumph than a consolation.

The English in India were thus in a much weaker trading position than the Dutch in Indonesia. Unable to impose monopolies, they were obliged to compete with local merchants and European rivals. That in turn forced them to become experts in the patterns of local trade. These 'country' trades were all the more vital because of the need to reduce the much-criticised drain of silver bullion from home. Though India took some British cloth, metals such as lead, tin and mercury, as well as mechanical toys, tapestries and ivory, these goods were never sufficient to balance the cost of the Company's purchases. Therefore, they acquired a knowledge and expertise in bargaining with Indian clients never achieved by their European competitors. By mid-century, however, they were still in a very precarious position, and compelled to operate in the shadow of a powerful and expanding empire.

PART III

Expansion

1651-1713

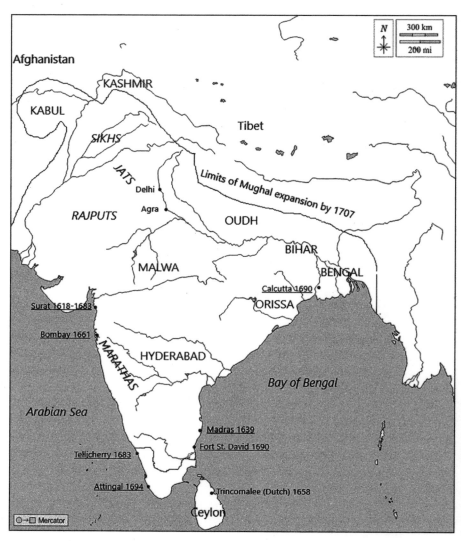

Mughal expansion and English enclaves in India by 1707.

8

Republic, Restoration and War

1651 was a turning point. The final defeat of Charles II at Worcester virtually ended the British civil wars, removed the threat of a Stuart-dominated Scotland and established a united British republic. Within a year Scotland had submitted and Ireland was subdued. At last the Commonwealth was fairly secure within the British Isles. The new Model Army now expected the Rump to carry out the godly reforms for which the soldiers believed they had been fighting, including a radical religious settlement. First, however, external dangers had to be faced. The great Catholic powers France and Spain were still at each other's throats, but both were potentially supporters of the Stuarts and enemies of republicanism. More immediately, there was real fear of the House of Orange's dynastic connections to the Stuarts, the Dutch republic's over-tolerant Calvinism and its considerable naval power. The Dutch, financiers of the Caribbean sugar revolution, were also serious commercial rivals. Dutch *fluyts*, designed to require small crews in relation to their tonnage, dominated the Atlantic carrying trades. There had also been violent disputes over North Sea fisheries. The Rump's response was a law with limited aims but with enormous significance for later imperial management.

At first sight the Navigation Ordinance of October 1651 might seem a purely commercial attempt to damage Dutch dominance of the seaborne carrying trade, and it would be easy to assume that it was passed to satisfy the demands of London merchants. Now, goods from Europe could only be imported into England in English ships, or in ships of the country of origin of the freight. Fish and any cargoes from Africa, Asia or America could arrive only in English vessels. Thus, Dutch ships could legally import Dutch products, but not (for example) Russian flax and timber, or Barbadian sugar, or Asian spices.

It is arguable that the real aim of the law was national security. If trade into English ports was limited largely to English vessels, English shipbuilding – and therefore English naval capacity - would prosper. More English vessels on oceanic routes would mean more trained deep-water sailors, again a vital naval resource. The Dutch Stadtholder, William II, was Charles II's cousin and sympathetic to the Stuart cause – the royalist assassination of the English ambassador to the Hague was attributed to Dutch complicity – so the intended relative weakening of Dutch naval capacity was crucial. War was in the air and the Ordinance was less a cause of the First Anglo-Dutch War than a reaction to its imminence.

Nor, despite being later understood as the first step towards a comprehensive system of colonial regulation, was it conceived primarily as an empire-building measure. Religion, internal security, and relations with European powers all played more important roles. At the same time, however, it marked the beginning of an effort to secure greater control over existing colonies and to acquire new ones, in order to weaken enemies, protect trade and to maximise the state's resources in relation to its Continental rivals. The emphasis on shipping was continued in the Tobacco Ordinances of 1652 and 1654, which (again) forbade the growing of tobacco in England, in order to protect the seaborne trade with Virginia.[1] This process survived the Restoration of the monarchy in 1660 and developed into the complex mechanism of commercial, maritime and colonial regulation known to historians as the Navigation System.

The First Anglo Dutch War
The First Anglo-Dutch War was a naval contest fought mainly in home waters. English fleets tried to intercept Dutch merchant convoys and Dutch fleets set out to see their ships safely home. Fighting was hard, fortunes wavered, and the Dutch drove the English from the Mediterranean. In the Channel and North Sea, however, the English had the advantages of deeper harbours and therefore of larger ships and heavier guns, together with a much more unified administrative system. By the autumn of 1653 the Commonwealth fleets had won three major fleet actions and blockaded the Dutch coast. The Dutch maritime economy collapsed and, with Cromwell now Lord Protector, serious peace talks began. In April 1654 the Treaty of Portsmouth brought the war to an end.[2]

Despite the victory, the treaty did not give England significant commercial or colonial advantages. Although the treaty enjoined respect for each other's trade laws, the Dutch denied that this implied acceptance of the Navigation Ordinance, which was in any case very troublesome to enforce. It was difficult to identify a ship's true ownership, beyond requiring the master to swear an oath on that point. Many ships, apparently English-owned, were of Dutch construction, and colonial producers still took now-illegal advantage of low Dutch shipping rates. The Dutch promise to prosecute the Amboyna murderers was meaningless as the perpetrators were already dead, and the East India Company was as far as ever from rebuilding its position in the East Indies. Cromwell's proposal for an Anglo-Dutch Protestant political union came to nothing. None of this mattered much alongside the Dutch promise to expel Charles Stuart, and their secret adherence to an annex called the Act of Seclusion: a commitment that the House of Orange would never again hold the office of Stadtholder. Security in Europe still trumped expansion abroad.

Cromwell's Spanish War

Expansion, however, was still on the agenda. Spain was the traditional enemy with an apparently vulnerable and fabulously rich empire, so holding out the Elizabethan dream of a profitable Protestant crusade. Some members of the Council of State, led by Major General John Lambert, were less certain of Spanish weakness and may have seen that France was the rising power, the real threat to English safety and European Protestantism. For a while the argument went Lambert's way and in October 1754 General at Sea Robert Blake was despatched to harry French movements against Spain in the western Mediterranean, followed by action against that perpetual menace, the North African Barbary pirates. But already Cardinal Mazarin had agreed to expel Charles Stuart from France, and even as Blake was sailing, a formal treaty deprived the Stuarts of all French aid. There was now no need to quarrel with France and a much stronger case for attacking the Spanish empire.

The Council heard the evidence of a supposed Caribbean expert – an ex-Dominican friar and former missionary, Thomas Gage – that the war could be confined to the West Indies, and that Cuba and Hispaniola were weakly defended. Thus, just as Blake was beginning the undeclared war with France, the council planned to seize Spanish Caribbean islands as both profitable colonies and as bases for further aggression. The so-called 'Western Design' was launched with ill-chosen troops, poorly supplied and stricken with disease. The land and sea commanders, Robert Venables and William Penn quarrelled. After failing to capture Hispaniola, and too weak to attempt Porto Bello or Havana, they captured the obscure, poorly defended and relatively unattractive island of Jamaica.

Jamaica was not enough to dress up the failed expedition as a success. The great prizes had been missed and Charles Stuart was already in the Spanish Netherlands, negotiating for a Spanish invasion in support of a royalist uprising. When Penn and Venables returned home they suffered a spell in the Tower for deserting their posts. Cromwell characteristically believed he had incurred God's displeasure, which may be why he willingly embraced the inevitable wider war with Spain. Blake, who had by now destroyed a Barbary squadron in Porto Farina near Tunis and ransomed English prisoners from the Dey of Algiers, was ordered to blockade Cadiz, prevent reinforcements sailing to the Caribbean, and to intercept the inward-bound treasure convoy from America should it slip past Penn. Exhaustion, shortage of supplies and need for repairs forced him to turn for home before the fleet arrived, but he and General Edward Mountagu resumed the blockade in the spring of 1656.

Effective blockade required a secure base for supplies and repairs. Portuguese-held Tangier was used but the harbour was too open to provide a permanent base. The Generals considered seizing Gibraltar, but found it too strongly fortified to be attempted without at least four thousand infantry. They had no such force available, and none could be spared from home because the Protectorate was already negotiating a French alliance aimed at the conquest of the Spanish Netherlands. The best that could be done was to pressure King John of Portugal into a firm anti-Spanish alliance, thus securing the continued use of Lisbon.

In September the need for a permanent base was underlined when, the main fleets having withdrawn to England for refitting, the small squadron blockading Cadiz intercepted and destroyed the incoming silver fleet. Although two of the seven vessels were sunk and three escaped, the other two yielded a haul worth £1,000,000 in silver, indigo, sugar and other goods. Yet the interception, coming after the English ships had been forced out to sea by a gale, had been fortuitous. It was fortunate, too, that the silver fleet had been without its usual formidable escort. The lack of a secure base to support a powerful fleet off southern Spain and into the Mediterranean was to plague strategic planners for many years.

The war now turned northward. As ever, the threat from the Spanish Netherlands, in the form of a Spanish army accompanied by Charles Stuart and his brother James, had to take priority over all other operations. An Anglo-French treaty of alliance, signed in March 1657 and valid for one year, committed England to providing a fleet and 6,000 troops to join France's 20,000 in an assault upon Mardyke, Dunkirk and Gravelines. Mardyke was taken in September and on the Protector's insistence Dunkirk became the first objective of the 1658 campaign. The siege opened on 15 May and on 4 June the Anglo-French army, supported by the artillery of English warships, defeated a Spanish relief force in the high sandhills to the east of the town. Dunkirk surrendered ten days later and, as the alliance treaty stipulated, was at once handed over to the English. England had once again a foothold on the continent, its first for a century, and had eliminated a nest of privateers.

Restoration and the Navigation System
Cromwell's death in 1658 led rapidly to the collapse of the Protectorate and a confused scramble for power within the army, during which it became clear that only a legitimate monarchy could restore stability. In January 1660, the commander in Scotland, George Monck, now the only general with a disciplined, paid and unpoliticised force at his back, marched on London. A Convention (a parliament not summoned by a reigning monarch) was elected, Charles issued a conciliatory declaration

from Breda in the Netherlands, and the monarchy was restored in all three kingdoms. On 29 May 1660, his thirtieth birthday, King Charles II entered his capital. The British republic was once again the three kingdoms of England, Ireland and Scotland.

With the Restoration, all laws passed by Interregnum parliaments became null and void. However, the perceived importance of the 1651 Navigation Ordinance was such that the Convention promptly re-enacted it and it was confirmed by the subsequent Cavalier Parliament (so called because it was dominated by royalists) in 1661. Moreover, the new law[3] addressed the weaknesses in the 1651 legislation. This was the work of New England-born Sir George Downing, Member for Carlisle, who saw that driving foreigners out of English seaborne trade was impossible without enough English and Irish shipping to take up the slack. Exports to the colonies could be carried only in English or Irish vessels. As for imports, the unenforceable blanket ban on foreign vessels was dropped. Instead, favourable customs tariffs were levied on specific 'enumerated' goods – including the sinews of naval power, timber, flax and hemp from the Baltic, amounting to about half of European trade – confined to English ships or ships of the country of origin. In addition, the number of items deliverable only to an English port rose from one to seven: sugar, tobacco, cotton wool, indigo, ginger, fustic and other dyeing woods. The master and three-quarters of the crew of every English ship must be English and all foreign-built ships owned in England had now to be registered. The latter measure was reinforced by the Fraud Act of 1662, which deemed all unregistered foreign-built ships alien.[4]

The next step was to reserve the colonial markets for English producers as well as for English shipping. In 1663 the Staple Act[5] required all goods bound for English colonies to pass through England; and in 1673 the Plantation Duties Act closed an important loophole by requiring duties on enumerated goods, for which a bond had not been deposited, to be paid before sailing. The result was a spectacular growth in English ship-building for long-distance trades, in the number of trained deep-water seamen, and consequently in English naval power. The Navigation System created a protected colonial market for English goods and thus an increasing income from customs duties, which by 1681 gave the Crown greater – but by no means complete – independence from parliament.

Charles II fought two expansionist Dutch wars, the net results of which were the acquisition of New Amsterdam, rechristened New York, and some embarrassing naval failures. Nevertheless, there was marked expansion of the empire from 1660 and a significant movement towards more centralised control. New settlement colonies were formed in North America, Carolina in 1663 and Delaware in 1664. In the Caribbean, the Cayman Islands, the Virgin Islands and the Bahamas were all in English hands by 1670. Charles's marriage to the Portuguese princess

Catherine of Braganza reinforced fears of his sympathy for Catholicism but strengthened the alliance with Portugal, and her dowry included two significant territorial gains. The island of Bombay, held outright by the Portuguese Crown through the *Estada da India*, became the first English sovereign possession in Asia, and was to have immense long-term significance in the building of British dominance in India. The other, Tangier, seemed at the time to be of far greater importance: it seemed to provide the permanent base so badly needed to support naval operations and defend trade in the Mediterranean.

Tangier and the search for a Mediterranean naval base
The maritime states of North Africa were a perpetual threat to trade passing in and out of the Mediterranean, and even raided the south-western coasts of Ireland and England. Their bases at Algiers, Tunis, Tripoli and Salé were well-defended and being on a dead lee shore for most of the year, were extremely difficult to blockade. Technically, they were not the 'Barbary pirates' as they were perceived at the time and by many historians since. They were in theory vassal states of the Ottoman empire, and in practice near-autonomous regencies waging declared war against Christian states. As N. A. M. Rodger has pointed out, their motives were very much like the Protectorate's: religion, a need to keep their Turkish garrisons busy, and to make warfare pay. They were prepared to make and adhere to peace treaties and alliances with states powerful enough to make their seaborne depredations unprofitable.[6]

The best strategy, therefore, was to patrol the Straits of Gibraltar so thoroughly that English convoys could pass safely, and Algerine vessels could be intercepted and destroyed. This, combined with the occasional bombardment or raid, might induce rulers like the Dey of Algiers to agree to leave the English alone while continuing to harass their rivals' shipping. None of this could be done without a secure and viable local naval base.

Tangier seemed heaven-sent to provide just such a base. Huge sums were spent on improving the open harbour by building a mole. The landward defences were repaired and improved, an arc of outworks was established to keep Moroccan batteries away from the core fortifications, and a garrison of about 3,000 men was installed.

Yet the outer defences were never quite complete and could be vulnerable: Moroccan troops proved extremely adept at siege works. As for the mole, after twenty years of work it was only 470 yards long, less than half its projected length, and it was already causing the harbour to silt up. Consequently, Tangier was never self-sustaining as a naval base because it never attracted the merchant and maritime community who could supply naval stores on the spot. Nor was there ever a real attempt to station an effective squadron on the island: a pair of slave-oared galleys were found but proved almost useless. Fleets operating in the Straits of

Gibraltar or the Western Mediterranean used other ports – Leghorn, Malta, Port Mahon in Minorca, Gibraltar - none of them English and all of them unsatisfactory in one way or another.[7]

A better-funded government might have been able to overcome the problems and sustain the base from home. But before 1681 Charles II's government was perpetually short of cash, partly because Charles himself observed no budgetary limits, partly because at the Restoration the Convention had given him a deliberately inadequate revenue of £1.2 million a year. It was not possible to properly maintain Tangier and complete the Mole in the face of two unsuccessful Dutch wars (the Second Anglo-Dutch War cost around £5 million while the Dutch spent £11m) and perpetual parliamentary suspicion of Charles's ambitions. The garrison itself was suspect: even after the passage of the first Test Act – reserving all Crown appointments to Anglicans who had to expressly deny the Roman doctrine of transubstantiation – Catholics could serve in the Tangier garrison, provoking a fear that he was building there a popish standing army in order to create an absolutist state.

Even in 1682, when his growing customs revenues were making him more financially independent, he could not undertake large naval or military expenditure without calling another parliament. And that, having just survived the Exclusion Crisis (1679-1681) in which three successive parliaments dominated by the 'Whig' opposition tried to remove his Catholic brother from the succession, he was most reluctant to do. Even in 1684, when under the Triennial Act another parliament became legally due, and in the face against cogent advice from councillors, he refused to order an election. With the support of the 'Tory' or royalist gentry and the Church of England he concentrated upon weakening the Whigs, revoking the charters of Whig-dominated boroughs, and pursuing Whig leaders through the courts. When in 1682 unsavoury but effective Admiral Herbert finally obtained a workable treaty with Algiers, it seemed only prudent to abandon a base that had proved useless and expensive. The defensive works were mined and blown up and the garrison was evacuated to the British Isles. The need for a Mediterranean base – under English control, close to the Straits, with a safe harbour and with easy access to supplies – was to dog strategists until the early eighteenth century.

The Second and Third Anglo-Dutch Wars

The first of the king's two Dutch Wars arose partly out of suspicion of the Calvinist and republican Dutch, but it also revealed a determination to continue the Protectorate's aggressive imperial expansion and enforce the Navigation System. On the West African coast there was intense competition for the lucrative West African slave trade. In North America some New Englanders were using New Netherland as an illegal export channel for their furs, and the Caribbean trades were still the objects of intense rivalry. In the East, the Dutch were threatening to extend their Indonesian dominance to India by acquiring the Portuguese settlements on the Malabar coast. While Charles II was not particularly anxious for confrontation, he allowed his brother James Duke of York and his adherents to pursue an aggressive and provocative policy. James was deeply involved with the incidents that triggered the war: a raid on Dutch factories in West Africa and the unprovoked seizure of New Netherland.

An escalating spiral of reprisal and counter reprisal led to a series of fleet actions in home waters, where two dramatic English successes were cancelled out by empty coffers and a humiliating Dutch raid on the Medway in June 1667. Charles had to make an immediate peace in which he gained no trade concessions at all and retained New Netherland, while the Dutch kept their much more lucrative conquest of Surinam. The third war of 1672-1674, as frustrating and ill-advised as the first, was only superficially about trade and colonies and changed nothing. A Dutch expedition retook New Netherland (now New York) and, having been defeated by France, yielded it up at the peace.

An imperial mechanism of government – state building
In 1650 the Commonwealth had established a Committee of Trade – with a paid secretary, one Benjamin Worsley – succeeded from 1653 by a succession of committees of the Council of State. At the Restoration a Council for Trade and Plantations took over imperial business, replaced in 1668 by a separate Council of Trade and in 1670 by a Council for Plantations, the two being united in 1672. There were ambitious plans for this body: a dedicated building, a permanent staff including Worsley, and a budget of £7,400. Though it only lasted two years, it provided a model for its successors, the Lords of Trade (1675-1696), and the Board of Trade.[8]

Thus, by the 1670s there was a strong central administrative structure in place and at the same time London seemed to be asserting tighter control over its colonies. New royal colonies were established, and charters were challenged with legal writs of *quo warranto* ('by what right'). Only two new major chartered companies were formed under Charles II: the Royal African Company (founded 1663 and reorganised 1672) and the Hudson Bay Company (1670), both to exploit trades in difficult and distant regions where the English controlled only tiny commercial enclaves. Even the granting of the royal island of Bombay to the East India Company 1668 can be seen in these terms, so that without ignoring earlier precedents and later inconsistencies, there is a strong case for seeing a turning point in colonial administration in the 1670s.

The process continued into the 1680s. James encouraged the 1684 abolition of the Massachusetts charter by *quo warranto* and after succeeding Charles in 1685 merged the New England colonies and New York into a Dominion of New England. Given time, the Crown might have tried to create three mega-colonies in North America – in New England, the middle colonies and the south – possibly without representative assemblies. In Ireland, James and his Deputy weakened the Dublin parliament, began the Catholicising of the Irish army, and set about restoring lands previously seized from Catholic owners. These projects collapsed in 1688-1689 when James, whose zeal and hurry made him appear to be planning to create a Catholic absolutism, was overthrown and replaced by his daughter Mary and her husband William III of Orange, the Dutch Stadtholder.

James and his followers (the 'Jacobites') went into exile in France, and a parallel upheaval in Scotland (involving a brief civil war) installed William and Mary as monarchs and Presbyterianism as the state religion. With Louis XIV of France supporting the Jacobite cause, both kingdoms were committed to war to save both the 'Glorious Revolution' and the Dutch Republic.

The 'fiscal-military state'
The strains of the wars against Louis XIV forced William (1689-1702) and Mary to seek more efficient means of finding the money to support their very large fleets and armies. In the process they made significant concessions to parliament, which began to transform England into a constitutional monarchy. A parliamentary committee was charged with reviewing government spending and a new Triennial Act (1696) obliged the monarch to summon a new parliament every three years, in place of merely meeting one. The quid pro quo was not merely parliamentary taxes but the underwriting of a new and sophisticated system of borrowing, which allowed William and his successor Queen Anne (1702-1714) to tap a far greater proportion of the nation's wealth than was available to Louis XIV in France. Its essential feature was the Bank of England, whose assets were guaranteed by parliament, and which became the agency through which money was lent to the government. Because investors' money was relatively safe from sudden or capricious royal bankruptcies (like Charles II's 1672 Stop of the Exchequer) the Crown could borrow at lower rates.

These funds, combined with the need to support huge armed forces, led to a rapid expansion of the state. In 1696 William III replaced the Lords of Trade with the Lords Commissioners for Trade and Plantations (popularly known as the Board of Trade), a body quite separate from the Privy Council, and which endured as a colonial office until 1782. A new Navigation Act closed loopholes in the existing system and the 1698 Woollen Act protected English producers by forbidding the export of wool from Ireland or any of the colonies, even to each other.

The evolution of this 'fiscal-military' state, which continued through the eighteenth century, has been brilliantly analysed by John Brewer.[9]

The wars against Louis XIV

The War of the League of Augsburg (1689-1697), sometimes called the Nine Years War, or King William's War by Americans, was fought to defend the Revolution Settlements against foreign and Jacobite attempts to restore James II, not to acquire overseas possessions. Indeed, its most notable 'imperial' event was the reconquest of Ireland from James II's supporters. James's Lord Deputy and the Catholicised Irish army rapidly established control over almost the whole island and, with the arrival of James and French troops, seemed poised to cross the Irish Sea. The Irish situation became so critical that William himself took command there himself, and in his absence the Royal Navy suffered a severe naval defeat off Beachy Head, leaving England open to invasion from two directions. William's much-mythologised victory at Battle of the Boyne (July 1690) was indecisive, and the war continued for a year until the Battle of Aughrim in July 1691 and the siege and Treaty of Limerick in October. The terms of the Limerick treaty were generous but were overridden by the new Protestant-dominated Irish parliament. The French advance on the Dutch Republic was slowed by William's Dutch and English troops but halted only by a bad French harvest and French financial exhaustion.[10]

The next round, the War of the Spanish Succession (1702-1713), was fought by a grand alliance of the British kingdoms and the Hapsburg Monarchy to prevent a union of the French and Spanish crowns under Louis XIV's grandson, Philip of Anjou, while Spain itself was divided by civil war. From the English perspective, defeat would not only mean Bourbon domination of Europe, but French possession of the much-feared springboard for invasion, the Spanish Netherlands, as well as active French support for the claims of James II's son to be King James III.

While John Churchill, Duke of Marlborough, won spectacular victories in Germany and the Low Countries, the lack of a permanent Mediterranean base hampered early naval operations. Though Portugal's entry into the war confirmed the use of Lisbon by the Royal Navy, a base inside the Straits was still essential to protect trade, watch Toulon and support allied land operations in Spain. In 1704, the capture of Gibraltar by an Anglo-Dutch force solved the problem of control and permanence, but not that of adequacy. The open harbour was unprotected save for a mole adequate to shelter a few galleys, it was negligible as a commercial port, and it was vulnerable to Franco-Spanish counter-attack. Indeed, a naval relief force appeared almost immediately, and a disaster was averted only by the mistaken French decision to withdraw. A clear strategic objective had been taken and held, but Gibraltar could never become home to a large fleet.

Republic, Restoration and War

In 1707 the allies even considered seizing Toulon, using Prince Eugene's Austrian army and the British fleet. The port was besieged and British bomb ketches panicked the French Mediterranean fleet into scuttling itself in harbour, in itself a major success. But the strength of the fortifications and the threat of a relieving French army forced the allies to withdraw, and the problem of a safe Mediterranean base remained unresolved. The difficulty was tragically underlined when Sir Cloudesley Shovell's flagship and two other ships of the line were lost on the Scillies on their way home to winter. The surrender of Sardinia, then a Spanish possession, to Admiral Leake in August 1708 gave a useful port at Cagliari but the real triumph came at the end of the month, when Leake seized Minorca. Port Mahon was the best harbour in the western Mediterranean, within easy range of Toulon and relatively immune to attack. For the time being, at least, a fundamental strategic problem had been solved.

The wider picture was not so satisfactory. In 1710, failure in Spain, stubborn French resistance to Marlborough's projected invasion, ever-rising taxation and suspicion that English resources were being used for foreign purposes, gave the Tories a decisive victory. Marlborough was sacked, the new ministry launched the only truly 'blue-water' operation of the war, a disastrous attack on Quebec, and peace negotiations were opened.

The Peace of Utrecht France gave Britain undisputed control of Newfoundland and Rupert's Land, as well as yielding Nova Scotia and the French part of St Kitts. However, these were subsidiary to the main issues: recognition of Queen Anne by France; British acceptance of Louis XIV's grandson as King of Spain, provided the two Bourbon kingdoms should never have the same ruler; and the transfer of the Spanish Netherlands to Austria, which removed the prospect of a Bourbon invasion, but not necessarily the threat of a Hapsburg one. Great Britain might have emerged as a Great Power but she was still highly vulnerable to shifts in the European power balance, and doubly so while the Jacobite threat lasted. Her empire remained a means of reducing her weakness, not an end or an expression of power in itself.

9

Mainland North America: The South and the Middle Colonies

The second half of the long seventeenth century saw an astonishing expansion of England's settlement colonies in North America and the creation of a powerful enterprise for exploiting the fur trade out of Hudson Bay. New Netherland was conquered and finally held, and the colonies of New York (1664) and New Jersey (1664) created. In 1681, Pennsylvania between Jersey and Maryland became a refuge for Quakers. To the south of Virginia, Carolina was founded in 1673 and, far to the north, Prince Rupert's Hudson Bay Company established fortified trading posts to tap the fur trade. All of these enterprises had initially to be carried out under royal charter, but as time passed the Crown asserted more and more direct control. In 1679 New Hampshire became a royal colony, and in 1684 Charles II proclaimed the Dominion of New England, uniting and abolishing the charters of all the other Puritan colonies. At James II's accession in 1685, New York joined Virginia and New England as Crown colonies. The Revolution saw the splitting up of New England into individual colonies again, and in 1691 Massachusetts received a modified self-governing charter; but the general trend was towards royal oversight, and the background to that was European power politics.

Carolina: invasion, settlement, initial conquest
Carolina was the brainchild of Sir John Colleton, a royalist refugee and one of the small landowners being edged out by the sugar revolution in Barbados. He had noticed that settlers were already moving into the region to the south of Virginia, where the climate favoured tobacco. He found a fellow entrepreneur in Governor Berkeley of Virginia who was aware of Virginians moving into what was to become the Albemarle

Mainland North America: The South and the Middle Colonies

region of North Carolina. Others had noted that New Englanders were going to the Cape Fear area and Barbadians were filtering into the Port Royal area still further south. Thus, it would be possible to populate a new colony without having the expense of bringing out settlers and servants from England.

Colleton and Berkeley used their London contacts to attract a small but powerful ring of investors. Two, Sir George Carteret and Lord Berkeley, were clients of James Duke of York, and Lord Berkeley was a member of both the Council for Plantations and the Royal African Company. Others included Edward Hyde, Earl of Clarendon and the king's Lord Chancellor; George Monck the general whose army had ensured Charles II's restoration; and Anthony Ashley Cooper, the later Baron Ashley, was already deeply involved in the administration of colonies and trade. The eighth partner, William Earl of Craven, a soldier rising rapidly in the royal service, was close to Prince Rupert. All were active in bodies administering trade, the navy or colonies, and every one of them had invested in commercial schemes such as the Royal African Company. Their interest was as absentee proprietors who expected incomes from rents, and who therefore had to find migrants who would actually settle in the new colony.[11]

The eight proprietors were granted a royal charter in 1663 closely based on that given to Maryland before the Interregnum. Stressing religious toleration, it strongly reflected the preferences of the king and Clarendon, and its town-based structure of government was designed to prevent dispersal of the population across a series of great plantations. That charter had now to be sold to four groups already in Carolina: the Virginians in the north, the new Englanders at Cape Fear and two groups of Barbadians, one at Port Royal in the far south. The New Englanders demanded self-government after the Massachusetts model, obliging the proprietors to offer a very considerable degree of autonomy. Land was distributed on a 'headright' system: 100 acres for each freeman, plus fifty for each male servant he imported and sixty for each woman. On discharge from indentures each male servant would receive ten acres and a female six. The concessions were accepted by both the new Englanders and one of the Barbadian groups, who settled at Cape Fear. The other Barbadian group accepted a second set of terms, the 'Agreement and Concessions', in January 1665. In the end, both the Cape Fear and Port Royal settlements failed, but the basic terms appeared in subsequent colonial constitutions, including Ashley's 1669 'Fundamental Constitutions'.

The Carolina economy at first depended more upon trade with the coastal Native nations, cattle and the production of naval stores, than upon tobacco. The hides of the whitetail deer were prized in Europe for making gloves and book covers, and the Yamasees living between Carolina and Florida were the key suppliers. The planters' demand for labour could also be met by Yamasee slaving raids upon weaker tribes. From the 1690s, however, planters turned increasingly to rice, exports rising from rising from 300 barrels in 1699 to 11,000 in 1714. The rapid expansion of rice cultivation, driven partly by planters' belief that rice grew best in hitherto virgin soil, pushed the colony's cattle and hogs further out, devastating the grazing and browsing of the whitetail deer and thereby the Indians' source of vital trade goods. At the same time the Yamasees' own raids had destroyed or driven away the nations from whom they took captives, reducing their purchasing power still further. From around 1710 the Yamasees began to fall into debt to traders, who insisted that they be paid in slaves taken from the Yamasees themselves. The consequences of this ecological and human disaster would be fully felt in 1715.[12]

Virginia: the Susquehannock War and Bacon's Rebellion
In Virginia the former royal governor, Sir William Berkley, was restored in 1660. War broke out with the Susquehannocks. It triggered a major revolt by white settlers, lasted longer, and arguably had a more profound impact. Yet most historians have been so preoccupied with the settler revolt, 'Bacon's Rebellion', that the Indian war is seldom mentioned in general works and is little understood. On the face of it, there was no need for conflict: the Indians' core territory lay in the Potomac Valley, sufficiently insulated by distance from expanding settlements and invasive livestock. One historian has suggested that the answer lies in internal tensions within both societies: the Indian practice of 'mourning war' – expressing domestic grief through outward violence – and class and gender tensions among the Virginians.

According to this interpretation, decades of war with the Haudenosaunees (the Five Nations, or Iroquois) had reduced the Susquehannock population from 5,000 in the 1650s to about 400 by 1675. This catastrophic loss turned 'mourning war' from a ritual outlet of emotion into a ruthless, pitiless form of conflict. Warriors as young as fifteen took over leadership roles; prisoners were slaughtered on the spot rather than being brought home as captives; and the ritual torture of captives became extended beyond all norms and provoked retaliation in kind. A further element was the aggression of frontiersmen, both fearful of raids and anxious to acquire the lands of even friendly Indians, and to whom the decentralised nature of Virginian government gave considerable freedom of action.

War broke out almost by accident. Virginian militia, pursuing some stolen hogs, attacked a Susquehannock camp in error, provoking an isolated and limited retaliation. A heavy-handed and murderous Virginian response led to a series of raids on the settlements. These in turn provoked panic and an unauthorised counter-offensive by the Virginian militia. The Susquehannocks scattered: some moving north, other to the west and another group returned to their town on the Potomac. For his part the

Mainland North America: The South and the Middle Colonies

Virginian governor William Berkeley condemned the militia action and replaced offensive action with the building of nine frontier forts. That in turn triggered a revolt by frontier settlers terrified of fresh raids, unwilling to distinguish between friend and foe, and who coveted the lands of all Indians whether hostile or not. However, it was not wholly about the Indian threat or even about royal government but aimed at the privileges of the planter élite: tax exemptions for members of the governor's council, a poll tax (paid in tobacco) for the upkeep of local government, measures enacted by a planter-dominated colonial assembly. The rebel leader was one Nathaniel Bacon, himself a well-off planter and member of the colonial council, who in April 1676 persuaded the friendly Occaneechee to help attack two Susquehannocks on the Roanoke river, and then turned on his allies. Disciplined by Berkeley, he raised two hundred men, forced the governor to flee and razed Jamestown. When Bacon died in October, Berkeley launched a counter-offensive, defeated what remained of the rebel forces and executed its leaders. The arrival of three royal commissioners backed by a thousand regular troops led to a reduction in the powers of the assembly, the replacement of the militantly anti Amerindian militia with a smaller, tamer force, and greater authority for the governor over the districts.[13] In May 1677 the Treaty of Middle Plantation between the commissioners and Indian leaders reduced the tribes to dependency in exchange for protection and limited hunting rights.

The Middle Colonies: New York and New Jersey

The conquest of New Netherland in 1664 was in part a move to tame New England and at the same time to enforce the Navigation Acts by eliminating clandestine trade with the Dutch. Under the proprietorship of the Duke of York until 1685, and thereafter as a Crown colony, the lower Hudson Valley became a land of large quasi-feudal estates, unattractive to would-be freehold settlers but with direct access to the fur trade through the Five Nations, which for a time dominated the economy. James granted the region that was to become New Jersey to two proprietors, Carteret and Lord Berkeley, who already had an interest in Carolina and who tried to attract settlers with land grants and religious toleration. Besides English families, New York and New Jersey attracted French Huguenots, Dutch, New Englanders, Scots Presbyterians and later, Palatine Germans. On the upper Hudson River, however, on the Iroquoian frontier, the population remained overwhelmingly Dutch. Despite temporary loss during the Third Anglo-Dutch War, New York became the key English colonial port of the north, and the hub of a vast traffic in food to the West Indies.

In the upper Hudson Valley, where the vast majority of the white population was still Dutch, the Iroquois had to confront the unwelcome arrival of the English. As Ian K. Steel points out, they had three choices. The first was to make peace with the traditional enemy, the French; but that would mean the return of Catholic missionaries, expelled in 1658 for bringing cultural contamination and internal conflicts. The second was to hope that the Dutch would continue to dominate the fur trade through Albany (formerly Fort Orange) and keep missionaries out. The third option was to try a neutral balancing act between English and French, and trade with both. The first option was, to begin with, the most popular.[14]

The Five Nations made peace in 1665-1666 at the cost of readmitting French missionaries, who were able to baptise about a fifth of the Iroquoian population. However, their old habit of demanding the segregation of converts made them increasingly unpopular and the emigration of Christian families to French-controlled territory eventually gave tradition-minded Iroquois the upper hand. By 1675 Edmund Andros, the governor of New York, was able to offer the Mohawks guns and land claims in New England in return for attacking Metacom's winter camp, and afterwards to offer asylum to the fugitive. In this way he built up the numbers of Indians willing to defend New York's eastern frontier, while encouraging the Iroquois to attack their enemies – French and Indian – further west. By 1678, the Iroquois had established land claims from Carolina to Maine.

The heavy casualties that were the price of this violent expansion induced the Five Nations to turn towards neutrality, a policy no more acceptable in Quebec than in New York and difficult and dangerous to maintain. Nevertheless, it enabled them to avoid over-dependence upon one source of guns and to replace their losses with adopted captives. All this was facilitated by the peaceful commercial approach of the Albany Dutch, in contrast with the aggression of settlers lower down the Hudson. In the coming Anglo-French struggle for the fur trade much would depend upon New York's ability to draw the Iroquois out of their neutrality.

The Middle Colonies: the founding of Pennsylvania

The Restoration shattered the confidence of the once powerful and violently radical Society of Friends. The return of the monarchy and the re-establishment of the Church of England seemed to be God's will. Fearful of their subversive past, the Cavalier Parliament passed a Quaker Act, the only new law imposing penalties for membership of a specific Dissenting sect. Though unevenly enforced, zealous local magistrates could use it to impose fines and imprisonment upon those whom they regarded as dangerous radicals. Gradually, the Friends lost their revolutionary zeal and turned to pacifism. In place of the fiery leadership of Fox and Naylor came the royalism of a convert to Quakerism: William Penn, a friend of both Charles II and James Duke of York, and son of their distinguished admiral.

Assisted by Charles II's own sympathy for religious toleration, Penn used his position to mitigate the enforcement of the Quaker Act and to encourage Quaker emigration to North America. Penn and other

Mainland North America: The South and the Middle Colonies

Quakers saw America not only as a refuge but, like the New Englanders, a place where a holy commonwealth could be constructed. They built up very considerable Quaker influence in West New Jersey and in 1682 purchased the proprietorship of East New Jersey outright. The next step was to acquire a new province south of the Delaware. Penn may have exploited Charles II's sympathy for religious toleration, debts the Crown still owed to his father and – despite the Lords of Trade's growing unease with proprietary colonies – a willingness to encourage Dissenters to leave the kingdom. Whatever the motivation, or combination of motives, in 1681 Charles II issued a charter making Penn proprietor of a vast tract of North America below the Delaware River.

Penn wanted to call the new colony 'New Wales' or 'Sylvania' (Woodland), but Charles insisted on 'Pennsylvania' in honour of Penn's father, the admiral. As the older Penn had never been a Quaker and was always a Tory, it seemed a strange name to give to a province intended for a holy experiment in egalitarianism. Perhaps, as Angus Calder suggests, Charles was mischievously 'teasing the well-bred Dissenting bore'.[15]

Penn landed in his chartered Promised Land in 1682 and began the building of its capital, Philadelphia, the city of brotherly love. His land policy, a mixture of large grant and attractive leasehold terms, attracted 3,000 settlers within a year. Religious toleration was another attractive feature: any believer in one God was welcome – thus in theory embracing Jews and Muslims – and all Christians could vote and hold offices. Thus, while government was inefficient and faction-ridden, the white population grew rapidly, agriculture thrived, and Philadelphia rapidly became a prosperous port.

Such success could only be at the expense of the Lenape, or Delaware Indians. To his credit, Penn was determined to acquire Indian land through treaty and fair purchase, and he may also have benefitted from the 'covenant chain' of interlocking alliances of which New York was already a part. Of particular significance was the growing Iroquois influence over the Delawares, reducing them to client status, dominating their foreign policy and claiming the right to dispose of their land as Onondaga saw fit. The gradual dispossession of the Pennsylvania Delawares was therefore slow and peaceful, but it was dispossession all the same.

10

New England, Hudson's Bay and the Clash with New France

For thirty years after the end of the Pequot War, southern New England enjoyed peace. Though the population had doubled by 1660, nearly all that growth was from natural increase, while immigration from the British Isles was outweighed by the emigration of adult Puritans keen to fight for Parliament in the Civil War or to enjoy the fruits of victory later. With so young a population there was less pressure on land and therefore less pressure upon the Native nations. While there was little demand for new land, the existence of the United Colonies of New England may have restrained frontier aggression by imposing a need for consensus. Moreover, Amerindians and whites were economically and to a limited extent culturally interdependent. Plymouth provided wampum, beads made from whelk shells, drilled with steel drills and strung together for sale inland to the New England Algonquians and through them to the Mohawk, who paid in furs. Puritan missions made slow but real progress from 1649 and founded a few towns of 'praying Indians'. Finally, neither side was sure it could safely make war on the other: the Indians had vivid memories of the fate of the Pequots, while the colonists feared the Narraganset-Mohawk connection.[16]

King Philip's War
The pressure on Indian land built up after 1660 and within a few years became intolerable, as a new colony-born generation came of age and increased the demand for new farms. The violence of local clashes increased as settlements came closer and closer to Indian towns and settler cattle damaged Indian crops. The most threatening of these settlements was the township of Swansea, which dominated the neck of land between the Wampanoag peninsula homeland and the mainland. Indians could not understand the idea of private and exclusive property in land and saw no reason why they could not hunt or farm on 'sold' land neglected

New England, Hudson's Bay and the Clash with New France

by the English. At the same time a profound economic and diplomatic revolution made war seem a viable solution. As the fur trade declined and the Mohawk directed their trade to Albany, the Wampanoags and Narragansetts became closer and turned their diplomacy towards anti-Mohawk and pro-French Algonquian tribes to the north. Determined to preserve their cultural and political unity, the Wampanoags became increasingly resistant to Christian missions. From the English point of view, all this presaged a wide-ranging hostile conspiracy, producing recurring war scares from 1664. By the mid-1670s the English were terrified by increasing Indian intransigence and Indians saw they must choose between moving westward, reduction to servants of the English, or a war of resistance. Indian nations were now much better-armed than in 1637, in the long term through illegal trade, and in the shorter term as the New England colonies relaxed their laws against trade in munitions from 1669. Most warriors now possessed firearms, very often flintlocks, which colonists were slower to adopt to replace the less efficient matchlock. To Metacom, 'King Philip' to the English and Wampanoag chief since 1662, war may have seemed worth the risks.[17]

The trouble began in June around the settlement of Swansea, beginning with armed demonstrations by bands of Wampanoags, proceeding to looting abandoned houses, and – when one of the looters was shot dead – the killing of nine settlers. Plymouth and Massachusetts militia responded in force and marched through the Mount Hope peninsula hunting for the Wampanoags who had already escaped into Pocasset by canoe. Now reinforced, free to choose his targets and use his superior mobility to evade colonial forces, Metacom began a devastating campaign against frontier settlements. These attacks encouraged the Nikmucks to start an offensive of their own, combining with settled Indians to ambush militia and burn towns in the upper Connecticut River Valley. That winter the Narragansetts, who had been hovering between peace and war, were driven into the conflict by the approach of a pre-emptive punitive expedition. The United Colonies may have been partly motivated by fear that they were conspiring with Metacom, but the 1,000 soldiers they raised were motivated by the prospective prizes – slaves and land. This column, reinforced by some Pequots and Mohegans, found and stormed a fortified refuge in the Great Swamp – but suffered over twenty per cent losses in the process. The surviving Narragansetts escaped north-eastward. From February to April the Indians burned towns to within twenty miles of Boston and as far as the coast of Massachusetts, as well as uncomfortably close to Plymouth. The colonial militias responded amateurishly, failed to co-operate properly, failed to pin down their enemies, performed poorly in woods and swamplands, and were repeatedly surprised or ambushed.

By April, however, Philip's forces were worn down hunger, disease and death. Rapid movement might foil pursuing militia but it also exposed

Indian cornfields to destruction. Their smaller numbers could not sustain losses at the same rate as the colonists, and even using forges for repair work, useable muskets and ammunition were in increasingly short supply. Morale fell, the militias improved their tactics, numbers of warriors gave up and even changed sides. When in August 1676 Philip himself was killed, the war was over. Many Indians fled north while others were enslaved or executed, and the colonists celebrated their return to God's grace.

For the Indians, the war was a demographic disaster. The numbers of Natives in southern New England fell from 11,600 to 3,700 through battle, disease and exposure, captivity, execution and permanent displacement. Those who fled north sought refuge with the Mohegans, Mahicans and Abenakis, leaving open vast areas to white penetration; in Douglas Leach's words, 'Philip's great gamble sealed the fate of all the tribes from the Merrimack River to Long Island Sound.' The refugees established themselves within the French sphere of influence, nursing an anti-English revanchism that would fester. The white colonists had also suffered a heavy blow. Of ninety towns, fifty-two had been attacked and seventeen destroyed; the numbers of dead were almost certainly well in excess of the early estimate of 800, and large numbers of settlers were now destitute refugees. The process of reconstruction took another two decades to complete.

Had God deserted them? In the long run, the settlers' Calvinist self-confidence was probably not reinforced by victory, as one historian would have it, but permanently undermined. Subsequent events would shake it further.[18]

The Glorious Revolution in America

The war had a different effect in Restoration England where, along with Bacon's rebellion in Virginia, it suggested that the colonies could not manage their own internal defence and invited closer supervision by the Crown. In 1676 the Lords of Trade sent an agent, Edward Randolph, to investigate New England's evasion of the parliamentary statutes and prohibition of Anglican worship. Having seen the destruction caused by the war, he reported that it was hight time to bring the autonomous colony to heel. In 1679, New Hampshire, the only New England colony not directly involved in the King Philip's War, became a royal colony. In 1684, at the very time of the *quo warranto* proceedings against defiant English boroughs, the Court of Chancery annulled the Massachusetts charter, after which Charles and the Board of Trade pushed ahead with plans to combine the American mainland colonies into two or three vice-royalties on the Spanish model. The next year, after Charles's death and James II's accession, Massachusetts, Connecticut, New Hampshire, Rhode Island, New York and New Jersey were designated as the Dominion of New

England, with a Crown-appointed governor and without an elected assembly.[19]

The Revolution of 1688 prompted an American revolt that ousted Edmund Andros. The Dominion broke up and in 1691 Massachusetts received a new charter which imposed a Crown-appointed governor and widened the franchise, but allowed it to swallow its old rival Plymouth. The original six Puritan colonies were reduced to four. Nevertheless, the whole episode – King Philip's War, the Crown's confiscation of the original charter, the imposition of the Dominion and the promotion of Anglicanism – had shaken old Puritan certainties to the core. Such fears, along with socio-economic rivalries, especially masculine fears concerning female sexuality and resentment of women of property, led to the infamous Salem witch trials of 1692-1693.

Rupert's Land

The vast region to the north of New France was icy, challenging and only accessible by sea. Agriculture was impossible and its Native inhabitants were migratory hunters and gatherers, whose homes were tipi-like lodges, quick to build and easy to dismantle. In winter the Cree, hardy Algonquians of the forests bordering Hudson's Bay, moved south to hunt bison in the more open 'parkland' region bordering the prairie, where they rubbed shoulders with the Siouan-speaking Assiniboin. The Company's trading partners, the Amerindians around Hudson Bay, west to Lake Winnipeg and south to Lake Superior, were more fortunate than their brethren further south, in that the temperature appears to have limited the effects of imported diseases, and there were no European settlements competing for their land. The Cree of Hudson's Bay, somewhere between 2,200 and 6,800 strong, valued European metal goods above all for the fishing and gathering season of spring and early summer. Guns for hunting were important, of course, but steel knives, hatchets, cooking pots and fishing hooks were infinitely superior to bark, wood, stone and bone. The London committee, realising the long-term importance of harmony with its suppliers, insisted that the Indians be treated well and honestly. The Cree liked Charles Bayly, the Quaker first governor of Fort Charles, and trade grew steadily with benefits to both sides.

In the autumn they began to move south, wintering with the Assiniboin, hunting for furs, trapping waterfowl and learning from their hosts how to 'pound' bison. South of the Cree lay Cree's allies the Objibwa, and their enemies the Assiniboin, originally a Siouan people, became drawn into the Cree trading network. Around 1690 when the English fur trade started to push into the interior and Algonquian-Sioux hostilities intensified, the Assiniboin may have decided to ally with the Cree.[20] Travel was on foot or – in the few months when the lakes and rivers were unfrozen – by canoe. Starvation was never far away.

The First British Empire

Yet this uninviting space yielded the finest furs on the continent. The potential of the northern fur trade was first realised in the 1650s by two Frenchmen, the combative Sieur des Groseilliers ('Lord Gooseberry Bushes') and his voluble companion Pierre Esprit Radisson. They approached the governor of New France with the idea of a direct trade through Hudson's Bay by sea, only for him to insist on the traffic being via Canada so it could be taxed. When he capped insult with injury by defrauding the pair of their trading profits, they went straight to London and the court of Charles II.

There was at once a great deal of interest. The expansionist band around the King – including his cousin Prince Rupert and his brother the Duke of York – were enthusiastic. Not only did the Bay promise profits but there was a strategic dimension. Russia, now a major importer of beaver, was also a key supplier of crucial naval stores: the tar, pitch, hemp, mast timber and flax (for sails) needed to keep the Restoration navy afloat and at sea. But the Baltic trade was dominated by the Dutch, who bought Canadian furs from the French and sold them in Muscovy. Thus, England's naval security was to an alarming degree dependent upon a potential (and already once an actual) enemy; but if England could break into the fur trade, and supply superior furs, this dependency would be drastically reduced.

The consortium of courtiers found investment in such a risky trade hard to come by – by 1668 they had raised no more than £10,000 – and one of the two ships sent out that year was lost en route. But the one vessel that reached the Bay with Groseilliers on board, the *Nonsuch*, achieved a dramatic success.

Groseilliers erected a fortified house named Fort Charles at the head of James Bay where the traders wintered. The Indians brought in furs of astonishing quality, which they exchanged for metal goods at what the whites thought bargain rates. The most prized of all were 'castor gras', beaver robes worn by an Indian headman for so long that they lost their outer hair and exposed the soft down beneath, prized for hatting. Even the fresh pelts, 'castor sec', were of superb quality. In the summer of 1669, taking advantage of the narrow window of opportunity when Hudson Strait was clear of ice and currents and winds were favourable, the *Nonsuch* sailed for home, bearing a cargo that sold in London for £1,379 6s 10d. The profit was not breathtaking, but it was substantial. The strategically desirable Hudson's Bay trade could also make money.

The charter Charles gave to the Hudson Bay Company in 1670 awarded it a monopoly of the trade over 'Rupert's Land', an area of 1.5 million square miles. Its first president was Prince Rupert, who was to be succeeded after twelve years by the Duke of York, supported by a governing committee of seven. It allowed the Company to establish a settlement colony, a highly unattractive prospect which came to nothing, and there was even talk of finding a workable land and water route to Asia. It quickly became apparent that furs were the only practical objective and the Company set out to make that trade pay.

The physical and financial risks were considerable – the Company generally lost one of its three to four ships a year and did not declare a dividend until 1684 – but the physical hazards made the monopoly self-enforcing. Interlopers generally came to grief or they lacked the staying power and the steadily gathered experience of the Company's men.[21]

By 1684 there were several trading posts on the Bay. Three were on James Bay: Fort Albany, Moose Factory and Rupert House were at the mouths of the rivers of the same names. York Fort was a considerable distance to the north-west, on the Bay proper. These stations employed only eighty-nine men in some of the most rugged conditions on earth – which meant men with sturdy characters and great physical toughness. John Nixon, who succeeded Bayly in 1679, urged the employment of Scots in place of the committee's 'London childring' and in the long run the Bay's trade was dominated by hardy Orkneymen. Those who stayed the course could forge satisfying and even lucrative careers. James Wright, who came to the Bay in the early 1670s as an apprentice shipwright, rose to become governor of all the posts there and a member of the governing committee in London. The experience, hardihood and special skills such men developed stood the Company in good stead against French- and New York-based rivals.

The French were deeply alarmed by the Company's modest success. They could not find the ships to regularly exploit the Bay trade by sea, nor goods as cheap as those offered by the English. In 1682 they founded their own Compagnie du Nord, which recruited frontiersmen called *coureurs de bois* ('wood runners') to take goods direct to the tribes, thus offering the Indians an alternative to the long trek to the English posts. The French traders were also more likely to speak the natives' languages and better understood the Indians' economic thinking. Moreover, though English goods were generally cheaper and more abundant, some French products were superior in quality. For example, the Indians rightly preferred French gin to crude English rum.

This was the long-term threat, but in the meantime the French were inclined to direct aggression. The pugnacious governor, Denonville, organised coureurs and experienced peasant militiamen, combined with Indian allies, to harass the Company forts mercilessly. In 1686 Pierre de Troyes led a surprise attack on the three James Bay posts and took them all. Two years later a naval expedition led by Pierre Le Moyne d'Iberville surprised and captured three Company ships trying to recover the forts. In 1690 he failed to take York Fort but captured the newly constructed Fort Severn, only to lose it again in 1693. The following year he was able to muster enough ships to take York Fort; the English retook it in 1695 but lost it again in 1697. It was not to be restored to the Company until the Treaty of Utrecht in 1713.

The wider casus belli
From 1689 the hostilities around Hudson Bay merged into the wider War of the League of Augsburg, known in the Americas as King William's War. As soon as hostilities broke out in Europe, France authorised the newly reappointed governor of New France, the Comte de Frontenac, to begin a major offensive against the English colonies. In February 1690 a party of Indians and Canadian militia destroyed the New York frontier town of Schenectady. On 18 March they struck Salmon Falls in New Hampshire, and in May a mixed band of French and Abenakis raided Casco and massacred the garrison at nearby Fort Loyal (now Portland) in Maine. A co-ordinated British response was almost impossible to organise. In 1690, Massachusetts forces sacked Port Royal in Acadia without support from other colonies and an intercolonial conference at New York attracted delegates only from only New York, Massachusetts, Plymouth, Connecticut and New Hampshire. What was supposed to be a combined assault on Quebec attracted only 285 militia – all from New York and Connecticut – and a few hundred Indians; an even smaller number reached La Prairie on the St. Lawrence opposite Montreal. Montreal itself was too strong to be attacked. The seaborne assault on Quebec foundered for want of coherent leadership, lack of ammunition and an outbreak of smallpox.[22]

Despite the formal ending of hostilities in 1697, this pattern of Canadian attack and incoherent English response persisted. In these operations much depended upon the attitudes of the Native American nations. Abenakis resentful of the English penetration of Maine, the Christianised tribes of New France, and the Great Lakes nations all tended to side with the French. Together they repeatedly raided the Iroquois country, devastating Onondaga, Oneidas and Mohawk towns. The Iroquois made their own dramatic incursions into New France, but were very wary of their English allies, who seemed incapable of stopping French retaliation. Consequently, the federation as a whole moved toward neutrality, while the Senecas in particular edged towards the French. In 1701 the Iroquois formally sought peace with both the French (at a meeting at Quebec) and the English (at Albany), their neutrality effectively shielding New York from attack for the next twelve years.

It was therefore the New England colonies that bore the brunt of raids during the War of the Spanish Succession – fortunately these were few and soon ceased. In Maine, French-led Abenakis attacked and sacked settlements, and in Massachusetts the town of Deerfield was destroyed and the village of Haverhill was attacked. Massachusetts,

New England, Hudson's Bay and the Clash with New France

Rhode Island and New Hampshire launched an unsuccessful attack on Port Royal in Acadia, a base of privateers harassing Boston fishermen. A New-England-New York assault on Quebec came to nothing because, preoccupied with the war in Europe, London could spare neither soldiers nor naval support. In 1710, however, Port Royal fell to colonial forces supported by 500 British marines, and in 1711 – with the Tories in power at home and a blue-water strategy once more in the ascendant – a major combined expedition was sent against Quebec. It failed and thereafter the peace negotiations ended active operations.

The Peace of Utrecht gave the northern mainland colonies greater security but not invulnerability. Possession of Acadia, now Nova Scotia, and of Port Royal (now Annapolis Royal) provided a buffer against Franco-Abenaki raids, and the cession of Newfoundland gave some protection to the New England fishermen. However, France still had possession of Cape Breton Island, which dominated the approaches to the St. Lawrence estuary and was to prove an irritating base for privateers. Further north, the Hudson's Bay posts and the valuable fur trade seemed secure. More importantly, while colonists – the New Englanders in particular – now depended upon the metropole for their defence and expansion, they were affronted when London chose to put imperial interests ahead of parochial ones.

11

The Caribbean: Sugar, Slaves and Conquest

The conquest of Jamaica
This 'Western Design' was to be executed by a powerful fleet carrying a strong infantry force for land operations. The next question was how the land force should be chosen. Instead of assigning whole regiments to the expedition, regimental commanders were required to provide drafts to create five new units. Predictably, the colonels made sure that they chose their undesirables, misfits and troublemakers, and supplied only the minimum numbers: only about 1,000 veterans were found. The new regiments had to be made up to strength from untrained recruits, so that the 2,500 soldiers were mostly inexperienced and all were ill-disciplined. The land force commander, Venables, was an experienced soldier and objected to the low quality of his men, but without effect.

The fleet reached Barbados in January 1655 where up to 4,000 local recruits were added to make six regiments, while a seventh was composed of volunteer seamen. Money from the island's treasury was seized and because supply ships due from Britain did not appear, local supplies had to be used. None of this pleased the local planter élite, especially as the Barbadian recruits included servants still bound by their indentures. Moreover, many were convinced that any colony the expedition should conquer would become Barbados's competitor. Thus, the usual particularism of colonial societies was already rearing its head in the English Caribbean.

Here the commanders, Venables and the competent naval General at Sea, William Penn, decided that their target should be Santo Domingo, the capital of the island of Hispaniola. At the time it seemed a reasonable choice. With the troops from England and Barbados, the plus another 1,300 from the Leeward Islands, they had the best part of 10,000 men. Unfortunately, the quality of the troops was still very uneven and the division of command between Venables and Penn transmitted downwards

The Caribbean: Sugar, Slaves and Conquest

into deep distrust between fleet and army. The food supply was still inadequate, knowledge of the geography and terrain of Hispaniola was sketchy at best, and the army was unused to tropical conditions. The planning took no account of the substantial strengthening of Spanish defences since Drake's successful raid of 1586 and following more recent Dutch assaults; and the long sojourn at Barbados had given the Spaniards ample time to prepare. It is hardly surprising that two attempts to take Santo Domingo were miserable failures.

On 13 April the expedition made landfall off Hispaniola. Venables wanted to land near the River Jaina, where Drake had disembarked in 1586. But with the surf too high for a safe landing, the fleet moved on to the River Nizao, thirty miles west of Santo Domingo. Some 7,500 men were landed, far too many for the resources available to them, and out of all proportion to the few hundred Spanish defenders. They struggled for three days towards their objective, without water bottles and through baking savannah and dense tropical bush. Disease thinned the ranks and Venables himself came down with dysentery. When at last the column approached the bastions of Santo Domingo it fell into an ambush. Perhaps 150 Spaniards routed the unseasoned and undisciplined advanced guard – but the veteran troops behind checked the outnumbered attackers and the 'sea regiment' pursued them down the road.

Instead of pressing their advantage, the English rested at a sugar plantation for a few days before they tried again. This time the troops took a mortar with them while the fleet began to bombard the seaward defences. Once again, they failed. The land force ran into another ambush in almost the same place as before. Fired upon from cover and then ridden down by lancers, hundreds of men died before the eighty Spanish attackers could be stopped by the sea regiment. The fleet found the batteries facing it powerful and effective and could not get close enough to do significant damage. At least 1,700 men had been lost and the survivors were demoralised and exhausted. After a brief conference, the commanders decided to cut their losses and withdraw.[23]

Two things were now clear. A renewed effort, an assault on Cuba or Puerto Rico, was out of the question; at the same time, it was also inadvisable to return home without making at least a minor conquest. The choice fell upon Santiago, later called Jamaica, a thinly settled and poorly garrisoned island, of no great importance to the Spanish American empire, and without modern defences. On 9 May the fleet sighted the town of Santiago de la Vega, and the next day 7,000 men, supported by gunfire from a galley and a ketch, stormed ashore nearby. Having swept the feeble Spanish resistance aside, however, Venables decided to rest his men overnight. It was a poor and in some ways fateful decision. Next day they covered the five miles to Santiago and occupied the town without meeting any resistance, but by then most of the population had fled.

Unwilling to pursue into unknown country without assured water supplies – very understandable in the light of recent experience – the English leaders were forced to negotiate. The terms they demanded at the subsequent meetings reflected those imposed on the Providence Island settlers in 1643. All the inhabitants who would not submit were to be deported, with clothing and whatever food they could carry. Those prepared to live under Protestant English rule were welcome to stay – artisans were to be particularly welcomed. Meanwhile they were to provide food for Venables's sickly and hungry army. A very few did submit but the majority were defiant.

The question was how to resist – by flight or by fight? Most decided to flee to Cuba by whatever means they could find, while others began a guerrilla war against the invaders. In due course the guerrillas divided, too, the slaves and free blacks moving away to set up their own camps.

This was only beginning of a prolonged guerrilla resistance supported from Cuba and Hispaniola. A settler leader, Maestre de Campo de Proenza, retired to Guatibaco in the jungle-clad mountains, where he made contact with Maroon communities led by Juan de Bolas and Juan de Serras. In May 1757, Proenza's successor, Cristobal Ysassi, received reinforcements from Cuba to make up a force of 300 soldiers and about 100 irregulars. Ysassi was defeated at Las Chorreras (modern Ocho Rios) but in 1658 he tried again at Rio Neuvo with about 550 Spanish troops and around 50 Jamaican guerrillas. Again, an English force of 750 men arrived by sea, defeated the Spanish and stormed their fort. That ended Spanish attempts to land forces on the island, but Ysassi fled into the mountains and fought on.

The end did not come until 1659 when an English patrol entered a previously unknown valley and found an African village with extensive gardens. Now threatened with the destruction of this precious food supply, De Bola was forced to negotiate. In return for promises of freedom and control of their own villages, De Bola's men undertook to root out the Spanish and other black resisters. Ysassi realized that it was impossible to fight any longer and fled to Cuba. Even that was not the end of resistance. A small Maroon band led by Juan de Serras held on and proved impossible to uproot. Jamaica was to be the scene of ongoing frontier resistance as well as a developing plantation economy and a naval base.

Buccaneering and consolidation
Meanwhile Jamaica had adopted a new industry and means of defence: buccaneering. These were groups of generally non-Spanish who lived in the uninhabited parts of the islands and lived on wild cattle and pigs, and by raiding. They were especially strong in Hispaniola, where they sold hides and smoked meat to local planters and passing ships. The majority were not pirates, being land-based marauders who used

The Caribbean: Sugar, Slaves and Conquest

shipping as a means of transportation; but more and more may have taken to piracy as the Hispaniolan herds declined. Pirates or not, they needed access to ports where they could sell plunder and purchase supplies. In 1657, Governor D'Oyley, having little naval protection, invited them to make their base at the new town of Port Royal, an arrangement kept up by successive governors as a source of both income and protection. During the Second Anglo-Dutch War they were the only means the English possessed of attacking Dutch Islands and protecting their own. However, they set their own price, and Governor Thomas Modyford paid them with letters of marque against Spanish shipping. They attacked towns as well as shipping, a habit connived at and copied by the small English naval squadron on the West Indies station. In 1659, for example, Captain Christopher Myngs entered Port Royal with £2-3 million worth of loot, most of which was never declared to the port authorities. However, what was declared by buccaneers and naval captains was sufficient to fund the island's administration, bribe Modyford, pay the royal levy of ten per cent and the Lord High Admiral James Duke of York's fifteenth.

Henry Morgan, the buccaneering chief with whom Modyford did business, was a power in his own right. In 1668 he attacked Porto Bello and took it with only 460 men, allegedly resorting to measures such as blowing up a garrison inside their own fort, using monks and nuns as human shields, and threatening to slaughter all his prisoners unless paid a ransom. This ruthless expedition yielded £60 a man: it was the buccaneers most profitable achievement. It was also a turning point: Spain declared war on all English ships and settlements south of the Tropic of Cancer, the region in which she still claimed a legal monopoly.

Modyford responded by commissioning Morgan as naval commander-in-chief with a brief to attack the Spaniards everywhere. But in 1670, by the Treaty of Madrid, Spain at last recognised the legitimacy of English Caribbean settlements. The buccaneers had to be reined in, but Morgan had already sailed to capture and sack Panama. It was a spectacular feat but his last. Profits worked out at only £50 a head. Modyford was recalled in 1671, Morgan was sent home, and a new governor Sir Thomas Lynch offered the remaining buccaneers land and a pardon.

That, however, was not the end of Morgan. He combined ruthlessness and greed with a charm that earned him a knighthood and the post of lieutenant governor, while Modyford also returned to Jamaica as chief justice. When Lynch went home in 1678, Morgan was acting governor, giving him an opportunity to allow a former colleague, one Captain Coxon, to raid and loot the Spanish Pacific colonies. After a second treaty with Spain in 1680, however, he seems to have actually worked to suppress buccaneering; and in 1682, when Lynch returned, he was driven from office, dying two years later overweight and sodden with drink.

Buccaneering was now in rapid terminal decline, though piracy was a problem for many years to come.

Many ex-buccaneers, unable to settle to a disciplined lifestyle, moved to the logwood camps of the Honduran coast. *Haematoxylum campechianum*, logwood, was a bent flowering tree valued for its versatile uses in textile dyeing. For decades, gangs of largely non-Spanish cutters had worked there, harvesting the wood, cutting it into yard-long lengths, piling them on the beach and selling them to visiting ships. The influx of buccaneers boosted production and attracted a lot of shipping from Jamaica, and especially from New Englanders, who were now the West Indies' principal suppliers of food and timber. Inevitably, the Spanish, who still claimed exclusive rights on the mainland, objected, while the English retorted that the 1670 Treaty of Madrid gave them every right to be there. The governor of Jamaica extended a kind of protectorate over the Moskito Indians who lived there, inspiring their leader to call himself 'King Jeremy' and wear a laced English hat as a crown. From time to time the Spanish would commission privateers, such as the Corsican Juan Corso in 1680, to clear out the logwooders; but although some of the cutters may have been persuaded or forced to go to sea with pirates, little damage was done before 1715.

While the buccaneers had brought some spectacular, ill-gotten wealth to Jamaica, this could not create a permanent stable economy. By 1692 Port Royal was the largest English settlement in the Americas, boasting a population of 10,000, hundreds of four-storeyed brick buildings, and spectacularly expensive rents. A permanently stable economy could only come from sugar planting and that was retarded for lack of slaves. The Royal African Company could not supply enough, and in Jamaica it was all too easy for slaves to escape to the maroon bands in the mountains. The point was dramatically and brutally underlined in June 1694 when an earthquake destroyed Port Royal in a couple of hours. Piracy, logwood and a beehive of a town were no substitute for an agricultural staple.

Servitude and resistance

Buccaneering may not have overwhelmed the Leeward Islands, but they still faced a significant amount of Carib resistance. As late as 1676, exposed planters in Antigua and Montserrat lived in constant fear of sudden canoe-borne descents. As in Jamaica, this terror combined with a rapidly increasing reliance upon black slaves to encourage an already obvious siege mentality among the planter elite. Indentured workers, too, were known to plan revolts, or run away: in Barbados, in 1649, they had plotted to seize the whole island. Especially worrying were the large numbers of Irish. From 1661 the islands began to introduce legal codes intended to define and regularise relations between workers and masters. Barbados led the way in 1661 with a Slave Code and a Servants' code, defining both as chattels and prescribing essentially the same types

The Caribbean: Sugar, Slaves and Conquest

of discipline. Jamaica followed suit in 1664 and the Leeward Islands in 1669. In 1670 Montserrat made this colour-blind approach explicit with a single law governing the discipline of both servants and slaves. This was perhaps inevitable at a time when, on the big plantations, white servants and black slaves worked in the same gangs.

In theory, indentured men and women had protections not available to slaves. The Barbadian Act of 1661, for example, contained clauses intended to restrain brutal masters. Significantly, the Lords of Trade, who vetted colonial legislation, sometimes objected to suggestions that servants were not ultimately free. In 1676 they criticised the word 'servitude' in a Jamaican Act, because it implied slavery. Their Lordships suggested the word 'service', pointing out that servants were not slaves but 'apprentices for years'.[24]

Recruitment of indentured servants was already in decline, however, and the number of black African slaves increased as sugar production expanded. The old insistence that the British Isles were overpopulated was being reversed, and the drain of manpower to the Caribbean colonies was increasingly deplored. Moreover, the American mainland colonies presented much greater opportunities for discharged servants to acquire their own land, so there was a critical retention problem. The Caribbean assemblies' attempts to encourage white labourers by halving the length of indentures merely doubled the cost and made black slave labour significantly cheaper.[25]

Slaves could not legally own property and could be sold with the plantation on which they worked. A slave who murdered a white person was hanged, whereas a white who unlawfully killed a slave was merely fined. Slave codes, while giving slaves marginal legal protections, were heavily loaded in favour of giving the planters security. Loud instruments, such as horns and drums, which might be used to organise uprisings, were banned. Harsh punishments were provided for low-level types of resistance, such as burning sugar cane fields (to make the harvest easier), flight and sabotage. A slave who stole or struck or threatened a white was put to death. Moreover, any planter who employed, aided or sheltered a runaway, failed to properly police his slaves, or allowed them to acquire ideas of equality and freedom, was guilty of a crime.

Historians are divided upon the effectiveness of slave resistance. It is arguable that the lesser forms, which might include retention of African cultural practices, temporary absence without leave, or developing their own trade and barter networks, had considerable success. On the other hand, violent revolts were hard to organise, often detected in advance (and consequently often limited to a region or even to a single plantation), and usually quickly suppressed by planter militias. In crowded Barbados and the Leewards, where rebels must either seize their whole island or submit to brutal punishments, there were a number of plots but only one actual revolt.[26]

Flight was generally a more practical and a more successful option. Refugees from Barbados and the Leewards sailed to other islands. Only in

Antigua, where the Shekerly Mountains provided a refuge, did a band of fifty blacks hold out until 1687, when a planter militia onslaught forced the survivors to escape by sea. The Kalinago communities in the Windwards – still unconquered and still launching raids against the Leewards – were favourite destinations. Joint African-Kalinago raids became common, 'miscegenation'(a word that first appears during the American Civil War) was widespread and by 1700 the mixed-blood 'Black Carib' population on St Vincent outnumbered both Africans and 'White' Caribs. In Belize and Jamaica, however, the proximity of formidable forest-clad mountains provided the ideal sanctuary for escapees or 'Maroons'.[27]

The formidable terrain may explain why in Jamaica there were more revolts than elsewhere, six major ones between 1673 and 1694. In 1673 some two hundred Coramantees (prisoners of war enslaved by their African captors on the Gold Coast) seized control of their plantation, armed themselves, and took to the mountains of the north-west. In 1675, on another northern plantation, the pattern was repeated. Another revolt in 1678 was suppressed, but in 1685-1686 a year-long insurrection spread from the south of the island to the north, and rebels who escaped planter retaliation – those taken were burned alive, torn apart by dogs or drawn and quartered – joined the Maroons in the mountains. In 1690, after yet another rebellion, they were joined by a further two hundred Coramantees whose leader became the headman of the entire community. This headman's son, Cudjoe, succeeded his father and became something of an absolute monarch. Smaller outbreaks in 1694, 1702 and 1704 sent even more recruits to the Maroons.[28]

Tariff protectionism and sidestepping the Navigation Acts

In theory, the 1651 and subsequent Navigation Acts ensured that West Indian products – sugar, tobacco, cotton and indigo – went direct to Great Britain for re-export. In return, the planters were given a heavily protected market: the 1661 Tariff Act created a duty of one shilling and five pence on British sugar, compared with thirty-five shillings and ten pence per hundredweight for the foreign product. However, while the colonists were happy to accept this protection – even insisting upon it – they wanted free trade in imports, especially slaves, and dealt so readily with interlopers that in 1698 the slave trade was opened to all comers. As for exports, the law was frequently broken.

All the islands were involved in evading the Navigation Acts. As late as the 1680s the English had not fully overtaken the Dutch in sugar refining, Dutch processes were cheaper, and their shipping costs lower; they could offer good prices to the planters and still make a handsome profit. Homeward-bound Dutch vessels would visit all the English islands, ostensibly to water but in reality to deliver illicit European goods. As one naval officer put it, 'The Dutch ships send their longboats to St. Christopher's once or twice a week on pretence of getting water, though one boat load of water would last them a month.' They would then move on to St Eustatius, where the English planters had already sent their molasses and sugar, load their cargoes, and sail for the Netherlands. It was a trade almost impossible to check, there being so many islands with innumerable coves and bays, and too few customs officers and vessels for efficient patrols. Governors, officials and even the courts often turned a blind eye: one Jamaican jury accepted the evidence of a witness who swore that Irish soap was a food and therefore a legitimate import.[29]

Defence depended upon local militias. Before black slavery and big estates became common, the rank and file were drawn from the smaller farmers and their servants. As the big estates grew, the militias became increasingly dependent on white servants – so much so that West Indian colonies passed 'deficiency laws' compelling planters to retain a fixed ratio of white employees, usually one white to ten black slaves. These arrangements could produce very large forces: in 1669 Barbados could call on 6,000 men, including 800 cavalry. Assemblies were resentful and suspicious of governors' control of these forces and in emergencies often resisted the imposition of martial law. In peace time they resented paying for the upkeep of fixed fortifications and in wartime resisted providing housing for regular garrisons.[30]

Continual wars and underlying weakness

In 1689, with the outbreak of the War of the League of Augsburg, warfare returned to the Caribbean and would not depart – barring one five-year break 1697-1702 – until the War of the Spanish Succession ended in 1713. The British islands suffered from raids, attempts and conquest and the devastating attacks of French privateers upon merchant shipping. In 1694 a massive French raid upon the eastern end of Jamaica destroyed plantations and carried off 2,000 slaves, 1,200 head of cattle and 420 horses. The threat of further raids from St. Domingue compelled the Crown to station 3,000 regular troops in Jamaica, who of course had to be fed and housed by the colony. Jamaica had also to raise, arm and train its own militia and to find money to pay for expensive fortifications. As if this was not enough, there were annual conflicts with the Maroons from 1700 onwards. The spectre of slave revolt combined with French invasion and a Maroon onslaught was never far away.[31]

Further east, the Leeward Islands, less well fortified than Barbados, suffered heavily. In 1706 the French carried off 3,187 slaves from Nevis to Martinique, and in July 1712 a privateer expedition overwhelmed the defences of Montserrat and Antigua.[32] The capture of the French half of St Kitts in 1702 – confirmed at Utrecht in 1713 and the only permanent territorial change in the Caribbean – could not conceal the fundamental weakness of Britain's fragments of Caribbean empire.

12

West Africa and the Growth of the Atlantic Slave Trade

Before the mid-seventeenth century, most English commerce with West Africa was in commodities other than slaves. As early as 1587 English ships visited Senegambia for hides, gum arabic for sizing cloth, and some gold from the interior. From 1607, John Davies, a London merchant, was active in buying redwood, used to produce a red dye for cloth, on the coast of Sierra Leone, and established an apparently short-lived trading post there in 1611. Gold was the main interest of 'The Company of Adventurers of London Trading to the Parts of Africa', more concisely and commonly known as the Guinea Company. Chartered in 1618 to trade with 'Gynney and Bynney', that is to Guinea and Benin, its efforts were in practice limited to Senegambia and Sierra Leone. Three early voyages to the Gambia River, which was supposed to give access to the inland gold fields, were failures: no gold was offered for sale and the ventures ran up a considerable loss. More profitable was the redwood at the Sierra Leone River – where the Company sublet its monopoly to Davies – and further east at the Sherbro River, where in 1628 the first permanent English factory was established. Despite these efforts, the Company was never able to enforce its monopoly and it was undermined by interlopers. In England its status as a royal monopoly left it open to parliamentary attacks, and the Anglo-French war of 1627-1629 inflicted serious forfeitures. In the short term, it was rescued politically by Charles I's resort to personal rule in 1629, and commercially by one Nicholas Crispe, who in 1631 bought a controlling interest and relaunched it as the Company of Merchants Trading to Africa.[33]

This new Guinea Company's charter gave it a theoretical claim to the whole African trade of Guinea and Angola, together with a promise of government support against competitors. While the redwood trade was retained, Crispe directed his main energies towards the Gold Coast, the main source of African gold, and where the Portuguese were being ousted by the Dutch. The Company established its fortified headquarters at Kormantin and built five other Gold Coast factories, where it focussed upon the gold trade. Even the Company's coastal trade with Benin was for cloth with which to purchase gold. It failed to make serious inroads into the Dutch West India Company's business and it was as vulnerable as its predecessors to interlopers. Nicholas Crispe was a Royalist and the Civil War of 1642-1646 saw control of its operations pass to supporters of Parliament. By 1651 it had lost £100,000 and its monopoly was restricted to twenty leagues either side of Sherbro and Kormantin respectively, securing its control of the gold and redwood trades but effectively cutting it out of the slave traffic to the east.

Even then it was bedevilled by competition and violence. Prince Rupert's fleet descended upon Company vessels on the Gambia in 1652 and many more of its ships were lost in the Anglo-Dutch War of 1651-1654. In 1657 it gave up direct trade altogether and leased its rights to the East India Company, which wanted ivory and gold for its purchases on the subcontinent. The EIC had no interest in slaving and forbade its servants to trade in slaves on their own account.[34]

Thus before 1660 the English share in the slave trade was carried on not by the chartered companies but by interlopers. Before the 1640s, when the Caribbean sugar revolution created a larger demand, that share was exceedingly small, but between 1640 and 1650 it grew significantly. Sources are incomplete and often unreliable but the following estimates, based on rigorous statistical work by a team led by David Eltis and David Richardson, cannot be very far from the mark.

Estimated numbers of slaves exported from Western Africa 1501-1650[35]
National totals include exports in colonial vessels.

	Spain	Portugal	British Isles	Netherlands	France	Denmark/ Baltic	TOTALS
1501–1525	6,363	7,000	0	0	0	0	13,363
1526–1550	25,375	25,387	0	0	0	0	50,762
1551–1575	28,167	31,089	1,685	0	66	0	61,007
1576–1600	60,056	90,715	237	1,365	0	0	15,373
1601–1625	83,496	267,519	0	1,829	0	0	352,844
1626–1650	44,313	201,609	33,695	31,519	1,827	1,053	315,050

Thus, when in 1660 the expansionists at Charles II's court formed a Company of Royal Adventurers into Africa, slaving was an important part of the new firm's business plan. The king himself was a shareholder and his charter gave it exclusive rights in West Africa for 1,000 years, but the need to negotiate away the existing rights of the Guinea and East India companies meant that initial operations were restricted to the Gambia.

An expedition led by Sir Robert Holmes, a veteran naval officer, secured a fortified base on James Island in the river mouth in 1661. Overall, by 1661 the Company had eighteen factories in operation and had sent over forty ships to service them. Two years later the Company was re-chartered as The Company of Royal Adventurers of England Trading into Africa, known as the Royal African Company. Taking over the Gold Coast factories and with the Duke of York at its head, and already engaged to supply 3,000 slaves a year to the Caribbean plantations, it was the first such company to have an explicit monopoly of the slave trade. It established a base at Allada on the Slave Coast in 1663 and its vessels made use of the Niger Delta ports of New and Old Calabar. However, this did not mean that slaving had now replaced gold as the Company's main pursuit. By 1665 it was making £200,000 a year from gold and only half that from slaves. A further £100,000 came from commodities such as ivory, redwood and pepper, so that in terms of income the slaving was only a quarter of the Company's business.

Its ruin was conflict with the Dutch, who resented the Company's intrusion into their own self-proclaimed monopoly in the Gambia. In 1661-1662 they seized some Company ships and tried to blockade some of the factories. The Company retaliated in 1663-1664 with a naval expedition led by Holmes that took several Dutch trading posts, including Cape Coast Castle, which the Dutch had earlier seized from the Swedes, and Gorée. Retribution was, however, swift and decisive. In 1664-1665 Admiral De Ruyter captured every English factory except the now-refortified Cape Coast Castle, which had replaced Kormantin as the local Company headquarters. After that the Company could do little business itself, licensing private traders from 1667 and devolving its Gambia interests to a new company of Gambia Adventurers in 1669. It 1672 it was dissolved and re-placed by a new Royal African Company, again under the Duke of York, with a monopoly of all African trade until 1688, and the right to levy a licence fee on independent traders thereafter.[36]

The RAC depended far more upon slaving than its predecessor, although it continued to trade in ivory, redwood, and other products. Its five posts were on the Gold Coast, with its headquarters at Cape Coast Castle, together with fifty soldiers and thirty resident slaves. It had a burst of real prosperity after 1678 when it took over the Gambia Adventurers' operations, which continued into the 1680s when it was allowed to raise its sale prices for slaves, established a new post at Dixcove west of Elmina, and began to out-compete the Dutch. Nevertheless, from its beginning it had serious underlying weaknesses. Undercapitalised and continually in debt, it was burdened with rebuilding its Gold Coast factories and rashly paying out in dividends as much as it borrowed. Trade goods of acceptable quality – cloth and iron bars for example – were expensive and could only be purchased in the Netherlands and the Baltic, and the purchase and transportation of the slaves themselves was costly. It was pestered by unlicensed interlopers from the start and after the Revolution in 1688, its monopoly – granted by its erstwhile head, the now exiled James II – became wholly unenforceable. For a short time after 1696 it even faced competition from the newly formed Scottish Company Trading to Africa and the Indies, the firm which came to grief in Darien. In 1698 the monopoly was formally ended: independent traders were supposed to pay a ten per cent levy towards the costs of maintaining the Company's bases in Africa, a payment that was seldom collected. By 1708 the free traders had exported around 75,000 slaves to the Americas against the Company's estimated 18,000.

Even for interlopers, with no posts or forts to maintain, the export of slaves to America was not only brutal but hugely inefficient. Of the 584,297 slaves embarked in British vessels between 1651 and 1713, only 459,690 reached their destinations alive. Transatlantic seaborne commerce was expensive and risky enough in peacetime, even for carriers of non-human cargoes, while to guard against revolt, slavers' crews had to be double normal size. Supplies for large crews and their prisoners were expensive, and equipment such as shackles added to the cost.

The RAC was thus ill-placed to withstand the impact of the Nine Years' War of 1689-1697 and the War of the Spanish Succession of 1702-1713. Fighting on the West African coast itself was indecisive: the English took French Fort St Louis on the Senegal River in 1692 (and lost it again the following year) and seized Gorée; the French took Fort James on the Gambia and held it until the Peace of Ryswick in 1697. More damaging were the hugely successful French privateering campaigns against English merchant shipping, which accounted for about one in four of the Company's vessels. Worse still, the Dutch – allied to the British in Europe – were not above using African auxiliaries or even taking direct military action against their RAC rivals. By 1712, when the 1698 Act expired and even the notional levy was abolished, the Company was in terminal decline.

Barriers to conquest: biological and African
Why then were plantations not developed in West Africa, at the source of the slave labour required for a sugar economy? William Reinart and Lotte Hughes point out that European powers made a number of attempts to do just that, and David Eltis has argued that 'what happened in the Americas was what Europeans wanted to happen in Africa but could not bring about.' The English efforts in this direction included the Royal African Company's attempts to introduce sugar, cotton, indigo and ginger, especially around Cape Coast Castle. For that matter, why were Europeans unable to control the gold-producing areas (as they would have liked to) by pushing a short distance inland? After all, Denykira and Axim, two of the most important gold fields, were only a few days

march from English Cape Coast Castle or Dutch Elmina. Why were their ambitions and efforts so abortive?

Alfred Crosby and others point to powerful biological factors, namely the tropical diseases which killed about half of all Europeans within a year of arrival; only ten per cent of all white men who worked in West Africa lived to go home.[37] That made European management of plantations, let alone settlement, very difficult. Conversely, Africans had immunities to tropical diseases such as yellow fever, and they already been exposed to European and Middle Eastern diseases through early maritime links, the trans-Sahara trade and migration. That is why contact with Europeans did not, as in the Americas, bring devastating epidemics which cleared the land for foreign settlement. While slaving may have had a demographic effect in some areas, it did not destroy whole populations.

This, however, is not the whole story. As Reinart and Hughes point out, environmental factors provide a background and framework for historical events, rather than directly causing them. David Eltis argues that in the early seventeenth century, disease notwithstanding, the European trading organisations maintained up to 1,000 men on the Gold Coast alone. While their careers were certainly short, they were replaceable – there were always people willing to go – so that there were always enough whites to supervise slave-manned plantations. (Indeed, for whites West Africa was not much less healthy than the West Indies). In terms of climate and soil, West Africa could offer as much cultivable space as the Caribbean.

Much more important was the power balance. The large African populations, already organised into powerful states, confined Europeans to their tiny coastal enclaves, unable to press inland or to conquer wide swathes of territory. In the face of such difficulties, the Atlantic wind patterns which facilitated the triangular trade in slaves beckoned irresistibly.

Even the small coastal states were quite powerful enough to keep Europeans on the back foot, levying port dues and customs duties and often dictating the terms of trade. In the Gambia and Senegal, the RAC agents were forced to buy overpriced slaves and hides in order to obtain the ivory and gum arabic they really wanted. The rulers of Benin refused to deal in male slaves, a move which was unsustainable in the long run but which forced slavers to look elsewhere until the 1720s. To the west of Benin, on what was becoming known as the 'Slave Coast', Benin's reluctance was exploited by the rising state of Allada, created by 1600 out of a loose federation of Aja states. By 1660, Allada was a highly centralised polity able to field at least 40,000 troops. In Whydah, which later overshadowed even Allada, the king had near-complete control over external trade. Recalcitrant traders, including in 1682 and 1692 chief factors of the RAC, were deported, and conflicts between rival European powers were restrained. During the War of the Spanish Succession the king imposed neutrality upon all the Europeans on his coast. On the Gold Coast, where English garrisons were larger and African rivalries stronger, Europeans could exercise some influence and intervene in local conflicts, but even here they were weak. Everywhere local rulers levied rent or tribute in return for allowing forts to be constructed on their territory, and almost all of them were vulnerable to African attack. Designed more to resist European than local assault, most of their batteries pointed out to sea, and while Cape Coast Castle was strong enough to survive a siege in 1688, those at Winneba (1679) and Sekondi (1694) were destroyed by local forces. At Dixcove Fort in 1712, African assailants blew up the powder magazine. West and north of the Gold Coast, most forts survived only because they were located on islands – and leaving those islands could be perilous. As David Eltis puts it:

> African resistance resulted in Europeans taking slaves away in ships as a second-best alternative to working slaves on African plantations or mines. From this perspective the slave trade was a symptom of African strength, not weakness.[38]

Although expanding states often took advantage of the slave trade to obtain European goods, deep-rooted pre-existing African conflicts and climate change seem to have been more important reasons for its development. By about 1486, when the Portuguese arrived in the Niger delta, the state of Benin was already expanding at the expense of weaker neighbouring polities. By the mid-seventeenth century, when English trade there first became significant, Benin controlled the whole delta, including the ports of Bonny and Lagos, while the inland city of Benin was large and flourishing. By this time a global 'mini-ice age' was disrupting agricultural production and provoking wars and political crises around the world.

Dr Toby Green points out that this general crisis had as profound an effect upon Africa as it did elsewhere. It is usually attributed to a decline in sunspot activity, and so to a fall in average temperatures. Alternatively, or indeed additionally, it may have been related to the drastic decline in Amerindian populations, resulting in reforestation and carbon capture. Whatever its origins, climate change wrought havoc upon mid-seventeenth century African economies. Rainfall varied unpredictably, flood alternated with drought and crop failures led to food insecurity and violent conflict. This may have led to a greater reliance upon imported European goods and to the rise of states prepared to supply the slaves demanded in payment.[39]

It may be no coincidence, then, that the kingdoms of Allada and Dahomey arose around 1600, possibly as a tripartite partition to settle a succession dispute in the forest state of Ardra. Allada certainly exploited Benin's refusal to trade in male slaves, but there is no significant evidence that its rulers conducted aggressive war to obtain them. Not until late in the century, when Europeans were already buying slaves from Allada and Whydah, did Dahomey begin to supply this traffic by conquering small tribes to its north. It did not at this time break through to the sea, though by 1708 its ruler, King Agaja, was casting covetous eyes upon the Whydah middlemen's profits.

Much the same was true of the two great forest empires of Oyo and Asante. Oyo, to the west of Benin and the most extensive and powerful forest state of all, had its origins in the savannah country to the north, where its formidable cavalry was used to devastating advantage against invaders from beyond the Niger. Later, it adapted its military methods to forest warfare and began to expand southwards. Never a coastal state, it conducted its trade through client or allied states, including Benin.

The Asante (Ashanti) Union emerged around Kumasi in the rainforest hinterland of the Gold Coast at the same time as large quantities of flintlock muskets were imported in lieu of the cumbersome and less efficient matchlocks, with the English rapidly overtaking rivals to become the principal supplier. Yet at this time Asante armies did not rely heavily on firearms. Originally a defensive union of weaker Akan states against the dominance of Denykira, about 1695 the Union became an efficiently centralised state with the Kumasi chief as its overlord (Asantehene), Osie Tutu. Six years later, Osei Tutu smashed Denykira power, reducing it to an Asante tributary, and thereafter the Union continued to expand. Powerful enough to survive Osei Tutu's death in ambush in 1717, Asante dominated the supply of gold and slaves to the coastal Fante states and therefore the reverse stream of firearms, cloth and iron.[40]

It has been argued that while Africans retained their independence, they also benefitted from the rapid expansion of world trade. There is some evidence that the inward flow of European firearms, cloth, iron and beads did not at this stage overwhelm African producers. Rather, it seems that traditional crafts, most famously Benin's bronze casting, continued to thrive alongside the use of imported products.

Far more secure than Amerindians from the ravages of disease, Africans were usually able to set the conditions of trade and always to confine the English and other Europeans to their tiny coastal posts. Such tenuous toeholds hardly amounted to 'empire', though some of their posts were to be continually occupied until the British conquests of nineteenth century. Not even in the very limited sense of a trade monopoly did the English or any other European power achieve dominance anywhere on the coast. There was only one real attempt, by the English in the Second Anglo-Dutch War, and that we have seen ended in disaster. As for 'informal empire' exercised through economic dominance, even on the Gold Coast local influence did not amount to political dominance.

13

Asian Enclaves

Bombay, acquired by the Crown through Charles II's marriage in 1661, and transferred to the East India Company in 1668, was the first outright English possession in Asia. On a group of islands and easily fortified, it was a far more secure port than Surat. But unlike Surat, it was nowhere near the textile-manufacturing regions of Gujurat and its own hinterland produced little of value. Consequently Surat-based merchants were reluctant to relocate to Bombay, so for a long time it was underused and underdeveloped.[41]

On the east coast, Around Fort St George and the former fishing village of Madraspatnam, the town of Madras was growing. As Moghul power pressed south, merchants were attracted to the security of the EIC's fortified stronghold, and a 'black town' of Indian merchants and craftsmen grew up around the largely separate 'white town' of the Company officials. However, its lack of a proper port, which meant cargoes had to be loaded and unloaded by boats working through the surf, was a major drawback. In 1651 there was no such secure enclave in Bengal. The Company's first and unfortified factory was established in 1651 at Hugli in the Ganges delta, on the river of the same name. At the same time the Mughal empire was pushing aggressively southward, so that the Company was to become more dependent than ever upon the emperor's goodwill. In the shorter term, however, the disruption created by the Deccan campaigns forced the Company to take defensive action and to assume, with disastrous results, that the empire could be coerced.

Mughal expansion, Islamisation and resistance
Aurangzeb's remarkably vigorous reign (1658-1707) saw a dramatic expansion of the Mughal empire eastwards into Assam, northwards into the Himalayas, and – most spectacularly of all – southwards into the Deccan. By 1707, only the Polygars' domains at the very tip of the

subcontinent lay outside his dominions. It has been argued that this enormous growth marked the beginnings of Moghul decline, thereby creating an opening for the European powers to expand their enclaves into dominion. The new territories were poorer than the old provinces to the north and therefore unable to pay for their own conquest. Moreover, it is argued, Aurangzeb's less tolerant religious attitudes sparked widespread revolt, which sapped the resources of the empire. But until the early eighteenth century, these appearances were very deceptive.

Aurangzeb found that attempts to secure his frontiers and expand beyond them could be costly and provoke fierce resistance. In 1660-1661 a new viceroy tightened Mughal control of Bengal, Orissa and Bihar in the north-east and in 1663 began an invasion of the states of Assam along the Brahmaputra River. Initial success, achieved with a formidable land army and a fleet of heavily armed river boats, was followed by prolonged resistance and defeat in the 1680s. To the north-west, in Afghanistan, a series of Pathan revolts in 1667 and 1672 1675 cost the emperor two whole armies ambushed and wiped out, and a third badly mauled. His viceroy was obliged to intervene in Pathan politics, using a divide and rule policy instead of one of conquest. The episode firmly deterred Aurangzeb from further Central Asian campaigns.

Internal resistance was stirred by the emperor's increasingly intolerant attitude to non-Muslims, aiming (it seems) at the eventual conversion of all his subjects. His tendency to appoint more and more Muslim officials narrowed the career paths open to non-Muslims since Akbar's day. The Mughal empire was to become a Muslim state under Shariah Law. In 1659 he created the post of *mutasib, or censor,* whose main function was to enforce Sharia Law in public places. From 1665 the toll levied on non-Muslims at internal customs posts was double that charged to followers of Islam. Four years later he ordered the demolition of recently built or recently repaired temples. Pilgrims travelling to Hindu holy places were taxed. At the behest of the court theologians, but ignoring the warnings of experienced administrators, he decreed a *jiziya*, a tax on all non-Muslims. In rural areas an additional 2.4% was added to their land tax assessments. These laws were unevenly enforced but where they were applied they provoked mass protests. In Surat, where enforcement was accompanied by extortion, 8,000 Banias, men of the merchant community, left the city, forcing Aurangzeb to compromise. In 1675, alarmed by some conversions from Islam, the emperor ordered the demolition of new Sikh temples, and had the Sikh Guru arrested and executed.

Worse still, he signalled that he was about to replace Hindu subject rulers with Muslim ones. In 1679 he clumsily intervened in a succession dispute in the Rajput state of Marwar, agreeing to accept the infant heir preferred by the Marwar court only on condition that he was raised as a Muslim. The result was a fierce revolt which Aurangzeb countered with an army of occupation, thereby provoking the ruler of neighbouring Mewar to join the resistance. The Rajputs had heroic cavalry but not field artillery and Mewar was quickly overrun. But that did not prevent the Rana from carrying on a prolonged guerrilla resistance from the hills.

The most effective and dangerous resistance came from the Marathas of the western Deccan. Here Shivaji Bhonsola (1627-1680) had been carving a separate kingdom out of the state of Bijapur since 1645. In 1657 he murdered the Bhijapur military commander at a peace conference and slaughtered his army. The Sultan's counter-offensive was cut short by other distractions, leaving Shivaji as a clearly independent ruler, a status that brought him face to face with the might of the empire.[42]

Unable to make much impression upon Shivaji's network of hill forts, the Mughal commander resorted to scorched earth tactics, while Shivaji launched spectacular cavalry raids. In January 1664 he struck at Surat. The town was overrun and only the fort and the English and Dutch merchants in their fortified compounds held out against the Marathas, who looted it for six days. At sea his fleet intercepted ships carrying Mecca-bound pilgrims and extorted ransoms The following year, finding himself close to defeat by a determined Mughal commander, he made his peace with Aurangzeb, but in 1670 he attacked Surat again. His 15,000 men easily overcame resistance at the newly constructed city walls and again spent days plundering the town. The lesson for the English, Dutch and Portuguese was clear: Aurangzeb could no longer defend the busiest port on the west coast and Bombay and Goa might also be vulnerable.[43]

From 1670 to 1674 Shivaji waged an energetic war of movement, raiding and fighting pitched battles in which Maratha mobility outweighed Mughal heavy cavalry and artillery. In 1674 he was crowned as the Maratha king and in 1677 he made an anti-Bijapur alliance with the rich and powerful Deccan state of Golconda. Within another year he had seized the fortresses of Jinji and Vellore, and annexed a swathe of rich lands which he declined to share with his ally.

When he died in 1680, after a brief succession dispute his son Shambhaji inherited the Bhonsola kingdom, which now extended some 400 miles along the coast and between 50 and 100 miles inland. In alliance with Aurangzeb's rebellious son, Akbar, but unwilling to commit to a concerted advance on Delhi, Shambhaji raided north into Khandesh, attacked the tiny state of Janjira, a Moghul tributary, and assaulted Portuguese enclaves including Goa. The East India Company officials at Bombay prudently made an alliance with the Marathas, supplying them with much-needed artillery and gunpowder. Aurangzeb and his commanders ravaged the vulnerable parts of the Maratha country but could not take the scores of hill and island forts that protected the bulk of the population. Nor could they lure Shambhaji into a decisive battle. In 1685 the emperor turned instead to the conquest of the two remaining Deccan sultanates,

Bijapur and Shambhaji's ally Golconda. The significance of these events was not wasted upon the East India Company: if the Mughals were tied down in vast internal and frontier conflicts and could no longer protect Surat and Bombay, they had better take their own defensive measures. It might even be possible to obtain better concessions by force.

The First Anglo-Mughal War

Already the EIC directors in London sensed that the Mughal empire was now weak enough to be bullied. Moreover, increasing competition from interlopers and the Dutch VOC, not to mention political opposition from Whigs at home, threatened the Company's business, its monopoly and potentially its very existence. This was certainly the view of Sir Josiah Child, the chairman, and his opinion held sway at the courts of Charles II (1660-1685) and his successor James II (1685-1688). Child thought the trade of Bengal could be opened by force and he may have thought that the company was strong enough to turn its rambling network of enclaves into imperial fortresses. His plan was to seize Chittagong, a city with a fine natural harbour to the east of the Ganges delta, a region where interlopers were particularly busy, and the Company's business was also threatened by Dutch competition. Meanwhile, the Company would wage maritime war of on Mughal commerce, and so force the empire to come to terms. He was given some royal troops and royal warships for the project, and there is some congruence between James II's support for this project and his plans to discipline the American colonies.

It is, however, going too far to assert that by 'by the eve of the Glorious Revolution, the Company's aggressive imperialism formed part of a wider political project to create an absolute monarchy in England and to establish an autocratic English empire overseas.'[44] There was certainly some alignment of objectives. The Crown's growing financial independence from 1681 rested on swelling customs revenues and it was in the royal interest to back chartered trading companies. It is also true that Charles used the EIC as a kind of bank, from which he could borrow money in return for defending its privileges. However, there is little evidence of a concerted 'absolutist project' in Stuart England. On the contrary, Charles feared that the Whig movement to exclude James from the succession might fatally undermine the monarchy and even lead to a second republic. His only illegal act was to ignore the Triennial Act's requirement for a new parliament in 1684, and that was probably out of fear of the Whigs rather than out of strength. His authority rested on the consent and support of the landed gentry and the Church of England; his income could sustain a modest standing army only as long as there was peace; his personal interest in the resumption of borough charters was limited to a few Whig strongholds, particularly London. There is a stronger case against James II but even here modern research has shown that he was really after civil and religious equality for Catholics. He made surprisingly little effort to Catholicise the Church of England and Catholic evangelising efforts were remarkably feeble. Nor, despite his sustained attempt to manage elections to a new parliament, is there any evidence that he aimed to abolish that institution. The contention that King and Company worked hand in hand to create an absolute monarchy in England and an 'autocratic' empire in India cannot be sustained.

The military and naval expedition sent against Chittagong and Salstee in 1685-86 was a fiasco, and a second one in 1687-1689 found the city's defences far too formidable to be attacked. Aurangzeb struck back by attacking all the Company's trading posts and expelling the English from both Bengal and Surat. In the west, hostilities arose from the Company's habit of intercepting Mughal merchant vessels, including in 1689 a convoy carrying supplies to an army operating against the Marathas. Realising that massive retaliation was not only possible but likely, Bombay hurriedly came to an agreement with the Marathas: the latter would supply military assistance in return for regular and substantial subsidies. They provided only about 2,000 mercenaries before the Mughal attack came. Bombay Fort was besieged for fifteen months and was finally forced to surrender. The terms were humiliating, granted no new advantages, and the English envoys had to enter the emperor's presence kneeling and with their hands bound.[45]

A stronger Mughal empire?
On the surface, it might seem that the Company had gained everything it wanted. Having paid a fine of £15,000 it recovered its privileges and in 1690 was allowed to build a factory, at Calcutta. By 1698 it was recognized as the *zamindar* – land-holder with responsibility for revenue and administration – of the three settlements which constituted Calcutta and had begun to build Fort William. At last, the EIC had its fortified enclave in Bengal and it began to acquire and fortify enclaves elsewhere: at Fort St David near Madras and in 1694 at Attingal on the Malabar coast, where within two years a fort had been built. It was now in a far stronger position than any of its European rivals.

The Portuguese were by now minor rivals on the subcontinent, despite clinging on to their base at Goa, while the Dutch presence on the Indian subcontinent was limited – their real centre of operations was Batavia, modern Jakarta, in Java. The Danes had a presence in the south but were far more interested in Catholic missionary work than in business. The French East India Company founded in 1664 by Louis XIV's minister Colbert was far too dependent upon the political fortunes of ministers at court. After 1720, with the arrival of two very talented local representatives, the French company became very dangerous, but in the late seventeenth century it struggled.

Yet the English were still at the mercy of a strengthened Mughal empire. In the year Calcutta was founded, Aurangzeb's estranged son Akbar, left in

The First British Empire

the lurch by the Marathas, escaped by sea to Persia. Soon after, the Maratha leader Shambhaji was captured, tortured for two weeks, hacked to pieces and fed to dogs. The Maratha kingdom, like the Deccan Sultanates, was overrun and annexed to the empire. By 1707 only the very southern tip of the subcontinent was outside the emperor's control.[46] Consequently, the Company had to woo and appease its overlord by supplying munitions, food and sometimes troops. The building of Fort William was approved only when the Company sacrificed two fleeing rebel *zamindars* and their escorts. When Anglo-American pirates fleeing the Caribbean appeared in the eastern seas, and the emperor held the Company responsible, the EIC asked the Crown for naval assistance and in doing so compromised its own independence.[47]

Even the now-chastened Company's commercial activities seem, on balance, to have been beneficial to India and strengthened the Mughal empire. Around Surat, in two regions on the Coromandel coast and in the Ganges delta peasants, textile workers and imperial officials thrived on the growing European demand for textiles. In Bengal, English and Dutch demand supported almost one in ten cloth workers, and peasants who changed from rice to mulberry production could quadruple their incomes. Dutch and English factors bought enormous quantities of saltpetre for gunpowder manufacture, a great deal of it from imperial lands. Most goods were purchased with precious metals, which were minted into rupees by imperial mints and used to pay Indian suppliers, employees, Mughal customs duties, and local officials. Such advantages were well worth the exemptions from internal duties and the extra-territorial privileges granted the British as *zamindars* within their enclaves, including the right to local revenues.[48]

As for the Company itself, it was very nearly fatally vulnerable in England itself at the time of the Revolution of 1688-1689. Unpopular with those merchants excluded from its narrow oligarchy, and suspect because of its close association with Toryism, in 1697 it was given notice to disband within three years. For a time the 'Old' company operated alongside a 'New' one, while it vigorously manoeuvred and lobbied for its survival. When it bought a large portion of the 'New' Company's stock, abolition became impossible, and they found a common interest in seeing off the Scottish Company's plan for its own Indian enclave. In doing so, both sides called upon the aid of Crown and Parliament and under Queen Anne a compromise was reached. In 1709 the two companies merged but at the price of accepting some state regulation. Gift-giving and receiving, crucial in Asian negotiations, were restricted; the new Charter was given a life of only eighteen years, ensuring regular reviews; and as the country felt the strains of the War of the Spanish Succession, the Company's capital was taken into the National Debt.[49] In effect, and even though its privileges would be only gradually worn away, and although it was to survive as an entity for another century and a half, the Company was becoming part of the war-fuelled expansion of the state.

PART IV
Global Power?
1713-1763

14

From Utrecht to Paris

The Utrecht treaties were overwhelmingly concerned with the European power balance, to which their overseas colonial provisions were more or less peripheral. France merely confirmed British possession of Rupert's Land and Newfoundland, and yielded Nova Scotia and the French share of St Kitts. Arguably, the Spanish cession of Gibraltar and Minorca was more important, giving Britain permanent bases in the Mediterranean from which to protect her trade, blockade the Toulon squadron, and hamper Bourbon military movements. Fifty years later, the imperial dimensions of the Peace of Paris were far more dramatic. Britain gained the whole of North America up to the Mississippi, West Indian islands and West African trading stations, while Minorca, lost in 1756, was restored. Spain lost Florida (but gained Louisiana west of the Mississippi as compensation) and was allowed to ransom back Havana and Manila. Now possessing global power that made her a front-rank European power, Britain was consolidating her extended but loosely governed imperium. Over the half-century between Utrecht and Paris, London moved from a preference for 'salutary neglect' to a policy of centralisation of the North Atlantic empire, and towards direct interference in the East India Company's territorial possessions.

Why this profound shift? The answer as ever lies in the European power balance. Britain had risen from second-rank status to that of a Great Power because her colonial empire compensated for her relative weakness in Europe. The Navigation System protected her foreign trade and maritime resources, while her innovative fiscal reforms allowed her to punch above her economic and demographic weight. This did not prevent some, Tories at first and then Whigs out of office, arguing for a maritime non-interventionist approach, but once apparent sceptics such as William Pitt found themselves in office they sang a very different tune. This is not a new revelation but easily lost sight of. Although the case has been made repeatedly for over half a century, at least one recent scholar has declared 'the primacy of foreign policy' at this time as a new discovery.[1]

There can be little doubt that in the aftermath of Utrecht most minds were on the danger of renewed war inside Europe. Elizabeth Farnese, consort to Philip V of Spain, was profoundly dissatisfied with the territorial distribution and wanted to regain parts of Italy for her sons. Moreover, it was far from certain that Philip would respect his renunciation of the French throne, especially while Louis XV was still a minor and without a male heir. Neither Britain nor France could allow such claims, so they combined against Spain in a short war. Finally, most major powers regarded the post-Revolution British regime as regicides and republicans, a view not much softened by the accession of George I in 1714 and the consequent British link to Hanover. The Hanoverian succession brought the Whigs and their Eurocentric foreign policy to the fore once again, to defend and manage the fallout from a continental settlement devised by their Eurosceptic opponents.

Internally, the Jacobite threat was still strong enough to be very dangerous when supported by foreign intervention. Louis XIV gave covert aid to James II's son, the Pretender James 'III'. The most dramatic uprising was in Scotland and northern England in 1715, where resentment of the Revolution, the religious settlement, the Union and the Hanoverian succession combined. It failed partly because of inept military and political leadership, but fundamentally because foreign help was not forthcoming. In 1719 Spain landed a handful of troops to support a rising at Glenshiel in Scotland, and the Swedish ambassador was implicated in a plot involving English Jacobites. In 1722, the government detected a plot, involving the Jacobite Bishop of Rochester, to seize London and the royal family with the aid of Irish exiles from France and Spain. The Hanoverian regime was therefore far from secure, and prudence dictated that Bourbon powers and their allies should not be tempted to support Jacobite ambitions. That, to the mind of Sir Robert Walpole, First Lord of the Treasury and effectively principal minister from 1721 to 1742, meant a peaceful, even isolationist, foreign policy. For him, its fundamental aim should be to protect the king's principality of Hanover without getting involved in the affairs of other countries. It followed that Great Britain should not entertain colonial expansion at the expense of any important European state.

Yet the threat of foreign combination against Britain was very real. For the time being, France was opposed to Spanish ambitions. After the death in 1715 of Louis XIV, with his heir Louis XV a childless minor and Philip V likely to claim the throne if the new king died without an heir, France had every reason to work against Spanish revanchism. However, Madrid could still find allies elsewhere. At Vienna in 1726 Spain aligned with the Hapsburg emperor Charles VI, agreeing to support the Pragmatic

Sanction (allowing Charles's daughter Maria Theresa to succeed to all his dominions) in return for Austrian aid in recovering the lost Mediterranean territories. Austria's possession of the former Spanish Netherlands, the creation of the Ostend Company as a possible trade rival, and the possible development of Ostend as a naval base made this alignment particularly worrying. The British reply, the Treaty of Hanover, linking George I's domains with Prussia and France, was unstable and in 1726 Russia joined the Vienna allies. The subsequent short Anglo-Spanish war of 1727-1728 saw Gibraltar half-heartedly besieged while the Royal Navy attacked Spanish shipping – and Charles VI refused to support his ally's apparent aggression. The rapprochement with France seemed more secure than ever, and the wisdom of an integrated European policy was apparently vindicated.[2]

The other side of this coin was a reluctance to become too embroiled in colonial affairs. Secretaries of State for the Southern Department, albeit with support and advice of the Board of Trade, had to manage relations with France and Spain as well as colonial affairs. Naval resources, for example, had to be concentrated in European waters, and colonial governors were mostly left to look after themselves. Between two and nine warships were stationed in the North American colonies, mainly for anti-piracy operations; by the late 1720s piracy had been largely eradicated, leaving commanders there with little to do. Nor could ministers interfere too fussily in the internal affairs of individual colonies, which were left to make whatever local laws they pleased. 'Salutary neglect' – the Duke of Newcastle's expression – became the broad attitude of London's policy makers. Conflicts in the colonies themselves were unlikely to lead to a general war: the foundation of Georgia in 1732 was an irritant to the Spaniards but provided a welcome buffer for South Carolina and was not enough to cause conflict by itself.[3]

Colonies were nevertheless valuable assets, so their economic development was left alone unless it competed with home industry or with the prosperity of other colonies. The Navigation Acts were amended where it seemed necessary to protect British producers against colonial competition, just as the 1699 Woollen Act did already. Laws restricting the colonies' right to export beaver hats and caps and their right to build new steel works were passed in 1732 and 1750 respectively. Arguably, these laws did not affect existing businesses, did not interfere with local markets and could not be adequately enforced.[4] A 1733 Molasses Act, meant to support West Indian producers by imposing a duty of a shilling a gallon on foreign sugar products, was widely ignored.

In 1733, with Louis XV now secure on his throne, France saw considerable strategic advantages in a Spanish alliance. The first 'Family Compact' pledged France to help Spain recover Gibraltar and committed Spain to supporting the claim of Louis XV's father-in-law, the deposed

Stanisław Leszczyński, to the throne of Poland. The French were less interested in Poland than in weakening the Hapsburg Monarchy and thereby discomfiting Britain. That was why Walpole refused to assist his ally, the Hapsburg emperor, when he became embroiled in the War of the Polish Succession (1733-1735), even though it meant letting down his Austrian ally, and why he refused to become embroiled with Spain over the commercial concessions in the Utrecht agreement.

Both positions, however, became harder and harder to sustain as the 1730s wore on. Even with royal patronage at his disposal, Walpole could not reward everyone he would have liked to keep committed to his government, so there emerged a group of ambitious office-hungry politicians, among them one William Pitt. Fanning fears of Hanoverian influence, condemning Spanish violence against British smugglers, and reviving the alleged mutilation of a Captain Jenkins, the opposition whipped up demand action. In March 1739 Walpole had to submit. Consenting to war against his own better judgement, he sourly informed the Duke of Newcastle, his Secretary of State, that it was his war and wished him well of it.[5]

He was quite right. Despite an early success at Porto Bello, in the Caribbean this 'War of Jenkins' Ear' was a disaster matched only by the failure of Cromwell's Western Design eighty years before. An attempt to harass the barely defended Pacific coast of South America was no more successful. Commodore George Anson's circumnavigation of the globe and capture of the Manila galleon hardly obscured the fact that he returned with only one ship and very few of his men.[6] Worse still, by 1740 there were clear signs that the French were about to intervene with a major West Indian expedition of their own. Britain was about to be confronted with the nightmare of a purely naval war against both Bourbon powers at once.

The day was saved by the outbreak of war in central Europe: young Frederick II of Prussia attacked the Hapsburg province of Silesia on the ground that Maria Theresa, being a woman, could not succeed there. France seized what appeared to be a God-given opportunity to dismember the Austrian empire at last. But the threat of French domination in Europe, especially the danger to the Austrian Netherlands – and the apparent danger of an invasion of Britain herself – brought even more wrath down upon the Walpole ministry. In the 1741 general election the ministry's majority shrank to nineteen seats. In December, the opposition gained control of the Committee of Privileges and Elections, the body charged with deciding disputed election results. Two petitions were quickly decided in the appellants' favour, and when the Committee overturned a third result (in Chippenham) Walpole found himself with a mere sixteen-seat majority; and as the Committee decisions might ultimately adjudicate up to thirty seats, the government was doomed. On 2 February Walpole resigned, making way for the interventionist Lord Carteret.[7]

From Utrecht to Paris

Carteret immediately set about sending a substantial British contingent to an allied 'Pragmatic Army' to defend the Austrian Netherlands. This was not a declaration of war. For the time being, Britain maintained the fiction that she was not at war with France, but merely Maria Theresa's ally in defending the Pragmatic Sanction, just as France affected to be Frederick II's mere auxiliary. Disputes about whether to invade France – preferred by Lord Stair, the veteran allied commander in chief – or to intervene in Germany as George II demanded, meant that nothing was done in 1742. But in 1743 the army did march into Germany and won a very lucky victory over a French army at Dettingen on the River Main. Next year the war came closer to home as a French invasion force commanded by Maurice de Saxe assembled at Dunkirk, its landing to be facilitated by a combined French fleet seizing control of the Channel, and co-ordinated with a formal declaration of war and a Jacobite rising. The French plan miscarried from over-complexity, mismanagement, British naval action and storms which destroyed Saxe's barges. Saxe then turned north into the Netherlands and in 1745 gained a significant victory over the Pragmatic Army, now led by George II's son the Duke of Cumberland, at Fontenoy.

Then came the news of Prince Charles Edward's landing on Eriskay off the west coast of Scotland, followed by the rising of a number of Highland clans, their seizure of Edinburgh and subsequent defeat of Sir John Cope's government forces at Prestonpans. To meet this sudden peril, Cumberland and most of the British regiments were withdrawn from Flanders. While he defeated the Jacobites decisively at Culloden in April 1746, Saxe was free to overrun the Austrian Netherlands and threaten the Dutch Republic. In February 1747 his subordinate Lowenthal stormed the supposedly impregnable Dutch fortress of Bergen-op-Zoom, before two striking British naval victories redressed the balance. In this crisis, colonial operations were less than sideshows.

Colonial clashes were therefore almost wholly locally inspired by and served local rather than imperial strategic interests. Forces from the southern American colonies raided (and were raided in return) by the Spanish in Florida. There were clashes in the Hudson-Lake Champlain corridor between New York and New France; on the New England frontier, and on the isthmus between New France and Nova Scotia. The most dramatic and successful British offensive was the capture of Louisbourg in 1745 by the New England colonies and a small British naval squadron. In India the following year, indecisive naval clashes led to the French capture of Madras. New Englanders were anxious to retain Louisbourg and so eliminate the threat it posed to their fishing fleets; but at the 1748 Peace of Aix-La-Chapelle the British plenipotentiary gratefully surrendered it to secure the evacuation of the Netherlands by France, and incidentally the return of Madras.

The First British Empire

In terms of issues, these colonial clashes were a continuation of the fighting that had flared up during the wars against Louis XIV. However, the forces involved were on a larger scale than ever before, and their combats were more numerous and intensive. Nor did they end because of a peace settlement arrived at in Europe. In India, continued conflict was the outcome of a conscious policy launched by the French governor, Dupleix. In the Americas it was largely because the expanding French and British colonies were now rubbing up against each other and competing for land and the Indian trade. Moreover, Aix-la-Chapelle had illustrated the usefulness of colonies as bargaining counters. Both Britain and France were aware that if the French could defend their possessions successfully, the British would be unable to buy back any fresh conquests in Europe. The dynamics of colonial conflict were becoming enmeshed with the strategic interests of the metropoles.

In fact, it was a skirmish in the American wilderness in 1754 which sparked off the next war, two years before fighting began in Europe. It demonstrated that Virginia alone could not repel French penetration of the Ohio Valley. The Board of Trade ordered the colonies to meet at Albany, hoping that concerted action could be agreed, but inter-colonial rivalry proved stronger than fear of New France. There was now no alternative to direct imperial intervention. In 1755 two regular regiments were deployed to North America for a major campaign against New France, and Major General Edward Braddock was appointed to the new post of commander-in-chief in mainland North America. At the same time Admiral Edward Boscawen was ordered to intercept a French convoy carrying reinforcements to New France. The result was the worst of both worlds: Boscawen engaged the convoy – thus making open war all but inevitable – but failed to stop all the transports. In 1756 the so-called 'Diplomatic Revolution' realigned the great powers and set off the conflict called the Seven Years' War. In a complex set of manoeuvres France and Austria, the two Catholic powers, combined against Prussia; consequently, Britain became allied with France's enemy, Prussia. War erupted in 1756 when Frederick II launched a pre-emptive attack upon the ring of enemy states about to engulf him.

At sea, the key strategic problem was to prevent the Brest and other Atlantic port squadrons from combining with the French Mediterranean fleet at Toulon. In theory the British Western Squadron should have been able to cover all the Atlantic ports. But the Atlantic squadron could not be everywhere at once, and its primary role was still to contain the Brest squadron. In 1756 and 1757 it failed to stop further reinforcements, military and naval, from reaching Canada. In the Mediterranean, possession of the excellent harbour at Port Mahon in Minorca should have provided a base from which to blockade Toulon; but Minorca was almost unmanned. Peacetime economies had dictated that there should be only a few vessels left in the Mediterranean – and for the same reason the garrison was too small to defend the whole island in the face of a passive population. There was clear evidence of a French expedition preparing at Toulon, probably against Minorca, but with a French army gathering on the Channel coast priority had to be given to the Western Squadron. Not until March 1756 were there enough ships available to make a Mediterranean fleet.

The chosen commander, Vice Admiral John Byng, who had extensive Western Mediterranean experience, was given ten ships of the line and orders to convey an infantry regiment from Gibraltar to Minorca. Byng, however, was in pessimistic mood. At Gibraltar he heard (falsely) that the French had already landed and gave way to despair, declining to embark troops as Minorca was as good as lost. He picked up three more sail of the line and sailed for Minorca as ordered, but with very little expectation of success.

After Byng sailed but a month before he sighted Minorca, the French expeditionary force landed and opened the siege of the formidable Fort St Philip. When he appeared, the French army was in a difficult position, having to dig approaches through solid rock, with limited supplies and with a covering fleet possessing no nearby port of refuge. Everything would turn upon the outcome of the naval battle. Yet Byng managed the engagement with notable incompetence: only part of the British fleet engaged, and the French squadron remained intact. Byng might still have redeemed the situation by attacking again, simply maintaining the threat, or by harrying French supply ships: had he done so, the siege would have collapsed. N. A. M. Rodger is to the point: 'The only hope for the French was for Byng to withdraw all British ships from the Western Mediterranean, and this he obligingly did.'[8] On 28 June, Fort St Philip was forced to surrender.

The disaster brought down the government and William Pitt to power for the first time. Pitt and his colleagues tried to save Byng, but it was all too clear that he had breached that part of the articles of war which prescribed death for failing to do his utmost to take or destroy enemy ships. He was shot on his own quarterdeck on 14 March 1757. As Rodger remarks,

> As a surprising number of historians, seemingly unaware of the fall of the Newcastle ministry, have attributed Byng's death to political persecution, it is worth repeating that he died while his political friends were in office, and in spite of their efforts to save him from the anger of the king, the fury of the public, and the disgust of his naval colleagues.[9]

He may be only partially right, however, about the effects of the execution. While it may well have engendered a more aggressive mentality among sea officers, and thus given the British a decided psychological advantage, there is some evidence that it made commanders on the spot hesitate before ignoring misconceived, potentially disastrous and out-of-date orders from London.

With invasion looming, forces were mustered in the usual camps in southern England and a lieutenant colonel rode along the coast from Dover to Dorset evaluating possible landing beaches. In America and India, the French were on the offensive. In Germany an Anglo-Hanoverian force led by Cumberland was defeated at Hastenbeck and subsequently forced to capitulate at Klostersevern. Hanover was now knocked out of the war. In January, Russia, Poland and Sweden joined the anti-Prussian coalition. In the spring the beleaguered Frederick expelled a French army from Prague but then suffered near-fatal defeats at the hands of the Austrians and the Russians. The only bright spot in these months of disaster was Spain's failure to join her Bourbon ally.

Recovery came in part from the tenacity of Frederick II, subsidised heavily by Britain and supported by a new allied army under the Prussian Duke of Brunswick. William Pitt, once vehemently opposed to continental commitments, and now Secretary of State, saw the necessity of a European ally to divert French resources from naval warfare. At the same time he set out to weaken France by blockading her ports, seizing her colonies and launching diversionary raids against the French coast.

There was little that was new in this approach. Nor could it have been realised without the ability of Newcastle, now First Lord of the Treasury, to muster crucial parliamentary majorities, nor the talents of other ministers and advisers, notably Anson at the Admiralty and Lord Ligonier at the Horse Guards. Not all of his strategic interventions and military appointments were wise, but what Pitt contributed was an overall strategic vision and a relentless co-ordinating energy. The wonder is not that he made mistakes, but that he made so few.

At sea, the key strategic problem was, as always, to prevent the French Toulon and Brest fleets from combining, and beyond that the challenge was to use blockade to prevent French troops and warships from reinforcing New France and the West Indies. However, until the Navy was able to build up its strength, neither goal could be easily achieved. Not only could Minorca not be saved, but in 1757 a planned amphibious attack on Louisbourg was frustrated by local French naval superiority. But in 1759 the Toulon and Brest fleets were smashed at the battles of Lagos and Quiberon Bay respectively. In 1759, Quebec in New France fell, Montreal the following year, and the whole of New France by 1761. In India Robert Clive's victory at Plassey won a substantial territorial foothold in Bengal. In 1761 Pitt had intelligence that Spain was about to declare war and advocated a pre-emptive strike against the incoming silver convoy. By then the war had become so expensive, and Pitt's ambition so huge and

From Utrecht to Paris

so manifest, that his Cabinet colleagues vetoed the move and Pitt resigned. However, when Spain joined the war in 1762 she promptly lost Havana and Manila, only adding to the British triumph.

The Peace of Paris confirmed Britain's new status as a Great Power. In North America, France surrendered the whole of New France, all of Louisiana east of the Mississippi and Cape Breton Island, as well as Tobago, Dominica, St Vincent and the Grenadines in the Caribbean, and Senegal in West Africa. The French factories in India were restored with the provisos that they could not be fortified and that France recognised British dominance in the Carnatic and Bengal. Minorca was restored and Spain gave up Florida and recognised British possession of the Honduran logwood settlements. These breathtaking gains secured Britain's strategic position in the Mediterranean, gave her dominance in America and greater strength in Asia, and confirmed her naval supremacy. Her ally Prussia had survived and by a separate treaty Frederick's possession of Silesia was confirmed. However, there was a price to be paid and Britain's supremacy was largely illusory.

Guadeloupe and Martinique, with their superior sugar production, and the slaving port of Gorée were returned to France, so theoretically restoring her most valuable maritime trade and naval resources. French footholds in India could be refortified and used to support Indian states hostile to the East India Company. Spain was given western Louisiana and New Orleans on the Mississippi's west bank as compensation for Florida, while the strategically important Havana and Manila were handed back. Although the concessions were meant to deflate Bourbon revanchism, they left open the possibility of an overwhelming Franco-Spanish naval combination. This was all the more threatening as Britain faced a period of diplomatic isolation: Prussia, the Hapsburg Monarchy and Russia now being more worried about each other's ambitions in Eastern Europe than about France. The British Isles and the British empire were still highly vulnerable.

15

Mainland North America: From Salutary Neglect to Imperial Intervention, 1713-1754

The Peace of Utrecht did not remove the potential for conflict in mainland North America. A rapidly growing British colonial population, pressing inexorably inland, was coming into conflict with a tightening arc of French-controlled territory, stretching from Canada through the Great Lakes and the length of the Mississippi. The construction of Louisbourg from 1720 on Cape Breton Island, where it could guard the mouth of the St. Lawrence, the expansion of the Illinois settlements and the 1720 building Fort Chartres there, and the 1718 foundation of New Orleans to command the entrance to the Mississippi, all seemed to signify a French determination to pen the British colonies to the coast.

In particular, the peace of Utrecht left four potential flashpoints of conflict. In the north, there was the question of the border between New France and Nova Scotia, and within Nova Scotia resistance by parts of the French-speaking population. Further south, British expansion along the Hudson-Lake Champlain corridor threatened to bring them up against the French to the south of Montreal. Third, Pennsylvanian traders and Virginian settlers were taking an interest in penetrating through the Appalachians into the Ohio Valley. Finally, the expansion of South Carolina exacerbated pre-existing frontier tensions with Spanish Florida. In all of these critical places the situation was complicated by powerful Amerindian groups determined to resist dispossession by playing the European invaders off against each other.

Population growth and frontier friction
The white population grew through both immigration and natural increase. The natural growth, probably due to low child and female

mortality and the availability of land and food, was the more significant of the two. Immigrants accounted for perhaps 300,000 people, 15-20% of the total increase before 1775. Most of these new immigrants were English, and there were some Scots. But about 125,000 newcomers were Presbyterian Ulster Irish ('Scotch-Irish') who, finding themselves unwelcome in Congregationalist New England, moved south into the Middle Colonies. From there some filtered, by way of inland valleys, into the frontier regions of Virginia and the Carolinas, while in the 1730s other sailed direct to Charleston. Perhaps 100,000 German speakers (including some Swiss) formed inland communities in Pennsylvania, eventually forming one-third of that colony's population.

Slavery was yet another source of population growth, especially in the south. The black population of the mainland colonies grew from around 9,000 in 1710 to 40,500 in 1740 and to 58,500 by 1750. In the southern colonies they formed an ever-increasing proportion. By 1740, two-thirds of South Carolina's people were black, 30,000 compared to 15,000 whites. Carolina's hunger for slaves, and their value as exports, had led to a thriving trade in Indian captives, in which the Yamasees of the southern frontier were principal suppliers. By 1713, however, their very success had led to a dearth of new prey, at the very time that the trade in deerskins, the Indians' only alternative source of trade goods, was in decline. Consequently, the Yamasees were falling into debt with the traders who supplied them with all kinds of European goods, including guns and ammunition. At the same time, frontier settlements and expanding rice production were encroaching on Yamasee lands. By 1713 a reckoning was not far away.

The Tuscarora War and the Yamasee War

A war of conquest was already underway in North Carolina, officially separated from South Carolina in 1710, although controlled by the same proprietors. The Tuscaroras had been diminished in numbers by smallpox, raided by Susquehannocks and Senecas, deceived by South Carolina traders and slavers, and encroached upon by North Carolina land speculators. The last straw was the intrusion of a new Swiss settlement, New Bern, in 1711. The Tuscaroras slaughtered the surveying party and systematically attacked intrusive farms. South Carolina raised an army of Amerindians which stormed only one Tuscarora town before disintegrating and taking its loot home. Fighting continued and in 1713 South Carolina raised a second force of a hundred whites and eight hundred Creeks, Catawbas and Cherokees. The Tuscaroras were overwhelmed, three thousand being killed or enslaved and two thousand fleeing northwards to become the sixth nation of the Iroquois confederacy. [10]

That was not the end. By 1715 the expansion of Carolina to the south, with its destruction of the Yamasee Indians' hunting grounds had ruined

The First British Empire

their ability to pay for trade goods, and traders had been taking slaves instead. The tension erupted into war between South Carolina on the one hand and the Yamasees and their Creek allies, soon joined by coastal plain Catawbas, mountaineer Cherokees, Savannah Shawnees and Guale from Florida, on the other. Armed with guns supplied by Virginian traders, their war parties swept through South Carolina, pushing the frontier back to the fringes of Charleston. They routed a colonial counter-offensive and kept a newly raised army, including 500 blacks, at bay. The colony came close to destruction, the five hundred black troops it raised testimony to the settlers' desperation. It was two years before the Yamasees' allies, realising that Virginia would not continue to supply them with firearms, abandoned the cause, the Cherokees actually changing sides. The refugee Yamasees and Guales retired to Florida where, now under Spanish protection, they launched repeated raids to northward for another decade.[11]

Afterwards, South Carolina traders were less demanding of their Amerindian customers and after 1717 new forts were built to watch the traders as much as to defend against the Indians. The proprietors, having been severely discredited by the war, lost the Carolinas to the Crown in 1719. The European wars of 1718-1721 and 1727-1728 against Spain were times of heightened tension in which both Carolina and Florida felt vulnerable, and in the second conflict Carolinians made an unsuccessful attack on St Augustine. The volatility of the southern frontier was such that in 1732 the imperial government authorised the creation of a buffer colony to be named after George II.

Georgia

Georgia, first settled in 1733, amounted to a British annexation of Florida's now depopulated Guale province. Spanish objections were rejected, and Spanish retaliation was expected. In 1734 the British government provided £25,800 to build forts, and a further £20,000 in 1737 as relations with Spain deteriorated. General James Oglethorpe, the colony's founder and first governor, cultivated good relations with the Creeks and other Natives, thus consolidating these defences. Originally conceived by Oglethorpe as a slave-free refuge for British debtors, it became a slave economy in the 1740s as landowners scented the higher profits. By 1750, about a quarter of Georgia's 5,200 people were slaves.

Slavery was both the economic strength and the Achilles heel of these southern colonies. As in the West Indies, slave economies brought with them the perennial danger of revolt, a peril exacerbated by Florida's offer of freedom and land for runaways. In November 1739, just as the War of Jenkins' Ear began, a revolt at Stono in South Carolina was attributed to this offer, as was a fire in Charleston soon after. Southern planters had already been developing a siege mentality very like that to be found in the West Indies, and their legislatures had introduced draconic slave codes.

Revolt combined with the threat of foreign intervention confirmed and strengthened this state of mind.

Further north, in the middle colonies of Pennsylvania, New Jersey and New York there were fewer slaves and no plantations, but Philadelphia was the biggest city and most important port in North America, followed closely by New York. By mid-century Pennsylvania and New Jersey were developing a thriving iron and steel industry, successful to the extent that the 1750 Iron Act forbade the construction of new steel works to protect Britain's own growing enterprises. That did not check colonial growth because existing mills were able to supply demand until the 1780s. On the frontiers, Pennsylvanian and Maryland traders and settlers were pressing inexorably inland at the expense of the Lenape (or Delaware) and Shawnee Indians. As we shall see, it was in the upper valley of the Delaware River than Pennsylvanians committed one of the most outrageous land frauds of the century. In New York, settlement was pushing up the Hudson north of Albany, into the valley of the Mohawk River and pressing on the lands of the Mohawks, the most easterly of the Iroquois nations. Here relations were managed by a colourful Irish trader, merchant and land speculator called William Johnson, whose wife was a Mohawk.

Boston was the main outlet for New England's exports of food and timber to the southern colonies and West Indies and their illegal imports of Dutch, French, and Spanish sugar products, in almost complete disregard of the Molasses Act. Inland, ever since King Philip's War the New Englanders had entertained a deep suspicion of all Algonquians, including the Abenaki of Maine and the Mi'kmaq of Nova Scotia. During the wars against Louis XIV the eastern Abenaki had allied with the French and raided invasive New Englander settlements. On the Indian side, suspicion and violence continued well into the post-war period. In 1722 Abenaki and Mi'kmaq attacked settlements in Maine, Massachusetts, New Hampshire and Nova Scotia, briefly blockaded Annapolis Royal, and were not repelled until 1725.

Acadian complexities

In Nova Scotia there were peculiar problems of governance due to the presence of a French Catholic population, the Mi'kmaq and a substantial number of mixed-race people. Mi'kmaq determination to retain their independence was aided by the British decision to treat Acadians and Mi'kmaq as separate communities. But as there was so much intermarriage and everyday interaction, and the fact that a substantial number of Mi'kmaq shared the Acadians' Catholic faith, meant that no clear distinction was possible. The situation was further complicated by Acadians who chose to refuse (as they were entitled to do under the Treaty of Utrecht) to swear allegiance to the British Crown unless they were exempted from military service. Anti-Catholic New Englanders with

The First British Empire

their eyes on Acadian land pressed for the expulsion of French speakers and their priests.

The Louisbourg expedition

The fortress of Louisbourg on Cape Breton Island was begun in 1720 and finished twenty years later. Its walls, thirty feet high and notionally mounting 250 guns, enclosed a small town and dominated a small harbour. The harbour entrance was commanded by a separate battery on a small island and a Grand Battery on the northern shore. This impressive fortress guarded the approach to the St. Lawrence while providing a forward base for potential attacks on Nova Scotia and New England, and a haven for privateers preying on their fishing fleets. It is hardly surprising that in the War of the Austrian Succession New England targeted Louisbourg.

On receiving news of the formal outbreak of war the governor at Louisbourg launched a surprise attack against Canseau (Canso), capturing the village and its eighty-man garrison of Massachusetts militia. A follow-up assault on Annapolis Royal failed in the face of a determined defence, indecisive French leadership, the refusal of French Acadians to join in, and the unwillingness of two French warships at Louisbourg to support an unauthorised local adventure. These moves were intended as the prelude to taking back Acadia from the British, but they turned out to be serious strategic errors. Massachusetts declared war on the Mi'kmaq and issued a scale of bounties for Native prisoners and scalps. New England privateers swarmed into the fishing grounds, taking hundreds of French vessels, while French ships preyed on English fishermen. Finally, New England launched a massive assault on Louisbourg itself.

The expedition was intended to eliminate the privateer nuisance, as well as being – at least for the Congregationalist clergy – something of an anti-Catholic crusade. Moreover, Louisbourg was believed to be vulnerable. A Lieutenant Bradstreet, one of the repatriated Canseau prisoners who had seen the state of the fortifications, thought the place could be easily taken. He claimed that there were no more than 600 regulars in the garrison and that the Cape Breton militia might produce only 1,800 men more; that the bastions mounted less than a hundred guns between them; and that there were two unrepaired breaches in one of the key batteries. He convinced William Shirley, the Governor of Massachusetts and a client of the Duke of Newcastle, and the assembly was forced to agree by a surge of popular enthusiasm. Shirley then wrote to London, asking for naval support, and appealed to the other British colonies as far south as Pennsylvania.

The response was determined by geography as well as resources. Massachusetts raised 3,000 men, Connecticut sent 500, New Hampshire 450, and little Rhode Island produced an armed ship. New York, conscious of its own frontier with New France, sent ten 24-pounder pieces of siege artillery, almost a third of the expedition's entire battering train. Colonies further south saw little or no benefit for themselves. New Jersey and Pennsylvania offered only supplies and in Philadelphia Benjamin Franklin sounded a note of warning: 'Taking strong places is a particular trade, which you have taken up without having served an apprenticeship to it.' Between them, the participating colonies found 100 transports and fifteen armed ships as escorts.

The expedition assembled at Canseau in 1745, where Commodore Peter Warren from the West Indies appeared with one ship mounting sixty guns and three with forty apiece. The landing at Gaburus Bay near Louisbourg was virtually unopposed, the militia took possession of the Grand Battery after the French abandoned it, and the besiegers began a steady bombardment from the landward side. The damage was not all inflicted upon the French: over half of the New Englander's casualties came from clumsy amateur handling of big guns. However, storming the place with a drunken and ill-disciplined militia proved to be a different matter: two attempts to take the island battery were disasters. Warren's blockade and the consequent hunger – by the end he had twelve ships seizing inward bound supplies – were more effective: the fortress surrendered.

On the face of it Louisbourg was a great triumph, or so New Englanders boasted to themselves: amateur soldiers had taken a Vauban-style fortress and the possibility of an attack on Quebec had been opened up. In the year of Fontenoy and at the beginning of the great Jacobite rebellion, successes were urgently needed and newspapers on both sides of the Atlantic trumpeted its glories. Warren was promoted Rear Admiral and made governor of New York, while Shirley was given the colonelcy of a new regular regiment to be raised in America. Plans were afoot for attacks on Montreal and Quebec in 1746.

In fact, it was something of a Pyrrhic victory. Disease decimated the victors as they struggled to repair the crumbling fortifications and the two-pronged assault on New France was never launched. Shirley managed to assemble about eight thousand militia from New England, New York, New Jersey, Maryland and even Virginia. But the expected regulars never arrived – for London, the Netherlands, the Jacobite revolt and diversionary raids on the French coast were greater priorities – and formal operations in North America came to an end.

War in the forest
The real war was fought in the woods of Nova Scotia, and on the frontiers of New England and New York. French and Indian raiders struck at forts on the New England frontier, clearing settlers out of Vermont and the Connecticut Valley, and driving into the Massachusetts frontier. They overwhelmed a militia detachment in unfortified Grand Pré on the Bay of Fundy and sacked undefended Saratoga on the upper Hudson

River. Mi'kmaq and Abenaki warriors pressed forward in Nova Scotia, intimidating the Acadian settlers into co-operation. Sudden encounters, ambushes and post-raid pursuits were frequent.

The danger did not produce mutual co-operation between periphery and metropole but rather increased tensions between New England and London. In Massachusetts there was resentment at its troops being detained to garrison Louisbourg, the non-arrival of the regular battalions to attack Quebec, and the rising cost of the war. This resentment expressed itself in riots against impressment. Towards the end of 1747 Boston was wracked by three days of violence when Admiral Charles Knowles attempted to press local seamen into his under-manned ships. In Nova Scotia the war made more urgent the question of how to deal with a conquered colony containing an unfriendly, if not wholly hostile, white community and a resentful Native population.

The Peace of Aix La Chapelle did nothing to end these clashes. Louisbourg was restored and with it the standing threat to Nova Scotia and New England shipping, not to mention French intrigues with Acadians and Indians. To counter the threat, the British established a new naval base, Halifax, at Chebucto Harbour on the south coast of the peninsula, and subsidised Protestant migrants from Britain and Europe. The policy was supported by William Shirley, who wanted land for settlers from Massachusetts, and implemented by George Montagu Dunk, Earl of Halifax and now President of the Board of Trade, who was alarmed at French activities on the American frontiers.

The building of Halifax in 1749 breached an implicit agreement of 1726 that this area was in Mi'kmaq territory, and there is some evidence that Indian hostility was expected and prepared for. The first violence seems to have come from Massachusetts settlers at Canseau and quickly escalated into an Indian war of resistance. Settlement was quickly confined to the vicinity of Halifax. French soldiers entered the peninsula to support the Mi'kmaq and to force Acadians to move.[12] In 1750 the French built new fortifications to secure the St Johns River area and Fort Beauséjour to dominate the isthmus of Chignecto. The commander of a force sent to capture Beauséjour found it too strong to attack and instead constructed Fort Lawrence opposite it. In effect, France was taking military action to shut the British out of a region they had claimed since 1713 and appeared to be threatening the peninsula itself. Meanwhile an even more dangerous conflict was about to spread through the Ohio River valley.

The Ohio powder keg

For the American historian Fred Anderson, Iroquois claims to the Ohio Valley were central to the outbreak of the Seven Years' War. The original Five Nations were the Mohawks, located on the river of the same name, a tributary of the Hudson; the Oneidas; the Onondagas, whose chief town was home to the confederacy's central council; the Cayugas south of Lake Ontario, and to their west the Senecas. The Tuscaroras, refugees from their war against North Carolina, arrived and settled between the Onondagas and Oneidas in about 1720, converting the Five into the Six Nations. The Six Nations claimed suzerainty by right of conquest over the Delawares and Shawnees. Advancing British settlement was pushing them out of the Susquehannah Valley into the Ohio. In the Ohio towns the confederation was represented by mainly Seneca 'half-kings'. All this placed the Iroquois in a position to sway the balance between French and British interests in a strategically crucial region.[13]

For the French, use of the Ohio waterways was essential to communications between New France and the food and fur-producing Illinois country, and with the new settlement of New Orleans at the mouth of the Mississippi. From Paris, the creation of a solid arc of settlement would confine the British to the seaboard and, in wartime, oblige them to divert naval and military resources from Europe. For the British, Anderson argues, the Ohio represented an outlet for the burgeoning population of their seaboard colonies, and thus the means to keep American colonial wages high enough to preclude competition with British manufactures.[14] This last argument is debatable – London also feared losing control of inland colonies – but the aims and fears of the French are beyond dispute. Until mid-century, neither side could afford the expense of direct occupation, so control had to be exerted through Amerindian intermediaries.

This allowed the Iroquois to position themselves as those intermediaries. By the early eighteenth century the Iroquois were divided between those who favoured France, those who saw security in a British alliance, and those who saw the future in neutrality. Defeats in the wars of 1689-1713, combined with internal divisions and disillusionment with the British as allies, led to a policy of neutrality after 1713, although the Mohawks still leaned towards the British at Albany and the Senecas towards the French. Having painfully established that neutrality, they set out to play the French and British off against each other. They claimed the Ohio as theirs by right on conquest – an assertion given colour by the wars of the late seventeenth century and by the Valley's depopulation. From the late 1730s, however, Iroquois dominance was declining and the League was losing its independence of action. One event that had a striking effect over Iroquois prestige was the Walking Purchase of 1737.[15]

The Walking Purchase was an astonishingly blatant piece of chicanery by the no-longer Quaker-dominated colony of Pennsylvania. The scene was the Delaware Valley, and the occasion was an apparently reasonable agreement between the Delawares and representatives of the Penn family. The Penns claimed land in the valley under a deed which ceded a tract extending as far west of the Delaware River as a man on foot could travel in a day. Deceived by a misleading map, the Delawares thought that forty miles would be the maximum distance that could be covered in that time. In fact, the Pennsylvanians prepared a path and brought in three athletes to run the distance. Only one runner finished but he had covered about eighty miles. The supervising Pennsylvanian official then drew a perpendicular line back to the river and claimed all the enclosed 1,200,932 acres (4,860 km^2). Outraged, the Delawares protested to the British and asked the Iroquois for help. Onondaga had other ideas: they had already agreed the cession with Pennsylvania, a deal later confirmed by the 1742 Treaty of Easton. Groups of angry Delawares and Shawnees migrated to the Wyoming Valley and to the Ohio regions, where they were beyond effective Iroquois control.

Iroquois influence was further undermined by the 1744 Treaty of Lancaster, by which the Iroquois gave Virginia (wittingly or unwittingly) the whole Ohio basin, in return for £1,110 in cash and gold, recognition of their suzerainty over several southern nations, and free passage for their war parties moving against the Catawbas and Cherokees. The treaty was concluded without the consent, or even consultation, of Delawares, Shawnees or any other Ohio people. By 1745 a group of about twenty Virginian speculators had obtained from their colonial assembly a grant of 350,000 acres in the upper Ohio basin. Although exploitation of the concession was halted by the formal outbreak of war between Britain and France, the consortium was to re-emerge as the Ohio Company, including among its investors the Virginia governor Robert Dinwiddie, Arthur Dobbs the governor of North Carolina, a London merchant John Hanbury, and a young tobacco planter called George Washington.

In 1748 Hanbury persuaded the Board of Trade to authorise a 200,000-acre grant on the Ohio, with the promise of 300,000 more should it settle a hundred families and build and garrison a fort.[16] Pennsylvanian traders had already penetrated the Ohio and established themselves among the Native populations. At Pickawillany, a large Miami town commanding three canoe routes between Lake Erie and the Mississippi, they helped the headman, Memeskia (or 'Old Briton'), to build a defensive palisade. From there they sent boats far down the Ohio, drawing trade away from the French and undermining their Indian alliances.

The French response was to assert their sovereignty over the whole Ohio drainage system. In 1749 Pierre Joseph Céleron de Blainville led an array of French troops, Canadian militia and Indians through the basin, expelling Pennsylvanian traders and burying engraved lead plates asserting the French claim. The Ohio nations made plain their hostility to French pretensions, especially at fortified Pickawillany, but Céleron lacked the force to proceed to confrontation. In 1752, French-inspired Ojibwa and Ottawa warriors surprised Pickawillany, killed Memeskia,

Mainland North America

destroyed the traders' storehouses, and raised the French flag over the stockade before withdrawing. The intimidation had its effect – this time the traders did not return in strength and the Miami Indians could get no aid from other nations. The following year the governor of New France, Marquis Duquesne, sent 1,500 regulars and militia to build a defensive line of forts from Lake Erie to the Ohio. From Presqu'ile on the lakes southern shore, where they built their first fort, they pushed overland to a tributary of the Allegheny River. There they constructed Fort Le Boeuf to protect the portage before descending to the Allegheny at Venango, where they transformed a British trading post into Fort Machault. Their target, of course, was the Forks, at the confluence of the Allegheny and Monongahela rivers. From Virginia, Pennsylvania, and indeed from London, this looked like planned aggression.

Dinwiddie sent Washington to Fort Le Boeuf to order the French out of 'British' territory and sent to London for permission to use force. When Washington returned empty-handed, and having received London's permission to use force, the governor ordered building at the Forks to begin immediately and prepared an expedition to reinforce the garrison there. Virginians, however, were unenthusiastic for a war to safeguard the Ohio Company's ambitions, and most of the 159 men who finally marched with Washington were penniless conscripts. In any case, it was too late. Long before Washington could cross the mountains a powerful French force has descended the Allegheny and forced the Virginian fort at the Forks to surrender. A formidable fortification, Fort Duquesne, rose in its place. From there the French commander, Contrecoeur, sent a party under Ensign Jumonville to locate Washington, seek a conference and warn him to retire.

For Tanaghrisson, the Half King who had encouraged the Virginians to fortify the Forks, and whose authority depended upon keeping the French at bay, this was a disaster. Needing to bounce Virginia into an all-out military effort to dislodge the French, he and a handful of Mingos (Ohio Senecas) joined Washington and persuaded him to surprise Jumonville's party. After an initial exchange of fire, Jumonville called a truce, whereupon Tanaghrisson tomahawked the ensign and his followers massacred the French prisoners. Virginia was certainly now committed: in effect, Tanaghrisson had precipitated a transatlantic war two years before it broke out in Europe.

Already the Board of Trade had ordered all the colonies from New Hampshire to Virginia to send delegates to a conference at Albany in New York.[17] There, it was hoped, the colonies could agree a common frontier policy and combine to see off a French threat that was beyond Virginia's resources to stem. In fact Virginia, the colony most urgently concerned, did not send delegates, nor did New Jersey. Assembling in June 1754, the seven delegations present, instead of planning urgent military co-operation, adopted a plan for a colonial federation put forward by Benjamin Franklin of Pennsylvania. Predictably, the plan was rejected by every colonial assembly to which it was put, and a concerted colonial war effort was as far away as ever. The home government was left with no alternative but to send a substantial force of British regulars and to appoint a commander-in-chief to co-ordinate the military resources of all the colonies. In this way a combination of parochial economic ambition, colonial disunion and Native politics propelled London into a war on either side of the Atlantic.

16

Mainland North America: The French and Indian War, 1754-1763

In dispatching two regiments of regular troops to North America, the ministry may have been simply responding to an emergency, as had been done in belated response to Bacon's Rebellion.[18] The appointment of a regular major-general as commander in chief of all forces there, British or colonial, was a different matter. The creation of two superintendents of Indian affairs for the northern and southern colonies, both responsible to the commander-in-chief, reinforced what was beginning to look like a vice-regal role. It was the most ambitious attempt to assert greater central control over the colonies since James II's ill-fated Dominion of New England. Consequently, the path to victory was paved with increasing Anglo-American tensions.

The key ministers concerned all feared French aggression in America as well as in Europe. Thomas Pelham-Holles, Duke of Newcastle and First Lord of the Treasury, favoured a softly-softly approach, containing France with allies in Europe while taking stealthy action to check her forward movement in America. In that way he hoped to avoid letting an American confrontation turn into a European war. Robert D'Arcy, Lord Holdernesse and Secretary of State for the Southern Department, was of a similar mind. But Halifax was more ambitious and had the support of the Duke of Cumberland, the king's uncle and commander-in chief of the British army, and Henry Fox, Secretary at War, responsible for military administration. Together they transformed Newcastle's modest plan into four separate but co-ordinated thrusts at every point of perceived French intrusion. Though the overall aim was probably still defensive, the new scheme had a distinctly aggressive aspect.

One column of regulars and provincials was to attack Fort Duquesne, while another force would make an amphibious attack on Fort Beauséjour. The other two forts targeted were not recent constructions. New France's links to Louisiana would be severed, and her own western back door threatened by taking Fort Niagara on Lake Ontario. Though now being rapidly expanded, Niagara was on a site well within the recognised French sphere, and the fort itself was almost thirty years old. In the same way, a fourth expedition was to take Fort St Frédéric at Crown Point on the shores of Lake Champlain, which like Niagara had been established for decades. Its capture would not only secure Albany against attack but also open up the Hudson-Champlain corridor to further settlement, and perhaps even threaten Montreal. The commander-in chief would thus have to co-ordinate four widely distanced campaigns, persuade the colonies to raise and pay for considerable numbers of troops, and find all the supplies and transport required. It was a formidable task, requiring considerable military skill, logistical ability and careful diplomacy.

Braddock

The task fell to Major General Edward Braddock, who – despite having never led troops in action – knew his profession well. Braddock's reputation once suffered from an undeserved image: stout, ageing, stuck in the rigidly linear tactical world of Europe, haughty, blustering, and unable to adapt to American conditions. Thankfully, conscientious research has long consigned that caricature to the historical dustbin, not least by his biographer, Lee McCardell.[19] Braddock turned out to be an able strategist who thought seriously about the management of a forest war: gathering information about how to campaign in the woods, evaluating the logistics of crossing a wilderness before he could engage his enemy; and considering how to secure his flanks in wild, closed country.

Unfortunately, and quite understandably, he was no diplomat. His commission authorised him require rather than request co-operation, much to the annoyance of colonial governors and legislators accustomed to substantial autonomy. James Glen of South Carolina saw to it that the Cherokee auxiliaries Braddock had been expecting remained in the south. Braddock had real doubts about the worth of provincial officers, and he expressed them bluntly, though he did not condemn them wholesale. He even allowed the recently defeated George Washington to wheedle his way onto his staff. Braddock was no less blunt with his potential Indian allies, refusing to guarantee the Delawares continued possession of their lands in exchange for their military assistance. Between Braddock's tactlessness and Glen's provincialism, the Fort Duquesne expedition had to march with only eight Indian scouts.

Despite that, his strong flanking parties kept the watching war parties at bay until he reached the Monongahela River, only a few miles from Fort

Mainland North America: The French and Indian War, 1754-1763

Duquesne. The disaster which followed arose not from incompetence on Braddock's part, nor from lack of courage on the part of his troops, but from the momentary carelessness of a subordinate officer.

When he was close to the fort, Braddock took a light column on ahead of the main body. Crossing the Monongahela and moving uphill through dense forest with ravines on either side of the track, his advance guard ran headlong into a force of French and Indians. A British volley shattered the French charge, but Lieutenant Colonel Thomas Gage failed to immediately seize a hillock dominating the path. The Indians and French secured this high ground. Streaming down the ravines and firing into the column from cover, they trapped the strung-out redcoats in the open. Braddock was mortally wounded while encouraging his men, who stood their ground for hours before giving way. When the fugitives appeared to his front, the commander of the rear column panicked and ordered a precipitate retreat. The main British effort had comprehensively failed.

Indeed, the only clear-cut success of 1755 was, significantly, the seaborne attack on Fort Beauséjour, soon followed by the beginning of the wholesale expulsion of the Acadians. Further south, the Niagara and Fort St. Frédéric expeditions – both of which involved difficult and dangerous woodland approaches – collapsed.

The Niagara enterprise led by the governor of Massachusetts, William Shirley, foundered on the logistics of wilderness campaigning. Poaching men from the Crown Point mission, and being in return prevented from recruiting Mohawks, was a bad enough start. Then Shirley heard that Admiral Boscawen, posted in the Gulf of St. Lawrence to intercept French reinforcements, had managed to take only two ships carrying a mere 400 of the 2,000 French regulars in the convoy. Short of supplies, Shirley nevertheless pushed on to Fort Oswego on Lake Ontario to find it too weakly fortified to serve as a base. He had to spend the rest of the summer strengthening Oswego in preparation for an offensive in the spring.

The Crown Point expedition was led by William Johnson, invaluable for the Mohawks he attracted but a hesitant amateur commander supported by ill-trained provincials from New York and New England. Reaching the portage far upriver from Albany, Johnson's regulars, provincials and Indians built a post he named Fort Edward and began to haul supplies, boats and ammunition overland to the lake he planned to rename after King George. At the lake end of the portage they made a camp, unfortified but with the trees cleared around it to provide a field of fire. Unknown to Johnson, the failures of Braddock and Shirley had allowed the newly arrived French commander, Baron Jean-Armand Diskau, to concentrate his forces at Crown Point. Already his regulars, Canadians and Indians (including Canadian dwelling Mohawks) were stealthily advancing through the woods towards Fort Edward.

The First British Empire

Diskau's plan was to cut off Johnson's retreat by taking Fort Edward before attacking the British camp. His Indians refused to attack a fortification and Johnson, belatedly warned, sent a scouting party almost as large as Diskau's whole force towards the Hudson. Diskau ambushed them on the road and pursued the broken troops towards Johnson's now hastily fortified camp. His Indians encircled the camp and opened fire from the woods while he charged with a deep column of regulars. Grape shot from Johnson's four cannon tore through the column and sent it reeling back in retreat. Diskau was mortally wounded and the siege broke up. Though the Battle of Lake George was later trumpeted as a triumph, the lesser general had won and Fort Frédéric stood unconquered.

By September the French had begun to build a new fort at Ticonderoga, dominating the channel between Lakes George and Champlain, and the threat to Fort Edward and Albany became plain. In response, Johnson began to construct Fort William Henry on his lakeside campsite and was made a baronet – some slight compensation for a major strategic failure.

Lord Loudoun 1756-1758

Shirley, who filled in as Braddock's temporary replacement, prepared a provincials-only expedition against Crown Point but could do little to stem the coming enemy counter-offensive in the middle colonies. French and Indian war parties swept back the frontiers of Virginia, Pennsylvania and Maryland. The forty-odd forts built by these provinces were nearly all too tiny or too rudimentary – blockhouses or simple stockades – and too feebly manned to effectively patrol the twenty-odd mile gaps between each of them. At best they were emergency refuges, at worst easy targets for enemy marauders. Maryland simply pulled its frontier defences back seventy miles and Virginia failed to recruit enough men – in both cases because the governing coastal elite feared slave revolts more than they did Indians. The Quakers in the Pennsylvanian assembly were unwilling to take effective military measures and finally withdrew from public life, while French and Indian parties captured forts and raided settlements to within seventy miles of Philadelphia. A Pennsylvanian expedition which attacked the Delaware town of Upper Kittanning suffered three times more casualties than it inflicted. Further north, in March 1756, raiders destroyed Fort Bull at the head of the Mohawk River and in July 1756 the Marquis de Montcalm, Diskau's successor, descended upon Fort Oswego. The New York and New England frontiers were now also wide open to attack. Much would depend upon reinforcements from Britain and the new commander-in-chief, John Campbell, Earl of Loudoun.

Loudoun reached Albany to find Shirley's Lake George provincials ready to go home if obliged to serve under lower-ranking regulars or brought under regular army discipline. Annoyed but recognising reality,

Mainland North America: The French and Indian War, 1754-1763

he compromised on both: regular officers below the rank of major could no longer issue orders to their provincial seniors, and he allowed the provincial Crown Point expedition to proceed once the officers had sworn to submit to royal authority. The New Englanders' contractual conception of military relations was completely outside Loudoun's experience,[20] but he was willing to adapt his received attitudes in a way they were not. He found assemblies had refused to find quarters and food for regular troops, and that Shirley had emptied the military purse by paying the going rates for these items. Even in his base at Albany he had to use force to get his men housed, and a battalion he sent to Philadelphia was treated in the same way. Americans seemed far keener to protect their rights and freedoms than to serve the common cause. He warned London to find to find a source of funding outside the assemblies' control and to 'remodel' colonial governments at once, or find the colonies ungovernable after the war. Of course, such sweeping reform was out of the question, but his assessment was to be proven quite correct.

In 1757, Loudoun not only had to deal with provincial obstruction but with orders to attack Louisbourg and Quebec by sea, so leaving the frontiers unprotected. Worse still, the Royal Navy had not yet established local control of the sea. Loudoun took the calculated risk of taking the bulk of his army to Halifax, but once there he waited to ascertain the French naval strength at Louisbourg. It was just as well: the French had managed to concentrate three squadrons there and an attempted assault was likely to cause the loss of the American field army at sea. He prudently withdrew to New York to find that in his absence Montcalm had taken Fort William Henry on Lake George, threatening the New York frontier. Loudoun pushed his men up the Hudson to defend Albany and planned a new offensive for 1758, clashing with the Massachusetts assembly over troop numbers. But his fate was sealed. In March he was recalled for a failure that was not his doing, leaving the army that he had meticulously organised and trained for forest warfare to his successor Major General Abercromby.

At the same time as sacking Loudoun, Pitt threw aside centralising measures to offer to reimburse the assemblies for the arms, powder and ball and tents for troops they might raise. The colonies would still have to cover the men's clothing and pay but a massive rebate could now be expected from the British taxpayer. Moreover, provincial officers would now be junior only to regulars of the same or higher rank. At a stroke he had cut through all the problems that had bedevilled Loudoun and ensured that even Massachusetts would raise men and money aplenty for the coming campaign. He had done so because he cared nothing for reform or the long-term coherence of the empire, but only for winning the war.[21] He kept one card firmly in his own hand, however: grand strategic planning.

1758: three victories and a catastrophe

The plan London imposed for 1758 was a four-pronged attack on Canada. If earlier operations had had a defensive component, this was now a war of conquest. One of Pitt's chosen generals, Jeffrey Amherst, was plucked out of the army in Germany, promoted over others' heads, and sent across the Atlantic to attack Louisbourg and Quebec. Abercromby was to take Ticonderoga and Crown Point and advance on Montreal, while a smaller force was to march against Fort Frontenac on Lake Ontario by way of the Mohawk Valley. Loudoun's former adjutant general, Brigadier General John Forbes, was to march on Fort Duquesne. The Ohio, originally the main theatre, was now a side show, presenting the most difficult logistical problems yet last in the queue for resources. 'Mr Amherst,' Forbes told Abercromby, 'has come to lick the butter of both our breads.'[22]

This time there were three striking successes. Amherst, ably seconded by James Wolfe, took Louisbourg in an essentially formal operation. In August a task force dispatched from the Hudson captured Fort Frontenac at the point where Lake Ontario drains into the St. Lawrence, so opening New France's back door. Forbes, dying of what may have been bowel cancer, held together a disparate force of regulars and provincials as it hacked a new road through the Pennsylvanian wilderness, while his diplomacy detached the Delawares and Shawnees from the French. His chosen route from Pennsylvania suited Pennsylvanians, but not Washington, who intrigued to change Forbes's strategy to serve Virginia. Progress was slow: it was November before the French commandant at the Forks was forced to blow up and abandon the fort, which Forbes ordered rebuilt as Fort Pitt before being carried back over the mountains to Philadelphia to die.[23]

Abercromby, however, suffered a disastrous reverse largely of his own making. Finding that Montcalm had reinforced Ticonderoga and strengthened it with a thick abattis of felled trees, he chose to attack without waiting for his artillery. Wave after wave of infantry was mown down as it struggled through the abattis. Abercromby, commanding from a post out of sight of the slaughter, ordered fresh assault upon fresh assault until nightfall when the number of dead and wounded was near 2,000. In a moment of panic, he withdrew his army to Lake George and the unused artillery, leaving Montcalm's much smaller force securely in possession. The consequence was predictable: Abercromby was dismissed, Wolfe took command at Louisbourg, and Amherst became commander-in-chief at New York.

1759: annus mirabilis

In the spring of 1759 the campaigns resumed. Wolfe's task was made much harder than expected by twenty-six French ships that slipped into the St. Lawrence as the ice broke up. They carried some five hundred troops and enough food to allow a prolonged defence, despite a poor

Mainland North America: The French and Indian War, 1754-1763

harvest in New France itself. It was June before Admiral Saunders took Wolfe upstream to besiege Quebec, to find that bluffs and two tributaries presented formidable obstacles for miles below the city, which was three hundred and fifty feet above the river. Montcalm had carefully fortified the most likely landing places below the town, where he repelled Wolfe's first attack at the end of July. The ailing Wolfe was reduced to bombarding the town and ravaging the countryside in the hope of luring the enemy out. Montcalm refused the bait and Wolfe spent weeks trying the patience of his three brigadiers as he searched for new ideas.

At the end of August these three advised him to look for a landing place upstream from the city, where he could cut off Montcalm's supplies from the west. Instead, without consulting or informing them until the last moment, he chose a pathway up the cliffs before Quebec itself. Preparations for an up-river landing became a feint designed to draw off Montcalm's troops.

What could have been a disaster miraculously became a triumph. Boats sent upstream in daylight fell downriver after dark to land troops at the cove called L'Anse au Foulon. Light infantry swarmed up the cliff to surprise and overwhelm the little French outpost at the top, and before Montcalm could react Wolfe's infantry had formed a line of battle across the Plain of Abraham. The French general had to engage his enemy – his town was short of food and the British ships now upstream severed his hope of further supplies, and Quebec's walls would not withstand a siege – but he did so without waiting for the return of troops earlier sent upstream to meet the expected landing. Against Wolfe's more professional and better disciplined troops the outcome was predictable. Accurate volleys and a determined charge swept the French from the field. Both commanders were mortally wounded, Quebec surrendered, and Brigadier General James Murray took command.

Even then the story was far from over. Lacking adequate supplies, Saunders had to withdraw his fleet before they became iced in for the winter, leaving Murray and his garrison isolated. In April a French force marched from Montreal to retake Quebec. Murray, worried about the weakness of his walls, came out to fight just as Montcalm had done. An attempt to envelop the French column as it moved up from the cliffs became bogged down in deep slushy snow and mud. After two hours of fighting Murray was forced back into Quebec. With supplies running out and the French constructing siege lines, all would depend on whose ships first came upriver when the ice melted. That issue had already been decided far away, with the destruction of the Toulon and Brest fleets at Lagos and Quiberon Bay. The French coast was now effectively blockaded and the Royal Navy had overwhelming superiority in the Gulf of St. Lawrence. The first sails to be sighted on the evening of May were British. The siege disintegrated and by 27 August Murray was outside Montreal.

The First British Empire

While Murray laid siege, Amherst's forces approached in two columns, one via Lake Champlain and the Richelieu River, the main force by way of Oswego and the upper St. Lawrence. By 5 September all three armies were united before Montreal. Lévis, the French commander, still harboured ideas of a counter-offensive using Indians and troops outside Montreal, but the former had seen the writing on the wall for New France. Impressed by the £17,000-worth of gifts and money in the hands of Amherst's 700 Iroquois, they decided that their futures lay with the British, not in defending a lost cause and bringing on their own destruction. In this roundabout way the Iroquois, whom Amherst regarded as greedy and expensive savages, forced Vaudreuil to capitulate on quite generous terms on 9 September.

The outlying French posts were occupied in 1761 and at the Peace of Paris Britain was confirmed in possession of all French lands, New Orleans excepted, east of the Mississippi River. The problem now lay in conciliating the Indians in that vast area, a task requiring tact, diplomacy, a proper understanding of Amerindian cultures and viewpoints, and a determination to keep white settlers out of Indian territory. Failure would produce expensive and bloody frontier wars – like the one already in progress between the Carolinas and the Cherokee nation – which might encourage Bourbon attempts at reconquest. Given settler land hunger and Amherst's opinion of Indians that danger was very real.

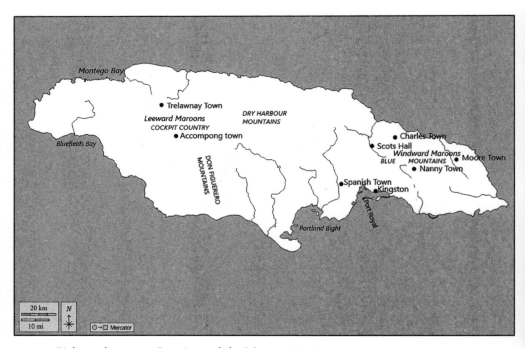

Eighteenth-century Jamaica and the Maroons.

17

The Caribbean: Slave Economies and Great Power Contests

Early in the eighteenth century the British West Indian colonies fell behind the French islands in sugar production. Guadeloupe and Martinique were larger and more productive than Barbados and the Leeward Islands, whereas Jamaica, larger than all the others put together, was slow to develop its potential as a sugar producer. French and Spanish sugar pushed the more expensive British product out of the European market and confined it to the heavily protected home market. With prices falling, British planters were strongly opposed to more Caribbean territorial acquisitions which might become competitors within the Navigation System.

This slow growth in production was due in part to the way land had been distributed among a restricted number of proprietors who did not necessarily cultivate all they owned. This was especially true of Jamaica, where it was a key cause for that island's slow development. By 1748 Jamaica was producing 17,399 tons per annum, a fourfold increase over 1700, but barely equal to that of the Leewards, which had a tiny fraction of Jamaica's area.

Another factor was the New England trade in fish, flour and timber with the West Indies. Yankee captains and merchants were not slow to realise that the molasses they wanted for distillation into rum was cheaper in the French islands. This was partly because French sugar products were cheaper to produce, partly because rum was banned in France to protect brandy producers. The English islands could sell in the home market as well as to the New England colonies, so their prices tended to be higher. The result was that the planters and their mercantile and parliamentary supporters in Britain campaigned for a legal check on peacetime trade with foreign islands.

The Molasses Act of 1733, passed against furious North American protests, imposed a duty of nine pence per gallon on all foreign spirits, six pence a gallon on molasses, and barred all French sugar products from Ireland. It was followed six years later by an Act allowing British planters to ship their products directly to Europe, a deliberate attempt to drive London prices up. The Molasses Act failed to check the New Englanders, who simply resorted to smuggling, but the legislation did give the West Indians a much larger protected market and made them more competitive in Europe. Nevertheless, the superior productivity of the French islands was a constant concern, economically and strategically.

The slave trade and resistance
Far more central to the islands' prosperity was the supply of slaves, a supply complicated by the Peace of Utrecht under which Britain was granted the *asiento*. The new South Sea Company was now allowed to send one ship and 4,800 slaves to the annual Porto Bello fair in modern-day Panama. Thus, there were two British importers of slaves to the Caribbean, the South Sea Company and the Royal African Company. The South Sea Company factors based themselves at Kingston, taking over much of the business of illicit traders and threatening the livelihoods of 1,200 men. It was also alleged that the South Sea men bought slaves imported by the Royal African Company and re-exported them, thus driving up prices on the island, and the Jamaican assembly retaliated by imposing a heavy export duty on slaves, a law later disallowed by the Board of Trade.

Slaves were not passive. Resistance of all kinds took place, the most feared but least frequent being mass rebellion. In April 1760 a major revolt known as Tacky's Rebellion erupted in St Mary's parish in northeastern Jamaica and uncomfortably close to Kingston itself (see page 158).It was defeated with some difficulty, after which measures – in the form of anti-runaway patrols and greater attention to slave discipline by magistrates – were improved. A second unexpected revolt in St Mary's 1765, and a planned insurrection detected in 1776, were quickly crushed.

At the lower level, slaves might malinger or commit acts of sabotage, ranging from breaking tools to damaging machinery. Running away was common: at any one time, two per cent of slaves were absent and a tenth of slaves ran way at some time or other. This might be for only a few days or weeks – to visit family on another plantation, perhaps – and was so common that planters found they had to live with it. Historians of slavery differ over how effective such resistance was. Writers such as Michael Craton stress the variety of forms of resistance to argue that slaves were successful in modifying their relationships with their masters. Others, while taking this on board, point out that there was not a single successful uprising in the British islands in the whole 200 years of slavery. Both points need to be acknowledged: the plantation system,

The Caribbean: Slave Economies and Great Power Contests

though far from invulnerable, was too powerful to be easily overthrown, and usually the best slaves could do was to oblige their masters to make concessions.

More dramatically and effectively, slaves might decamp *en masse* to the Maroon communities that formed in the hinterlands of every settlement with adjacent rugged territory, notably French Guadeloupe, Martinique, French St. Domingue, Spanish Cuba, British Belize and the adjacent Spanish territories, and Jamaica. As the numbers of escapees rose, Jamaican Maroon raids upon the plantations became so frequent and destructive that in 1730 the British began military operations against their towns.

The First Maroon War

The War (1730-1739) was a long grinding duel. Maroon determination, skilled guerrilla tactics and frequent ambushes turned what was supposed to be a brief campaign into nine years of attrition. Oral traditions still recall the Maroon soldiers' use of lookouts on mountain tops, war horns and conch shells to give warning or to co-ordinate tactics, camouflage, luring troops into narrow defiles where they could be attacked with rolling boulders, logs, arrows and bullets. All this was apparently informed by memories of their African warrior cultures. In 1732 the British captured Nanny Town, only to lose it in 1733 and recover it again after a five-day battle in 1734. The survivors split up, Nanny leading her people to a more secure refuge further east. Others travelled west to join Cudjoe in the cockpit country, only to be refused permission to settle there because they would not submit to his rule and be forced to return east in a much-reduced condition. Militia incursions repeatedly forced Maroon communities to relocate their provision gardens, acutely reducing their food supply. The British, on the other hand, could not defeat their determined and skilled enemy fighting an unconventional war, and rightly feared Spanish intervention. By 1739 both sides were exhausted, and Governor Edward Trelawney concluded that clemency and concession were the only answer to this kind of insurgency. With some difficulty, he opened negotiations with Cudjoe and on 1 March a treaty was signed. Nanny and her people held out for several months, but without Cudjoe's support they were eventually obliged to make their own peace. The Maroons secured recognition of their independence, 1,500 acres of land for each of the two communities, the right to hunt to within three miles of any plantation, licensed access to local markets, recognition of the life-long tenures of their headmen, and the right of those headmen to impose any penalty short of death for crimes committed in their communities. In return the Maroons were to accept residential superintendents as liaison officers, cut a road to Cudjoe's main settlement (renamed Trelawney Town), pledge to hunt down and return future runaways and to agree that the headmen should be nominated by the British Jamaican authorities.[24]

Superficially, the Maroons had won: after all, it was the British, not they, who had sued for peace. The roads built to weaken Maroon independence may have had a contrary effect, in that they gave the slaves who made them a much clearer idea of the island's overall geography, and possibly encouraged revolt and flight. Maroon communities certainly tried to prove their value to the white planters: in 1742 they intercepted fugitives from a failed slave rebellion and in 1744 they were the first to encounter a small band of rebels from the Port Royal dockyard. However, the terms undermined the authority of the headmen – especially as political discipline rested upon their autonomy and use of the death penalty.

There were also economic disadvantages not obvious at the time. The land they were ceded was only a small part of the regions in which they were used to hunt, fish and farm; but now planters felt entitled to encroach on those undefined lands. As more British settlers arrived In Jamaica, so the friction grew, while in the Maroon towns factionalism thrived. The Jamaican assembly was quick to exploit this factionalism by extending the powers of British superintendents resident in Maroon towns, imposing white leadership on Maroon bands hunting escaped slaves, and in 1744 organising Maroon soldiers into companies under British command. It is scarcely surprising that new wars broke out; it is extraordinary that the first came as late as 1795.[25]

Indeed, Helen McKee has shown that after 1739 there was a great deal of collaboration and co-operation between Maroons and many white planters. Whatever may have been true of Portuguese Brazil or the Danish islands, in Jamaica these alliances were not only with poor whites and plantation overseers, but with very wealthy and powerful men. Interactions seem to have been especially common in north-eastern Jamaica, where the planters had a great deal to gain from amicable relations, and a great deal to lose from provoking violence. Moreover, there was plenty of better land available for plantation expansion other than that held by the Maroons. Disputes over land arose less from deliberate encroachment on either side but from ambiguities in the treaties and long delays in surveying the relevant boundaries. They were settled by discussion and compromise. There was also social interaction: perhaps to associate themselves with the planter elite, and to dissociate themselves from connotations of slavery, Maroons increasingly abandoned African names in favour of English ones. Maroons in military dress travelled freely through the island, greeted warmly by whites they met on the road and even being entertained at plantation houses. When it suited them, individuals and gangs of Maroons took work on plantations on the same terms as free whites.

The Caribbean: Slave Economies and Great Power Contests

Knowing that Cudjoe would protect them against casual violence, planters visited Trelawny Town, where they took part in dances and ceremonies, and slept with and sometimes married Maroon women. While the potential threat of another Maroon War frightened planters, both officials and settlers saw the Maroons as an essential component in Jamaica's internal and external security.[26]

The War of Jenkins's Ear in the Caribbean

The Maroon treaties of 1739 and 1740 came just in time. At the outset of the War of Jenkins's Ear, Britain was very poorly placed to mount a campaign of Caribbean conquest and her own possession were vulnerable. Large squadrons could not be maintained there for long, largely because of the devastation wrought by the *terrido navalis*, the worm that thrived in tropical waters and burrowed into any submerged timber. All the local dockyards, except those of Spanish Havana, were inadequate and ill-stocked. English Harbour in the Leewards was still under development and was lightly fortified. The main British base at Port Royal in Jamaica had basic careening and resupply facilities but was far downwind of the vulnerable Leewards. During the hurricane season the nearest secure and adequate bases were Boston and New York. A further obstacle to a prolonged Caribbean campaign was disease in the form of malaria and yellow fever.

By contrast, Spain was stronger than she looked. Possession of Havana, guarding the principal exit from the Caribbean, was a major advantage, despite its leeward position. Moreover, since 1714 Spain had been building up a naval force designed not to secure command of the sea but to inflict unacceptable losses upon a more powerful British or French enemy. Substantial, sometimes quite elaborate, fortifications protected the main bases and settlements, and lesser ones covered the more obvious landing places. An enemy determined to capture any of the major centres would have to mount large, unwieldy amphibious operations which would be unlikely to succeed before disease ruined them. Thus, though the Spanish colonies might look ill-protected, they were in fact very formidable targets.[27]

The Walpole government and its First Lord of the Admiralty, Charles Wager, were well aware of the difficulties and of the danger of French intervention in home waters. Wager's proposed solution was to keep the main fleet for defence and raid vulnerable points in Spain's Caribbean, American mainland and Asian possessions with smaller, fast-moving forces. The first such blow was struck by Vice-Admiral Edward Vernon, commander of the Jamaica station, against Porto Bello. Using only six ships, he appeared off the port on 29 November, landed and attacked on the 30th and accepted the Spanish surrender on the 31st. He stayed for three weeks, levelling the fortifications designed to control external trade. Unfortunately, Vernon's very success seemed to prove that major expeditions would have even greater success, claims which the ministry was ill-placed to resist. Worse, it provoked France into despatching a major squadron with orders to combine with the Spanish fleet at Havana and pounce on Vernon before he could be aware. The nightmare of a Bourbon combination in a purely maritime war was about to be realised.

Fortunately, the Spanish admiral refused to conform to French plans, and the French squadron ran out of food. Sir Chaloner Ogle was despatched with twenty-five of the line and 8,000 troops, with orders to join Vernon and attack major bases such as Cartagena and Havana. Vernon was appalled but agreed to attack Cartagena, rather than Havana with its powerful fortifications and resident Spanish squadron. The expedition was a disaster. Vernon's domineering personality alienated the military commanders, so army-navy co-operation was fractious. While the shore batteries were silenced and taken, the inner defences held firm. It was April before they were able to attack the San Lazar fortress and the attack was a dismal failure. Already, many of the soldiers and seamen were ill, so the British had to retire to Jamaica. Vernon's attempts to attack Santiago de Cuba were frustrated. He and General Wentworth could no longer work together, and there were only 2,000 troops still well enough to fight. Expeditions against places on the Venezuelan coast came to nothing. Thus, the Spanish Caribbean empire remained intact and the British had suffered heavy losses for no territorial gain.[28]

Tacky's Revolt
The Seven Years' War brought shortages and hunger to Jamaica's slaves and by the end of 1759 an island-wide revolt had been planned. This development coincided with the arrival of thousands of slaves from West Central Africa, so diluting the Coromantees' domination in Jamaica. Whether the planned insurrection was meant to salvage the Coromantee position, or whether the newcomers identified with the existing leadership, is unknown and may be unknowable. Nor do we know the ultimate aims of the rebellion or how united the plotters were in their ambitions. Whatever the case, as Vincent Brown argues, African cultural and military experiences combined with Jamaican circumstances to produce an existential threat to the colonial plantocracy.

The rebellion broke out prematurely at an estate in St Mary's parish, a mountainous, jungle-covered region on the north-east side of the island. One version has it that the local leader, a man called Tacky, got drunk and struck too soon. Another, more likely, contention is that the Africans confused Easter Sunday with Whitsun, when the co-ordinated rebellions were supposed to begin. Whatever the trigger, the revolt unfolded at first with rapid efficiency. On the night of 7-8 March about a hundred slaves swarmed over undermanned Fort Haldane at the entrance to an inlet called Port Maria Harbour, killed the lone sentry and seized about forty muskets, two barrels of gunpowder and a keg of bullets. They then swept through the narrow valleys, surprising and plundering plantations, burning houses, mills and crops, killing ten whites, slaughtering thirty blacks who would not join them, and rounding up recruits. By noon on 8 April, when the insurgents halted in a forest clearing, four hundred or so rebel men and women were under arms.

Already, however, forces were gathering against them. As the insurgents feasted on a roasted ox and obeah men and women administered oaths of allegiance, about a hundred and thirty militia – white, free black, mulatto – appeared and fighting ensued. The wooded terrain suited the rebels' African experience, but their improvised ammunition was inaccurate, and they retreated deeper into the forest. Meanwhile, Lieutenant Governor Henry Moore declared martial law, called out the whole island's militia, directed regulars of the 49th and 74th regiments towards St Mary's and called on the Maroons from as far away as Trelawney town in the west. On 14 April, Maroons and militia defeated the rebels. Tacky and Jamaica, the two principal leaders, were killed.

As the captured rebels were interrogated and tortured, more and more information came to light about the intended scale of the rebellion, information apparently confirmed by further outbreaks. On 15 April in Kingston a white man was shot at and a sword with ritual markings was discovered. In St Thomas at the very eastern tip of Jamaica, a planned uprising was betrayed by a man called Cuffee, a piece of treachery that did not spare him execution alongside his fellows. At that moment another and larger revolt, involving no fewer than 600 slaves, broke out in Westmoreland parish at the western extremity of the island.

Within a day, revolts had broken out on all the plantations at the foot of the Hanover Mountains. It may be that some insurgents aimed to capture a deep-water harbour and establish a free sugar-exporting state. If so, they were overborne by less ambitious participants who first wanted a refuge safe from white or Maroon attack. About 1,200 rebels retired deep into the Hanover range and fortified a narrow defile with a breastwork behind which they began to construct their new village. On 29 May they repelled a series of attacks by militia units. Already, however, regular troops were scouring the woods and the next day a Maroon contingent arrived. On 2 June the Maroons surrounded the rebel village and a combined assault carried the barricade and overran the settlement. Naval forces appeared and landed parties while confused fighting continued in the woods, the rebels ambushing soldiers but being themselves driven back by the Maroons. Some rebels withdrew eastward, attacking plantations as they went, while others fought it out in over twenty widespread clashes. By early August it was over: the last of the rebels had been killed, committed suicide or surrendered. The principal leaders, including Apongo, were taken and executed. Many planters believed that an island-wide conspiracy had existed and that it had failed thanks largely to the Maroons.

Assault on the French West Indies 1756-1762
By the outbreak of the Seven Years' War in 1756, rising sugar prices and growing markets had made planters less wary of new conquests that might mean new competition, while privateers based on the French and Spanish islands were a constant irritant. Merchants complained that the British islands were incapable of satisfying domestic and re-export demand. Even before the war, Pitt was keen to undermine French naval and economic power by seizing Guadeloupe and Martinique. Moreover, the memory of Vernon's expedition had taught the need for harmonious military-naval co-operation, and Pitt's raids on the French coast showed how that could be achieved.

For all these reasons, the Seven Years' War saw sweeping British conquests in the West Indies. Until 1759, other theatres – home waters, Europe, North America – took priority for resources and attention, but by then the situation had changed. Pitt's strategy was being undermined by slow progress in North America, the probability that at the end of the war newly conquered Louisbourg would have to be sacrificed to regain Minorca, and the failure of the diversionary raids on French ports. Already William Beckford, a prominent Jamaican planter, had persuaded Pitt that the French islands were vulnerable, and the seizure of Gorée and Senegal gave hope that such operations were feasible. Moreover, Spanish neutrality, dictated by naval weakness in the Caribbean and by the wishes of Ferdinand VI (r.1746-1759), was unlikely to end soon, so the French forces in the islands would be on their own. Anson and Ligonier gave their consent, subject to the expeditionary force being of adequate size, and in January 1759 7,000 troops, their transports, nine ships of the line, some frigates and four bomb vessels assembled at Bridgetown, Barbados. Their target was Martinique.[29]

The expedition appeared off Fort Royale on 15 January, achieving complete naval supremacy and successfully landing the troops three miles away at Cas Navires Bay. Getting the army to Fort Royale was more difficult. The French militia fought doggedly to hold the forested ridges between bay and the town, the road soon proved impracticable for artillery, and the army re-embarked. St Pierre, a reputed privateer base twenty miles to the north, was even less approachable, so the sea and land commanders decided to attempt Guadeloupe instead.[30]

John White painted numerous images of Amerindian people, villages and artefacts at Roanoke, North Carolina. Mrs. P. D. H. Page after the originals by John White. (George Mellon collection, Yale Centre for British Art (YCBA))

Pocahontas, dressed and presented as royalty, in an early example of Eurocentric interpretation of indigenous political structures. Unknown artist. (YCBA)

King Charles I, who granted the charter for Maryland and tried to centralise control over Ireland and New England. (Metropolitan Museum of Art)

Left: Henrietta Maria, Charles I's French wife, after whom the Catholic-refuge colony of Maryland was named, with court dwarf Sir Jeffrey Hudson. Painting by Sir Anthony Van Dyck, 1633. (National Gallery of Art, Washington (NGA))

Below: Cecil Calvert, Baron Baltimore, and his wife Anne Arundel on the Maryland Medal, struck to mark the granting of the colony's charter in 1632. (NGA)

Above: Prince Rupert of the Rhine, Royalist cavalry commander, admiral and founder member of the Hudson Bay and Royal African Companies. Portrait from the studio of Peter Lely. (YCBA)

Below: Charles II and his bride Catherine of Braganza, whose dowry included Bombay and Tangier, depicted on a silver medal of 1662. (NGA)

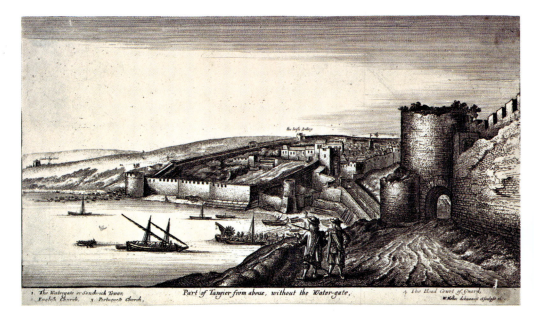

Above: Hopes that Tangier would provide a much-needed Mediterranean naval base were frustrated by its inadequate harbour and the cost of its defence. The dilapidated state of the fortifications on the right and the tiny outlying fort to the left testify to the problems. Part of Tangier from above, 1670, print by Wenceslaus Hollar. (Metropolitan Museum of Art)

Left: The Mughal emperor Jahangir liked James I's emissary, Sir Thomas Roe, but shrewdly denied him the exclusive treading rights he sought. Unknown artist. (Smithsonian American Art Museum)

Above: Elihu Yale, here seen with two aristocratic guests, was an early example of the 'Nabob', an East India Company servant who had grown rich enough to set up as a gentleman at home. The black child slave, whether in the household or in iconography, was a symbol of conspicuous wealth. (YCBA)

Right: A disdainful little white girl ignores the fruit offered by an improbably delighted black slave, representing one of thousands serving in eighteenth-century British families. (YCBA)

Britain's reliance upon seaborne defence, which in turn depended upon colonial trade, is reflected in this c. 1720 allegorical design by James Thornhill for a panel of George I's state coach. (YCBA)

A print of Fort St. George, Madras, by Gerard van der Gucht about 1736, showing the beach to which cargoes and passengers were carried through the surf. (YCBA)

Inflated public confidence in the power of the Royal Navy is reflected in this early eighteenth-century painting by Peter Monamy. The size and apparent power of these ships of the line is emphasised by the sloop and small boats in the foreground. (YCBA)

Vernon's capture of Puerto Bello in November 1739, an initial triumph in an otherwise dismal Caribbean offensive. (YCBA)

Cape Town in 1736. Long before its final capture by the British the Dutch-held Cape was a vital refreshment port for outward-bound East Indiamen. (YCBA)

Above left: A young New England officer showing off his new martial finery in 1756. Portrait by Joseph Blackburn. (NGA)

Above right: Reynolds' painting of General John Burgoyne, dashing cavalryman, playwright and man about London, whose surrender at Saratoga in 1777 changed the course of the War of American Independence. (Frick Collection)

Colonel Guy Johnson, nephew to Sir William, with his Mohawk friend Karonghyontye (Captain David Hill), expressing the wartime interdependence of British and loyal Amerindians. The portrait was painted by Benjamin West in 1776, while Johnson was in London to secure appointment as northern Superintendent of Indian Affairs. (NGA)

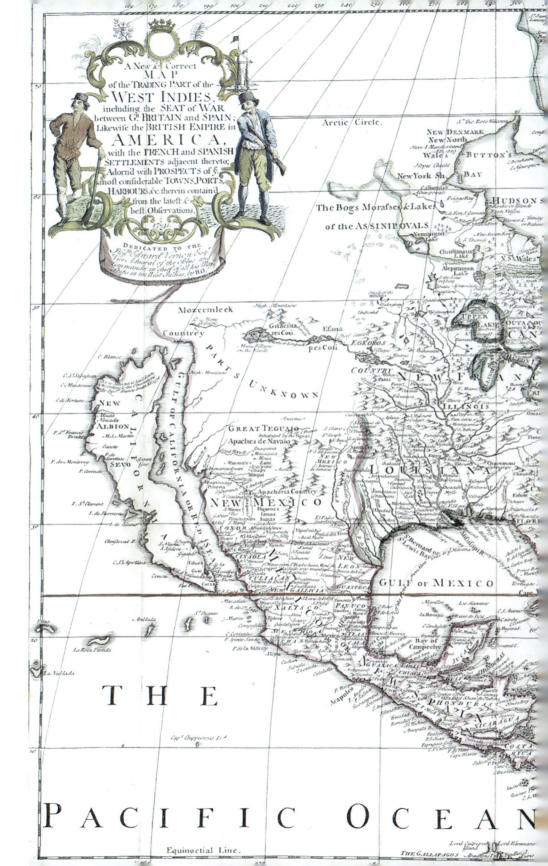

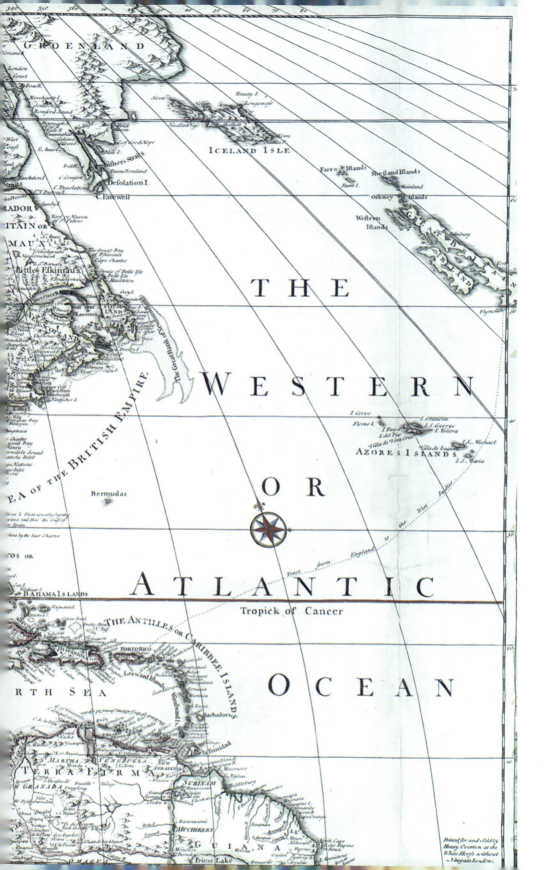

Lieutenant Colonel Banastre Tarleton, the gambling-addicted and vigorous commander of the British Legion of southern Loyalists. Son of a ship owner, he entered Parliament for Liverpool in 1790, allied with Charles James Fox and strongly defended the slave trade. From a 1782 portrait by Sir Joshua Reynolds now in the National Gallery, London.

Above: A modern artist's impression of the Battle of the Virginia Capes, which sealed the fate of Cornwallis at Yorktown.

Right: Thayendanegea (Joseph Brant), a Mohawk leader who fought against the American rebels and later emigrated to Canada, in dignified pose during a visit to Albany in 1806. (National Portrait Gallery, Smithsonian Institution)

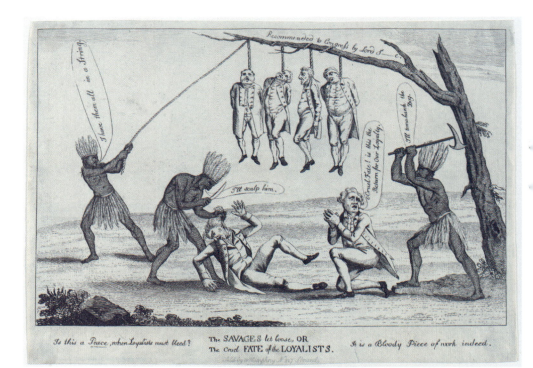

Above: White Loyalists were sometimes less dignified in bewailing their poor post-war treatment. Here faithful American gentlemen, abandoned by Shelburne, are hanged and scalped by victorious rebels represented (with unconscious irony?) as savage Amerindians. 'The Savages Let Loose, or The Cruel fate of the Loyalists', William Humphrey, 1783. (Metropolitan Museum of Art)

Right: The ancestors of this peaceful-looking Caribs family, portrayed by Agostino Brunias about 1780, had long resisted the European invasion of the Lesser Antilles. (YCBA)

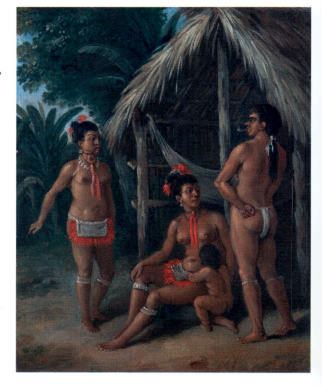

The Caribbean: Slave Economies and Great Power Contests

Guadeloupe was essentially a small archipelago, of which the closely adjoining Basse Terre and Grand Terre were the main islands. The town of Basse Terre, the only fortified port, was quickly taken, followed on 14 February by Fort Louis guarding the narrow crossing onto Grand Terre. The inland resistance on Basse Terre was now isolated, the militia were short of food, and British raids devastated their plantations. On 11 May 1759 the French governor surrendered. A relief expedition from France was too weak and arrived too late.[31]

News of this success when it reached London in March made the ministry more ambitious. Now that the British had a bargaining counter to secure Louisbourg, any further gains might be kept for the British empire. A proposal to attack St Lucia proved abortive, because those troops not garrisoned on Guadeloupe had already returned to North America; but at the end of 1760 with Montreal fallen and continuing success in Germany, plans were laid to attack Dominica and, if possible, St Lucia, using Amherst's troops from the north. The fall of Dominica in June 1761 was followed by a second attempt on Martinique in January 1762.[32]

Once again, the army, numbering up to 16,000 men, was landed at Cas Navires Bay after naval gunfire had neutralised the batteries there. This time, however, the advance was more systematic and determined. The French defenders, threatened on both flanks, were pushed back until the British held the high ground dominating Fort Royale. The ridge was too far from the town for an effective bombardment, so guns were brought round by water and began to batter the walls from close-to. On 3 February Fort Royale quickly surrendered, leaving the governor with no choice but to yield the whole island nine days later. As at Guadeloupe, a French relief force arrived too late to intervene. British forces went on to attack the French-settled 'neutral' islands: Grenada was taken on 5 March, followed by St Vincent, St Lucia and Tobago.[33]

The assault on Havana 1762

By now war with Spain had broken out and the ministry was planning an attack on the greatest Caribbean fortress of all, Havana. It was a formidable undertaking: the fortifications were powerful and there were no fewer than fourteen Spanish ships of the line there and seven more close enough to have joined, against nineteen British. The usual and safer approach, along the south coast to round the western tip of Cuba, and then taking at least a week to beat east to Havana, would give the defenders ample warning. As Anson appreciated when he worked out the details, the British descent would have to be sudden, overwhelming and brief, if the men were not to be decimated by disease in the coming wet season. At first all went well. Surprise was achieved by sailing along the north coast, through the dangerous Old Bahama Channel, and on 7 June 1762, 12,000 men were landed successfully a short distance to the east of the city. By the end of the day they were at its gates. On 9 June troops landed to the west, and a few days later seized the Cabana heights, the highest point of which overlooked the El Moro fortress at the harbour entrance. The landings were unmolested because the Spanish commanders had sunk three of their ships of the line behind the boom across the harbour mouth, leaving the other eleven trapped inside. This allowed the ships' seamen and artillery to reinforce the defenders of the city and El Moro, but it handed the initiative to the British.[34]

At least two eminent historians have concluded that the British, so pressed for time, should now have stormed the town without further ado. The military commander, Lord Albemarle, opted instead for a formal siege of El Moro, avoiding heavy immediate casualties but guaranteeing a long operation, sickness and debilitation. The ground was so rocky that breastworks had to take the place of approach trenches, the first battery was ruined when its breastwork caught fire, and courageous Spanish sorties had to be beaten off. A combined naval and military bombardment silenced most of the Spanish guns on the landward side, but the ships lay too far below the fort to do much damage while sustaining heavy losses themselves. When the breastworks reached the lip of the ditch, a long arduous process of mining (with the help of Cornish miners among Admiral Pocock's seamen) was begun. Not until 30 July was the mine detonated, a practicable breach made and the Moro stormed. By 13 August, when the city finally surrendered, barely 3,000 of the attackers were fit for duty. Had the garrison held out a little longer, the whole operation would have collapsed.[35]

Yet it was in many ways a resounding triumph. The strongest and richest city in the West indies, indeed in Spanish America, had fallen, and the British now commanded the vital outlet from the Caribbean. Almost a fifth of the Spanish navy had been captured intact and Admiral Pocock and Albemarle netted £122,657 of prize money apiece. Although it proved impossible to subdue the rest of the island (which the British thought had been included in the surrender terms), the occupation helped to compel Spain to recognise the Honduras and Mosquito coast settlements, and to yield Florida in return for the western part of French Louisiana.[36]

The Caribbean and the Peace of Paris

There was a powerful case for retaining most, if not all, the Caribbean conquests within the British empire. Guadeloupe and Martinique would provide additional sugar for the expanding imperial and European market, a British-dominated Caribbean would check American breaches of the Molasses Act; and Guadeloupe alone would yield revenues to defray part

The Caribbean: Slave Economies and Great Power Contests

of the costs of war. Moreover, there was something to be said for Pitt's argument that retaining Havana as well as the French sugar islands would permanently weaken the Bourbon powers. From this perspective, yielding up Canada was a small price to pay. Yet the Peace of Paris returned all the West Indian territories except the economically insignificant islands of St Vincent, Dominica, Tobago and Grenada.

The Caribbean provisions of the Peace of Paris have often been attributed to the so-called West India interest, the wealthy absentee planters who did not want new sugar supplies to undermine their profits, and who commanded a substantial block of votes in the House of Commons. In fact, there were only about twenty representatives of absentee Caribbean interests out of 558 MPs, far too few for success, had not their wishes chimed with wider policy considerations. As we have seen, the desire to secure a lasting peace dictated generous terms and vast gains in North America had to be balanced by concessions in the West Indies. Thus, despite the apparent triumph, Britain's Caribbean empire remained economically insecure, strategically vulnerable and internally fragile.

18

The Indian Bridgeheads, *c.* 1713-*c.* 1765

Without Moghul decline the British rise to prominence would not have been possible. As we have seen, the East India Company's late-seventeenth century attempt to achieve autonomy in Bengal was swiftly and effectively quashed. The British did not consciously accelerate the disintegration, though they certainly exploited it, and the Moghuls felt far more threatened by Afghan and Persian incursions than by a handful of troops employed by a European trading company. Yet by 1765 empire had all but dissolved into a kaleidoscope of successor states and the East India Company, no longer held back by Moghul might, was a significant Indian power.

The Mughal decline was slow and many explanations have been offered. Perhaps the most fundamental was the emperors' failure to integrate the myriad states and faiths into a coherent whole. Hindus had never become fully reconciled to Muslim rule and the emperor Aurangzeb seems to have wanted to create a wholly Muslim state. While too clever to try forced conversions, he did impose a tax upon unbelievers, making all non-Muslims into second-class subjects. That was enough to provoke both open and passive resistance. By 1657 the great Maratha leader Shivaji was openly at war with Aurangzeb and by 1700 a coherent Maratha state in the west formed a base for persistent raids across northern India. The Rajput states became more restive. In the far north-west a formidably militarised Sikh state evolved.

Distance was another factor, enabling Muslim provincial governors to attain autonomy while formally acknowledging the sovereignty of the emperor. The critical turning point was the Nizam of Hyderabad's virtual secession from the empire, creating a vast and powerful state in the Deccan. Within the two spheres of influence the lesser governors, notably the Nawab of Arcot in the Carnatic, the hinterland of Madras, tried to assert their own independence. In due course the Nawabs of Bengal also

The Indian Bridgeheads, c. 1713-c. 1765

broke away from direct Mughal control. There is no doubt that this fragmentation was crucial to British success. Did the British exploit a process outside their control, or did their driving ambition help to create the fragmentation in the first place?

Aurangzeb's death in March 1707 at his camp near Ahmednagar triggered the usual short, vicious succession war. Within a year his eldest son emerged as victor, having slaughtered two brothers and four nephews on the battlefield. Styling himself Bahadur Shah, he set out to address divisions within the empire by accepting the submission of nobles who had opposed him, and by quietly dropping collection of the jiziya, the religious tax, and by a relaxed attitude to Islamic doctrinal purity. No longer could loyalty be formally identified with Islam.

Unfortunately, the change came rather late. Continuing Hindu resistance by Rajputs, Jats and Marathas was compounded by a fresh and fanatical Sikh insurgency. Sikh rebels came within a few days march of Delhi before Mughal forces pushed them back and overran the Punjabi plains; and even then, it proved impossible to stamp out guerrilla bands or to capture Banda, its charismatic leader. Meanwhile Maratha cavalry swept across the Deccan, further disrupting an empire already overextended by the conquest of poorer southern provinces. As the emperor proved unable to provide protection, the jaghirdars in those parts increasingly held back the revenues they collected. Already used to retaining the same jaghirs (assigned revenues from a region) for long periods, these nobles were becoming increasingly independent.

Early in 1712 the Mughal effort was interrupted by Bahadur Shah's death and a new succession war. A powerful noble, Zulfikar Khan, enthroned the most pliable of the dead emperor's three sons, but he and his candidate were dead within a year and internecine struggle went on. By 1720, after the blinding of one emperor and the installation of a puppet under the thumb of his ministers, the fabric of the empire was in tatters. Three years later the Nizam of Hyderabad, with some Maratha assistance, shattered a Moghul army and set up a virtually independent state in the Deccan. Bengal and Orissa broke away, paying only nominal tribute to the new emperor, and Oudh was beyond Delhi's control. The Marathas continued their depredations, avoiding pitched battles but using their swiftly moving cavalry to harass, sever lines of supply, and starve their opponents. This was a form of warfare to which Mughal forces consistently failed to adapt, and which even the Nizam found too formidable to crush. By 1738 they were operating in the vicinity of Delhi. The following year a Persian army poured into India, used its camel-mounted swivel guns to rip through Moghul heavy cavalry, and sacked the city. When the Persians withdrew, leaving only the shadow of Moghul authority behind them, the Maratha leaders thought they might succeed to the paramount power in India.

The First British Empire

Local initiatives

Maratha ambition was not matched on the British side, and certainly not in London. Left to themselves the directors and shareholders in London would have been content to go on trading peacefully and avoiding expensive political commitments. In 1717 they were delighted to receive autonomy in their trading enclaves and freedom from internal taxes in return for paying the emperor 13,000 rupees a year. Not until mid-century was it clear to them that the Mughal empire was about to collapse – so until then there was no point in taking military action against it. Nor did ministers, though they regarded the Company's trade as a national interest, have plans for expansion. When, from the late 1740s, they responded to the Company's pleas for military support, they ordered their commanders to follow the Company's instructions. Instead, initiatives came from the men on the spot, a powerful example of what has been termed 'sub -imperialism'.

The men on the spot were certainly readier to take advantage of opportunities but their aims were limited and commercial. In any case, they lacked the military wherewithal to embark upon adventures of conquest. As late as 1748 they had only a handful of troops, native and European, dispersed between the enclaves around Madras, in the Bombay region and in Bengal. The new successor states, on the other hand, were in some ways more powerful than the Moghul authority they replaced. While outwardly retaining Moghul forms of government they maintained large military forces, which they began to train in the European manner; and to maintain those forces they introduced more direct and efficient tax regimes.

French intervention in the south

The trigger was French ambition. By the 1730s the French East India Company had recovered from a disastrous financial crisis and its most intelligent and active servant, Dupleix, the governor of Pondicherry, could see advantages in making alliances with the Mughal's vassals. Although earlier historiography credited him with planning to drive the British out of southern India, his primary goal was to exchange military aid for commercial privileges. The British and French companies remained on good terms during the early years of the War of the Austrian Succession, but the appearance of British and French naval squadrons on the Coromandel Coast made that truce very fragile indeed. When the British took some French merchant ships, the French retaliated by descending upon Madras and capturing it. Some of the Company's men, including a quarrelsome, depressive and egotistical clerk called Robert Clive, escaped south to Fort St David. The fort held out, and in recognition of abilities displayed during its defence, Clive was given an ensign's commission in the Company's army. He was one of a small number of able British

The Indian Bridgeheads, c. 1713-c. 1765

leaders whose energy ultimately made the difference between victory and defeat.

The British tried to hit back. Major Stringer Lawrence, with Clive under his command, beat off a French attack upon Cuddalore in June 1748. When Admiral Boscawen arrived with a formidable naval squadron, artillery and military reinforcements, the British even attempted to seize Pondicherry. None of this was enough to offset Dupleix's regional gains and the threat to the British company remained critical. The EIC had begun to recruit and train Indian infantry (sepoys), but by 1748 it still had only 3,000 troops in the whole of India. Although Madras was returned under the Peace of Aix-La-Chapelle, the fighting and peril in India continued.

In 1749 Shaji, the deposed ruler of Tanjore, a small but wealthy Hindu state within the Carnatic, appealed to the Madras council for military aid. He offered in return to pay the expenses of the war, which might defray the cost of maintaining the expanded Madras army and line the pockets of the men most deeply involved: the governor and deputy governor, Boscawen and Clive. Moreover, Shaji was prepared to cede the fort at Davakottai, one of the very few natural harbours on the Coromandel coast and only fifty miles south of Fort St David. The intervention in this exceptional case could be (and was) retrospectively justified to the Directors as replacing a pro-French prince with a British client. In short, changing Indian circumstances, not British contrivance, had presented an opening too good to miss. An expedition led by Lawrence and Clive seized Davakottai on the second attempt and, although the reigning raja won the civil war, he allowed the British to keep the port. At this point, however, the Madras council had nothing near the grand strategic vision of Dupleix. The Council did not envisage a systematic intervention in the wider politics of the Carnatic.

Dupleix had vaster ambitions. His aim was to exploit succession disputes in both the Carnatic and the Deccan to place his own candidates upon the *musnuds* (thrones of cushions) of both Arcot and Hyderabad. His opportunity came late in 1748 with the death of the Nizam ul-Mulk, and his succession by his second son, Nasir Jang. Nasir Jang was immediately challenged by his brother Salabat Jang, and a nephew, Muzzafar Jang. Meanwhile, a similar dispute had arisen in the Carnatic, where one Chanda Sahib challenged the Nawab, Anwar ud-din. At Pondicherry in June 1749 Dupleix conspired with Muzzafar Jang and Chanda Sahib to overthrow their rivals. Success would give the French command of the hinterland of Madras and Fort St David, potentially cutting off the presidency from the inland textile trade.[37]

Success was dramatic and almost immediate. A native army accompanied by a small French contingent commanded by Dupleix's general, the Comte de Bussy, defeated and killed Anwar ud-din and captured his eldest son

The First British Empire

at Abur. The younger son, Mohammed Ali Khan, no soldier and with less popular support, fled south to the great rock fortress of Trinchinopoly, where he proclaimed himself Nawab. In the north, Muzzafar Jang entered the capital Arcot, where he proclaimed himself Nizam and Chanda Sahib the new Nawab. When in December 1750 Nasir Jang, the incumbent Nizam, intervened in support of Mohammed Ali, Dupleix procured his assassination. He may also have been behind the subsequent slaughter of Muzzafar Jang by the same trio of conspirators and his replacement by his brother Salabat Jang; at all events Dupleix backed the new Nizam, eventually with 5,500 French and Indian troops, and ensconced Bussy as his adviser at Hyderabad. In return, the French received control of the revenues in the Northern Circars, a narrow coastal territory to the north of the Carnatic.

Up to this point, the British at Fort St David, with few troops and little money, had been unable to intervene. Now, very reluctantly, and well aware of French military superiority, they decided to back Muhammed Ali in exchange for the revenues of one of his provinces. It was a near-disastrous choice. Two botched attempts to relieve Trinchinopoly ended with nearly all the Madras forces shut up in the fortress. All the council could do was to send Robert Clive with 200 white troops and 300 sepoys to make a diversionary attack upon the Carnatic's capital, Arcot. This was a measure of desperation. It looked as though the EIC's presence in the south was doomed.

Astonishingly, Clive managed to surprise and capture the fortress at Arcot and to hold onto it for fifty days against a much larger force sent against him from Trichinopoly. With the failure of the final assault, and news that a powerful Maratha force was marching to Clive's relief, the siege broke up. Clive followed up his success with a victory at Arni and the capture of some French-held towns. British prestige was now on the rise, Mysore had already joined Mohamed Ali's cause, and the chiefs commanding the supply route from Davakottai had followed suit. Chanda Sahib had been seriously weakened.[38]

But the siege of Trinchinopoly was not over. Indecisive skirmishing continued and it was not until the following year that Lawrence and Clive defeated Chanda Sahib and put Mohammed Ali on the throne of the Carnatic. Chanda Sahib fled to the raja of Tanjore, who promptly beheaded him. The French no longer had a credible candidate for the *mansad*, the regal cushion at Arcot, but even then the fighting went on into 1753 and 1754. Stringer Lawrence and Clive achieved some minor successes, but they were unable to win a decisive victory. In August 1754 both sides received reinforcements from home, but the British government's contribution was formidable: a naval squadron built around four ships of the line and a whole royal regiment of foot, the first ever deployed to India.

The Indian Bridgeheads, c. 1713-c. 1765

By 1754 the company directors in London and Paris, horrified by falling dividends, were anxious for a compromise peace. The French company recalled Dupleix, perhaps less for embarking on risky and expensive projects than for failure, and instructed his successor, Charles Godeheu, to negotiate a compromise based on the *status quo ante bellum*. By the end of the year a truce, subject to ratification in London and Paris, left the French in a dominant position in the Deccan while implicitly accepting Mohammed Ali as Nawab in the Carnatic. The French were thus left with considerable political gains, immediate relief from ruinous military expenditure, and the option of undermining Mohammed Ali in the future. The British gained a precarious security in the Carnatic, but one upon which they must build. Thus, while in Europe the governments were drawn towards war by events in North America and the outstanding question of Silesia, in India the men on the ground behaved as if there had been no truce at all.

Bengal and Plassey

The next crisis concerned the Company's factory at Calcutta. In 1756 Alivardi Khan, Nawab of Bengal, died and was succeeded by his grandson, Siraj-ad-Daula. Within a few months this unstable young man had, by repeatedly veering between aggression and conciliation, alienated Hindu merchants and bankers as well as some of his Muslim army commanders. One such action concerned the British factory at Calcutta and the French base upstream at Chandanagore, where the outbreak of the Seven Years' War prompted both companies to begin building fortifications. Siraj-ad-Daula ordered them to stop and to demolish the defences already built, claiming he would protect each from the other. Probably the Nawab was following his late father's sage advice to get a firmer grip on the European companies, which were becoming too independent and too prosperous for the security of the state. His mistake was to confront the British without conciliating the many enemies he had made at home. However, while the French manged to persuade him that their preparations were not a threat, the governor of Calcutta responded in terms that were insulting and defiant. When he ignored the Nawab's order to desist – a perfectly reasonable request – the Nawab attacked and easily captured Calcutta. His prisoners were locked in a small windowless cell for the night, where about a hundred of them suffocated.

Later imperial historiography represented this 'Black Hole' as a terrible atrocity, one which seemed to prove the barbarity of oriental despotism. It also seemed to show that, when the Company later struck back and unseated the Nawab, it was acting in self-defence. In fact, the deaths were a consequence of carelessness and neglect, not malice, and at the time the Company did not seem to think it important. Though the improved military situation at Madras enabled them to send Clive north with a small army, they negotiated amicably with the Nawab who readily returned

Calcutta and paid some reparations. He even allowed Clive, with British naval support, to capture Chandanagore from the French in March 1757.

However, the episode had convinced the Nawab's critics that he was hopelessly unstable and had to go. They had a ready candidate in Mir Jafir, a Bengali general and uncle to the Nawab, and in Clive they found a willing ally. One of the very few Company officials prepared to interfere in Bengal politics, he was careful to ensure that the conspirators would support him before he took military action. On 23 June 1757 his army of 3,000 Europeans and sepoys met Suraj-ad Daula's 60,000 at Plassey. On the battlefield Clive was hesitant and the fighting consisted mainly of a half-hearted exchange of artillery fire. Though the French guns were silenced, the day was carried not by superior British skill at arms, but by conspiracy. Mir Jafir held back his men and the Nawab's army disintegrated. Mir Jafir was installed as Nawab, only to find himself wholly dependent on British support to stay on his newly won throne.[39] The rewards for Clive and the Company were enormous, but he did not remove the Nawab and annex Bengal, though the idea certainly crossed his mind. The settlement with Mir Jafir was essentially conservative, giving the Company no new formal privileges except the right to attack French bases in eastern India.

Clive's next move was to send Colonel Forde into the Northern Circars to exploit an anti-French revolt in October 1758. In May 1759 Forde took the French base of Masuliputam and stood firm against an expedition sent from the Deccan by Salabat Jang. In the end the Nizam changed sides and awarded the French concessions in the Circars to the British East India Company.[40]

While Clive conquered Bengal, the initiative in the Carnatic had swung to the French. Having recovered Arcot, their new commander, the Comte De Lally, besieged Madras from December 1758 until February 1759, when lack of progress and lack of pay for his troops forced him to withdraw. Now, with the revenues of the Northern Circars available, and with reinforcements from home, the British took the offensive. In 1760 their new commander, Sir Eyre Coote, defeated Lally in a pitched battle outside Wandiwash and moved on to encircle Pondicherry, forcing its surrender on 15 January 1761.[41]

Muhammed Ali was now effectively a British client. Required to pay for the forces raised to protect his throne, he borrowed vast sums from British sources, not least from the Company's own servants. But the dependency was two-way. Because these creditors now depended on Muhammed Ali's land revenues to repay their investment, they had a vested interest in encouraging him to expand his effective control of the province. As he had territorial ambitions beyond his own frontiers, and because Hyderabad, the Marathas and Mysore all had designs on the Carnatic, he had the power to pull the Company into further unwanted conflicts. In this way the ruler of the Carnatic exercised a powerful influence over future British policy, an influence reaching even into the House of Commons.[42]

The Indian Bridgeheads, c. 1713-c. 1765

Bengal: from client state to conquest

For a time Bengal was an independent state under British patronage. Mir Jafir, the new Nawab, set about rewarding those who had supported him. Anyone who needed favour at court, bankers and businessmen prominent among them, rushed to purchase the favour of those with influence. This was a transformative process: for many Company servants the road to great riches was no longer private trade but Indian politics. Clive himself was given the equivalent of £240,000 and lands worth £28,000 a year in rents. By his estimate, the Company and its most ambitious servants made £3m out of the revolution in Bengal.

Clive returned home after collecting his rewards, but others stayed on.[43] Having learned that money could be made out of deposing one Nawab and installing another, and after Mir Jafir tried to use the Dutch to dislodge the British, they removed him in favour Mir Qasim. It has been argued that this plunder would have been more tolerable if – like the Afghans and Persians who periodically plundered Delhi – the British had left for home with their loot. Instead they stayed, not merely looting Bengal but threatening to destabilise its neighbours, particularly the Muslim state of Oudh. Company servants claimed that the Company's exemption from internal trade taxes granted in 1717 now applied to their own private transactions and those of their Indian agents. Mir Qasim responded by abolishing all such taxes, thereby cutting the Company's commercial advantage; and when the Company objected, largely on behalf of its servants, he secured a military alliance with the Wazir of Oudh, Shuja-ud-Daula, and the Mogul emperor Shah Alam II himself. Three Muslim armies totalling perhaps 40,000 men marched to expel the British from Bengal.[44]

On 22 October 1764 the alliance's army was met by 10,000 British troops and sepoys at Buxar, a small fortified riverside town in Orissa. The encounter was hard-fought and proved, once again, that while individual arms of an Indian force could be formidable, command and co-ordination were fatally flawed. The Mughal forces attacked first and alone and were pushed back by disciplined firepower. The British commander was then able to defeat his opponents in detail.

The overthrow of Mir Qasim and the flight of Shuja-ud Daula gave the British effective control of the lower Ganges valley and forced Shah Alam to come to terms. By the Treaty of Allahabad of 12 August 1765, the emperor granted the Company the *Diwani*, the right to collect the revenues of Bengal, Orissa and Bihar in return for an annual tribute of 26 lakhs, 2.6m rupees, equivalent to £260,000. Shuja-ud-Daula was restored to Oudh but had to surrender Allahabad and Kora to the emperor and 50 lakhs in reparations to the Company. In effect, the Company now governed Bengal and had become a major territorial power in India. Buxar, not Plassey, was the real turning point in the building of British India.

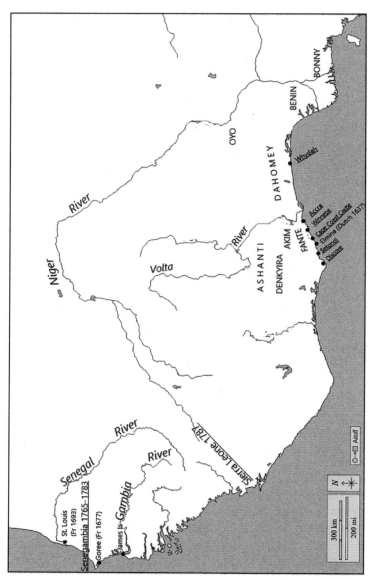

West Africa: powerful kingdoms and embattled enclaves.

19

West Africa, 1713-1763: Slaves, Guns and Wars

The Royal African Company's troubles did not end with the Peace of Utrecht. There was some recovery in its slave trading activities in the mid-1720s, peaking at around 1725, perhaps partly due to the contracts it agreed with the South Sea Company. However, the costs of maintaining its forts and factories were now prohibitive; combined with the competition of interlopers this meant that it could only trade in slaves at a loss. In 1728, its post at Bence Island in the Sierra Leone River estuary was sacked by African attackers, after which it was left to interlopers from London and was then obtained by a private Scottish company. In 1731 the RAC stopped slaving altogether and concentrated upon buying gold and pepper.

The Atlantic slave trade, and Britain's share in it, grew substantially in the early eighteenth century and coincided with aggressive wars of expansion by Oyo, Dahomey and Asante. Were these conflicts begun mainly or wholly to obtain slaves in exchange for goods such as guns, gunpowder, cloth and iron bars? Was there what has been called a 'gun-slave cycle', in which guns made slaving possible and the new captives were exchanged for more munitions? Or has the power of firearms in West Africa been exaggerated? Did the British become more secure in their coastal enclaves? Finally, did the economic power of Europeans lead to indirect political control in some coastal states, establishing what has been termed 'informal empire'?

Guns and African warfare
In the 'Benin Gap' in the rainforest along the 'Slave Coast', where the open plain came down to the sea, possession of firearms did not necessarily translate into military success. After his succession around 1708, Dahomey's King Agaja had created an army well-equipped with firearms, possessed of a training and discipline that impressed European observers, and supported by a very effective intelligence service. His

intention was to conquer neighbouring Akan states and to break free of subordination to the Alafin of the great Yoruba empire of Oyo. More immediately, the rulers of Allada and Whydah interrupted the slave trade to the Atlantic coast by insisting on their monopoly rights. In 1724 he overran Allada, an Oyo tributary, capturing its small train of artillery, and in 1726 tested the water by sending Oyo a reduced tribute. The Alafin responded vigorously: his cavalry swept into northern Dahomey, destroyed Agaja's army in battle, and sacked the capital, Abomey. Agaja was forced to submit and was obliged to resume paying tribute. In this case, guns were of limited value against traditional cavalry, at least on an open battlefield.[45]

However, defeat by Oyo did not prevent Agaja from conquering Whydah in 1727 and reducing it to tributary status. He had warned the European traders to remain neutral and to drive the point home he burned their forts. At least the British and French forts were soon rebuilt, for when enemy fugitives took refuge there in 1728, he burned the French post and came close to doing the same to the British one. Agaja was careful to follow his conquest by sending valuable presents to the Alafin, but the question of regular tribute was insoluble: in essence, Agaja wanted Dahomey to be an independent power controlling the trade routes to the sea, something which the Alafin could not allow. In March 1728 Oyo again invaded Dahomey.[46]

Agaja was ready. He buried his treasure, abandoned his capital and retired into marshes where the Oyo cavalry could not follow, and where his superiority in guns and field fortifications would be most telling. In the end the numerically superior Oyo army retired for lack of supplies and Agaja reoccupied his capital. He repeated the performance in 1729 and 1730, but in the latter year he was lured out of the marshes into an ambush and heavily defeated. Once again, he made terms, agreeing on a regular tribute and – significantly – to facilitate the through-trade in slaves, in return for it being a royal monopoly. Forced to move his capital to Allada, he built up a centralised bureaucratic administration to incorporate newly conquered Allada and Whydah. Centralisation provoked some chiefs to revolt and in 1737 rebels forced him to open the slave trade.

By 1739, however, Agaja either felt strong enough to deny tribute to Oyo or failed to keep up with the Alafin's demands; or Oyo may have taken exception to his 1737 attack on the nearby state of Badagry. Whatever the cause or causes, Dahomey was again invaded in 1739. Agaja died the following year, but Dahomey kept up a spirited resistance until being forced to submit in 1747. The mighty Oyo empire now not only controlled the inland supply of slaves but had its own outlet to the sea and was in a position to eliminate or allow the British presence on the Slave Coast. (In the same way, in the 1750s Dahomey blocked supplies of guns to its northern neighbours the Mahi people but was still unable to conquer them). No doubt Oyo's triumph had been delayed by Dahomey's superior firepower and fortifications, but numbers and wealth had told in the end.

The direction of Oyo's triumphant expansion was probably conditioned by two factors: its cavalry-dependent military techniques and economic motives. The plains of the Benin Gap suited horsemen, but they also allowed Oyo to establish control of the trade routes from the Atlantic coast to the interior. The wars did produce prisoners of war who were enslaved and sold on, but Oyo was not constantly at war with its southern neighbours. The tribute demanded of subdued states included slaves, but the numbers of tribute slaves were generally very small. From 1730 Dahomey, for example, was expected to provide eighty-two slaves per annum. It seems that most of the slaves sold by Oyo agents on the Slave Coast were purchased from northern regions. Oyo was in the re-export business: imported slaves were sold on to British and other European dealers, in return for guns, gunpowder, cloth, iron bars, cowrie shells (for currency) and other goods, which in turn were re-exported to pay for the slaves and cavalry horses. Taxes levied on this trade formed a substantial part of the Alafin's income and therefore his ability to support a large army and an expanding civil service.[47]

Similar patterns can be discerned on the Gold Coast, where the number of forts made British and other European powers more influential, and where guns were more readily available to the coastal states. Neither European intervention nor possession of guns saved small forest states from the expansionist depredations of Asante, which had developed a formidable political and military organisation. In the early eighteenth century, Asante traders became frequent and valued visitors to the British posts and in 1722-1733 the federation continued its northern expansion by overrunning Bono-Mansu. In 1726 however, Asante armies moved south against the Wassaw, a forest people led by one Ntsiful, who used the forest to slow the enemy advance. Fighting a determined and effective rear-guard action as he led his whole people towards the coast and aided by an ultimately unsuccessful Asante war with Akyem from 1742, by 1745 Ntsiful had occupied the passes giving access to the coastal enclaves. Together with new allies, Denkyira and Twifo, the Wassaw effectively cut off Asante's hitherto profitable trade with the British posts at Dixcove and Cape Coast. Asante traders now took to the longer, more dangerous and difficult easterly routes through hills and marshes to Accra; but even there they were cut off when the Wassaw concluded alliances with the Akan states of Akim and Akwamunow. Asante now aimed to force its way through to the coast. Despite British and Dutch mediation, tension between the two states grew amid frequent threats of war, war which was probably only delayed by the indolence and alcoholism of the reigning Ashantene, Kusi Obodum, and a challenge to his rule about 1760.[48]

While these conflicts had their roots in African conditions, a major strategic objective was now control of the trade routes to the coast, and they were fought in part with large quantities of imported firearms. Most of the slaves seem to have been imported from the savannah states to the north, where guns were of limited military value. However, as the supply of guns and gunpowder increased, so did the numbers of slaves brough to the coast for sale. The British share alone in this traffic rose from 554,042 in 1726-1750 to 832,047 between 1751 and 1775, but the supply of guns given in exchange rose eightfold. In Senegambia, where slave trading was far less important, the volume of guns and gun powder traded was far lower.[49] The complexities of this 'gun-slave cycle' are still being unravelled.

Anglo-French competition and conflict 1750-1763
By 1750 the RAC's income could no longer sustain their dilapidated forts and trading stations. One possible solution was to give up those little enclaves altogether – after all, interlopers had set up their own establishments in various places. That, however, would have hampered trade, since the assembling, purchase and embarkation of human cargoes took some time to accomplish, and the credit relationships between African merchants and British dealers required a permanent coastal presence. Alternatively, the Crown could have taken over direct control of the forts, no doubt in part to establish some kind of sovereignty, but that attracted little political support.

The solution adopted was a ramshackle compromise: a new Company of Merchants Trading to Africa, funded by Parliament to the tune of £13,000 a year (or more when the structures needed repairs) was given the role of maintaining the forts, posts and canoes. Composed of all merchants involved in African trades, it was forbidden to trade itself, attract outside investment or run into debt. Although the Company of Merchants built a new Gold Coast fort at Anamabo, it was a less than perfect way of maintaining a West African presence.[50] Its territorial toeholds could hardly be described as fragments of empire.

Nor was there a West African empire in the very limited sense of the exclusion of European rivals. African rulers preferred to have more than one set of trading partners, appreciating that competition kept slave prices high – and they were adept at playing one set of Europeans off against another. In 1750, Dutch traders incited an African attack on Dixcove, and when the pugnacious British president responded aggressively he found himself attacked and under African siege for eight months. Nor could a monopoly have been enforced through naval supremacy. The British frigate, sometimes accompanied by a sloop or other smaller vessel, which visited the British posts once a year, was forbidden to engage in conflicts without explicit orders from London. At Gorée, however, the French sustained a seventy-four-gun ship of the line and a couple of frigates, each more powerful than the usual British patrol. In the years between the Peace of Aix-la-Chapelle and the outbreak of the Seven Years' War, as tensions rose in Europe, India and America, both states became more confrontational in West Africa.[51]

A pre-war crisis arose at Anamabo on the Gold Coast, where the British claimed exclusive trading rights. The French had been trying to establish a post since 1730, where the local headman Eno Baisie Kurentsi, 'John Currantee' to the British, had been playing the French and British off against each other for years. In January 1751 a French seventy-four and a powerful frigate appeared and sent a delegation ashore to negotiate for a settlement. Currantee not only refused but fired on boats from which French seamen were fishing. A year later another small squadron arrived, quickly followed by a stronger British force sent from Britain to counter it. When Currantee declined to break off his talks with the French, the British commander informed his French counterpart that the British claimed 'sovereignty' over the whole Fante country by virtue of a ground rent and threatened to treat any attempt at fort-building as an act of war. The French departed, but although the Fante agreed a treaty giving exclusive commercial rights to Britain, as Currantee refused to sign, no-one on the British side took it seriously. A second British squadron arrived just in time to counter a third French attempt to negotiate from strength.[52]

While the Gold Coast slave trade was the main source of Anglo-French tension in West Africa – in 1757 a French squadron battered and almost captured Cape Coast Castle - in Senegal the key factor was competition for supplies of gum Arabic. The French claimed a monopoly of that trade and Dutch and British competitors allegedly needed the protection of armed convoys if they were to infiltrate it. When the Seven Years' War began, and with William Pitt advocating a strike against Guadeloupe and Martinique, a merchant named Thomas Cummings argued that an assault on St Louis and Gorée Island in Senegal would have an equally devastating effect. Cummings claimed to have learned from traders with experience of the Emirate of Trarza, and from the Emir himself, that Trarza was likely to use its cavalry to support a British incursion. Nothing if not persistent and hoping to secure a legal trade monopoly for himself, he pestered the Board of Trade until his case was accepted and Pitt authorised an attack on St Louis in 1758. When the expedition reached Portendick on the Trarza coast, they discovered that the emirate had no interest in helping one group of Europeans overthrow another, which could only depress prices – only in appeasing the victor (if there was one) while keeping the trade as open as possible. The British decided to go it alone and took St Louis at the end of April. A subsequent assault on Gorée was a failure, but Pitt's response was to send a major naval expedition under Admiral Keppel, which arrived off the island in December and forced its surrender in January 1759. Gorée, basically a naval station, was returned to France by the Peace of Paris, but St Louis, an important commercial base, was retained.[53]

Thus, acute European competition for control of the West African trades, with all their implications for wealth, shipping and naval security, was set to continue. African states, far from becoming auxiliaries to this rivalry, retained their freedom of action, and the European enclaves were ultimately at their mercy. If this was empire, it was extremely fragile.

PART V
Crisis
1756-1783

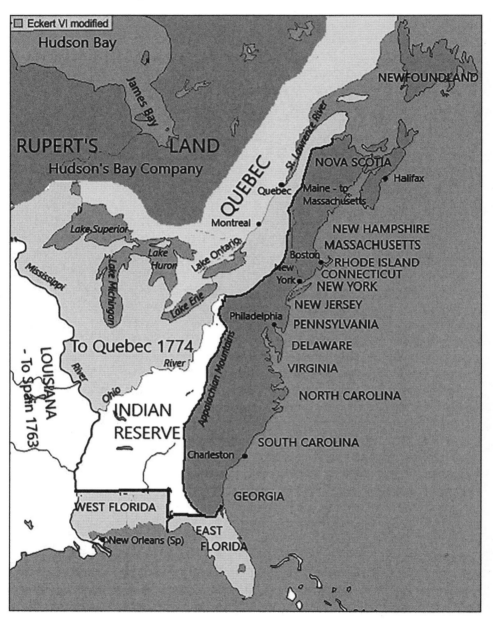

Eastern North America, 1763.

20

From Triumph to Defeat, 1763-1783

For the political elite, the financial heritage of 1763 was terrifying. The National Debt now stood at £132.6 million, compared with £76.1 million in 1748 and £74.6 million in 1756, a fact which dominated foreign and domestic policy for over a decade. The Whigs were deeply divided between Pitt's supporters and his 'Old Corps' opponents, while the Tories were still too weak to govern alone. No ministry between 1762 and 1770 could rely on a comfortable majority, and none of the premiers could command the consistent confidence of George III.

Consequently, administrations were unstable and short-lived, and the independent country gentlemen on the cross benches, whose main aim was to drive down the land tax, had to be placated. One result was headlong demobilisation, which left Britain and her colonies exposed in a world where the Bourbon powers were eager for revenge and where none of the major European states stood to gain by a British alliance. A second was the ill-fated but rational attempt to tax America, which all but destroyed the Atlantic empire, and a third was an unedifying readiness to tap the wealth of India without any concern for the plight of overtaxed and exploited Indians. Meanwhile, two significant court cases – one English, the other in Scotland – cast doubts over the future of slavery.

Ministerial fragility 1762-1770
King George III spent a decade looking for a prime minister with whom he could work, who at least partly shared his vision of a government freed from party, and who could sustain a parliamentary majority. His attempts to be rid of 'faction', his later association with the loss of America, and his porphyria-driven descent into apparent insanity once gave the King a very bad press. Far from being, or planning to be, a tyrant, he had a powerful – at times over-rigid and over-literal – respect for the constitution, parliament and the electorate. He was also intelligent, if not

quite brilliant. Carefully educated by John Stuart, the Scottish second Earl of Bute, he created a remarkable botanical collection in his Kew garden, loved music, supported the astronomer Herschel, founded the Royal Society of Arts, built up an impressive library, and under a pseudonym wrote informed articles on agricultural improvement. It is possible that many modern historians have overreacted in his favour, but it is surely going too far to see in his ideals– as one scholar does[1] – an absolutist ambition at least as great of that of James II.

He was glad to be rid of the Duke of Newcastle, who resigned in May 1762, and appointed Bute in his place. Bute was deeply respected and trusted by his former pupil, independent of party, an elected Scottish peer and already Secretary of State for the North. But Bute lacked a solid following in either House, and he came under savage attack for giving France a soft peace. The abuse came not only from Pitt, which was to be expected, but from beyond Westminster as well. Public prints depicted him as a Tory, a Scot (Scots were supposed to be poverty-stricken, avaricious place-seekers), the lover of King George III's mother (titillating but false) and a friend of France (wholly untrue). The most cutting attacks came from an occasionally unsavoury Englishman, John Wilkes, MP for Aylesbury. Number 45 of Wilkes's journal *The North Briton* – the title itself was a jibe at Bute and Scots – claimed that the King's speech to Parliament, written by Bute, contained lies about the Peace of Paris. The government counter-attacked with charges of seditious libel, but by then Bute had had enough and resigned in April 1763.

His successor George Grenville was left to deal with Wilkes, who was arrested under a general warrant for the unnamed authors, printers and publishers of the offending article. This raised questions as to the legality of such broad warrants and about the privileges of MPs. Acquitted, he in turn prosecuted the officials concerned with his detention and the seizure of his papers. Among those papers, however, was a copy of an obscene satirical poem claiming a living bishop as its editor, enabling the government to get him expelled from the Commons for blasphemous libel. Wilkes fled to France, was convicted by the House in his absence, and outlawed when he failed to appear for sentencing. Wilkes's behaviour was a challenge to the supposed self-serving, corrupt and incompetent world of Whig insiders, a challenge which was to emerge even more colourfully in 1768. Wilkes's career was followed approvingly by many in the American colonies.

The Wilkes affair was a serious distraction from Grenville's main business, which was to reduce the National Debt and to get the colonies to pay some of the continuing costs of empire. In 1764-1765 he reformed the Molasses Act, introduced a colonial stamp duty, regulated colonial currency and required colonies to provide shelter and fuel for British troops. The reforms raised a storm in America, but Grenville's Achilles' heel was his relationship with George III, who insisted on privately consulting Bute. In 1765 George managed to get rid of him by assembling a new administration led by the young Marquis of Rockingham.

The short-lived Rockingham ministry achieved little more than the repeal of Grenville's Stamp Act, while reserving Parliament's right to tax the colonies. The King detested Rockingham almost as much as he disliked Grenville and got rid of him as soon as he could. It was left to the cross-party 'patriot' ministry led by the ailing William Pitt, now Earl of Chatham, to grasp the twin nettles of colonial taxation and tapping the resources of the East India Company.

While Chatham took the waters at Bath, the government was led nominally by the Duke of Grafton, and in practice by the Chancellor of the Exchequer, Charles Townshend, and the Southern Secretary, the Earl of Shelburne. From the Stamp Act crisis, Townshend concluded that while Americans objected fiercely to internal taxes, they had no objection to external ones, such as the Navigation Acts. He therefore persuaded his colleagues, and subsequently Parliament, to impose a range of customs duties upon various items imported into the colonies. Townshend failed to realise that by now any parliamentary revenue-raising tax which was anathema to many colonists.

The subsequent resistance damaged the government's standing in Britain and compounded many other problems it faced. Two regiments sent to Boston to enforce the legislation were legally impotent to act and became walking symbols of tyranny. The Whigs were still deeply divided, Pitt's acceptance of his peerage had cost him popularity, and ministers were deeply embarrassed by the dramatic reappearance of John Wilkes.[2]

Wilkes returned to England in November 1768 and announced that in the approaching general election he would stand for the county of Middlesex, which embraced London and had an unusually wide franchise. He won the poll comfortably and dramatically surrendered to the Court of King's Bench, which imprisoned him pending trial. The prison became a focus for popular demonstrations and on one occasion for a violent clash with troops. When Parliament assembled it nevertheless voted to expel him and declare the election void. The process was repeated twice more before, on the fourth occasion, MPs declared his defeated opponent the winner. Here was Parliament brushing aside the choice of the people of Middlesex – just as it was trying to bypass colonists' elected representatives.

Wilkes was to triumph in the end. In 1771 he successfully championed the cause of two printers accused of illegally publishing parliamentary proceedings, after which reporting from Parliament became free and uncensored. At the general election of 1774 there was no stopping him. He stood again for Middlesex and was elected to the seat he held until 1790.[3] Thus a man who had no sympathy with the economic grievances of poor Londoners, and who openly mocked his own supporters, became a radical hero on both sides of the Atlantic.

Lord North, whose administration took office in January 1770, brought some stability. He worked well with the King and he was skilled in keeping Commons majorities together. However, the price of placating competing factions was financial stringency and meeting the American challenge to parliamentary sovereignty was now a political imperative.

Regulating 'John Company'
While America was a constant headache, all these fragile ministries had to confront the fact that the East India Company was now a major territorial power in India. Was that permissible or desirable? The Chatham administration of 1766-1767 started from the premise that direct Crown administration of the Company's territories was impractical, both for lack of resources and personnel and because taking over the Company's vast resources of patronage would have been politically disastrous. While Chatham favoured challenging the Company's legal right to territorial revenues, other ministers such as Charles Townshend feared being seen to attack chartered rights; and Chatham's physical and mental infirmity allowed them to carry the day.

By an Act of 1767, the Company was obliged to agree to pay £400,000 annually and to cap its dividends at 10 per cent, without any other restrictions on its operations. However, once the Crown had a stake in the Company's financial viability, it continued to legislate to keep its expenditure and dividends under control. To avoid a dispute over the charter, ministers and their adherents began to buy up Company stock, thus forming a ministerial bloc, managed from 1768 by the Earl of Sandwich, in anticipation of new legislation in 1769.

The outcome in 1769 was a five-year agreement between Crown and Company, formalised by Act of Parliament, continuing the 1767 arrangements with the proviso that the payments to the Crown would be reduced in line with the reductions in the dividend, and cease altogether if the dividend dropped below 6 per cent. On the other hand, the dividend could now be raised by 1 per cent annual increments to a maximum of 12.5 per cent, without incurring any increase in the payment. Moreover, the Crown could borrow at 2 per cent any profits remaining to the Company after payment of debts.

During the term of this agreement some unpleasant developments underlined the need to regulate the Company's finances within the Indian subcontinent itself. In 1769 news that Madras had lost a war against the rising state of Mysore caused a sudden slump in the price of East India stock and brought many shareholders to the brink of ruin. This, combined with a story of a French naval and military build-up at Mauritius, raised the spectre of a Bourbon attack which a weakened

Company would be unable to repel. Meanwhile the Company recklessly raised its dividend although its income was falling, and in 1772 a wider financial crash threatened the Company's existence, a substantial portion of government income, and a mainstay of the country's prosperity. Public outrage at stories of misrule in Bengal added to the urgency. The North ministry had no option but to intervene and the Company was in no state to resist.

From November 1772, a secret Commons committee gathered the information the ministry needed to take effective action. North would have liked to nationalise all the Company's possessions. However, ministers were in no position to advocate annexation of Bengal or any other of the Company's territories. Shareholders with corrupt dealings to conceal had joined forces with the opposition Whigs led by the Earl of Rockingham, who played upon the persistent fear of an excessively powerful Crown, and who raised the spectre of a secret cabal directing operations behind the scenes. This may have been at least as important as the fact that over 200 MPs owned East India Company stock. North therefore edged his way towards an agreement with the directors, but the shareholders in the general court proved so irresponsible and truculent that a settlement had to be forced upon them by law.

The Regulating Act of 1773 set about establishing stability in the Company's management by doubling the shareholders' voting qualification from £500 to £1,000 worth of stock, which must be held for at least a year instead of the previous six months. The practice of splitting stock to create votes was restrained. The twenty-four Directors were to be elected every four years instead of annually. As for control of policy in India, the Treasury and Secretary of State were entitled to receive copies of all incoming correspondence within a fortnight of its arrival. The Governor of Bengal now became the Governor General of all the Company's Indian possessions and was to be nominated by the Crown; but this centralisation was to be balanced by a Bengal council of four members with the right of veto. The Crown would also appoint the four members of the Governor General's council. To protect Indians against exploitation by Company servants, a new Supreme Court of four judges, all Crown appointees, was to hear cases brought against British subjects in Bengal.

That done, the government was willing to forego its claim to an annual contribution from the Company and to otherwise help it out of its financial morass. It was obliged to accept a government loan of £1,400,000 and to limit the dividend to 6 per cent until the loan was repaid and the overall Company debt reduced. Company servants could no longer easily lend money to the Company in order to transfer their gains back to Britain.

There were also plans to alleviate the depression caused by high customs duties in the sale of the Company's tea – perhaps half the tea consumed by Britons was smuggled – by allowing its sale in the colonies with full drawback of duties. The Tea Act of 1773 would, it was thought, render the Company's prices so low that the North American smugglers would be put out of business. The momentous political consequences, beginning with the Boston 'Tea Party' of 1774, were not foreseen.

The reform was nevertheless well-intentioned and did indeed begin the process of bringing the Company's political affairs under control. The new governor general, Warren Hastings, was an old India hand, already governor of Bengal, and a workaholic known for his intelligence, linguistic ability, and sympathetic interest in Indian cultures. During the War of American Independence, he successfully preserved the East India Company as a major Indian power. However, as we shall see in a later chapter, the Act had serious weaknesses.

Slavery and the Mansfield judgement

By the 1770s there were between 15,000 and 20,000 Africans living in Britain, out of a population of over 8,500,000. Most were slaves but a significant number, including a few student sons of West African rulers, were free. The most famous free African was Olaudah Equiano, seaman, businessman, abolitionist and author, who had settled in Britain by 1768.[4] The legal status of those held as slaves was already a contentious issue. Quakers on both sides of the Atlantic had been campaigning against slavery for some time, and more recently their voices had been joined by the Anglican evangelicals Granville Sharp and John Wesley (who was charged with hypocrisy by American 'Patriots' who objected to being 'slaves' of Great Britain). Courtroom verdicts in 1697, 1701, 1707 and 1762 held that, as slavery was obnoxious to English common law, any slave brought into England automatically became free. However, these were challenged not just by common belief but by two contrary judgements of 1729 and 1747.

The problem appeared to come to a head in 1772 with the case of James Somerset, a slave brought from Jamaica by his master and who ran away rather than be returned there. Recaptured, but supported by Sharp, Somerset appealed to the Court of King's Bench. The Lord Chief Justice William Murray, first Earl Mansfield, was deeply opposed to slavery, at least within Britain; but he was equally convinced that the law must protect private property, and that he must not overstep his judicial functions by attempting to change the law through his decision. After three lengthy sessions, long consideration, and using strongly abolitionist rhetoric, Mansfield ruled that no man might be sent abroad against his will, and therefore Somerset could remain in England. He did not say that slavery could not legally exist in England, and his verdict did not – as has frequently been alleged – lead to the immediate freeing of 15,000 slaves. Masters soon learned to get around the Mansfield judgement by binding their slaves as apprentices as soon as they landed in England. Nevertheless, the popular perception was that slavery did not exist in England, and British blacks and their white abolitionist supporters were greatly encouraged.[5] Moreover, a subsequent Scottish judgement of 1777 held that slavery was contrary to the law of Scotland, meaning that any slave living in or brought into North Britain automatically became free.

Diplomatic isolation

The fundamental diplomatic problem was that Britain's potential allies – Prussia, the Hapsburg Monarchy, Russia – no longer saw Bourbon France and Spain as major threats. Each was worried about the others' ambitions in Poland, while Austria and Russia were rivals for gains at the expense of the declining Ottoman Empire. Prussia, wary of Austrian revanchism, opposed Hapsburg manoeuvres to strengthen their position in Germany, especially attempts to exchange the Netherlands for Bavaria. This left French governments led by Choiseul and Vergennes free to build up the French navy preparatory to a seaborne war of revenge with Britain, possibly in alliance with Spain. In 1768 the French annexation of Corsica, uncomfortably close to Minorca, was a straw in the wind, and in 1770 a Spanish attempt to reclaim the Falkland Islands almost made this nightmare into reality. Yet in the mind of Lord North, whose great strength was his talent for reconciling competing factions, the need for low taxation trumped real recognition of the danger. In the few years after the Falklands crisis, Lord Sandwich, First Lord of the Admiralty, worked hard to build up an adequate stock of seasoned timber and to expand the capacity of the dockyards. But as the sense of emergency waned, there were fewer and fewer funds available to keep building and repairs to a safe level. This was to have serious consequences once the War of American Independence broke out in 1775, and especially after France joined the Americans in 1778.

War

Once hostilities began in the spring of 1775, the danger of French and perhaps Spanish intervention presented critical logistical and strategic problems. Sandwich was always more worried about Bourbon invasion than about the American war and wanted to keep adequate naval forces in home waters. The new Secretary of State for the Colonies, Lord George Germain, wanted more ships in American waters to protect troop convoys and to make the most of Britain's water-borne mobility. The result, as we shall see, was delayed campaigns, short campaigning seasons and missed opportunities for early victory. When France did enter in February 1778, it proved impossible to achieve the quick, annihilating victory that the situation demanded.

Immediately Britain faced her usual naval problem of keeping the Brest and Toulon squadrons apart, but this time she had not a single European ally to distract the enemy. When the Toulon squadron escaped and sailed for New York, it could not be pursued in strength until its destination became obvious – and the arguably necessary pursuit by Admiral Byron ruined Sandwich's successful concentration of superior numbers against the Brest fleet. The subsequent Battle of Ushant on 27 July was indecisive, an excellent result for France but potentially disastrous for Britain. Now she would be hard put to guard against invasion and protect her Atlantic convoys, guard the Mediterranean bases, defend the West Indies, support the army in America and counter the French in Asian waters all at once.

When Spain declared war in 1779, disaster came perilously near: Gibraltar and Minorca were besieged, numerical superiority in home waters was lost, and a Franco-Spanish fleet entered the Channel intending to attack Portsmouth. Only the debilitated condition of the French (not the Spanish) ships, and Admiral Hardy's refusal to be drawn prematurely into battle, saved the day.

After that the Bourbons seemed unable to exploit their advantage. Admiral George Rodney was freed to sail to relieve Gibraltar and Minorca and reinforce the West Indies, and on 16 January 1780 he surprised and mauled a much smaller Spanish squadron in the so-called Moonlight Battle off Cape St Vincent. Even the advent of an Armed Neutrality of the North, to resist British searches for military contraband by force, and a declaration of war on the Dutch before they could accede to it, was not overwhelming. For over a year Britain's enemies failed to concentrate their forces in any of the key theatres – North America, the Caribbean, and India – and in home waters another combined Bourbon armada entered the Channel, only to be deterred by the defensive posture of a smaller British fleet. In America, the British managed by switching naval forces between the West Indies and North America as need and opportunity arose. But even the most skilful juggling could not keep all these maritime balls in the air at once, and in May 1782 they began to fall.

Radicalism
The War of American Independence divided Britons, not because many people sympathised with the revolt, but because interrupted trade, consequent inflation and unemployment, soaring taxation, and apparent military failure seemed again to reveal incompetence and corruption in the charmed circle of Whig politics. Provincial gentry who had strongly supported the North ministry and the war wanted to free the House of Commons from executive influence and make members more responsive to voters. In December 1779 Christopher Wyvill, a Yorkshire cleric and country gentleman, led the formation of a county association, the first

of many across the country. Wyvill and his followers demanded an end to rotten boroughs, more seats for the counties, and a return to triennial parliaments. By the spring of 1780 his movement had produced thirty-six petitions from counties and larger boroughs.

A more radical movement was led by John Cartwright, a militia officer, whose 1780 Society for Constitutional Information favoured universal manhood suffrage, the secret ballot and annual parliaments. News of the fall of Charleston to British forces in May 1780, and the fright administered by the six-day Gordon riots in June, temporarily derailed the reformers, but the election of 1780 brought into Parliament the younger William Pitt, who sympathised with Wyvill, and one of Cartwright's key allies, the playwright Richard Sheridan.

Grattan's parliament and the Volunteer movement
In Ireland, the war ended a long period of economic growth and introduced increased unemployment, high prices, and shortages of all kinds, which led to threatening political action. The Patriot group in the Irish parliament declared openly for the American rebels. Anger at tithes payable by Catholics to the Church of Ireland fed recruitment into the secret Whiteboys association. The Whiteboys attacked landlords, tenants, their animals and hayricks, provoking the formation of a Protestant terrorist organisation, the Steelboys. In 1778, with invasion a real threat and Ireland denuded of troops, Ulster Protestants created a paramilitary force called the Volunteers. 40,000 strong by 1780, the Volunteers broadened their appeal across Ireland to embrace Catholics as well as Protestants in demanding economic and political reform.

The North ministry responded with a series of economic concessions: Ireland could now export its wool and glass, import precious metals, and trade with the British empire (the East India Company's monopoly excepted) on equal terms. Irish merchants could join the Turkey Company and Irish ports were opened to Levantine trade. Moreover, the regulation of Anglo-Irish trade was devolved to the Irish parliament. However, if ministers thought that these changes would defuse the Irish question, they were sadly mistaken.

The real issue was the status of the Irish parliament. The British defeat at Yorktown in November 1781, followed by a great Volunteer convention at Dungannon in 1782, forced Rockingham's government to repeal Poyning's Law and the 1720 Declaratory Act, thus granting the Irish parliament equality with Westminster. In practice, the Dublin assembly was elected by a minority, excluded Catholics and Presbyterians from its membership, and the Anglo-Irish elite continued to dominate its sessions. Yet 'Grattan's Parliament' was strong enough to challenge Westminster on some salient issues and to develop in some of its members a new Irish nationalism.[6] One can think of this as the first colonial constitution to achieve equivalence with Britain's, but it should also be seen as a move towards greater equality and autonomy within the imperial 'core'. Unfortunately, it was to be short-lived.

Defeat, peace and imperial survival

In May a West Indies convoy was lost in the Channel approaches and a week later Pensacola in Florida was taken by Spanish forces. A victory over a small Dutch squadron in the North Sea in August was dwarfed by the capitulation of Minorca. In September, the French at last achieved a powerful concentration in Chesapeake Bay, forcing Lord Cornwallis's army to surrender at Yorktown on 18 October. Yorktown utterly demoralised the government: Lord George Germain was dismissed in January 1782, North informed George III that he would no longer wage war against the Americans, the King considered abdication, and some cross-bench MPs withdrew their support from North. In March, North pressed his resignation upon his reluctant sovereign, Rockingham accepted the seals of office and Britain entered a new period of confusing political instability.

Rockingham rightly distrusted the King, who was determined to be rid of him again and was not best pleased by sweeping reforms intended to restrict royal patronage. Colonial administration was entirely restructured with the abolition of the Board of Trade and the post of Secretary of State for Colonies. The Northern and Southern Secretaries became the Home Secretary and Foreign Secretary respectively. Meanwhile, peace talks with both the Americans and the allied European powers began.

After Rockingham's sudden death the peace negotiations were carried on by his successor, Lord Shelburne. His position had been strengthened in 1782 by a dramatic West Indian naval victory and the collapse of a final Spanish attack on Gibraltar using covered floating gun batteries. More important even than the psychological advantage of these successes was the near bankruptcy of the Bourbon powers. Consequently, Britain was able to secure a separate peace with America (the Treaty of Paris) and the Treaty of Versailles with France and Spain of 20 January 1783 was far less damaging than it might have been. France gained only Tobago, recovered Senegal in West Africa, and achieved expanding fishing and trading rights in Newfoundland and India. Spain recovered Florida and Minorca, but not Gibraltar. The Dutch were lucky to retrieve Trincomalee in Ceylon (Sri Lanka), which had been taken by the British and recaptured by France. Though most of Europe, and not a few at home, thought Britain had forever lost her Great Power status, she had the means for a powerful recovery.

The poor provision in the treaty for up to 100,000 American loyalist refugees – the United States was supposed to seek compensation from its

From Triumph to Defeat, 1763-1783

constituent states – weakened Shelburne's support. He gave way to an opportunistic, unlikely – and many thought unholy – alliance between the radical Whig Charles James Fox and Lord North. Fox introduced a Bill which would have transferred control of the East India Company's territories to the Crown, but his opponents secured its defeat by raising questions about extended royal patronage and the violation of charters. In December 1783, George dismissed Fox and North and bestowed the office of First Lord of the Treasury upon the younger William Pitt.

21

The Origins of the American Revolution, 1755-1775

In 1783, just twenty years after the triumphant conclusion of the Seven Years' War, and after another bloody eight-year conflict, Britain was forced to accept the independence of the new United States. It was essentially a clash between two opposing world views. Many, though far from all, Americans identified their colonies' autonomy with the liberties of Englishmen, liberties which they saw as increasingly under threat from an imperial government determined to impose an absolutism backed by a standing army. These fears were linked to local economic interests, which London seemed eager to curtail through unconstitutional taxation and restraints upon westward settler expansion at the expense of Native Americans. The Navigation System, which gave American producers heavily protected markets as well as imposing irritating restrictions, was probably less important.

From London, it seemed that a violent minority of parochially minded colonists was determined to tyrannise a loyal majority and frustrate governments trying to discharge wider imperial responsibilities. If the Navigation System imposed some economic restrictions, it gave American insiders considerable advantages, such as security against foreign competition. Though Parliament might wish to assert its sovereignty over the colonies, and sometimes aggressively, there was never any intention to permanently remove representative assemblies, the rule of law, trial by jury and other constitutional rights. As one British historian has put it:

> It would not be altogether wrong – though it would be an oversimplification – to see in the growing difficulties faced by Lord North's government in the 1770s a general confrontation between a national government trying to discharge imperial responsibilities and irresponsible sectionalism and self-interest assuming rather different forms in different sectors but linked by similar problems and deploying similar arguments and tactics.[7]

Though it should be added that ministers consistently failed to accurately anticipate American reactions to their policies – and they might have acted differently had they done so – that assessment may be very close to reality.

The relative significance of the Seven Years' War
Modern scholarship tends to see the Revolution originating in the strains upon metropole-periphery relations growing out of the Seven Years' War. The war saw significant centralisation of imperial authority at the expense of colonies with a long tradition of internal self-government. The creation of a commander-in-chief of all forces, regular or provincial, in mainland North America was a considerable intrusion upon the military autonomy of the thirteen colonies. At the same time, the two new Superintendents of Indian Affairs undermined each colony's control of frontier policy. Colonial assemblies generally opposed regulation by the Superintendents and military officers on the spot, and colonial governors tended to identify with the interests of their provinces. Yet some British officers seemed determined to side with Native Americans against settler expansion. In 1758, Brigadier General John Forbes facilitated his advance on Fort Duquesne by winning over Indian nations in the region. In 1760 and 1761 regular troops were sent to South Carolina, at the colony's request, to support the southern colonies' forces against the Cherokees; in both cases the commanding officers sympathised with the Indians and limited their operations in hopes of achieving a lasting peace. On the second occasion Colonel James Grant negotiated a treaty that fell far short of the vengeful demands of many colonists, and he and his men were hissed on the way to their ships when they withdrew.[8] In 1761, Colonel Henry Bouquet forcibly removed Maryland intruders from the Forks of the Ohio, and a treaty signed at Easton fixed the Pennsylvania frontier at the height of the Appalachian Mountains.

Moreover, imperial demands that colonial assemblies vote higher taxation to support the war effort were rejected until London promised to repay a very large proportion from the pocket of the British taxpayer. This opposition might be partly explained by the relative lack of circulating currency in America, and there were already ideological objections to standing armies.[9] Nevertheless, the fact remains that colonial taxes were far lighter than those levied in Britain, and colonists were content to enjoy the benefits of the war.

Imperial frontier management
It is now clear that post-war frontier policy was a very important part of the mix. Having driven the French away, colonial settlers, land speculators and traders expected to be able to expand into and across the Appalachian mountain barrier. British ministers, on the other hand, saw peace with Amerindian nations, many of whom had recently been allied with the French, as key to avoiding costly backwoods wars, keeping the Bourbons at bay and

protecting Indian lands against acquisitive intruders. Lord Egremont, Pitt's portly and pleasure-loving successor as Secretary of State for the Southern Department, concluded that the only way to achieve this was to create a continuous boundary between white settlements and Indian lands. He took advice from Henry Ellis, the perceptive governor of Georgia, and assumed direct personal control of colonial affairs from the Board of Trade. When an unexpected Cherokee delegation appeared in London, he ensured that the three warriors met the King, and were feted, entertained and shown all the impressive sights of the imperial capital.[10] Early in 1763 he persuaded the Privy Council to issue an Order-in-Council establishing a boundary line along the Appalachian watershed, ordered Sir Jeffrey Amherst to treat the northern nations with consideration and justice, and instructed John Stuart, the second southern Superintendent of Indian Affairs, to convene a congress at Augusta, Georgia. There he was to assure the Creeks, Cherokees and others that, although the British had taken over former French forts, this did not presage a wholesale seizure of their lands, a promise to be backed up by the distribution of a shipload of presents being sent from Britain.

The Congress was a success, at least in the short term, and thereafter Stuart pursued a dynamically protective policy, designed to keep settler intrusion at bay and to prevent traders from demanding land in payment of debts. In the north, however, Amherst ignored the spirit of his orders and ceased to distribute presents, hoping thereby to reduce recently hostile nations to impotence.

Here, too, the result vindicated Egremont's policy. In May 1763 an Ottawa war chief named Obwandiyagtiac (or Pontiac), led a coalition of the Amerindian nations around the Great Lakes and down into the Ohio Valley in a sudden and ferocious attack on the forts occupied by the British. Every post between Detroit in the west and Pitt at the Ohio forks was captured, most by deception and surprise, a few by direct assault. Detroit and Fort Pitt were closely invested, the Natives displaying great skill at siege craft, digging approach trenches and using fire arrows and heated lead to set wooden buildings ablaze. Beyond Fort Pitt on the Forbes Road the garrisons at Forts Ligonier and Bedford were attacked. There was no French intrigue behind this war, though there was a concerted attempt by the Indians to draw the Illinois French into the fray. Amherst, who apparently had instructed his commanders to distribute smallpox-infected blankets in an attempt at ethnic cleansing, was immediately recalled. [11] The account is in fact disputed, though Philadelphia-based Colonel Henry Bouquet did write to Amherst during the siege of Fort Pitt by Pontiac, describing the dire situation of the cramped fort, itself beset by smallpox, and Amherst replied:

> Could it not be contrived to Send the Small Pox among those Disaffected Tribes of Indians? We must, on this occasion, Use Every Stratagem in our power to Reduce them.

The Origins of the American Revolution, 1755-1775

Egremont did not live to see the end of the bloody and destructive war, which dragged on until 1766. But even his fatal heart attack brought on late 1763 by excessive eating, did not derail the constructive frontier policy he had launched.

The weaknesses of this paternalistic approach were threefold. First, it provoked resentment from settlers: Virginians, Pennsylvanians and Marylanders assumed that their wartime efforts entitled them to treat the Ohio lands as conquests. Second, it was largely unenforceable: the frontier forts being too far apart and their garrisons too small, and by 1766 it was clear that the coastal cities were under-garrisoned. The policy therefore promised the Indians far greater protection than an early modern Atlantic empire could deliver, while settlers, merchants, traders and speculators learned that they could defy the imperial will with near impunity. New land companies mushroomed, involving men as prominent as George Washington and Benjamin Franklin. Third, it was not proof against the decisions of future ministers, or against the corrupt activities of some local officials.

In 1768 – when more troops were already needed in the coastal cities – the North ministry recognised reality and withdrew from the frontier military posts. At the same time, it agreed to compensate traders, merchants and speculators for their supposed wartime losses, and authorised Sir William Johnson to purchase the Kentucky region south-east of the Ohio from the Iroquois. Once the cession was agreed by the Treaty of Fort Stanwix, three land companies pursued claims there. Joining hands in 1772 as the Grand Ohio Company, they obtained a huge grant, which was to become a new colony called Vandalia. The Indians actually living there had not consented, an inland colony would be even harder to manage than coastal ones, and it was very clear that the new frontier would not be respected by settlers and speculators. The only Cabinet voice raised in protest belonged to the Secretary of State, Lord Hillsborough, who resigned.

The Fort Stanwix boundary also violated a border just agreed with the Cherokees at Hard Labor, South Carolina. In 1770 John Stuart concluded a new pact, the Treaty of Lochaber, which restored and revised the Hard Labor line but won few friends among southern frontiersmen, speculators, and traders keen to be paid in land. Stuart, the most persistent advocate of firm frontier management, now symbolised obstructive imperial authority.

The boundless ambition of the speculators was confirmed in 1773 by the new Illinois Company's attempt to illegally buy land from Indian tribes further west. When their first purchase was blocked their agent turned to his kinsman, Lord Dunmore, the governor of Virginia. Dunmore then became a shareholder in a new land purchase firm, the Wabash Company, which made purchases of its own. At the same time, Dunmore used the Virginian militia to crush Shawnee and

Mingo resistance to the Kentucky settlers. By then the Quebec Act had transferred the lands north-west of the Ohio to Canada. The returning Virginian militia men made their attitude very clear by threatening to use force of arms against the Crown. Not even the Continental Congress had gone quite that far.

The 'Sugar' and Currency Acts

The under-taxation of the colonies contributed to the unprecedented National Debt, and hence London's anxiety to avoid costly and dangerous frontier wars. The acquisition of the whole continent up to the east banks of the Mississippi, the need to garrison newly conquered Florida and Canada, and the need to police the frontier meant that economy through wholesale military demobilisation was not an option. Ten thousand men would be required for North America and the West Indies, and from London it seemed only just and fair that Americans should pay a proportion of the cost. Many Americans, on the other hand, had strong seventeenth-century ideological objections to a standing army, to any taxation not primarily intended to regulate trade, and to any measure tending to undermine the autonomy of their elected assemblies.

Grenville's first fiscal measure, the American Duties Act of 1764, often misleadingly called the Sugar Act, tried to square this circle. It replaced the Molasses Act, slashing the sixpenny duty on foreign sugar products to threepence, while taking steps to enforce its collection and suppress smuggling. It also banned the import of foreign rum, so undermining the French Caribbean distillers who depended upon the North American market and forcing down the cost of molasses imported by New England rum producers. British West Indian planters were protected by raising the duty on foreign sugars from five to seven shillings per hundredweight (112 lbs or 51 kg), while to benefit British manufacturers duties were also raised on foreign silk, calico and linen textiles. More innovatively, British wine merchants were assisted by a new duty on direct imports of Portuguese Madeira, the colonial elites' favourite wine and hitherto imported without charge. Grenville's aims were both mercantilist and fiscal: to create or reinforce protected markets throughout the empire, and to bring in revenue, an estimated £70,000-80,000 from the molasses tax alone.[12]

Simply imposing duties would have no effect without rooting out the institutionalised corruption evident everywhere in the colonial customs service. Since 1733 foreign molasses had been imported more or less openly, the officers being paid off with a 'composition fine' of up to two pence a gallon. Now governors had to take oaths to enforce the law and customs officers became liable to heavy punishments, including dismissal and exclusion from all future appointments. To aid them in their work

The Origins of the American Revolution, 1755-1775

they were protected from lawsuits by imposing a very low cap on costs and damages. Defendants could no longer choose to have a case heard in a common law court, with a jury sympathetic to smuggling, rather than in one of the eleven American vice-admiralty courts, where a judge sat alone. Because those same judges could be intimidated by hostile crowds, a new vice-admiralty court for the whole of America was to sit at Halifax, well out of the way of popular violence. Coastal trades were to be much more rigorously supervised than before. Captains of ships of under 100 tons had to post bonds of £1,000, masters of larger ships twice that, and even coastal cargoes had to be verified by a system of sealed manifestos called 'cockets'. All this was thought to bring the American colonies into line with British practice and to ensure that colonists paid their fair share of the costs of empire.

In colonies with such a long tradition of autonomy, this tightening of control was bound to arouse opposition. In particular, Americans had always accepted duties intended to control the flow of trade, but this Act was intended partly to raise revenue and was therefore objectionable. Moreover, Boston businessmen like John Hancock who had routinely ignored the Molasses Act were resentful that the law was at long last about to be enforced, and represented the tax on sugar as a sop to the West Indian interest in the House of Commons.

At the same time, a Currency Act, arising from a private Member's Bill, stopped colonial debtors paying British creditors in depreciated colonial currency, by banning the issue of paper money. Although aimed squarely at Virginia, it was generally irritating because there was still a shortage of coin in North America, and even local payments could be affected.

It has been argued that Grenville and Halifax were wrong to reject co-operation as a means of getting America to pay its way,[13] but the colonies had refused to pay their way in the war until Parliament had agreed to shoulder much of the burden. Ministers had no reason to expect different attitudes now.

Massachusetts reacted first in the form of a protest by the Boston town meeting, with radicals like Samuel Adams – failed brewer and incompetent tax collector – raising constitutional as well as economic issues. In the assembly, committees were formed to correspond with other colonies and James Otis persuaded them to send out his pamphlet *The Rights of the Colonies* in which he contended that parliamentary sovereignty was limited by the natural rights of the subject. Though it was popular in Boston and elsewhere, its argument was legally feeble: only Parliament could alter its own laws or amend the constitution. Economically, only rum distillers, coastal traders and purchasers of imported luxuries had anything to fear. In New England an attempted boycott of British luxuries soon broke down, and of all the colonial legislatures only Massachusetts and New York made official protests.

The Stamp Act crisis and the Quartering Act

The Grenville ministry concluded that an internal tax would also, in the end, be acceptable. The Stamp Act of 1765 demanded that all legal documents and many others, including newspapers, must be printed upon paper bearing an official stamp showing that duty had been paid. It provoked widespread and violent resistance, partly because it invaded the sacred prerogatives of the colonial assemblies, but also because it affected the pockets of a very wide band of the population. Tavern licences required the stamp, as did playing cards. Patrick Henry, a radical back-country lawyer, persuaded the Virginian assembly to pass five resolutions condemning internal taxation. The fifth was withdrawn and a sixth, which declared that Virginians could legally refuse to pay an internal tax imposed by Parliament, was too extreme for most deputies and never passed. Nevertheless, a radical gauntlet had been thrown down. While nine colonies sent delegates to a Stamp Act Congress in New York – a rare sign of inter-colonial cooperation – a new organisation, the 'Sons of Liberty' appeared in New York and rapidly spread to other colonies. In every colony but Georgia, violent mobs organised by the 'Sons' forced stamp agents to resign. The insignificant imperial forces in these colonies – essentially a headquarters in New York and a string of isolated wilderness forts – were quite inadequate to restore order.

The resistance was sharpened by a Quartering Act passed in May 1765 which required each colony to house the King's troops in vacant buildings, provide those quarters with fuel and halved the fare they would pay at river crossings. Many colonists thought this taxation in kind as blatant an attack on colonial autonomy as the Stamp Act. New York, where the new rules were most likely to be applied, bluntly refused to comply. Yet the measure was very moderate. It addressed the persistent decade-old reluctance of colonial assemblies to provide shelter, fuel and candles to the King's men. In deference to American feelings, it stipulated that the soldiers' food would be paid for and excluded billeting troops in private homes. In this it was less than Thomas Gage, the commander in chief in America, had wanted. If colonists saw the quartering obligations as analogous to robbery by a 'mugger', as one historian claims, they were rather missing the point.[14]

Rockingham, the Townshend legislation and resistance

In 1766 Grenville's ministry fell over an unrelated matter, and the new Rockingham administration had to concede that the Stamp Act was unacceptable in the colonies and opposed by commercial interests at home. There was no thought at his stage of reacting to American opposition by force, but rather of finding a mutually acceptable form of parliamentary taxation. Parliament repealed the Stamp Act, in the face of Grenville's prescient warning that retreat would only tempt the radicals to demand more. However, this was not the same as surrendering the right to tax the colonies, a point spelled out by Parliament in an accompanying Declaratory Act. It was assumed that taxation would now have to be done through an external levy. A Revenue Act, intended to regulate trade as well as to raise revenue, was actually accepted by colonial assemblies and the crisis seemed to have passed.

However, the constitutional genie could not be so easily put back in its bottle. New York continued to defy the Quartering Act. Chatham, who replaced Rockingham in May 1767, was unwell and the resulting power vacuum gave opportunities to more aggressive younger men. While Chatham recuperated, the Chancellor of the Exchequer Charles Townshend persuaded the Cabinet and then Parliament to impose duties on goods imported into the colonies ranging from tea to printer's ink. This Revenue Act, of course, ignored the radical objection to any measure aimed at raising a revenue. At the same time a Suspending Act forbade the New York Assembly to conduct any other business until it had implemented the Quartering Act. In America, the Townshend legislation was greeted at first with calm but defiant moderation, and later by outrage and renewed violence.

It began, rather slowly, in Massachusetts, when the town meeting agreed a new non-importation agreement. In February 1768, Samuel Adams and his radical friends persuaded the assembly to send a circular letter to the other colonial legislatures to plan concerted action. However, there were protests elsewhere as other colonial assemblies petitioned the Crown; already a Pennsylvanian, John Dickinson, had produced his *Letters From a Farmer in Pennsylvania* condemning the Acts, which was reprinted in every colony and in Britain. However, it was the circular letter that got attention from ministers. Lord Hillsborough, occupying the new post of Secretary of State for the Colonies, ordered Governor Francis Bernard to get the Massachusetts assembly's letter withdrawn, and told all other governors to dissolve assemblies which discussed it. The result was outrage and defiance and crowds began violently to harass customs officers.

Hilllsborough had been more provocative than the Cabinet intended, but the government's collective patience was now exhausted. It seemed that concession and conciliation only begat more demands and violence, so that if a stand was not made Parliament would lose even its power to regulate trade. Military action was taken. In 1768, the frontier garrisons were withdrawn and two battalions were sent to Boston, reputedly the core of the trouble and the smuggling capital of the Americas. This was a serious miscalculation, which ministers were to repeat time and time again.

First, resistance was not confined to Boston or even to New England. Moreover, the move overlooked an obvious legal difficulty. In the colonies, as in Britain, troops could be sent to support civil authority only at the request of the local magistrates, and they could use force only with the specific consent of those magistrates. No Massachusetts justice was about to make such a request or to authorise violent action. Sentries were placed on the Neck, the narrow isthmus connecting the town to the mainland, but smugglers simply walked past them. Worse, soldiers were allowed to supplement their wages with casual employment when off-duty, and at a time of depression and unemployment they accepted low wages at the expense of local labourers and craftsmen. In short, the occupation was provocative without being effective. Violence broke out.

In January 1770, a mob, secure in their knowledge of the law, threatened a detachment guarding the customs house. Snowballs were hurled, the crowd moved closer, muskets were beaten down with clubs. A volley was fired and the crowd dispersed. The troops had acted in self-defence, but Paul Revere, a printer, produced a broadside depicting the incident as unprovoked military aggression, labelling it the 'Boston Massacre' – a propaganda victory for the radicals.

The 'Massacre' came just before the news that parliament had repealed all the Townshend duties except that on tea. The tea tax, however, was widely resented as a symbol of parliament's claim to the right to tax, and smuggling continued apace. When in 1771 the revenue cutter *Gaspée* was boarded and burnt by Rhode Islanders, a commission of investigation could find no witnesses at all. In Britain, however, the North ministry was determined to give no further ground. Though they recognised the resentments of the New Englanders, they believed that many Americans were loyal and only needed to be liberated from the violent and tyrannical radical minority. The scene was set for a bloody collision.

The Coercive Acts

The trigger was the Tea Act of 1773, intended primarily to bail out a cash-strapped East India Company, but perhaps also to ensure that the tea duty was paid. In America, large-scale tea smugglers were under real threat and the radicals were alarmed by the constitutional implications: if the tea could be landed, Parliament would have re-established its right to tax colonial trade. The Sons of Liberty, now styling themselves 'Patriots', organised resistance in the major ports. In Charleston the tea was landed but not allowed to leave the wharf. In Philadelphia and New York, it could not even be landed. But in Boston there occurred the most spectacular protest of all.

Here the 'Sons' were able to prevent the tea from being landed, but the governor responded by refusing to let the three East Indiamen depart until the duty was paid. The impasse was resolved by a gang of masked men, symbolically dressed as Indians, who boarded the ships by night and threw the tea into the harbour. Once again, Boston was wrongly seen as the epicentre of radical violence: consequently, the government delivered its response too narrowly and in insufficient strength.

The famed 'Boston Tea Party' provoked a series of statutes designed to punish Massachusetts, and Boston in particular, and were to be withdrawn only when the ruined tea had been paid for. The Boston Port Act closed the customs house, effectively ending all legitimate traffic through that port. The Massachusetts Government Act suspended the colony's charter and put an end to assembly meetings. Town meetings were forbidden unless the governor asked for one. Officials and soldiers were protected against prosecution before biased juries by the Administration of Justice Act, which allowed them to be tried in another colony or in Britain. Finally, a new Quartering Act allowed the governor to house troops in empty buildings if no other suitable building was provided, in essence repeating the Act of 1765. Gage was appointed governor, effectively placing Massachusetts under military government, if not under military law. The Quebec Act, which gave Canada the coveted territories north-west of the Ohio, protected the right of French Catholics and failed to establish an elected assembly, was just as intolerable as the rest of these 'Intolerable Acts'.

Once again ministers had misunderstood the range and depth of American discontents. Their actions could be, and were, represented as a design to bring all thirteen colonies under a military absolutism – and once again they provoked disparate provinces into concerted action. Every colony but Georgia sent elected delegates to a Continental Congress which met in Philadelphia in October. Patrick Henry and Samuel Adams wanted an immediate declaration of independence, which would have been an effective declaration of war. The mood of the majority was, however, more cautious. The Congress finally resolved on a non-importation agreement against British goods, to be extended to West Indian products should the islands join the protest, until Parliament should repeal the coercive legislation. The boycott was ratified by all the participating colonies except the New York assembly, but there was no possibility that the North ministry would back down. By the spring, the Massachusetts and other New England militias were gathering arms and stores and drilling for war.

22

The Global War of American Independence, 1775-1783

What's in a name? One consequence of the war which began as an internal colonial skirmish in April 1775 was the independence of the United States of America in 1783, a fact reflected in descriptive names such as the Revolutionary War and the American War of Independence. Such labels also reflect the preoccupation of many historians, on both sides of the Atlantic, with the American theatre, which Americans tend to see ending with the surrender at Yorktown in 1781. This approach overlooks the fact that this was another a global war between contending empires which went on until 1783, by which time the conflict outside America had turned in Britain's favour. While this chapter discusses the war in America, it must be seen in the context of struggles in the Caribbean, India, the Mediterranean and the home waters of the British Isles. We can test the proposition that the global war was the decisive factor by asking two subsidiary questions: if open Bourbon intervention from 1778-79 was crucial to American insurgent victory, why was Britain unable to win a decisive victory before that date? And if Bourbon intervention was critical to the outcome of the war, why did it take so long (1778-1783) for Britain to be defeated? Then we might ask a third question: why wasn't the defeat worse than it actually was?

Logistics and elusive victory 1775-1777
The first question has been answered in numerous ways, often invoking incompetence and confusion on the British side and the heroism and tenacity of a people in arms on the other. The noble leadership of George Washington has been contrasted with that of a muddleheaded tyrant, George III, lazy and corrupt ministers, and ineffective military leadership in the field. At a lower level, the inherent guerrilla skills of rebel militia have been contrasted with the inflexible tactics of British regulars clad in absurdly visible red coats. Though such caricatures

The Global War of American Independence, 1775-1783

may linger in the public imagination, no serious historian would now subscribe to them.

More complex and convincing explanations would include the government's persistent assumptions about the revolt. The south was supposed to be fundamentally loyal. In fact, loyalists were strongest in New York, New Jersey and Pennsylvania, but they needed military support before they could come into the open. The area to be reconquered was huge and the British army never controlled quite enough territory for long enough to supply its daily needs from local sources. Food, wine, beer, clothing, tentage, cooking pots, candles, writing paper and ink, even firewood had to be shipped in across three thousand miles of ocean. Most of the war materials required by the rebels, on the other hand, with the notable exception of gunpowder, were available from within North America. That fact, and the sheer length and complexity of the coastline, made an effective blockade impossible. There was no alternative to a war of reconquest, and that meant relying on transatlantic shipping that was always vulnerable to French interdiction. The spectre of Bourbon intervention was effective long before it actually occurred

Lexington and Concord

Gage knew that he had too few troops to risk offensive action, but he was under orders to do something. Rather than risk his whole command he sent about 620 men under Lieutenant Colonel Francis Smith to seize and destroy the military stores known to be accumulating at the inland town of Concord. The movement on the night of 18-19 April 1775 was supposed to be secret but it was betrayed long before the troops reached the village of Lexington at dawn on the 19th. There, seventy or so tired and ragged militia men were drawn up on the village green. Samuel Adams, it has been suggested, knew perfectly well that these men could not withstand regulars. He really wanted American martyrs to galvanise the rebel cause. And he got them.

Summoned to stand aside, the militia began to move towards a wall on the British right, where the light infantry were to surround and disarm them. The incident might have passed without bloodshed had not a few rebels fired from behind the wall. The light infantry responded, several militia were shot down and the British column pressed on to Concord. There they destroyed some artillery, ammunition and flour and began to retire towards Boston. At once they were engaged by militia shooting from behind trees, fences, buildings and walls. Flanking parties fought back, but in peacetime the light infantry's training to deal with such tactics had been sadly neglected. Only the arrival of a relief column from Boston saved Smith's men from annihilation. The rebellion had won a minor battlefield success and a powerful propaganda victory.

The revolt spread throughout the thirteen colonies, and Boston was closely besieged. Ticonderoga, dilapidated and under-garrisoned, was surprised by New England militia, thus furnishing siege artillery for the makeshift 'Continental Army' of which George Washington became commander-in-chief. A winter invasion of Canada captured Montreal and besieged Quebec before being expelled in the spring of 1776. Everywhere governors fled, loyalists were intimidated, and the British scrambled to find local allies. In Virginia, after months of hesitation, and having been driven to take refuge in a British warship, Dunmore offered freedom for all slaves who would fight against the rebellion. Native Americans were divided. The Catawbas and the western Iroquois favoured the rebels, while the Mohawks and many other tribes decided that a British victory would better serve their interests. Others, including the older Cherokee leaders, chose neutrality, but it was the pro-war party that at first became very powerful.

Boston besieged

Reinforcements were sent to Boston and to Canada, and in May three Major Generals – William Howe, Henry Clinton and John Burgoyne – arrived to support Gage. A plan to seize Dorchester Heights was pre-empted by the American occupation of Breed's Hill on the other side of the harbour, a position from which they were able to fire into the town. Immediate action was essential and at 2 p.m. on 17 June, under the cover of a naval bombardment, Howe led a landing below Breed's Hill.

The narrowness of the ground frustrated a text-book outflanking manoeuvre and successive frontal assaults were repulsed before the rebel redoubt was taken. The battle, misleadingly named after neighbouring Bunker Hill, showed just how formidable colonial troops could be when fighting from behind breastworks, and that any British attempt to break out of Boston would be accompanied by unacceptable losses. It raised American morale and for the British raised the question of how long Boston could be held, and whether it should be abandoned in favour of New York. In August Gage asked for permission to move, only to find himself superseded by Howe. Howe received London's consent to an evacuation in October, too late in the season to be acted upon. Howe remained penned inside Boston throughout the winter of 1775-1776, but in February 1776 the guns from Ticonderoga finally reached Washington's army. By early March they were on Dorchester Heights, where the Americans were now too strongly entrenched to be dislodged without unacceptable losses. With American round shot striking ships and town, Howe had no alternative but immediate evacuation. Amid scenes of deliberate destruction and lawless plunder, troops and refugee loyalists were crammed into ships and by mid-March they were at sea en route to Halifax, where Howe hoped to reorganise and resupply his men before a descent upon New York.

The Global War of American Independence, 1775-1783

French involvement and a new strategy

The Second Continental Congress was not deterred by the Canadian fiasco. In March 1776, encouraged by Breed's Hill and by the defeat of the North Carolina Tories at Moore's Creek Bridge, it sent a Connecticut delegate, Silas Deane, to France, posing as a merchant buying Indian trade goods, but in fact to obtain artillery, muskets, ammunition, bayonets, tents and uniforms. His contact in Paris, Dr Edward Bancroft, was turned by a British agent so that by the summer the ministry knew that foreign Minister, comte de Vergennes was considering armed intervention and that Deane was handing out American commissions to numerous French courtiers.[15]

Lord George Germain, now Secretary of State for Colonies, pondered a new strategy for 1776. He accepted that Boston should be abandoned and that New York, with its central position, fine harbour and access to the Hudson was a much better proposition. Howe was therefore instructed to seize New York, whence reinforcements, equipment and supplies would proceed from Britain, while the force already in Canada under Guy Carleton would strike towards the Hudson by way of Lake Champlain. In this way New England would be severed from the rest of the colonies and overwhelmed in a pincer movement. However, Germain set the reinforcements under Major General Lord Cornwallis a double task. On the way they should rendezvous with Henry Clinton off Cape Fear and then, with Clinton in command, liberate the supposedly numerous Carolina loyalists beginning with North Carolina, before moving on to New York. Once again, that fatal ministerial misconception was to frustrate operations on the ground.

At the same time negotiation would not be abandoned: William Howe and his elder brother Vice Admiral Lord Richard Howe were named as commissioners empowered to persuade the rebels to submit. This was far from wishful thinking. In July 1776 the Second Continental Congress voted for independence but by a narrow margin and after considerable agonising by many delegates. Emotional ties and the clear economic benefits of remaining within the empire still had their appeal. It has been estimated that no more than a third of colonists actually approved of separation, perhaps a quarter remained actively loyal, and the remainder were undecided. Although the men at Philadelphia could not have known these proportions for certain, they must have been aware that support for their cause was very doubtful. A series of severe military defeats accompanied by a British olive branch might yet have swung the majority Congressmen back to reconciliation.

The New York campaign 1776

William Howe's caution in 1776 was forced upon him by logistics, the sensible wish to avoid another Bunker Hill, the knowledge that his trained regulars were precious assets not to be squandered lightly, and that – with numbers so heavily against him – moral ascendency must be established and maintained. Moreover, even a minor check might bring France in on the rebel side. Therefore, he must have adequate numbers of troops and adequate supplies to sustain them. Transatlantic logistics proved the stumbling block: some supplies did not arrive until May and the reinforcements had not appeared when he felt obliged to set sail for New York in June.

On 2 July he seized Staten Island and although Washington had dispersed his forces to cover as many landing points as possible, Howe was not about to sacrifice his precious regulars by a premature opposed amphibious landing. Howe waited on Staten Island for most of the summer, first for the reinforcements under Clinton and Cornwallis which had been so unfortunately diverted southwards, and then for the food, tents and cooking pots and other equipment essential to a successful offensive. At the very moment that a bold offensive might have ended the war, the British army was immobilised.

Clinton had reached Cape Fear as early as 12 March, but too late to save the North Carolina loyalists who had been defeated at Moore's Creek Bridge the previous month. His reinforcements under Lord Cornwallis appeared only in April, by which time any prospect of advancing into the back country was impracticable. Instead of sailing at once for New York, Clinton and Cornwallis made a protracted but futile attempt on Charleston in South Carolina before turning north. They did not reach Howe until July, by which time much of the campaigning season had been lost. His supplies, including his vital cooking pots, did not arrive until August. Howe and his brother employed the time in appearing to offer a negotiated settlement, on terms which they probably expected to be unacceptable but which kept the Americans in play until he was ready to move.

When Howe did move, he acted with determination, skill and flexibility. Landing on Long Island he easily outflanked Washington's position on Brooklyn Heights and forced him back into a small entrenched beachhead against the East River. The Americans were in some confusion and their defences far from perfect, but Howe, remembering Breed's Hill, refused to attack the American trenches frontally, enabling Washington to escape by water under cover of night.

Howe had then to plan an assault on Manhattan Island. That could not be done without running boats through the narrow strait at the southern end of Long Island, past the rebel batteries, and that was not possible until favourable tides coincided with a moonless night. This imposed another delay, often but wrongly attributed to a preference for negotiation over action, although once again the Howes used the time to put out feelers. When he did attack, his landing again turned the rebel flank and forced a hurried retreat. The next rebel position to fall was New York City itself. Further north at Haarlem Heights, Howe once again preferred manoeuvre to headlong attack, forcing Washington into a hurried retreat to White Plains. Here Washington made a stand, only to be turned and forced yet again into retreat. Cornwallis pursued him across New Jersey to the Delaware River.

At no point did Howe seek to trap Washington and annihilate his army: that Napoleonic conception was not available to the British commander, and he could not afford to take heavy losses among his precious regulars. His strategy was to drive the enemy from pillar to post, harrying him until his army fell to pieces. He very nearly succeeded in 1776: but for the lateness of the season he might have ended the war. Then at Christmas came a severe reminder of the need for caution and the danger of over-extending the outnumbered British army. In a daring raid across the Delaware, Washington overwhelmed Hessian garrisons at Trenton and Princeton and obliged Howe to pull his exposed New Jersey detachments back to the borders of New York.

Meanwhile, Carleton had every reason to be as cautious as Howe. At Lake Champlain, faced by an American flotilla led by Benedict Arnold, he halted to construct a formidable squadron, including a three-masted ship carried overland in pieces and reassembled on the lake shore. In October, Carleton's ships destroyed Arnold's flotilla and the Americans abandoned Crown Point. The season was well advanced, however, and Carleton did not feel strong enough to subdue Ticonderoga in the time left to him. By returning to the head of the lake he gave the Americans a much-needed respite, but he had avoided commitment to a winter in an isolated and vulnerable position, the lake frozen behind him.

As it was, a campaign had to be planned for 1777. Unfortunately for Howe, his flamboyant subordinate Burgoyne went home on leave and put his own plan to Germain. Germain and the King were impressed, perhaps because he seemed more adventurous than Carleton. This plan, which perpetuated the old misconception that New England was the heart of the trouble, required the army in Canada to march via Lake Champlain to the Hudson, this supposedly cutting off New England from the other colonies and so bringing about the demise of the rebellion. This would be supported by an Indian and loyalist force under Brigadier General Barry St. Leger, advancing from Lake Ontario via Lake Oneida to the Mohawk and so to Albany. How such a march would isolate New England or tempt Washington into open battle was unclear.

In any case, no-one – not Howe, nor Clinton, nor Germain, and certainly not Burgoyne – imagined that it would encounter severe resistance. Having first considered pushing north to meet Burgoyne near Albany, Howe concluded that it would be strategically pointless. A threat to Philadelphia would not only force Washington to accept battle and finally expose his army to destruction, but it would also prevent the Continental Army from moving against Burgoyne. The question was now how Philadelphia was to be approached, overland or by sea?

In June, Howe probed into New Jersey, hoping to lure the American commander from his fortifications at Morristown, and once almost trapped him by feigning retreat, but Washington's slipperiness and constant harassment by the New Jersey militia convinced him that an overland advance was impossible. Instead, he determined to attack Philadelphia by sea, but precious time had been lost. It was late July before the bulk of his army was embarked and sailing southward, unable to respond if Burgoyne needed substantial assistance.

The Philadelphia Campaign 1777

When Howe's convoy reached the Delaware the rebel defences looked too strong to be attacked directly, so the ships sailed round through the Chesapeake, to land on 25 August at Head of Elk, just a few miles from the original planned beachhead. Even then, his cautious advance on Philadelphia was very slow. Nevertheless, Washington fell into the trap and on 17 September tried to save the city by holding the line of Brandywine Creek – and almost lost the war in a day. While the main force pinned him down at the crucial ford, Cornwallis circled around his right wing and the rebel line collapsed. Fleeing in chaos down a single narrow road, the rebels should have been easy prey for Howe's two regiments of dragoons: but darkness was falling and two months at sea had so debilitated their horses that an annihilating pursuit was impossible. That did not check the American rout. Congress fled Philadelphia in panic and on 20 September an American rear-guard was surprised and destroyed in a night attack at Paoli. Within days, Cornwallis led the triumphant British army into the rebel capital.

Howe's arrival delighted local loyalists – but the Continental Army lived to fight another day. Washington planned to keep Howe pinned down in Philadelphia while the two American forts on the Delaware hampered British seaborne communications; and on 4 October he launched a surprise counter-offensive at Germantown. That attack was repulsed with heavy losses, but exactly two weeks later disaster struck Burgoyne on the Hudson.

Saratoga

Burgoyne had marched from Lake Champlain towards the Hudson, easily capturing Fort Ticonderoga. Preferring momentum to security, he then allowed his advance guard's pursuit of the garrison to drag him away from his preferred line of advance down Lake George, to a difficult road across country. It took him three weeks to reach the Hudson, having had to rebuild forty destroyed bridges and removes countless felled trees and

The Global War of American Independence, 1775-1783

other obstacles left by the Americans. When he reached Fort Edward on the Hudson on 30 July he was so short of supplies that he had to authorise a raid into the Connecticut Valley. At Bennington the detachment was trapped by a vastly superior force of militia and a relief force was also destroyed.

At once, local people who had rallied to Burgoyne when he first arrived changed sides. Meanwhile St. Leger, despite a victory at Oriskany, was unable to take Fort Stanwix and had to retire to Oswego. While Burgoyne was being steadily weakened, the Americans grew stronger. The new American commander, Horatio Gates, now had some 7,000 Continentals and militia at his disposal. A cautious commander would now have decided to withdraw while the road to Canada was still open.

But in Burgoyne, the dashing cavalry commander, dramatist and gambler were ever uppermost. Certain that a bold advance would force the Americans back without a serious fight, he crossed to the west bank of the Hudson at Saratoga Springs on 13-14 September. At Freeman's Farm his attempt to turn Gates's position on Bemis Heights clashed with a blocking force under Benedict Arnold, winning the day but suffering serious losses. Even now, clinging to news that Clinton was advancing from New York, Burgoyne pressed on in the teeth of his subordinates' advice to retire. Not until 8 October, having suffered further heavy losses, did he begin to retreat, only to find that Gates had blocked his way. Still able to mount a strong defence, but unable to reach the Hudson, he offered to surrender on condition that his army could embark for Europe and take no further part in the war. Gates, unaware that Clinton's advance had stalled, was anxious to comply. On 17 October, the British army at Saratoga was taken into captivity.

A new strategy
Saratoga transformed the war. Worse for the British than the loss of 5,000 men or a dramatic boost to American morale – and far worse than the resignations of William Howe and Guy Carleton – was the French decision to openly support the rebellion. The old British nightmare of a junction between the Brest and Toulon fleets was revived, with every prospect that Spain would soon join in, and with no European ally to distract them. An early encounter with the Brest squadron off Ushant was indecisive. British naval strength must now be mustered in home waters to prevent invasion, which meant that the loss of a whole transatlantic convoy was possible. Moreover, this would now be a global war, with British resources stretched to breaking point with commitments from the Mediterranean to the Caribbean, West Africa and Asia. British strategy had to be urgently reviewed, but coherence was bedevilled by differences between Germain and Sandwich, and by the inability of North to impose decisions.[16]

The First British Empire

The most radical option, abandoning the rebellious colonies, was considered but rejected. By early March 1778, the ministry had decided to adopt a largely defensive posture in America in favour of a naval war, in which Halifax and New York would be key bases. To free troops for a West Indian offensive, Clinton, Howe's successor as commander-in-chief, was ordered to abandon Philadelphia, thus deserting the loyalists who had openly welcomed Howe and giving the rebels an even stronger sense that they were winning. Moreover, his army was divided: 5,000 men were detached for an amphibious assault on St Lucia, and 3,000 went to garrison the Floridas. In the north, Indians were to be encouraged to attack the northern and western frontiers, using arms and equipment funnelled through Quebec and Fort Niagara, theoretically allowing Clinton to further subdivide his army to assail the supposedly loyalist-heavy southern colonies. At the same time a commission led by Lord Carlisle was despatched to make peace with the Americans on any terms short of independence – and without informing Carlisle of the evacuation of Philadelphia. Congress would not now accept anything but full independence and the British were clearly not negotiating from strength. Clinton was furious and managed to delay these detachments until November, but he was unable to reverse them.[17]

Why then, did French intervention not bring about a rapid British defeat in America? The war went on until 1783, marked by vigorous British campaigning and frequent battlefield success in the face of worsening conditions. The answer seems to lie in the failure of the French to co-operate efficiently and persistently with the Americans. Like the British, the French placed a high value on the West Indies and none upon the conquest of Canada, which they had promised to Congress. Without any prospect of territorial gains in North America, they gave campaigning there a low priority, so that until 1781 French aid to Washington was sporadic at best. Despite very serious strategic errors of their own, the British were able to exploit this lack of co-ordination so effectively that by 1781 the Continental Army was on the verge of collapse.

A drawn battle with the Brest squadron off Ushant was followed by the escape of the Toulon squadron into the Atlantic. It was shadowed by two fast frigates, but the British were on the horns of a very uncomfortable dilemma. A premature pursuit in force might have left the Channel unprotected, yet a belated response risked the loss of New York or even the whole of Clinton's army. By the time it was clear that their fleet was heading for North America, and Admiral John Byron was sent in pursuit, the French had an unbeatable head start.[18]

Clinton was warned in time and retreated from Philadelphia overland rather than risking capture at sea, and repulsed Washington's attack on his rear-guard at Monmouth Court House on 28 June 1778. Meanwhile the French squadron arrived off New York, penning Lord Howe's

The Global War of American Independence, 1775-1783

outnumbered and undermanned squadron into the harbour, but instead of persisting with a tight blockade the French admiral D'Estaing moved north to the apparently softer target of Newport, captured by the British in December 1776. His attack was to be co-ordinated with that of 10,000 Continentals and militia, but before either could strike, Lord Howe appeared. A storm prevented a decisive engagement but D'Estaing, fearful that Howe would be further reinforced and worried about damage to his own ships, retired to Boston. An independent American attack from the land side was a failure and the demoralised militia melted away. The British were able to sustain Rhode Island until October 1779 when they voluntarily evacuated it.

The British followed up this success with devastating raids on New Jersey and New England, while their Indian allies were already harassing the frontier settlements. In July 1778 the Mohawk leader Joseph Brandt and Walter Butler, son of an Indian department official, led an expedition of Indians and loyalist rangers against the Wyoming Valley settlements. In November, Butler and a largely Iroquois force attacked the New York village of Cherry Valley. In both cases, unprepared and incautious militia garrisons were overwhelmed. Substantial American forces had to be diverted to attack and burn Shawnee and Mohawk towns, depriving them of food – but failed to break their will and ability to fight on. Fort Niagara itself was beyond the Americans' logistical reach, and as long as Niagara could sustain the Indians they would fight on. More might have been done, but Clinton, preoccupied with vain efforts to tempt Washington into open battle, was unable to exploit their success.

Southern success

Despite a rapid Spanish conquest of the Floridas, the southern strategy got off to a promising start. On 31 December, Savannah was seized and by summer 1779 the British forces had penetrated into South Carolina and briefly threatened Charleston. In September, D'Estaing appeared off Savannah and landed 5,000 troops to support a Continental army led by Benjamin Lincoln. The British defence, however, was stubborn and the siege dragged on. By October D'Estaing was ready to leave. He had always intended to return to the West Indies at the end of the hurricane season, and he was deeply worried about the condition of his ships and disease ravaging his crews. A last-chance combined assault was repulsed with hideous losses and on 18 October the siege broke up. Once again, the failure of Franco-American co-operation had saved the day for the British.

In December, Clinton led a seaborne descent upon South Carolina and in April 1780 he took Charleston before returning with the bulk of his army to New York. Cornwallis, left to complete the conquest, defeated a counter-invasion led by Gates at Camden, and for the first time the British began to make themselves self-supporting through the management of confiscated tidewater plantations. However, he could not suppress persistent back-country guerrilla resistance, his irregular loyalist militia behaved like 'banditti', and on 6 October rebel bands overwhelmed a loyalist column at King's Mountain. So bitter and persistent now was the civil war in South Carolina that he could see no solution but an invasion of the North Carolina back country, where there were still supposed to be many loyalists awaiting rescue, and whence the southern guerrillas received aid and comfort. It was a strategic error comparable to Burgoyne's – and worse, because the French navy had occupied Rhode Island, where it was joined by a substantial land force commanded by the Comte de Rochambeau.

The road to Yorktown[19]

Cornwallis struggled through North Carolina, far from seaborne support and in a country almost bare of provisions. Harassed by guerrillas, weakened by the loss of a major detachment at Cowpens and by a hard-won victory at Guilford Court House on 15 March, he retired to the coast at Wilmington. In April, once sure that the South Carolina garrison was holding its own, he struck out for Virginia. In May, his bedraggled and hungry army, barely 1,500 strong, joined the British force of about 5,500 operating out of Petersburg on a tributary of the James River. Now with a respectable force and expecting the Royal Navy to protect his back, he harassed and almost destroyed an American detachment led by the Comte de Lafayette. This agile offensive was brought to an end by a fatal order from the north: Cornwallis was to secure a winter base for the navy. He chose Yorktown, a short distance from Williamsburg, with deep water close inshore and situated on an apparently defensible peninsula protruding into Chesapeake Bay. In fact, Cornwallis had been ordered into a trap.

Washington, Rochambeau, the French squadron from Newport and Admiral De Grasse's fleet from the Caribbean were already converging upon Yorktown. Clinton, fearing that they were about to attack New York, hesitated and the new naval commander in chief, Admiral Thomas Graves, felt too weak to intervene. Only the arrival of Admiral Samuel Hood with ten of the line persuaded them to sail for the Chesapeake at the end of August. De Grasse was there first and an indecisive battle off the Virginia Capes failed to dislodge him. Graves returned to New York for repairs, and Clinton determined to risk New York by embarking 7,000 men for Yorktown, the boldest move of his career. The dockyards worked slowly, however, and he and Graves were unable to sail until 19 October.

They were too late: two days earlier, under heavy bombardment, having lost two bastions and unable to break out, Cornwallis had offered to surrender on terms. On the very day that the British relief expedition left New York, Cornwallis's men marched out of their fortifications and grounded their arms. It was the last turning point of the war.

The Global War of American Independence, 1775-1783

The scale of the American victory was not at first apparent. The French, anxious to resume Caribbean operations, refused to help Washington capture Charleston and Savannah. The main British army at New York was still intact and formidable, if dispirited, and many loyalists still believed the war could be won. It was a loss of nerve in London that finally decided the issue. Carleton arrived in New York to replace Clinton in May 1782, bearing orders to end offensive operations.

Yorktown came just in time for the rebels. Penniless, leading demoralised troops, unable to sustain his numbers, and disappointed with the French, Washington had known himself to be on the brink of defeat. Even after Cornwallis capitulated, Clinton could have taken the offensive and the Royal Navy still had the capacity to win back control of American waters. For London, however, Yorktown was the last straw in a long, bloody, expensive and apparently futile war. George III at last allowed North to resign and the new ministry led by Shelburne set about peace negotiations with both the Americans and France. In May 1782, Carleton arrived in New York to replace Clinton bearing orders to cease all offensive operations.

Elsewhere, the war took a brighter turn when the siege of Gibraltar collapsed, Rodney won back naval dominance in the Caribbean, and the near-bankrupt French government forced Spain to seek peace without recovering the Rock. The Treaty of Paris formally ended the war with the Americans, recognising the independence of the United States of America and handing over the north-western territories formally denied them, though at the price of letting down loyal Indian allies. The subsequent agreement with France, the Treaty of Versailles, cost her less than might have been expected.

23

Canada and Florida: Colonies of Conquest

The 1763 Proclamation created three new colonies, East and West Florida and Quebec. How should such conquered colonies with potentially hostile Catholic populations be managed? By wholesale removal, as in Nova Scotia in 1755 – and if so, how were the empty lands to be re-peopled? With a heavy military presence and a powerful governor? In both Canada and the Floridas these questions would be answered in different ways, and in the former in a manner that presaged a new kind of imperial relationship.

Quebec
Newly conquered Quebec presented a serious problem. Its 79,000 settlers could hardly be expelled like the Nova Scotia Cajuns of 1755 – the cost of that much smaller operation had been huge. Nor could they be expected to leave voluntarily and at once, like the few thousand Spaniards of West Florida. About 1,600 people departed, mainly officials, army officers and merchants, only 270 of whom were native Canadians. Those who remained were a disparate lot: rural *habitants* holding farms from seigneurs, Catholic clergy with the right to levy tithes. Most of the citizens of Quebec and Montreal, and to the west, around the Great Lakes and beyond the Proclamation Line – the boundary marked in the Appalachian Mountains prohibiting Anglo-American colonists from settling on lands acquired from the French – roamed the French of the 'interior'. Together they presented a permanent threat of subversion, collusion with disaffected Natives and a magnet for French attack in a future war. Its semi-feudal social structure was unlike that of any other British possession, and the population was overwhelmingly Roman Catholic.

London expected British settlers to flood in and force the French to assimilate through sheer force of numbers; but although British merchants and traders were drawn to the fur trade and English speakers bought up some of the seigneuries, the majority continued to be French-speaking and Catholic. It was soon very clear that although English criminal law could be tweaked to suit Canadian circumstances, English civil law could not. Under the prevailing Custom of Paris seigneurial landed property, guaranteed to its possessors in 1763, should be inherited by the eldest son and non-seigneurial property divided among the heir's brothers. In such cases, and in those concerning the sale and transfer of property, Catholics were allowed to serve as jurors.

James Murray, now the first governor of Quebec province, therefore set about constructing a form of governance acceptable to French Canadian seigneurs, *habitants* and priests while appeasing London's desire for Anglicisation and giving reassurance to the British incomers. He suppressed a minor revolt as gently as possible and in 1765 he attempted to establish an elected assembly. Representatives assembled in Quebec, but Murray was caught between his duty to apply the oath demanded by the second Test Act, designed to confine elective offices to Anglicans, and the deputies' Catholicism. Murray, who was fond of the French Canadians and despised profiteering in-comers, refused to have an assembly dominated by the British Protestant minority and the experiment failed. Canada continued to be ruled by the governor and his appointed executive council.

However, the British settlers' protests to London, backed by their account of a minor civil disturbance in Montreal in 1764, undermined the governor's authority and led to his recall in 1766. His successor, Colonel Guy Carleton, inherited Murray's dilemma. He, too, had little time for noisy British merchants wishing to run the colony on their own terms and in their own interests – particularly by replacing seigneurial land tenure with freehold – and focussed upon conciliating the French Canadians. In an unusual role for a colonial governor, he travelled to London to argue for the retention of the seigneurial system, recognition of the Roman Catholic Church (including its right to tithes), the removal of reference to Protestantism from the oath of allegiance, and the retention of a paid Canadian militia. He also insisted upon the retention of French civil law in place of English common law. The result was the 1774 Quebec Act, which also extended the colony's boundary to the Ohio and the Mississippi. Above all, it established a new principle: a colony could be British without being entirely English in language, culture, law or government. Thus, while the Act angered anti-Catholic New Englanders and middle colonies expansionists, it ensured that there would be no rebellion in settled Canada. It was a formidable achievement and Carleton, now promoted major general, returned to Quebec to make it work.

The test came the very next year with the outbreak of the War of American Independence. The moment that hostilities erupted in Massachusetts the Continental Congress sent two invading columns in the confident expectation that the oppressed settlers would rise up in support of liberty. Major General Schuyler and Brigadier General Richard Montgomery were to push up the Hudson-Lake Champlain corridor, while Colonel Benedict Arnold marched overland through the Maine wilderness against Quebec. Carleton, expecting a thrust from the direction of Ticonderoga, based himself at Montreal, knowing he had the backing of the seigneurs, the Catholic hierarchy and the Scots ex-soldiers settled along the St. Lawrence, though he was far less certain of the *habitants*.

The Schuyler expedition successfully reached the head of Lake Champlain and began to push towards British-held Fort St Johns on the upper reaches of the Richelieu River. Here, Schuyler's health collapsed and Montgomery, who took over command, was held up for six crucial weeks by a stubborn defence. He did not occupy a near-defenceless Montreal until 13 November. Winter was closing in, there was no sign of Canadian enthusiasm, his own troops began to desert in droves, and there was smallpox in the town. Carleton, disguised as an *habitant*, had already slipped downriver by boat to strengthen the defence of Quebec.

Arnold did indeed receive some support in the form of supplies from the *habitants* whose homes he passed en route. When his 650-odd exhausted and hungry men appeared on the Plains of Abraham and summoned Quebec to surrender, the senior British naval officer in the city despaired of both Canadians and British settlers. 'The King's forces are few,' he wrote to the Admiralty, 'the Canadians generally in the interest of the rebels, many of the merchants indifferent so they can secure their property.'[20] However, Arnold does not seem to have attracted recruits. He withdrew to Point aux Trembles, some twenty miles to the west, commenting significantly that he had no hard currency to offer the Canadians and that they did not trust paper. When Montgomery arrived from Montreal and took command, the expedition was a little better off for supplies and ammunition and possessed field pieces, but there was no grateful influx of Canadian volunteers. Carleton had meanwhile expelled all waverers from the city, so Quebec was held only by those determined to fight to a finish. Barricades were erected in the narrow streets of the Lower Town and the walls of the Upper Town were impervious to the rebels' few small cannon.

A deserter brought Carleton the invaders' plan of attack on the Lower Town of Quebec with two converging columns, and when the rebels attacked on 31 December he was ready. Under cover of a snowstorm the rebel columns forced some barricades before being fought to a halt in a confusing maze of streets. Arnold was wounded at the outset and Montgomery killed when his advance party walked into a blast of grapeshot. Carleton pursued the retreating rebels as far as Lake Champlain, where he began to build a flotilla to take control of the lake and threaten Crown Point. In 1776, a revolt by a handful of Nova Scotia militia attracted no Mi'kmac support and was quickly suppressed. The following year Canada became the base of Burgoyne's disastrous march to the Hudson, but the American invasion was never renewed. The attempt to 'liberate' Canada was over.

The Floridas

Florida was a different proposition. Almost all the Spanish settlers left in 1763, despite being offered the option of taking the oath of allegiance and remaining, largely because the Spanish government provided the means of departure. The entire population of St Augustine was evacuated to Cuba and eight Spanish ships carried 600 Spaniards and Catholic Indians to Vera Cruz in Mexico. All but a handful of French families abandoned Mobile, hitherto part of Louisiana. The problem now was to fill the void these emigrants left behind.

The territory stretched from the Mississippi to the east coast of the Florida peninsula. Too large to be administered as one colony, it was divided by the 1763 Proclamation into two provinces. The peninsula with its capital at St. Augustine became East Florida; while West Florida with its chief town at Pensacola took in the Gulf coast with its northern border, the official limit of white settlement, fixed at 31° north, moved the next year to 32° 28' to suit local topography. Though both provinces were supposed to have appointed executive councils and elected legislatures, tiny populations and the autocratic instincts of the first chief executives meant that power was generally in the hands of the governors.[21]

Both governments took pains to attract settlers, publishing colourful accounts of the fertile land and endless opportunities in their respective provinces –omitting the extreme heat and humidity, the wet, cold winters, the tornadoes, insects and barren sandy stretches. The Proclamation imposed a headright system designed to create a self-sufficient society of small farmers, and although quit rents were prescribed, they were in practice deferred for periods of years.

Success was modest at best. While the fertile lands of West Florida adjacent to the Mississippi attracted migrants from the north, the Caribbean and even from Britain and Europe, there were never enough; while in East Florida only two settlements were established in the colony's first decade. Indentured labourers were hard to find and harder to keep. While the first governor of East Florida, James Grant, had no moral reservations about employing slave labour, a solution encouraged by the headright system, which awarded each settler additional acres for every dependent he brought with him, for some years there was little work for slaves to do. For years, Grant tapped South Carolinian expertise in indigo planting and established an estate of his own as a demonstration farm. By 1770, about eight plantations were in operation and the first cargo of indigo was exported, while subsidies were encouraging experiments with other crops. By the mid-1770s even West Florida had no more than 5,000 residents, many of them slaves, and more than half of those around Natchez on the Mississippi were slaves. East Florida by 1771 could boast only 288 whites but 900 black slaves, who were beginning to produce exportable quantities of indigo.[22]

These tiny settlements lived in the shadow of a regional Amerindian population of about 30,000. The Creeks, living to the north-east of the Floridas, numbered 15,000 people and could raise about 3,000 warriors. The Choctaws, to the north and west of West Florida, could field about 2,000 and the Chickasaws a few hundred. All resented the transfer of forts and territory from Bourbons to British and initial skirmishes soon revealed that their suspicions had only been partly mollified by the 1763 Congress of Augusta. The British diplomatically chose not to occupy Fort Toulouse in the Creek country and attempts to garrison Fort Chartres on the Mississippi were physically resisted by Choctaws and their allies until well into 1764. Clashes with encroaching settlers were common.

Yet the very existence of the colonies depended upon keeping the peace, as ministers in London well understood – particularly in the aftermath of Pontiac's War. When in 1766 West Florida's first governor, George Johnstone, demanded 2,500 troops for a retaliatory war against the Creeks he was quickly dismissed. Negotiation and conciliation, together with the importance of the deerskin trade to both sides, proved more fruitful and the Floridas did not experience a major Indian war.[23]

When war did come it was through the great American rebellion and even that was at first but a distant rumble of thunder. The struggling, tough and often illiterate Floridians were impervious to the propaganda of either side and there was little resistance even to the Stamp Act.[24] Theirs were bread and butter issues, not abstract constitutional reasonings, and they were content to remain loyal to an empire that seemed to be their only protection. For the rebels, on the other hand, Florida was no Canada, having little doctrinal, strategic or even economic significance. While a Florida campaign to open the Mississippi was mooted and discussed in Congress, there were simply too many other more urgent calls on its resources. In East Florida, in 1777 and 1778 St. Augustine repelled two rebel raids. When the war first arrived in West Florida in February 1778 it was in the form of a river-borne raid led by a renegade alcoholic debt-ridden Natchez entrepreneur named James Willing.

Willing's raid was little more than an essay in unrestrained plunder, destruction and revenge on personal enemies in the Natchez region, but it exposed the feebleness of British defences on the lower Mississippi. It was April before a handful of troops from Pensacola, a rag-tag makeshift militia and a few naval vessels were able to retake ground and threaten to cut off his return. More sinister than Willing's mosquito-bite was the refuge he was allowed in Spanish New Orleans. Though Willing himself

Canada and Florida: Colonies of Conquest

was taken as he attempted to sail north, most of his men were allowed safe passage overland through Spanish Louisiana. With France already at war and with Spain likely to follow, the North ministry moved to reinforce both provinces: 3,200 British regulars, German mercenaries and loyalists arrived in the autumn. Then in April 1779, Spain finally went to war as an ally of France, and the Floridas were in the front line.

Bernardo de Galvez, the governor at New Orleans, assembled some troops and picked off the British Mississippi settlements before taking Mobile in 1780. In the spring, with command of the sea and a besieging force eventually swollen to 7,000 men, he attacked Pensacola and after facing a dogged defence, accepted its surrender in May 1781. East Florida remained for the time being in British hands, but after Yorktown its fate was a foregone conclusion. The peace of 1783 transferred both Floridas permanently to Spain.

The attempt to replicate the re-peopling of Nova Scotia in the Floridas had failed as much for environmental as military reasons. With the very limited exception of the fertile lands of the Mississippi, few were prepared to brave the steaming, swampy, alligator-ridden and hurricane-prone lands of the Gulf coast, and fewer still were attracted by the peninsula. With so few settlers, and those so tepid in their loyalism, and with British forces occupied elsewhere, the two southern colonies were all but indefensible. The great Canadian experiment, on the other hand, had been a modest success. If French Canadians were not yet inspired to fight for their late conquerors, they at least felt that they were better off under British than under American rule. The first inklings of a Canadian identity within the empire were in evidence.

24

West Indies, 1763-1783

The triumphant end to the Seven Years' War did not eliminate the essential fragility of Britain's Caribbean empire. The return of Guadeloupe, Martinique and Havana restored the long-term Bourbon threat, as well as French dominance in the sugar trade. Even the expected expansion in the Ceded Islands could not compensate for the larger area and fertility of the French and Spanish colonies. Foreign sugars continued to out-compete the British product in European markets, making planters ever more dependent upon their protected home market. The consequent threat to British shipping and prosperity combined with the ever-present danger of slave revolts – Tacky's revolt left a long shadow – to produce an atmosphere of insecurity and fear: but that very fear may have spared the Caribbean isles from revolution in the darkest days the War of American Independence.

Although West Indian disputes with the metropole tended to be over executive powers rather than over the rights of the colonial assemblies, this was not entirely the case. In Jamaica and the Leewards the Sugar Act provoked protests because it reduced the duty on foreign molasses, rather than raising it to prohibitive levels. West Indians rioted against the Stamp Act and, as we shall see, West Indian assemblies vehemently insisted that only they could regulate the slave trade and the conditions of slavery within the islands. Like the mainland colonists, Caribbean planters refused to pay for the garrisons and ships required to defend them, but unlike the Americans, they knew they needed protection and often demanded it.

The Free Ports Act of 1766, which opened four free ports in Jamaica and two in Dominica, was intended to tap into legitimate trade with the Spanish Indies and to compete with French free ports at Martinique, Guadeloupe, St Luca and St. Domingue, as well as the Dutch entrepot at St Eustatius, and to draw foreign sugars into the British system. However, the Act provided substantial protection for Jamaican products, including sugar, ginger and tobacco – none of these could be exported in foreign vessels – while tobacco and naval stores were off limits in both islands. Once again, far from being weakened, the mercantilist principles of the Navigation System had adjusted to changing realities.

Slave unrest and Maroon allies
Jamaicans knew they had been lucky to survive Tacky's revolt – the militia had performed indifferently and only the presence of two battle-hardened British regiments and the active loyalty of the Maroons had averted catastrophe. Governor Moore did his best to ensuring that the island was not denuded of regulars and introduced a strict regulation of slave discipline and movement, but the most important security measure was continued friendly relations with the Maroons.

Short-lived revolts in St Mary's in November 1765 and in Westmoreland in 1766 underlined the need for constant vigilance; still more alarming was a conspiracy uncovered in 1776, meant to take advantage of the removal of troops to mainland north America, and involving perhaps 8,000 slaves across the island. In 1781, they tracked down and killed the troublesome escapee, bandit and guerrilla called 'Three Fingered Jack'. Co-operation with the Maroons was clearly vital to the colony's survival.[25] Yet at the same time relations between them and many planters and the colonial government were becoming increasingly strained.

White, red, black, Catholic
Britain's Caribbean conquests, like the Floridas and Quebec, raised the question of how to govern colonies inhabited by foreigners and Catholics. As in Quebec, the British government moved with caution. Following its surrender in 1762, Grenada was allowed to keep its existing forms of governance, French property there was protected, and freedom of worship guaranteed. All British subjects were allowed to buy land and, despite initial objections, French planters found they could easily sell their properties to incomers. However, the Proclamation of October 1763 erected the Ceded Islands – Grenada, Tobago, Dominica, St Vincent and the Grenadines – into a province of the empire, alongside the two Floridas and Quebec.

The new colony was modelled on the constitutions of existing royal American possessions: a governor and council to exercise executive powers, an elected assembly to make local laws and a system of British courts. These were established to encourage British settlers to buy property there, although French settlers were to be encouraged to stay. Adult male white freeholders, French or British, were given the vote subject only to an oath of allegiance. Catholics were initially excluded from election to the twenty-one-strong assembly, but in 1768 the Privy Council ruled that the

Test Acts and penal laws did not apply outside the British Isles. The result was to import into the Ceded Islands the confessional tensions already evident on the American mainland, and to promote – as in Quebec – Protestant incomers' resentment of French Catholics.[26]

Further tension arose from the problem of the existing Carib inhabitants. In the first five years St Vincent attracted land purchasers from all over the Caribbean and even from mainland North America. The few hundred 'Red' or 'Yellow' Caribs, so-called to distinguish them from the largely Africanised 'Black' Caribs, and now mostly confined to Grenada and St Vincent, had a sympathetic audience in Britain. Like mainland Amerindians, they were seen as creatures of nature, 'noble savages' who deserved protection from encroaching Europeans, while to planters, they were still cruel raiders and cannibals. The Black Caribs arose from the arrival of escaped African slaves. Whether by adoption, violence or a mixture of the two, the 'Black' mulatto Caribs came to dominate the eastern or windward side of St Vincent. They had never recognised French sovereignty and did not accept the transfer of their part of the island to the British. Numerous – there were about 5,000 of them in 1763 – and well-armed, they were in a position to resist settler intrusion.

The Black Carib War
In the first few years, over 12,000 acres on the leeward coast were alienated to incoming settlers from all over the Caribbean and even from mainland North America, intending to cultivate sugar cane. This side of the island was rugged and mountainous; the French had found it more suited to coffee and cocoa and sugar growing was possible only in the narrow valleys, so there was soon clamour for the flat and fertile lands on the windward side. While in London there was a presumption that the Caribs should be persuaded to sell their lands, there was a pronounced reluctance to sanction settler demands for expropriation and forcible removal of a free people. Not until 1768 did the government sanction surveys of the eastern half of the island, and then only with the provision of alternative lands for the displaced.

The commissioners, who seem to have absorbed the settler viewpoint, insisted that roads were necessary for the surveys, a demand which the Black Caribs wisely refused. In 1769 a surveying party sent in under military escort was blockaded and forced to withdraw, a humiliation which only fuelled settler demands for the expulsion of the entire population. The following year a consortium of unknown speculators, fronted by Richard Burke, Collector of Customs for Grenada and brother to the politician Edmund Burke, purchased from the Red Caribs a strip of largely uncultivable land on the north-west coast, abutting Black Carib claims and arguably overlapping them. The deal bypassed the government auction system with its fixed reserve price of £1 an acre, so that instead of a potential £1,200 or more, the Caribs were paid a paltry £250. Despite Burke's claims that the land was sold freely, this illegal and arguably fraudulent transaction ignored Black Carib claims altogether.

When speculators began to erect buildings on their new land, the Black Caribs made their feelings known by twice razing the works and in October 1771, led by Joseph Chatoyer, rejected the commissioners' attempt to negotiate a specific land cession. The commissioners now persuaded a reluctant London that British authority and honour were at stake. Troops from mainland North America and other Caribbean islands were ordered to St Vincent but with the caveat that could only be used with restraint and as a very last resort. The government's preferred outcome would have been Black Carib submission, a specific area set aside for their subsistence, and future co-existence.

When war did break out in September 1772 the British forces made slow progress through rugged and unfamiliar terrain, suffering heavy casualties in action and from disease. In February 1773 the Black Caribs were able to negotiate a settlement on reasonably favourable terms. They gave up most of their lands in eastern St Vincent and promised allegiance to the British Crown in return for guaranteed possession of a region in the north, including the areas claimed by Richard Burke's associates. Their autonomy was otherwise unaffected and once the troops had been withdrawn local officials had no means to make them abandon the region they had been obliged to yield. On balance, the First Carib War could be described as ending in a Carib victory.

The Bourbon counter-offensive
French entry into the War of American Independence brought the conflict to the Caribbean, where the British position was strategically difficult. By far the most valuable island was Jamaica, but as it lay a thousand miles to windward of the Leewards and Windwards, the main British naval force under Rear Admiral Barrington was based at English Harbour, Antigua. The best that could be done to protect Jamaica from surprise was to post a smaller squadron there under Sir Peter Parker. Between the Leewards and Windwards lay Dominica, encircled by a pattern of French islands, and a hundred miles to the east lay Barbados. Because the military garrisons were necessarily scattered and weak, the British islands' security depended wholly upon dominance of the sea – and that dominance was uncertain.

The first British move to secure that ascendancy was to attack St Lucia, conveniently to windward of Martinique, using the 5,000 troops taken from Clinton's army in mainland North America, under Major General James Grant. It was an enterprise of considerable risk. D'Estaing was at sea – indeed, he was already heading south for the Caribbean – and the naval escort commanded by Commodore William Hotham was small. Hotham was lucky to escape capture (one straggling transport was lost) and to successfully rendezvous with Barrington at Barbados. But while the Royal Navy was so preoccupied, a local French force seized Dominica, thus severing the fragile Windwards-Leewards link. The vulnerability of the scattered West Indian islands was exposed.

The assault on St Lucia also came close to failure. Barrington's warships covered the bay of Le Grand Cul de Sac while Grant's ten regiments landed and took possession. On 15 December, D'Estaing twice failed to break into the bay, after which he landed his 9,000 troops to turn the British position. Though this force had an overwhelming numerical advantage, it was thrice repulsed by three British battalions dug in across the neck of the Vigie Peninsula. With a third of his soldiers lost, and with the British naval defences looking stronger than ever, D'Estaing gave up and sailed for Savannah. When Byron belatedly arrived from North America, the British had, by a whisker, secured temporary superiority in the Caribbean.[27]

That dominance was, however, to be short-lived. In the early months of 1779, both sides sent reinforcements to the Caribbean, but the British faced more commitments and uncertainties. By June the French had a slight numerical superiority and Byron was distracted by the need to cover a homeward-bound convoy gathering at St Kitts. Immediately, a tiny French force descended upon St Vincent, where they had already been invited by Chatoyer; and the weak garrison, in fear of a new Black Carib war, surrendered at once. In July, D'Estaing followed up by taking Grenada. Then Byron appeared, with twenty-one ships of the line and a convoy of troop transports. Believing he was facing only part of the French fleet and seeing the enemy slowly emerging from the harbour and at an apparently fatal disadvantage, he signalled 'General Chase' to get his ships into action before the enemy could form line. His headlong attack was heavily defeated, his damaged ships were lucky to avoid capture, and only the French admiral's slowness saved the convoy. Grenada was lost and dominance in the Caribbean had now definitely passed to France.[28]

It was now impossible either to return six of Grant's battalions to the North American mainland, as had been planned, or to keep a mobile reserve at St Lucia ready to be transported to any danger point by sea. Dispersal across all the islands, on the other hand, would have left him weak everywhere. He chose to garrison only the most important British possessions, namely St Lucia, St Kitts and Antigua. Contradictory reports of D'Estaing's movements and the direction of possible Spanish offensives added to the confusion. At home, the demands of other theatres – America, Minorca and Gibraltar, home defence – delayed the scraping together of a relief force. Not until late January 1780 were ten battalions dispatched for the Caribbean and it was February when Grant's successor General Vaughan reached Barbados and set about re-concentrating the scattered garrisons at St Lucia. Plans for an offensive were checked by the arrival of French reinforcements, but the subsequent appearance of Rodney, coming from Gibraltar with four of the line, brought the British up to nearly equal strength. On 17 April 1780, Rodney surprised Admiral Guichen off Martinique.[29]

Rodney was a tactical innovator and his plan was to concentrate against the rear of the enemy fleet. But although he had explained his intention to his captains, he had not converted them to his doctrine and an ambiguous signal allowed them to engage all along the French line. The result was like that at Ushant: much smoke and noise, not a single French ship sunk or captured, and Rodney furious with his captains and with subordinate Admirals Parker and Rowley. Rodney then positioned himself between Guichen and Martinique, hoping to force a fresh action, but the French commander, under orders to avoid tactical risks, took refuge at Guadeloupe. In May, Guichen set out to take St Lucia; again Rodney intercepted him, and after two indecisive actions the French retreated to Martinique. The British had won a kind of moral victory, and Rodney had now imposed greater co-ordination and discipline on his captains, but overall naval superiority in the Caribbean was still in doubt.

Then a Spanish fleet arrived in the Caribbean, evaded Rodney's attempt to intercept it, and joined Guichen. The Bourbons now had twenty-seven effective ships of the line while Rodney could only muster eighteen. Immediate disaster was averted only because the Spanish admiral insisted on moving on to Cuba with a French escort. But this move posed another problem: although the threat of an unstoppable combined assault on the Leewards was temporarily removed, the forces at Havana posed a serious threat to Jamaica.[30]

Jamaica's garrison was reinforced and a premature expedition to Nicaragua was withdrawn, but the reinforcements were already sickly, the rains had arrived, and the Jamaican assembly, which had been demanding more troops, refused to pay for barracks and there were no billets to be had. By the end of December 1780, barely 1,500 men were fit for duty and Sir Peter Parker's naval squadron was too weak to defend the island against a major assault, let alone fulfil his other major responsibility, the protection of West Florida.

Meanwhile the war had been widened by the outbreak of war with the Dutch Republic. St Eustatius, a free port since 1753, for so long a thorn in the side of the British Navigation System, ill-defended, and now notoriously a route by which the American rebels obtained British gunpower and other supplies, became a prime target. When Rodney arrived in February 1781, the governor immediately surrendered, along with 130 merchantmen. The value of these ships and their cargoes, along with those of a convoy of thirty vessels and goods still on shore, promised prize money worth about £3 million, far too tempting a prospect for the grasping Rodney. Instead of delegating the task of identification and evaluation, he and the military commander undertook the task themselves, making little distinction between contraband and private property and treating Jewish residents, among them American loyalists, with particular contempt. Their avarice immobilised the main British West Indies fleet and leaving only a weak squadron under newly arrived Rear Admiral Sir Samuel Hood to cover Martinique.

Consequently, French reinforcements from France under De Grasse had only to fight a long-range skirmish with Hood before reaching Martinique. Within days the French commander was off to attack British islands. St Lucia held out but Tobago surrendered two days before Rodney's belated arrival on 4 June. Ageing and ailing, Rodney counted De Grasse's fleet, saw it outnumbered him twenty-six against twenty-four, and retired without risking a general action. He then sailed for home leaving his subordinate Hood with only fourteen of the line, while De Grasse sailed for Yorktown. At first, Hood failed to realise that De Grasse had taken his whole fleet northwards, and it was early August before he set out from Antigua to join Graves at New York.[31] Cornwallis's army was doomed in large part by strategic errors committed in the Caribbean.

By early 1782 Hood was back in the Caribbean with only twenty-two effective sail of the line against De Grasse with thirty, and with the islands' military garrisons so reduced by illness that their only defence was the fleet. De Grasse intended to attack Jamaica as soon as his stores arrived in convoy from France, and meanwhile he was able to attack the Leewards almost at will. Foul winds prevented a landing on Barbados, but on 11 January he attacked St Kitts. The garrison on Brimstone Hill put up a determined resistance, allowing Hood to sail to the rescue. When the enemy put to sea to meet him, he slipped into their old position, anchoring behind some shallow water so they could not engage him line to line. Next day he repulsed two French attacks before the French on shore, using captured artillery, pounded Brimstone Hill into surrender. Hood's position between the French fleet and shore batteries was now untenable: judging De Grasse too strong to be attacked, he slipped away quietly and undetected in the night.

After that, the possible targets were too numerous to be protected by an understrength fleet. De Grasse followed up by securing the surrenders of Nevis, Montserrat, Demerara and Essequibo. In all these places the colonial councils, not caring to risk dispossession, were all too willing to make terms. In March the convoy of stores and troops reached Martinique, and by 7 April De Grasse had sailed to join the Spanish fleet at San Domingo for the delayed attack on Jamaica. The fragility of the British West Indian empire had never been so rudely exposed.

West Indies, 1763-1783

The Battle of Les Saintes

By now, however, Rodney had returned with reinforcements, giving his command a slight superiority in numbers and firepower provided he could prevent a convergence of the two Bourbon fleets. Sailing from St Lucia in pursuit he quickly caught up with De Grasse, who was hampered by his cumbersome transports and storeships. After some skirmishing in the passage between Grenada and a group of Islets called Les Saintes, De Grasse was weakened by a series of collisions among his own ships and one ship had to be taken in tow by a frigate. On the morning of 11 April, Rodney, with thirty-six of the line against thirty, lured him into action by threatening the straggler.

The fleets engaged on opposite tacks, exchanging broadsides as they passed. The British, firing faster than the French and doing severe damage with their carronades, had the French penned against the coast of Dominica, and were in sight of a tactical victory. A curious incident then occurred at the height of the battle. The clouds of blinding smoke and a shift in the wind disrupted both lines of battle – or was it only the French line? – allowing the British to pierce the French line in three places. Whether it was a long-considered plan of Rodney's (or of someone else), or the result of chance and individual initiative, is still debated,[32] but the outcome was dramatic. De Grasse and his flagship were encircled and taken with four other sail of the line and his surviving ships fled. Rodney ordered a 'General Chase' but called off the pursuit (much to Hood's dismay) as darkness approached. Hood caught two of the fugitives a week later, bringing the bag to seven, and though the French fleet was still largely intact, the British had recovered local naval supremacy. And the very high number of French troops aboard ship meant that as many as 5,000 prisoners were taken.

The psychological results of the Battle of Les Saintes were greater than its immediate tactical or strategic outcomes. Combined with the failure of the last great assault on Gibraltar, it demoralised a French government already nearing the end of its financial resources. In Britain the new Rockingham ministry recalled Rodney and dispatched his successor Admiral Pigot just a day before the news of the Battle of the Saints arrived. The victorious admiral would now come home a popular hero and the government, having failed to recall Pigot, desperately tried to retrieve its error by giving Rodney a peerage. And well they might. Thanks to Rodney, most of Britain's Caribbean empire was saved and after the war the Pitt administration could set about protecting it – much to the chagrin of the planters – against commercial penetration by the newly independent United States.

25

India:
From Clive to Hastings

By 1763 the East India Company was a major territorial power, but this was very far from dominance. The Mughal emperor was still its legal overlord and the Company was expected to support him against his enemies and to govern their domains according to Islamic law and orders from Delhi. The Marathas, having recovered from their devastating defeat at the hands of the Afghans at Panipat in 1761, were also contenders for supreme power. In addition, Haidar Ali of Mysore had emerged as a serious military threat, building up not only armies but a fleet he hoped would one day wrest control of the sea from the British.[33] In 1767 he combined with the Nizam to attack the Carnatic, overrunning several fortified places, and achieving strategic surprise by continuing his campaign through the monsoon season. Though repulsed in 1768, by 1769 his horsemen were at the gates of Fort St George, forcing the Madras Council into a humiliating peace.[34]

Resistance, trade, corruption and war
This First Anglo-Mysore War was a significant straw in the military wind. Whereas hitherto superior co-ordination of infantry, cavalry and artillery had given the British spectacular victories over much larger Indian armies, their rivals were catching up, and the technological gap, never very wide, was narrowing fast. Even within Bengal, where the danger of serious insurrection was slight, persistent *dacoity* (banditry) and resistance to revenue demands severely limited the depth of British control.

Resistance within Bengal was strengthened by very high revenue demands and by the drain of wealth to Britain. Contemporary Indian commentators remarked upon the contrast between the relative prosperity resulting from the Company's earlier imports of bullion and the decline caused by its present exports of revenues. Monopolies of various commodities, including rice, were in the hands of Company servants and their Indian collaborators, who found export markets more profitable than feeding Bengal. The outward flow of wealth undermined commerce and drove up unemployment, ruining families at every social level. As noble households fell on hard times, their servants and craftsmen were turned out with little hope of finding other work. The dissolution of the Nawab's army made over 50,000 cavalrymen jobless, not to mention huge numbers of camp followers. In 1769-1771 all these factors exacerbated the effects of a great drought to produce a catastrophic famine, which killed perhaps a third of Bengal's population.

An alternative analysis suggests that economic development was stimulated from the growth of trade across the subcontinent and by the monetisation of business between successor states. It may well be that Indian bankers who serviced British financial needs, and the merchants who supplied their goods, did well out of the change of regime, but that probably did not outweigh the damage done by predatory administrators and the export of wealth.

Private trade, corruption and warfare were also damaging to the Company's profits. Moreover, although British demand for Indian cottons and silk rose sharply in the years after Buxar, the income from them usually failed to meet the Company's military outlay, civil administration and pensions. The sheer scale of these commitments was an important factor, but competition from independent traders and the private enterprise of the Company's own servants made a bad situation worse. Clive returned to Bengal in 1765 with a mandate to curb corruption and indiscipline. He made some progress: accepting bribes in return for political favours was forbidden, while the Company discouraged private trade by making its commercial servants shareholders in a subsidiary company.[35]

By 1773 the Company's financial problems, combined with disturbing stories of corruption and plunder, moved the British government to interfere. Three pieces of legislation followed. An Act to allow the company to borrow £400.000 was accompanied by a Regulating Act designed to bring the Company under some kind of centralised political control while not interfering with its commercial operations. A governor-general was appointed to oversee all three presidencies in India, but he was to be restrained by a council which would decide policy by majority vote. Company servants were forbidden to engage in private trade or to take bribes. A new supreme court was created to sit at Calcutta and British judges were appointed to administer British law there, apparently in an attempt to protect Indians against the machinations of their rulers and business partners. The Tea Act, which had such momentous consequences in North America, was meant to ease the Company's financial problems by allowing it to sell tea direct to British colonies instead of auctioning it in London.

The governor-general, however, had no means of enforcing his will over the Madras and Bombay presidencies, and the Act failed to separate administrative functions from commercial ones. Moreover, he was restrained from decisive action by a council of four (in addition to himself) whose decisions were to be by majority vote. Clearly and understandably designed to prevent one man from wielding excessive power, it turned out to be a ball and chain around the leg of the first chief executive, Warren Hastings. This was all the more unfortunate when the borders of Bengal, Bombay and Madras seemed particularly vulnerable.

In 1774 Hastings was sufficiently worried about Bengal's western frontier to be drawn into a war between Oudh and the Rohillas, an Afghan people who had established their own state, Rohilkhand, adjacent to Oudh. They were not a menace in themselves. But in the early 1770s they were attacked by the Marathas, who had taken Delhi in 1770 and were now advancing down the Ganges. Rohilkand appealed to Shah Shuja of Oudh. Oudh and EIC troops forced the Marathas to withdraw, but the Rohillas then refused to pay Shuja his promised forty lakhs of rupees. Shuja, a key ally, had to be supported. Oudh and Company troops took the offensive, the Rohilla forces were defeated, and most of Rohilkhand was annexed to Oudh. The reduced state entered a subsidiary treaty with the Company. Unfortunately for Hastings, his support for Oudh could be represented as hiring out Company troops to a vicious ally – and this was the line taken by most of his newly arrived councillors.

Phillip Francis and an obstructive council

Of the new councillors, only Richard Barwell was a Company man and had experience of India – he proved also to be the only one sympathetic to Hastings. The others – General Sir John Clavering, commander in chief and Hastings' deputy, Colonel Monson and Philip Francis – were all Crown appointees sent out from Britain. All three were convinced that the East India Company's rule was wrong in principle and criminal in practice. On the voyage out, Francis – clever, vindictive and ambitious – persuaded his two military colleagues to oppose the governor-general's measures as a matter of policy.

Upon landing, having complained about being given only a seventeen-gun salute and Hastings' failure to dress formally for their welcoming luncheon, they proceeded to attack him over the Rohilla War. Ignoring his strategic aims, they accused him of hiring out Company troops as mercenaries and thereby colluding in atrocities committed by Oudh troops. Francis went on to attack Hastings' 1772 revenue settlement. The governor-general was not to be rid of them until 1777, when Clavering and Monson were dead and Hastings could use his casting vote to break the deadlock between Barwell and Francis. The following year Hastings shot and seriously wounded Francis in a duel, whereupon Francis left India and Hastings could assume near-despotic power.

Meanwhile, as government in Bengal came to a standstill, Madras and Bombay became less and less amenable to direction from Calcutta. The resulting administrative paralysis opened opportunities for the renascent Marathas, the Nizam of Hyderabad and the rising power of Mysore – all of which coveted the British client state of the Carnatic.

The First Maratha War

Hastings, like all before and after him, had good reason to fear that the French would once again fish in troubled waters. The French East India Company had been wound up, but its military and naval assets were now in the hands of the French crown and a potentially a major threat to British India. Pondicherry was partly refortified and had a 1,000-man garrison, which could be supported from Mauritius, and the governor there was keen to ally with Indian powers seeking a counter-weight to the British.[36] News of the outbreak of war in 1778 reached India in sixty-eight days, giving the governor-general an initial advantage, but that was offset by his undefined authority over Bombay and Madras, by the vast distances between the three British power-centres, and by the rash behaviour of the Presidency of Bombay.

Bombay, well behind Bengal, Madras and China in terms of commerce, ran at a loss and had to be supported from Calcutta to the tune of £250,000 a year. It was worth keeping for the sake of its shipyards, the only ones the Company possessed on the west coast, but it needed access to more revenue-yielding territories. In pursuit of such concessions the Bombay Council intervened in a Maratha succession dispute, with inadequate resources and abysmal political intelligence.

It chose the already-declining cause of Ragunath Rao, the incumbent Peshwa of Poona, whose predecessor had been murdered in 1773, and who was opposed by Nana Farnavis, chief minister and protector of the dead man's infant son. In exchange for land in Gujarat, islands near Bombay and 150,000 rupees a month Bombay would provide 2,500 troops. When in March 1775 their client was defeated and fled to Surat, they extracted from him even better terms and committed more troops of their own and from Madras. The war in Gujarat now swung in Ragunath Rao's favour, but when Hastings heard of Bombay's commitment, he called a halt. A hastily negotiated Treaty of Purandar in March 1776 gave the British all the concessions they had asked for in return for deserting Ragunath Rao, who was to be bought off with a pension. Bombay's ambitions, however, were not to be checked by a treaty imposed from Bengal: in 1777 the Bombay army again marched on Poona.

It moved, however, with snail-like speed. Not until late in 1778 did 3,000 troops, encumbered with an artillery and supply train hauled by

19,000 bullocks, set out for Poona. Climbing at less than a mile a day through the Western Ghats, they gave their Maratha opponents plenty of time to resupply their forts and to prepare a large and mobile army of their own. When in February 1779 the British force descended at last into open country it was quickly surrounded by hordes of swift horsemen it could neither engage nor escape.

At Wadgaon the British capitulated, giving up all the concessions gained since 1773 and handing over Ragunath Rao to his foes. A force that came overland from Bengal arrived too late to do more than take refuge in Surat. Bombay was now exposed to a counter-offensive by the victorious Nana Farnavis. At first, Nana carried all before him and Bombay seemed about to be overrun. Only a forced march by Hastings's army from Bengal saved Bombay, but the power of the Marathas remained intact and threatening.

The Second Mysore War 1780-1784
Worse was to come. Nana Farnavis, having concluded that it was time for Indian powers to combine against the British, offered peace and a military alliance to Mysore. Hyderabad also joined and a little time afterwards a substantial consignment of French arms reached Mysore. In July 1780, Haider Ali launched 100,000 cavalry, European-style infantry and ample artillery against a wholly unprepared Madras. Rapidly overrunning the Carnatic, he prevented the junction of two British forces and annihilated the smaller one – some 3,800 strong – at Pollilur. The other army, led by Munro of Buxar fame, retired ignominiously to Madras. By year's end Haider had 7,000 prisoners. Yet, instead of storming Madras itself, he kept his army intact by resorting to harassing cavalry raids against British posts and communications. Had Haider pressed his advantage, the whole British foothold in southern India could have been eliminated.

Suffren versus Hughes 1783-1784
Haider's hesitation allowed Hastings to send reinforcements by sea and, by opening negotiations, to separate Haider from his allies. The safe arrival of those reinforcements was only possible because the French failed to achieve naval control of the Bay of Bengal. The inactivity of their Mauritius squadron allowed a small Royal Navy fleet under Vice Admiral Sir Edward Hughes to support an amphibious assault on the Dutch base at Negapatam, while Haider's own navy was annihilated off Mangalore. Early in 1782, Hughes seized the finest harbour in the entire region, the Dutch port of Trincomalee in Ceylon (now Sri Lanka). Only then did a reinforced French fleet led by Admiral Suffren appear on the Coromandel coast. In four fiercely contested battles Suffren failed to make his numerical advantage decisive, but he did retake Trincomalee. He was able to refit at Aceh, using material supplied the Dutch, while Hughes

had to retire to Bombay. Here was a moment of the greatest danger: with both Trincomalee and Aceh in their possession, the French could have built up an unshakeable naval dominance along the Coromandel coast. Meanwhile, reinforcements for both sides arrived from Europe. Everything would turn on the outcome of the next battle.[37]

The fleets met again off Cuddalore on 26 June 1783. For once Hughes had a numerical advantage – eighteen of the line against fifteen – and all his vessels were copper-bottomed and therefore faster. Even so, the result was indecisive and before the fleets could meet again, news of the peace treaties intervened.

With some justice, Hughes blamed his lack of success on the scarcity of Indian dockyards – the nearest proper one was Bombay – and more specifically upon the dearth elsewhere of masts, spars, cordage and canvas. If a shortage of naval stores had been damaging to British Atlantic operations, it came close to being fatal in India. The point was not lost on ministers, who began to think in terms of a new Pacific naval base positioned to take advantage of the flax and pines reported by James Cook.

The combination of Haider's restraint, allied disunity and Hughes's determination allowed Hastings time in which to detach Mysore's allies. By the 1782 Treaty of Salbai, a key Maratha leader, Mahadji Scindia, changed sides and joined the British,[38] but the very survival of Madras and Bombay was still in the balance. Haider's sudden death in 1782 and Tipu Sultan's succession to the throne of Mysore did nothing to improve the British position. The 1784 Treaty of Mangalore – essentially a mutual restoration of conquests – reflected the military stalemate, but the very fact that British negotiators had to travel to Mangalore, a recent Mysore conquest, underlined the company's weakness and vulnerability. The question of who was to dominate in southern India would not be resolved for another two decades.

26

West Africa, 1763-1783

The Senegambia experiment
What was to be done with Britain's new conquests in Senegambia? Forces pulled in different directions. Free traders argued that Fort Louis and Gorée should be opened up to independent traders outside the jurisdiction of the Company. Ministers and many MPs were thinking of supporting trade with political authority by making Senegambia a royal colony, a view endorsed by Dartmouth, Halifax and Townshend. In their view, completely free trade would only weaken British commerce in Africa, leave the forts unmaintained, and the terms of trade at the mercy of African governments. Townshend attributed the decline in the gum trade to excessive competition from free traders. Moreover, with a general tightening in imperial control over colonies in the air, it seemed irrational to allow too much independence to private traders. The result was a flawed compromise: Senegambia would become a Crown Colony, outside the orbit of the Company, but excluding Gorée, which had been handed back to France.

In fact, Senegambia never redressed the power imbalance between British and African. The colony never consisted of more than a few forts precariously linked by vulnerable waterways and by the sea. The two key forts, St James at the Gambia mouth and St Louis on the Senegal, were poorly constructed and British authority extended no more than a cannon shot from their walls. In 1768 the Fort St James garrison barely repelled a sustained African attack involving the use of scaling ladders. At Fort St Louis the *habitants*, resident African and creole traders and their families, were very independently minded – they insisted on making their own treaty with the incoming British in 1758 – and it quickly became clear that the island could not be held without their support.

Only a handful of Europeans lived among 1,405 free Africans, 223 people of mixed race, and 3,108 slaves. Though the colony was given a chief justice to administer English law, the traditional legal system tended to prevail. Disease quickly made the upriver forts, already mostly abandoned by the French, untenable and the river trade remained firmly in the hands of Africans. The idea of rendering the African polities dependent by making vast quantities of trade goods available at the forts never came to fruition.

Worse, the state of the gum trade was due not to the independent traders but to internal warfare, as Trarza and its neighbour Brakna fought for its control. Gold became scarce on the coast as the belligerents invested in cavalry horses brough in across the Sahara. African rulers consistently resisted British attempts to monopolise trade through agreement and, in at least one case, used an embargo to remind the British of their vulnerability. And without control of the hinterland, London's and O'Hara's plans to establish sugar, rice, cotton and indigo plantations in Senegambia could not be undertaken: the planters' property would simply become hostage to the wills of the African rulers. Even though in 1771 O'Hara began to build a plantation settlement at Podor on the Senegal, its prospects were far from assured. Brakna hostility, arising out of his military support for Trarza expansion, forced him to be give it up. By 1775 his attempts to encourage small independent farms by agreement with local rulers had clearly failed. Even competition from other European powers could not be excluded as a great deal of business went through Gorée, and Trarza dealt with French traders at uncontrolled points on the 'Gum Coast'.[39]

Unsurprisingly, the American War of Independence extinguished the colony of Senegambia. In 1779 a French expedition took St Louis – where the garrison quickly surrendered for fear of a *habitant* revolt – and captured Fort James, while American privateers sacked the private establishment on Bence Island. The Treaty of Versailles in 1783 saw Fort James returned but the mirage of British dominance in the region had finally evaporated.

The Asante problem on the Gold Coast
In the Gold Coast, war broke out when Fante and Asante attacked Wassu and its Akim allies in 1765. The Akim army was destroyed but the Wassu forces escaped and remained formidable. The Asante-Fante alliance soon broke down, leaving the Asante army too short of supplies, in the midst of too many enemies, and too far from home to embark upon a Fante war. The Asantehene therefore retired and the Fante moved quickly to make allies of their late foes. For the British factors, the prospect of an Asante-Fante war was alarming. On one hand, the opening of the closed trade paths would be welcome; but having Asante – regarded not unreasonably as a centralised despotism – in control of the whole coast would place the British and Dutch in a very precarious position.

It would be much safer to keep the seaboard under the control of the looser Fante confederation, whose members might be played off against each other. The Dutch, though at first outwardly co-operative, leaned to the view that it would be easier to deal with one polity instead of many, so were not fundamentally averse to an Asante conquest, and even tried to prevent the Fante-Wassaw alliance. On this divergence of views, Anglo-Dutch mediation foundered.

From 1766 to 1768 Cape Coast Castle was pulled further and further into open support for the Fantes, having even to consider the unpalatable possibility of having to give them military assistance. The crisis eased when the Fantes returned some hostages they had held since 1765, but when war again threatened in 1772 the Cape Coast British had to make their position even clearer. They would not take part in a general Asante-Fante conflict, but if defeated, the Fantes could find refuge under the guns of the British forts. That decision, made without consulting the Dutch, did not go down well with the Company of Merchants controlling committee in London, nor with the Board of Trade. Nevertheless, the realities of Gold Coast politics had made support for the Fantes inevitable.[40]

Further east at Whydah, in the shadow of triumphant Dahomey, trade was in decline. From 1764, British captains avoided the place partly because repeated raids by Whydah exiles and others made it unsafe. More importantly, skilful French competition and ample Portuguese imports of Brazilian tobacco made commerce unprofitable; in that year, some ships out of Liverpool made disastrous losses because the prices of slaves were now too high. Nor was Dahomey able to procure enough slaves, at first because it relied wholly on purchase from regions to the north, and then because its own raiding parties were repeatedly and humiliatingly defeated. No English ship was seen at Whydah until 1770 and from 1775 the War of American Independence so increased the threat from privateers, and so drove up insurance premiums, that owners laid up ships rather than take such risks.[41] Between 1765 and 1785 the British embarked only 36,635 slaves in the Bight of Benin (and delivered only 29,573 to the West Indies and the American colonies). By contrast, although all slave traffic was hit by the War of Independence, the Bight of Biafra produced 238,966, making it the single most important source of African captives.

In the five years 1761-1765 British ships carried away only 36,371 slaves from West Africa, but this rose dramatically to 215,915 in the five years before the War of Independence. Over the same periods vessels belonging to the American colonies took another 44,906. The British empire was now the biggest trafficker in human misery, having overtaken the Portuguese and acquired over twice their share. Though wartime British slave shipments were down to 85,408, and although much of the

West Africa, 1763-1783

lost business was taken over by the previously far less significant Danes, there was a sharp post-war recovery. Numbers climbed again to 125,313 between 1780 and 1785.[42] The upturn came just as the abolitionist movement was acquiring a strong voice in Parliament and in the public mind. If Britain were to outlaw her slave trade, she would have to do so as it reached the height of its prosperity: to commit, as one historian has put it, 'econocide'. (See chapter 29.)

27

Reconnaissance: British Penetration of the Pacific

At least two-thirds of the coasts of the Australian land mass were known by the end of the seventeenth century. There is some cartographical evidence that Portuguese navigators may have surveyed the outline of the southern and south-eastern coasts in the early sixteenth century. The Spanish explorer Torres passed through the strait that bears his name in the early seventeenth century, and Dutch captains, too eagerly seeking westing before turning north to Batavia, ran into the west coast. In 1627 a pair of Dutch ships even explored into the Great Australian Bight. Many mariners, like the company of the *Batavia* in 1629, were wrecked; others, like Dirk Hartog, who landed at Shark Bay and nailed up a copper plate in token of formal possession, were more fortunate. Abel Tasman, exploring from Batavia, sailed right round the continent, touching only at Van Diemen's Land and New Zealand (which he took for a peninsula), and found nothing inviting. Although the English pirate William Dampier recorded unattractive impressions of the north-west coast and its indigenous people, very little of this activity was English.

The east or Pacific coast, however, was an enigma. How far to the west of Tasman's track did it lie? Was New Zealand the tip of an even larger southern continent? What lay in the vast uncharted areas of the western Pacific? The Spanish, whose Acapulco-Manila galleons made regular crossings on a fixed track, were not interested in further exploration. Well into the eighteenth century, British interest in the Pacific was essentially predatory and focussed upon the Spanish colonies of the South American seaboard. Even Anson's circumnavigation was essentially a raid of the traditional kind.

However, the late eighteenth century saw an upsurge in Pacific exploration. The lure of the north-west passage, which might be explored from its western end, was still alive. The southern whale fishery and the opportunities for sealing and fur-trading on the American north-west coast were alluring, and the supposed southern continent – *Terra Australis Incognita* – might have crucial strategic significance in the continuing colonial rivalry with France. A series of naval expeditions were sent to investigate.

Byron, Wallis and Carteret 1764-1768

In 1764 Captain John Byron set out on what proved to be the fastest circumnavigation to date. Following the usual route from Magellan Strait to the East Indies, he failed to penetrate the south-west Pacific but somehow became convinced that there was a large land mass to the south of his track. In 1767 two vessels under Samuel Wallis and Philip Carteret were despatched to investigate Byron's report. Wallis, following the usual track across the Pacific, sighted what appeared to be mountains some sixty miles to the south. Carteret, steering further south, further reduced the possible limits of *Terra Australis*, paradoxically raising hopes of finding it. The circumnavigation of the French navigator Bougainville (1766-1769) underlined the urgency of pursuing this objective.

When Wallis and Carteret returned to Britain in 1768 the Admiralty was already fitting out yet another expedition, this time with a scientific brief at the behest of the Royal Society, to observe the transit of Venus from the Pacific. One location Wallis had reported, Tahiti, became the intended site of the observation and the aim of the voyage was extended: to reach down into 40° south and cruise westward to New Zealand in search of the southern continent. The personnel was swelled with the appointment of an official astronomer and two prominent botanists, the young Englishman Joseph Banks and the Swedish academic David Solander, together with their assistants, servants and artists to record their discoveries. The naval commander was the relatively unknown Lieutenant James Cook.

James Cook's first voyage

Cook was an extraordinary man. Born in 1728, son of a Yorkshire day labourer, he was briefly apprenticed to a draper and grocer before going to sea in Newcastle colliers bound for London. After nine years in this trade he had risen to mate and was offered the command of one of his employer's ships. Instead, he opted to begin his career again, as a humble able seaman in HMS *Eagle*. On the face of it this was a wild gamble, but Cook's established credentials as a navigator and pilot proved invaluable. Within weeks he was raised to master's mate – apprentice navigating officer – and in June 1757 passed the first examination for the warrant rank of sailing master. In 1759 he attracted notice for his part in charting of the navigable channel of the St. Lawrence and the anchorage opposite Quebec, and later for five summers spent carefully charting the coasts of Newfoundland.

His command, HM Bark *Endeavour* was a four-year-old Whitby collier, purchased specifically for this expedition. With a shallow draft for charting shallow coastal waters, a flat bottom to make her easy to beach for repairs, and a capacious hold for supplies, she possessed all the key qualities for a long voyage of exploration. Officially, Cook was to observe the transit of Venus from Tahiti, but his sealed orders, to be opened only after the astronomical work was done, required him probe far into the South Pacific to locate the southern continent.

After observing the transit, he turned due south, taking *Endeavour* down to 40° south before turning west for Van Diemen's New Zealand, still thought to be a peninsula. He sailed right round the North and South Islands, proving that they were not attached a southern land mass, and took formal possession, having misrepresented the process to a handful of bewildered Maoris. His orders to seek dialogue and consent were easier obey in the abstract than in the multi-cultural, multi-linguistic Pacific, where the sudden and unwelcome appearance of intruders worked against instant amity.

Cook then pressed further west in search of the east coast of New Holland. At first light on 20 April 1770, he sighted its south-eastern tip, Cape Hicks, and turned to follow the coastline northward, from time to time sighting columns of smoke indicating habitation, sometimes a fire glowing in the night, and at least once, tiny black figures moving on a distant beach. He pressed northward until at Stingray Bay he at last found a safe, capacious harbour, together with several streams which seemed to promise an assured supply of water for a settlement.

At this moment there was a significant encounter. A party of aborigines fled as the ship's boats approached, except for two men who stood their ground. Cook, Banks and Tupia, their Tahitian interpreter, tried to speak with them but to no avail. Some thrown nails and beads seemed to arouse interest and Cook misinterpreted the aborigines' gestures as an invitation to land. As his boat pulled in they brandished spears, making clear that the newcomers were unwelcome. Cook fired a warning shot between them, at which they fell back to their bundles of spears higher up the beach and one of them hurled a large stone. Cook fired again, wounding a man with bird shot, who then held up a small wooden shield for protection. As the boat touched, they hurled spears, a third shot was fired and both men made off into the trees, leaving the shield behind to be picked up as a trophy. Thereafter the Aborigines' reactions varied between flight, curiosity, shouted demands that the intruders be gone, and attempted violence. Naked, apparently sleeping in the open or in primitive 'huts', armed with 'darts' and 'wooden swords' (boomerangs), speaking a language not even Tupia could fathom, and evading all Cook's earnest attempts to communicate, as imperial collaborators they were sadly unpromising. For the aborigines, this terrifying irruption from beyond the known world was simply inexplicable. On 6 May, after nine days in the anchorage he had renamed Botany Bay, Cook took *Endeavour* to sea.[43]

Some twenty miles northward of Botany Bay, and from some three miles to seaward, he sighted what appeared to be a small but safe harbour he named Port Jackson, and next day he sighted and named Broken Bay. Although smoke was seen often enough – at least some of which must have been spreading news of the frightening apparitions from the spirit world – there was no further contact with the aborigines until June, and then only as the aftermath of a near fatal accident. Just before 11pm on 12 June, feeling her way between the shoals of the Great Barrier Reef, apparently in at least seventeen fathoms and between two casts of the lead, Endeavour struck the coral and stuck fast. With all useable pumps at work, stores and guns were jettisoned while repeated efforts to warp her off came to nothing. Work went on until, almost twenty-four hours after she had struck, she rose on the incoming tide and the water threatened to overwhelm the pumps. Cook was forced to choose between warping her off by main force, which might tear her right open, or see her founder on the reef. He chose to take the risk: hauling in on cables to two anchors, her people warped her off the coral, the pumps began to gain over the leak and a prepared sail was hauled under the ship to fother the hole, making a temporary repair. On Monday 18 June, after days edging her landward through a maze of shoals, Cook got her into the mouth of a river he later called Endeavour and beached her for repairs.[44]

The damage was severe and extensive. There were several holes and her sheathing had been torn, requiring her hold to be emptied and long careful repairs undertaken, so Cook was unable to sail until 4 August. Here the aborigines, the Kuku-yalanji, were at first as wary as the Cadigal and Gwiyagal around Botany Bay, but gradually they became more confident and curious. Cook saw at once that these were a different kind of people. They were shorter and darker than the Botany Bay people, their men's noses pierced for bone inserts, and did not have the missing front tooth noted by Dampier in the north-west. Though naked and armed with fishing spears and boomerangs, their material culture seemed a little more advanced than further south: at least one canoe was a sturdy wooden outrigger. Eventually a dozen indigenes were bold enough to come on board *Endeavour* as guests, but they made their expectations of their strange visitors very clear. Finding that the crew had been killing large numbers of green turtles – their clan's turtles, and one of their main foods in the coming wet season – they claimed their share and tried to throw two of the carcases overboard. When the sailors stopped them, they tried to seize everything they could lay hands on. Frustrated again, they went ashore and suddenly set fire to the grass around the ship's two landing parties. The first fire was extinguished but the second spread fiercely through the woods. Even then Cook did not give up: he and others

The First British Empire

followed the blacks into the bush and an uneasy reconciliation followed – but there was no possibility of mutual understanding. Cook sailed next day, his ship safe and seaworthy, but he was no nearer to persuading the aborigines to accept the sovereignty of George III.[45]

Thereafter *Endeavour* had to keep away from the coast and its reefs, a necessity emphasised by another near shipwreck when wind and current pushed her to within yards of a line of breakers. Though natives were sometimes sighted, there was no further opportunity for contact.

Cook had had orders to claim newly found lands with the consent of any peoples he should find there. But these natives of New South Wales seemed too primitive and without any visible form of government with which he could negotiate. As far as he could see, this was *terra nullius*, uninhabited land, which could be taken into the possession of George III without further ado. When he reached aptly-named Possession Island he formally claimed the whole coast for George III.

For two centuries that perception underlay the whole process of European colonisation, legal title and land management, and for a long time historians took it for granted. To take an extreme example, Sir Stephen Roberts's *History of Australian Land Settlement*, first published in 1924 and reissued as late as 1968, does not mention aboriginal possession once.[46] But of course, it was not *terra nullius* at all.

Cook's second and third voyages

Cook undertook his second great voyage (1771-1773) in not one but two specially purchased and refitted North Sea colliers, HMS *Resolution* and HMS *Adventure*, as insurance against shipwreck. His mission was to try to locate *Terra Australis* southwards of New Zealand and New Holland and incidentally to compare the performances of chronometers by Larcum Kendall and John Arnold. He trice penetrated the Antarctic Circle, eventually reaching 71° 10′ S without finding the elusive continent and describing a huge arc through the Pacific. Kendall proved better able to withstand the demands of this expedition than Arnold.

The third voyage third voyage of 1776-1779, ostensibly to look for the north-west passage, was almost certainly undertaken for strategic reasons. Originally commissioned in 1774, it coincided with the British withdrawal from Port Egmont in the Falkland Islands as the price of settlement after the crisis of 1770-1771. If Britain was to be denied a base close to the southern entrance to the Pacific, she might be able to establish dominance over the supposed shorter northern route. With his usual meticulous persistence, Cook charted the whole north-west American coast from the southern limits of Spanish exploration to the limits of more recent Russian discoveries. He did not, however, find a northern passage.

His geographical achievement has been overshadowed by a more spectacular and, in terms of the coming clash of cultures, significant incident – his death in a skirmish on a Hawaiian beach. Glyndwr Williams argues that he arrived at the 'Sandwich Isles' at a fortuitous time, the festival of the god Lono, and left at the end of this season in accordance with his worshippers' beliefs. Thus, when his *Resolution* suffered damage and returned for repairs, he was unwelcome, the season was now that of the war god, and lethal violence – almost incidentally over the theft of ship's boat – followed almost naturally. Others see him, rather simplistically, as a bad-tempered, arrogant outsider who tried to bully the islanders and paid the price. Whatever really caused the death of this great navigator, the Williams interpretation has the deeper grasp of how cultural misunderstandings could lead to tragic results.[47]

PART VI

Recovery and Survival

1783-1815

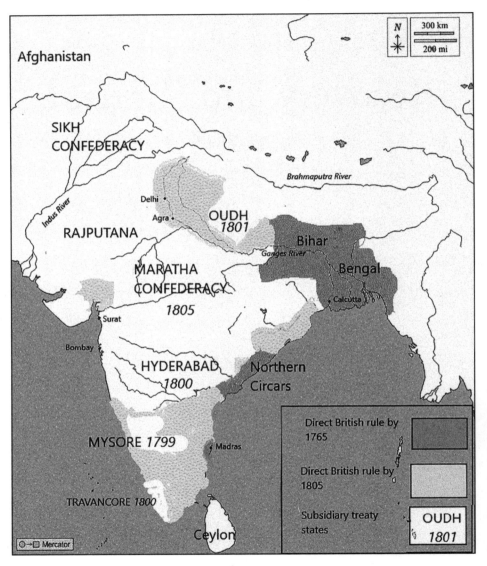

The expansion of British power in India to 1805.

28

From Crisis to Triumph

The king's appointment of the younger William Pitt, at twenty-four younger than any prime minister before or since, marked the beginning of an imperial recovery. The tasks confronting his ministry were to rescue the government's finances from the crushing effects of the late global war, restore the country's prosperity, and to repair Britain's role as a European and global power. Far from moving away from protectionism towards free trade, the new administration set about making the Navigation System more efficient, countering a possible French naval build-up in Asian waters, and establishing a firm British presence in the South Pacific. Having seen off Fox's India Bill, Pitt significantly tightened Crown control over the East India Company's governance and diplomacy in the subcontinent and cleared the way for the separation of commercial and administrative functions within its civil service. Less successfully, he supported Christopher Wyvil's last campaign for parliamentary reform and early attempts to outlaw the slave trade. He was not to know that this work was to be interrupted by a French revolution and a global war of survival; nor that, long after his death, his reforms would ensure not mere survival but Britain's emergence as the dominant global power.

Fiscal reform
At nearly £243 million and growing, the scale of the National Debt was far more frightening even than that of 1763, while savage spending cuts were even less of a serious option. Interest on the debt alone amounted to nine million a year, another million had to be found for ordinary civil administration, and millions more were needed to sustain the peacetime army and navy. The remaining North American colonies could not support their own governance and had to be subsidised. On top of all that, short-term funding was required to compensate refugee American loyalists. Cuts being out of the question, and the land tax being politically

untouchable, the only alternative was to improve the yield from indirect levies.

Crown revenue from customs duties had fallen dramatically as high wartime taxation had encouraged smuggling. Working with Charles Jenkinson, Lord Hawkesbury, at the Board of Trade, Pitt set about cutting duties and stepping up measures to intercept contraband. The Commutation Act of 1784 cut the tea duty from 119 to 25 per cent, imposing instead an increased window tax. Within a short time, the duties on imported wines and spirits were also reduced, and those on wine and tobacco were collected as excise levies, making them harder to evade. Smuggling was further undermined by the 1786 Eden Treaty with France, which reduced tariffs on both sides, and also opened up a large market for the increasingly mechanised textile industry. Further reductions in 1787 were accompanied by increasingly effective enforcement.

Beyond this systematic and effective reform, Pitt's ministry seemed to have little idea of how to go about raising more revenue. Taxes on luxuries such as hair powder, coaches, hackney carriages and servants, might be bearable, but other indirect taxes aroused furious opposition. In a flurry of what one historian has described as 'rather desperate and unsuccessful improvisation', it imposed heavy excises upon cotton textiles (rapidly repealed in the face of industry opposition) and a tax on coal (defeated by coal and iron interests). Taxes on ordinary items such as linen, ribbons and candles caused even wider indignation and were withdrawn in 1789. Nevertheless, the new taxes and increased consumption raised an additional three million pounds for the Treasury and enforcement saved a further million. In 1786 he restored the Sinking Fund, which by 1792 had reduced the National Debt by £10 million.[1]

A reformed fiscal system would count for little, however, without prosperity both at home and abroad. Pitt rejected Shelburne's proposed free trade arrangement with the United States in favour of the more popular position that the Navigation System must be reformed and strictly enforced. He began in 1783 with an Order-in-Council banning American shipping from the West Indian colonies, reinforced in 1786 by a new Navigation Act, redefining what was legally a British ship and imposing a register of British merchant shipping. When it became evident that American imports were reaching the West Indian colonies illegally through French and Spanish islands, an Act of 1787 restricted imports from those places. Though planters might complain that their supplies of food and other materials must now come from more distant and expensive sources, the British islands were partly compensated by bounties on the production of indigo and cotton. British shipping and shipbuilding boomed on the exclusion of the Americans and with it – it was widely assumed – the maritime resources essential to a major naval power. Britain's share of the slave trade peaked in this period.

In the same way, though economically negligible compared to the Caribbean, the timber and fur trades of Canada and Hudson's Bay, Canadian timber and the Newfoundland fisheries had an important strategic significance. Therefore they had to be protected against the territorial ambitions of the United States, and that in turn meant that their inner tranquillity was a matter of concern. Nova Scotia had become home to some 25,000 American loyalist refugees and another 20,000 had settled in upper Quebec. Not only did these settlers have the sympathy of British public opinion but should their demands for representative government be ignored they might move towards an American-style republicanism. Yet any alteration in the 1774 settlement, which guaranteed the rights of French-speaking Canadians and the Roman Catholic Church, might be equally dangerous.

The ministry first created a new colony, New Brunswick, out of the northern part of Nova Scotia and followed that with the Canada Act of 1791. This split Quebec into two provinces, Upper and Lower Canada, each with a bicameral legislature – an elected lower house being elective and an appointed executive council – and a deputy governor. A governor-general was appointed to co-ordinate the two. In this way, the French of Lower Canada would continue to dominate there, while the loyalists around Lake Ontario would have the institutions they desired. The effectiveness of this arrangement was to be tested in the Anglo-American war of 1812-1814.

Pitt's India Acts, 1784 and 1786
Whatever might be done to revive imperial prosperity in the Americas, there was no escaping that fact that the centre of imperial gravity had shifted decisively eastward. The most pressing need was to assert government control over the East Indian Company's dominions and patronage, but that was open to attack as giving far too much power and influence to the Crown. Having attacked Fox's Bill on those grounds in 1783, Pitt could hardly expropriate them himself. Instead, the India Act of 1784 created a modest structure of Crown supervision which could be extended as circumstances changed. A Board of Control of six privy councillors, including the Chancellor of the Exchequer and the Secretary of State for Home and the Colonies, was to supervise the Company's correspondence and it could insist that any new administrative appointments be matched with economies elsewhere. Moreover, the six board members included Pitt's close allies Henry Dundas and William Temple. For the post of governor-general the ministry lighted upon Lord Cornwallis, a strong personality who could be relied upon to put imperial interests first. Cornwallis, well aware of what had happened to Hastings, was reluctant. He accepted only when a new Act of 1786 allowed him tighter control over Madras and Bombay and permitted him to override his council.

The Pacific

Reforming the government of India was only part of a programme to extend British trade and influence in Asia and the Pacific, and to counter the danger of Bourbon build-ups at Mauritius and Manilla. Just as American vessels could not be allowed to supply the West Indian colonies, so New Englanders could not be permitted to supply the lion's share of Britain's imported whale products. The East India Company's Pacific monopoly was progressively reduced in favour of whaling and sealing enterprises, and whaling in the South Atlantic, the Pacific and around Greenland attracted government subsidies. So extensive did these activities become, alongside those of Americans and of Russians based in Alaska, that in 1789 a Spanish squadron seized three British ships at Nootka Sound, on the west coast of Vancouver Island. When the news reached Europe both sides mobilised their fleets and Pitt found himself under pressure from public opinion and from his own Foreign Secretary to use force. War was averted, partly because in 1790 revolutionary France was in no condition to aid her ally, but also because Pitt kept his head. Spain not only ceded compensation but the right of Britain to use the region for whaling activities.

There was also the problem of naval stores. The war had revealed in stark relief the perils of over-dependence upon Baltic sources of mast timber, hemp and flax, and nowhere more dramatically than during the Hughes-Suffren duel in Indian waters. As we shall see in Chapter 29, that need combined with a French naval build-up at Mauritius led the ministry to take a keen interest in the Pacific flax and timber sources noted by Cook, and in 1788 to establish a colony at Botany Bay.

The abolition of the British slave trade

With economic recovery in the forefront of his mind, it is curious that Pitt was sympathetic to the demands of William Wilberforce and his friends for the abolition of the slave trade. In 1783, a small group of Quakers presented a petition to parliament and from 1784 formed an alliance with an evangelical Anglican group centred on the village of Clapham, which included Thomas Clarkson, Granville Sharp, Henry Thornton (MP for Surrey), John Newton (slaver turned Anglican priest) and John Shore who served as governor-general of India from 1795 to 1798. Their parliamentary voice was William Wilberforce, heir to a commercial fortune, MP for Hull and a friend of the prime minister. The Unitarian pottery entrepreneur Josiah Wedgwood was another adherent. There is no doubt that these people were providentialists, who believed that abolishing the evil of the slave trade and slavery would save Britain from God's just wrath. Nor is there much doubt that by the 1780s many voters and Members of Parliament found the slave trade distasteful. The argument that abolition was driven by moral forces is therefore strong.[2]

However, a majority also thought slavery the trade a regrettable economic and strategic necessity, supporting the West Indies trade and providing a vital nursery of seamen. Pitt incited Wilberforce to propose abolition but could not adopt it as a government measure because of the hostility of many of his supporters, including some cabinet ministers. In 1788 Parliament agreed to ameliorate conditions on slave ships, not to outlaw the trade, and in 1791 Wilberforce's motion to introduce a bill for immediate abolition was crushingly defeated. His second attempt in 1792 seemed doomed to suffer the same fate, until Henry Dundas carried an amendment to make abolition gradual, not immediate, and later persuaded the House to set 1796 as the terminal date. Often accused of cynical obstructionism, Dundas may in fact have achieved the best possible outcome available in peacetime. The Lords refused to vote on the matter until it had heard evidence and the 1796 target was shelved altogether when in March 1793 Britain went to war with revolutionary France, reform of all kinds became suspect, and the West Indies slave economy once again seemed crucial to national survival.

The Williams thesis and its critics
There is therefore something to be said for the argument put forward by the Trinidadian historian and politician, Eric Williams, that the trade was abolished in 1807 not through moral outrage but because free trade became economically more attractive to a majority of MPs. However, from the 1970s other historians, less bound to Marxist materialism, demonstrated that Britain abolished her slave trade just as it was at its most valuable – committing what an American scholar, Seymour Drescher, called 'econocide'. As Eltis remarks, 'any economic interpretation of history risks insufficient probing of the motives of people.'[3] The truth seems to lie somewhere in between. Moral outrage was certainly there, but it could not take precedence over a war for survival. By 1807, with the war against Napoleon still hard-fought, but with the danger of invasion now minimal and the French Caribbean empire destroyed, the slave trade could be safely abandoned.

Williams also argued that the slavery provided much of the capital and markets necessary for the industrialisation of Britain, an issue taken up vigorously by the Nigerian historian, J. E. Inikori. Others, including David Eltis and Seymour Drescher, have pointed out that it is impossible to determine how much of the profits of slavery were invested in new industries and have argued that in any case it could not have provided more than a fraction of the necessary capital. As for markets, there can be no doubt that West Africa and the slave societies of the Caribbean were significant consumers of Lancashire cotton, light Yorkshire woollens, metals and metal products. Whether these markets were of lesser or greater significance than the expanding British domestic population is a matter of intense debate. It is now clear that the British share of the slave trade peaked in the 1790s, after the 'industrial take-off' of about 1780. Moreover, there is now powerful evidence that the domestic economy was more important.[4]

A 'blockade' of revolutionary exports
The revolution which began in 1789 and rapidly created a constitutional monarchy was at first welcomed in Britain. Mainstream Whigs saw it as a Gallic version of the Glorious Revolution, those on the left as a precursor of even greater liberty, and only a few like Edmund Burke an assault on ancient institutions that guaranteed stability, justice and social order. Most were probably confused by the events but pleased to see the old enemy reduced to geopolitical impotence. By February 1793 all that had changed radically.

Since the spring of 1792 France had gone to war with both Austria and Prussia, announced her intention to export the revolution everywhere, overrun the Austrian Netherlands, announced the expansion of France to her 'natural' frontiers including the Rhine, and overthrown and executed her king. The old expansionist France was back, in command of the essential springboard for an invasion, and with a frightening ideological edge. Then she went to war with Britain, Spain and the Dutch Republic, which, with Prussian and the Hapsburg monarchy, formed an anti-French coalition.

Although British troops did fight in the Netherlands and took part in the occupation of Toulon in 1793, the victories of the French armies towards the end of the year forced Pitt to focus upon maritime defence and colonial warfare. Consequently, he soon found himself opening negotiations with the United States to prevent a revival of the Franco-American alliance of 1778-1783. Outstanding issues included a continuing British presence north of the Ohio, the boundary with Canada, access to each other's markets, and wartime seizures of American merchantmen headed for French ports. The resulting Jay treaty did not settle all these disputes but did provide for compensation for ship seizures on the British side, payment of pre-1775 debts on the American, British withdrawal of garrisons, and access to each other's markets. These terms were sufficiently beneficial to the Americans to avoid war and Pitt could now focus upon defeating revolutionary France.

Meanwhile, the First Coalition was being destroyed as France resumed its career of conquest. France expanded her boundaries to the Alps and Rhine and by 1797 the Dutch Republic and much of Italy had been converted into French satellite 'sister republics'. Prussia and Austria had made peace and Spain had changed sides, threatening to repeat the Franco-Spanish combination against an isolated Britain. Bonaparte's 1798 Egyptian expedition threatened the overland route to India and

Britain's position in the subcontinent. Nelson's victory at Aboukir Bay was thus a strategic and diplomatic godsend. It not only isolated the French army in Egypt and encouraged the formation of a second anti-French coalition, but allowed the occupation of Malta, giving Britain a new Mediterranean base in a key strategic position. Here she could block the narrow straits between Sicily and North Africa, easily intervene in Italy, and check any new French incursion eastward. The loss of Minorca had finally been more than made good.

It did not, however, guarantee the British Isles against invasion, nor the victory of the Second Coalition, which after a promising start was broken up in the course of 1799. Nor did it weaken the perceived danger of Jacobin insurrection within the British Isles.

Irish reform and the Act of Union
Ireland was a particularly vulnerable spot. 'Grattan's parliament' represented neither Catholics nor Presbyterians and at least a third of its members were pensioners or officeholders. Nevertheless, the nationalist minority took an increasingly independent line and thought of themselves as leaders of national opinion. The French Revolution's emphasis upon republicanism and national independence appealed not only to Catholics but to Ulster Protestants as well. The United Irishmen, founded in Belfast and Dublin in 1791, advocated greater Irish autonomy and religious toleration.

At first Pitt was inclined to bully the Dublin élite into making concessions: in 1792 and 1793 Catholic Relief Acts gave Irish Catholics greater access to the legal professions, the right to bear arms, to own landed property, to jury service, to university education and to the vote. In 1795 the government even supported the establishment of a Catholic seminary. However, full Catholic access to Parliament and office under the Crown was not on the table, and a Lord Lieutenant who advocated it was promptly dismissed.[5] This was probably a mistake: the French Revolution had alienated at least half the French clergy and a large part of their flocks, and the Irish hierarchy was reluctant to support calls for revolution. Domestic conflict now invited French intervention.

As wartime economic difficulties deepened, violence between Catholic 'Defenders' and Protestant 'Peep O'Day' societies escalated. The Defenders' overtures to the French and their demands for independence frightened many Protestants among the United Irishmen, but by 1796 a hard core of the movement centred around Theobald Wolfe Tone, a radical Protestant. Tone and his followers were prepared to seek French aid to establish an independent republic, though France's behaviour towards her 'sister' republics in Europe should have been a warning.

With the Dutch and Spanish fleets now aligned with the French, a successful invasion of Ireland seemed more than probable – an attempted landing in December 1796 was prevented only by bad weather – and over 40,000 British troops had to be deployed there. Wolfe Tone went to France to agree joint plans, while outside their strongholds of Belfast and Dublin committed United Irishmen collaborated with the Defenders. The mutinies in the Channel and North Sea fleets in 1797 made the situation even more critical, and in 1798 both the Pitt ministry and the United Irishmen took Bonaparte's Egyptian preparations for an imminent new descent upon Ireland.

Overestimating their domestic support and without the backing of the Catholic clergy, the Irishmen prepared a widespread revolt, only for their plans to be quickly penetrated and their leaders arrested. The capture of Lord Edward Fitzgerald, their key coordinator, robbed the planned revolts of any chance of cohesion, and outbreaks around Dublin in Kildare and Wicklow were quickly mopped up. In Country Wexford some 30,000 rebels held out for a month in expectation of French help, until their defeat on 21 June at Vinegar Hill. One small French landing took place in August, far too late and in the wrong place, at Killala in the west. A further French attempt in October was taken at sea and with it the United Irishmen's leader, Wolf Tone.[6]

These events demonstrated conclusively that without radical reform Ireland could not be kept loyal. Yet wholesale Catholic emancipation might well produce an Irish parliament demanding independence and civil war between Catholic and Protestant; and in any case the Dublin administration was nearly bankrupt. Pitt and his ministers swung round from backing the Protestant Ascendency to work for a union of the two kingdoms. As early as June 1798, Lord Cornwallis, a Catholic sympathiser, was made Lord Lieutenant and commander in chief of the Irish army, and the ministry began to plan a union which would satisfy Catholics, British and Irish, by abandoning the Test and Corporation Acts. It was even suggested that the Irish Catholic clergy should receive some state support, as the Ulster Protestants did already.

The difficulty lay in getting the Union Bill through Parliament, where the Irish Protestant establishment had many friends, and also in winning over the King. When George III let it be known that he would veto a Bill that included Catholic emancipation –arguing that ratifying it would violate his coronation oath to protect the Church of England – Pitt dropped his plans and promised never to raise them again in the King's lifetime. Indeed, the King had not only the support of the majority in the cabinet, but of most of the political nation too. The emasculated measure then passed the Westminster parliament easily enough, the King gave his assent and in Ireland, where Protestants could see little alternative to union, the way was smoothed by compensation for deprived borough proprietors.

From Crisis to Triumph

The 1800 Act of Union, to be effective from 1 January 1801, gave the House of Commons a hundred Irish members and the Lords twenty-eight Irish peers and four Anglican bishops. Ireland was given free trade with Britain, twenty years' protection for its textiles, and its own exchequer until 1817, in return for paying twelve per cent of the Union's budget. Pitt resigned on principle in February 1801 – there is no reason to suppose that he deliberately misled Irish Catholics over emancipation, but their resentment was to have long-term and unforeseen consequences.[7]

The Peace of Amiens 1802-1803

Pitt was replaced by Henry Addington, whose government is often compared unfavourably to Pitt's, but which was not without achievements. In 1802 it took a war-weary and isolated nation out of the war through the Peace of Amiens, though admittedly on terms which mostly favoured France. All of Britain's colonial conquests except Tobago and Trinidad were to be restored and Malta was to be given back to the Knights of St John, depriving Britain once again of a sound Mediterranean base. The return of Cape Colony to the Dutch threatened her lifeline to India and cleared the way for possible French annexation. Egypt, where a British force had defeated the French occupying army in 1801, was given back to the Ottoman Empire and thus rendered vulnerable to a future French attack.

However, the government saw the treaty as no more than a truce, a breathing space in which Britain could prepare for Napoleon's expected resumed aggression. Meanwhile, the ministry pushed through some significant military reforms and introduced an income tax. Peace broke down in 1803, sooner than Napoleon had intended, because the British would not evacuate Malta in the face of France's annexation of Piedmont and her acquisition of Spanish Parma and Louisiana. Addington was no war minister and was opposed by powerful politicians who disapproved of the Treaty of Amiens. He resigned in 1804 and an ailing William Pitt returned to office, just as Napoleon had assembled a powerful invasion force at Boulogne waiting for the combined Franco-Spanish fleets to seize control of the Channel.

Renewed war, survival, victory

The invasion never came, thanks partly to the impossibility of Napoleon's many plans, and latterly to the formation of a third coalition of Austria, Russia and Britain against France. Napoleon turned east against his continental opponents, wining stunning victories at Ulm and Austerlitz in 1805, Jena and Auerstadt against the Prussians when they finally joined in 1806, and Friedland against the Russians in 1807. The treaties of Tilsit confirmed Napoleon's European dominance and Britain's renewed isolation, although Nelson's victory off Cape Trafalgar in October 1805 removed the invasion threat for some years. A depressed Pitt died in 1807, having never lost his 'Austerlitz face'.

Britain was able to survive Napoleon's economic blockade through expanding her global and colonial trades, while her own blockade inflicted far greater damage upon France. A brief war with the United States in 1812-1814, ostensibly about British trade restrictions but really caused by American designs on Canada, did not weaken British resolve. Napoleon's invasions of Spain and Portugal in 1808, and the determined popular resistance in both countries, enabled Britain to fight a long-drawn-out land war in the Iberian peninsula, the 'ulcer' that drained French strength steadily, little by little. His attack on Russia and resounding defeat in 1812 gave rise to another coalition, which brought him down in 1813-1814 and defeated his attempted comeback in the Hundred Days of 1815.[8]

Colonial acquisitions in his period were, as in every conflict, ancillary to this European strategic focus. The reconquest of the Cape and the seizure of Mauritius safeguarded the maritime link to India, while conquests in the Caribbean including Martinique, Guadalupe, St Lucia and Tobago inflicted economic damage on France. The occupation of Java had a similar purpose, as well as eliminating a threat to the annual China convoys passing homeward through the Indonesian straits. From 1808, Britain was once again able to use Spanish Minorca as a base, and in 1809-1810 Admiral Collingwood drove the French from the Ionian Islands. At the Congress of Vienna, as at Paris in 1763, Britain was careful not to antagonise other powers by retaining too much, but this time she did so from a position of far greater strength. Nearly all her gains had strategic rather than commercial significance. In the Caribbean, Martinique and Guadalupe were returned to France, though St Lucia (with its key harbour), Tobago and Dutch Guiana were retained. Java was handed back to the Dutch, but not the strategically important Cape; and France did not recover Mauritius. Malta was another vital strategic gain, as was the retention of the Ionian Islands conquered in 1809-1810.[9] The agreement was signed nine days before Napoleon's final defeat at Waterloo on 18 June 1815. Empire was still about the European balance of power.

29

India: The Rise to Dominance

In 1783 and for years afterwards, neither the East India Company's directors, nor their new masters in London, wanted to expand their territories in India. With the Company some £20 million in debt, and with the National Debt at ten times that figure, expensive wars and ambitious diplomacy had to give way to economy and consolidation. Yet India was now far more important to the surviving British empire, and in times of emergency British governments would be under pressure to defend the company's territories there, if necessary by aggression and expansion. For the time being, however, Company and Crown were set upon sustaining a balance of power in the subcontinent. Only after the outbreak of war with revolutionary France, and the advent of a consciously expansionist governor-general, did the British seek and achieve dominance.

Cornwallis, reform and a 'permanent settlement'
Cornwallis, a loyal servant of the Crown whose reputation was barely touched by his surrender at Yorktown, was determined to stamp out the widespread corruption he saw among the Company's servants and, so he thought, the Indian administrative class. His first step was to separate the Company's civil service from its commercial operations, and to professionalise it. High salaries and generous pensions made an administrative career attractive, but – as private commerce was forbidden – it was no longer a route to vast riches. He next began to remove all Indians from high positions, assuming that their corruption was rooted in their societies, and that British appointees would be more morally reliable. Anglo-Indians were also systematically removed from office and barred from the Company's service. To the same end, he also separated the judiciary from the revenue-collecting arm of the civil service, and – significantly – made it answerable to the courts. By 1791 he had introduced a new court system, with fewer Indian judges and in which

native law was amended according to so-called European principles. The *shari'a* principle that the family of a murder victim should have a say in sentencing, for example, was abandoned. In this way a much-needed attack on corruption carried with it a corrosive racial and cultural discrimination.

Finally, Cornwallis set about stabilising the government's income through a 'permanent settlement' of the revenue. The hereditary tax-collectors, the *zamindars*, were local gentry with whom the peasants could often bargain, and who in their turn could bargain with central government. This introduced a flexibility invaluable in times of dearth and sustained a close relationship between local *zamindar* and peasant. Enforcement might sometimes involve violence, but dispossession and enforced sales of property were rare. On the other hand – and this was Cornwallis's main concern – the system meant that government could not be certain of its income from year to year and involved what to Western eyes looked like corruption. Moreover, Cornwallis wanted to create an Indian class of improving landlords, very much on the model of his own background, and perhaps embodying physiocratic ideas of property, industry and progress. As with his administrative reforms, Cornwallis wanted to 'improve' India by creating an Anglicised hierarchical landed society.[10]

His solution was to fix for ten years the sum to be collected each year from each *zamindar*, from which he could deduct ten per cent as his commission. If the *zamindar* or peasant failed to pay the sum specified, his own land could be seized and sold. The result was financially successful but socially and economically damaging. High initial assessments drove out the old zamindari families in favour of new men, often Calcutta bankers and merchants who treated their new posts as investments, and effectively reduced peasants to tenants of the new *zamindars*.

All this was done while pursuing a balance of power policy. Cornwallis was well aware that the Pitt ministry wanted no disturbances in India, and he quickly found that the Company's armed forces were ill-prepared for conflict. Wars of conquest were therefore out of the question, which meant guarding exiting frontiers while establishing peaceful relations with the other subcontinental powers. Ideally, diplomacy would see to it that no one Indian power, or combination of powers, would be able to threaten the British position. But even Cornwallis was unable to ignore one serious threat to the stability he was committed to preserve.

Cornwallis and Tipu Sultan

Tipu Sultan, Haider Ali's son and heir, was intelligent, cultured, militarily gifted and ambitious. His twin aims were to drive the British from India and to secure for himself dominance of the west and south, perhaps even to replace the Mughal emperor himself. He appreciated that he would need French help and that he must also modernise his state's economy. His energy, talents and charisma have seduced some historians, who view him as a proto-nationalist. However that may be, he allowed impatience and ambition to trump discretion. Instead of waiting to rebuild Haidar's navy, he began to expand his kingdom northwards by land campaigns. He provoked the British by sending an embassy to France.[11] He ignored his father's advice to seek allies within India and by 1786 he was at war with both Hyderabad and the Marathas. Tipu compounded this folly by openly renouncing his nominal allegiance to the emperor Shah Alam, and finally, in December 1789, by striking southwards at the Company's ally, the Raja of Travancore.

Cornwallis had hitherto pursued a policy of studied neutrality. Already, and on orders from London, he had revoked his predecessor's unconditional offer of five battalions to support the Marathas. Whether he did so out of a conscientious observance of existing treaty obligations, rejection of wars of expansion, or simply an awareness of the unprepared state of the Company's armies is a matter for debate. However, it is striking that in 1789, with his ally threatened, Cornwallis saw no reason to intervene himself. Instead, he negotiated an alliance with Hyderabad and the Marathas, and instructed Madras to defend the integrity of Travancore. And it was very nearly enough.

Tipu's first attempt to breach the Raja's elaborate frontier defences – the 'Lines of Travancore' – was an embarrassing failure; at his second attempt he broke through, only to be held up by improvised stockades, monsoon floods and sickness. The news that Madras was assembling a large force at Trichinopoly forced him into a second retreat. Fortunately for Tipu, Hyderabad and the Marathas failed to move, enabling his nimble columns to easily evade the clumsy Madras forces and drive deep into the Carnatic. By early 1791 he was ravaging the coastal regions south of Madras.

Only now, when he could no longer treat the war as a local southern matter, did Cornwallis take the field in person to lead an invasion of Mysore itself. Bangalore fell after a short campaign, but Tipu frustrated the subsequent British advance on Seringapatam by a scorched earth policy. Only the belated arrival of forces from Hyderabad and the Maratha country, combined with Cornwallis's own tactical shrewdness, forced Tipu to terms on 18 March 1792.

The Treaty of Seringapatam deprived Mysore of about half of its territory, awarding substantial gains to the Marathas and the Nizam, while the Company took much of the Malabar coast. Tipu's two young sons were handed over to Cornwallis as hostages for their father's future good behaviour. It has been suggested that, by so weakening Mysore and dramatically expanding its own territories, the Company had moved from being a middle-ranking Indian power to a contender for paramountcy. At the time, however, Cornwallis deliberately ensured that Mysore would survive as a viable state. The alternatives as he saw them – either handing all to the Nizam and the Marathas or establishing a costly and inevitably corrupt puppet state – were equally unattractive. Tipu even kept a substantial stretch of coastline, including the important naval base of Mangalore, so his power was far from broken. Neither Cornwallis, nor his successor Shore, saw any reason to revise this settlement and until 1798 the Company continued to favour an Indian balance of power.

Revolution, Wellesley and conquest
The threat, however, was not removed. Hardly was the ink dry on the 1792 treaty than Tipu approached the Nizam for an anti-British alliance. He sent emissaries to Constantinople and to the French at Mauritius, employed French mercenaries to train and lead a powerful sepoy corps, and planned a naval expansion that would in time have given him local superiority at sea. In 1797 the threat became critical. The armies of the French Directory had swept across Europe, setting up satellite states – 'sister republics' – in conquered territories outside the 'natural' frontiers of France. Bonaparte had driven the Austrians out of Italy and imposed his own peace terms. In India, Mysore, Hyderabad and the Maratha Confederacy all employed considerable numbers of well-equipped French-trained troops, and Tipu had embarked upon his new naval programme, intended to provide him with a hundred warships, twenty of them of sixty-nine guns and upwards, which would have given him local superiority over the British fleets. Dundas instructed Shore's successor, Richard Wellesley, Lord Mornington, to clear out these centres of French influence as soon as possible. The mood in Britain was far more aggressive than in 1792, a mood personified in the person of Wellesley, with his aristocratic disdain for the Company 'cheesemongers' and their profit margins, and no belief at all in an Indian power balance.

On arrival in Calcutta early in 1798, Wellesley was confronted with the news that Bonaparte had landed in Egypt and defeated its Mameluke rulers at the Battle of the Pyramids. Wellesley, the ministry and even Admiral Horatio Nelson believed that he would establish a naval base on the Red Sea, whence French forces could link up with powerful anti-British states in India. Urgent action was needed and expansionist, aggressive Wellesley was just the man to take it. He quickly concluded a pact with the Nizam, who was afraid of Tipu and considered a British alliance the lesser evil. The French-trained corps were to be dismissed and replaced with 6,000 Company troops for whose services the Nizam would pay £41,710 per annum. For the first time, a major Indian state had been reduced to a client of the Company. The Hyderabad alliance secured, and having received news of the Battle of Aboukir Bay, which effectively cut Egypt off from France, Wellesley was able to arrange a similar treaty with the Peshwa of Poona, by which the Maratha Confederacy was to supply 25,000 troops for the war against Mysore.

Finding himself thus isolated, Tipu sought belatedly to conciliate the Nizam. There was no response: Tipu entered the Fourth Anglo-Mysore War with no allies and an army slightly outnumbered by Wellesley's. Driven back into Seringapatam, he conducted the defence with desperate courage and skill until Wellesley's artillery battered a breach which was stormed on 4 May 1799. Tipu, fighting to the last, was shot dead in the melee before the inner defences. The town was looted and sacked, and the power of Mysore was broken forever. Tipu's family was dispossessed in favour of a five-year old member of the Wadiyar family earlier overthrown by Haidar. Shorn of its last piece of coastline, Mysore was now a much smaller, wholly landlocked client state. The Nawab of the Carnatic, accused of conspiring with Tipu, was dethroned, pensioned off and saw his state annexed.

Wellesley now turned his attention to the Maratha Confederacy, the last remaining major obstacle to British dominance of the subcontinent. The Confederacy's key weakness had always been its lack of unified leadership, and at this moment it was particularly divided. The new Peshwa of Pune was at odds with the new leaders of the Scindia and Holkar dynasties, and all three of them were inexperienced young men with too much personal power and too little restraining advice. In 1802, the hard-pressed Peshwa appealed to Wellesley, only to decisively defeated by Holkar before British troops could interfere. Now wholly dependent upon British aid, the Peshwa accepted the Treaty of Bassein: Wellesley's troops in exchange for an annual cash payment and recognition of the Company as overlord.

Wellesley now planned to weaken Scindia by taking control of Delhi and the emperor Shah Alam, whose symbolic standing was still significant, bribing mercenaries in the Maratha armies, and detaching Holkar from Scindia and Bhonsle. When these two chiefs declared war in August 1803, Wellesley attacked them with a southern army under his younger brother Arthur, and a northern force under Lord Lake.

In the Deccan, Arthur engaged a powerful Maratha force at Assaye on 10 September. Avoiding a head-on attack, he achieved a surprise crossing of the Kailna River, forcing his opponent to redeploy at right-angles to the river, and secured both his own flanks on the Kailna and Juah streams. However, the Marathas changed front smoothly and their artillery opened a devastating fire on Wellesley's men, now wedged into the junction of the Kailna and Juah, threatening to blast a wide hole in the British line. The day was saved by a bayonet and cavalry assault on the Maratha guns, whose crews fought doggedly but who found themselves inadequately supported by the infantry to their rear. Even as the Maratha line crumbled, a final British cavalry charge was repelled by Maratha gunners.

At the end of November at Argaum, the pattern was repeated. Wellesley's advancing column was surprised by hidden guns that threatened to overwhelm his own artillery before it could unlimber; again, the British infantry advanced rapidly on the guns, to be met with ill-coordinated counter-attacks by Maratha infantry and the Maratha army disintegrated. Meanwhile Lake seized the fortress of Aligarh, swung past Agra and defeated Scindia in a bloody encounter near Delhi, before going on to take Agra and win another battle at Laswari. On 17 December, Bhonsle made peace at Deogaon, yielding up a swathe of territory south of Bengal. Thirteen days later at Surji-Anjangaon, Scindia followed suit, ceding a band of provinces reaching from the Ganges to Gujurat. Only then, too late, did Holkar decide to fight. His fast-moving and strikingly successful campaign of 1804-1805 could not compensate for his isolation and was doomed to ultimate failure.[12]

Why, despite the narrowing gap between the effectiveness and technologies of British and Indian armies, were the British so consistently successful? Clearly, the failure of Indian leaders to act together was a key factor: not being blessed with hindsight they did not appreciate the significance of the British threat until it was too late. Yet at times the British were close to defeat. At Assaye and Delhi the excellent Maratha artillery came close to winning battles. Part of the answer seems to lie in the failure of Indian states to reconcile European and Indian modes of warfare. Maratha field artillery was far superior to the British arm, and there were some well-drilled European-style infantry battalions. However, there were never enough trained officers for these battalions, and they had to operate with traditional Indian levies with even weaker command structures. Strategic and tactical doctrines were also problematic. While Maratha commanders opted for a policy of fighting pitched battles, its light cavalry arm, devastating when used to raid and harass and isolate an enemy, was never adapted to the shock tactics needed on the battlefield. Moreover, as we have seen, Maratha command structures were unable to fully co-ordinate infantry and artillery. Finally, there was a profound difference in military culture. Fortresses fell to Wellesley largely because the South Asian garrisons were willing to make a sensible financial settlement, especially if they had not been recently paid. The same was sometimes true on the battlefield: at Assaye some units seem to have stood aside because their pay was in arrears. The British were able to take advantage of these situations because they had greater access to credit.

These were not inevitable victories brought about by the superiority of the British, but they were decisive. Shah Alam was now the Company's client and pensioner, and the British controlled the Ganges Valley, the whole east coast, and most of southern India. Yet even this was not dominance. Bombay was still a vulnerable-looking enclave; the British had withdrawn from Rajahstan, Holkar was not bound by a subsidiary treaty, and the other Maratha chiefs had significant military resources of their own. It remained to be seen whether the peace of 1805 could be sustained.

Moreover, Wellesley's triumph had been costly. The Company's debt had risen from £17 million in 1798 to almost £31.5 million by 1803. The Directors were outraged and expressed their outrage to the Board of Control. Before Assaye and Delhi had been fought, London had decided to recall the governor-general. However, there was no going back on his conquests. Indeed, the third and last Maratha War, that of 1817-1818 may be seen as a consequence of his campaigns. The Company's future prosperity now depended heavily upon the extraction of revenues with which to finance trade and the armies which kept the revenue-producing territories secure.

The Company had vastly expanded its own domains and reduced most of the rest of the subcontinent to tributary status. Should an organisation with such enormous territorial obligations be permitted to trade in the same region? At home, the champions of administrative reform joined hands with free traders and evangelicals when the Company charter fell due for renewal in 1813. Although the Company kept its commercial monopoly in the Far East for another twenty years, in India it was entirely removed. The powers of the Board of Control were strengthened, and India was opened to Christian missionaries for the first time. It was to sustain and expand its role as the government of India for almost another half-century.

30

Australasia: Settlement, Invasion, Resistance

There were at least 200,000 Aborigines in Australia in 1770 and quite possibly thrice that number. Basically stone-age hunters and gatherers, Native Australians managed the land through regular burning of underbrush to renew grass and so attract game while encouraging useful plants to thrive – hence the lack of undergrowth noted by Cook. Coastal and riverine clans fished with specialised spears, hooks and lines, fish traps, and nets up to half a mile long, while inland water management may have included the excavation of stone-lined wells. Populations were kept in balance with the land's productivity through strict marriage rules, infanticide, and communal ownership. These people lived in a land enclosed by the sky, where sacred markers associated with ancestral spirits denoted clan boundaries.

It was a world governed by the Dreaming, a combination of religion, ancestral memory and traditional law, a world where innovation came second to tradition and societal needs came before those of the individual. Warfare, by European standards, was remarkably mild. Raids on another clan to obtain women and the subsequent revenge attacks seldom caused much bloodshed; occasional large-scale battles might result in one or two deaths, and wars of conquest were unknown. With over three hundred language groups, and innumerable ancestral clans governed by councils of elders, Aboriginal society possessed a nature and complexity almost impenetrable to outsiders. Land was the common ancestral possession of the clan: the idea that it could be alienated to individuals, let alone to foreign incomers with no spiritual connection to that land, was beyond comprehension.[13]

On his second and third voyages to the Pacific Cook discovered Norfolk Island and New Caledonia and revisited New Zealand. In all three places huge pines – potential masts and spars – were seen and in the former two locations wild flax – the raw material for canvas – was found. Neither New Zealand nor Norfolk Island were suitable for major settlement: Maori hostility told against the first, while Norfolk Island was tiny and lacked a safe harbour. New South Wales, however, seemed to be sparsely populated by a people unlikely to prove dangerous, and Botany Bay promised a safe harbour, fertile soil, ample water and a reasonably temperate climate. In 1786 the Pitt ministry decided to settle almost a thousand convicts there as the basis of a new British settlement colony. The motives behind this plan to colonise one of the remotest places on earth have been the subject of passionate debate.

The traditional interpretation holds that disposal of convicts was the first and only factor in the mind of government. From 1775, the American colonies were no longer a secure destination for felons sentenced to transportation beyond the seas and from 1783 they were not available at all. As a temporary measure, the Hulks Act allowed them to be housed in disused ships moored in the Thames and by 1786 the number of hulks and the numbers of convicts crammed into them became insupportable. Attempts to find suitable sites in western Africa having proved abortive, ministers hurriedly put together a fleet to carry almost a thousand convicts to a new prison in the remotest and least inhabited place imaginable: Botany Bay.

That view was first challenged in 1952 by Tasmania-based historian K. M. Dallas, and taken up more successfully in 1966 by Geoffrey Blainey, then Professor of Economic History at the University of Melbourne. In *The Tyranny of Distance*, Blainey inverted the customary hierarchy of causation: there was a strategic agenda behind the settlement and convicts were the only available means of its execution. To Blainey's mind, the American war had highlighted the importance of naval stores, especially in the East. After each of his engagements with Suffren, Hughes had found Indian dockyards without urgently needed masts, spars, canvas and cordage. And if the references to naval stores in the customarily available documents was scarce, this was because their importance, like that of oil in the twentieth century, was too obvious to need emphasis. For him, the main purpose of the 1788 expedition was to set up a secure base on a safely uninhabited shore, whence the flax and pines of Norfolk Island and New Zealand could be exploited. Moreover, opening the Pacific had tempting commercial possibilities, especially the southern whale fishery, which Britain could not allow to fall entirely into the hands of Frenchmen or New Englanders.

Blainey's contention aroused fierce opposition from established historians committed to the convict-dumping theory and from younger ones attracted to its implied Australian exceptionalism. At first, they had a telling argument: Blainey's case rested largely upon what the known sources did *not* say rather than upon solid, verifiable fact. In later years, however, Alan Frost demonstrated that, though real enough, the convict problem was never as serious as has customarily been claimed. The traditional image of a River Thames crammed with overcrowded and insanitary hulks was (and remains) simply wrong: by 1783 there were no more than three in use. Moreover, New South Wales was not the Pitt ministry's first choice for a convict settlement. Other sites, cheaper to reach and maintain, were considered first. The government's real problem was the French naval build-up at Mauritius. This, combined with the Spanish squadron at Manila and the Dutch flotilla at Batavia, could threaten the security of British possessions in India and cut off access to China; and after 1783 the annual China convoys were of greater economic importance than ever. Critics of this 'strategic outlier' theory – the main thrust of which rested upon a dearth of direct primary evidence – were seriously undermined when Frost's persistence produced a mass of new documentation, proving once and for all the narrowness and inadequacy of the traditional sources. As early as 1997, one eminent traditionalist was driven to brush aside the strategic argument rather than properly engage with it.[14] The debate rumbles on – Australian exceptionalism doing battle with a broader imperial perspective – but the strategic argument has become too powerful to be dismissed. It may be no coincidence that the officer chosen to lead the expedition and become the first governor of New South Wales was a naval captain, Arthur Philip, who had earlier been employed to spy on French naval preparations at Toulon.

Philip's 'First Fleet' reached Botany Bay in January 1788, at the height of the southern summer. The soil was poor, the abundant streams noted by Cook and Banks had dried up and the anchorage was badly exposed to the east. An alternative was desperately needed, and on 21 January Philip took three ships' boats northward to examine the inlet Cook had named Port

Australia: the first invasions, 1788-1815.

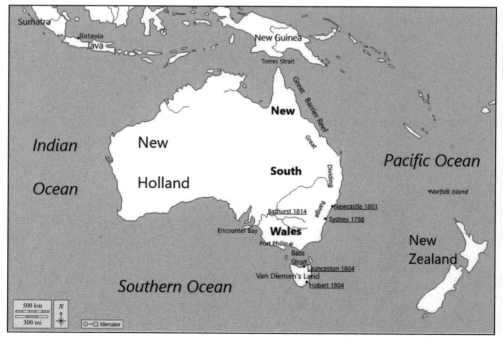

Jackson. There they came upon the flooded river valleys of Sydney Harbour, hitherto concealed by its three overlapping headlands. After examining many of the coves and inlets, Philip finally chose one on the southern shore, where there was abundant fresh water – the Tank Stream – and deep water close to shore. At a cove across the harbour he met Aborigines so dignified and confident that he named the place Manly. The ships were brought round and on 26 January the town of Sydney was formally begun.

Once ashore, Philip certainly behaved as though naval stores were a prime reason for his presence. Within a month he set about occupying Norfolk Island. The plan was to first clear land and plant crops for subsistence and then to focus upon the cultivation of the native flax. The first stage took longer than intended and was followed by an unexpected problem. The local plant had such long fibres that even the experienced flax dressers on the island struggled to separate them from the stalk. New Zealanders were known to be able to weave these fibres and the two finally recruited, hardly experts themselves, helped to improve quality and production, but the resulting canvas was disappointingly expensive and weak. The Baltic was not wholly closed to British ships after war broke out in 1793 and the project was gradually abandoned. Even the immensely tall and straight Norfolk Island pines were a disappointment: Many turned out to be rotten inside and too dangerous for use as ships' masts.

Yet, as Blainey puts it, the 'failure of flax and pine on Norfolk Island was less important than their initial promise.' Establishing a colony on such a remote coast at such a vast distance would have been unthinkable and unworkable without the prospective production of naval stores. Flax was indeed the 'hollow conqueror' of Australian remoteness.[15]

Collaboration and resistance
The Aborigines were far more numerous than Philip had been led to expect and the governor and his officers took very seriously their instructions to reconcile them to the invasion. Despite their best efforts, however, relations with the Aborigines were hard to establish and marked by very limited linguistic progress, mutual gift-giving, theft and occasional violence. For their part, the indigenes showed a real concern to get on with their new and unwelcome neighbours, sometimes helping to haul in fishing nets and being rewarded with part of the catch, but communication was so difficult that Philip resorted to kidnapping.

His first captive, Arabanoo, died in the first smallpox epidemic in 1789, and while two children proved to be adaptable and quick learners, they had limited utility as go-betweens. Two other adults, Coleby and Bennelong, proved more useful. Though both escaped, from time to time they came back to the Sydney Cove settlement as visitors, sometimes with women and children seeking food. Bennelong's family made a habit of camping and feasting in the governor's large garden. Bennelong's wife gave birth at the colony's hospital, and when both died the wife was buried in the precincts of Government house and the baby was cremated somewhere else in the settlement. In this way a kind of 'middle ground' grew up, the Aborigines relating the new landscape to their Dreaming. Just as in their world authority belonged to the elders, so here they saw power belonged with Philip. To those who allied with Bennelong at least, Philip became 'Father', just as Amerindians referred to the French and British monarchs.[16]

That did not mean that either side fully understood the other. Only Bennelong learned enough English to communicate, while Philip was able to learn Aboriginal words but not to use them accurately. Nor did it preclude violence. At an otherwise amicable beach meeting with Bennelong and others, where presents were offered and accepted, an elder was frightened by Philip's smiling approach and speared him through the shoulder. Nor did all local Aborigines follow Bennelong's conciliatory lead – violence and excessive trespass had to be avenged. Foraging convicts and marines were often less fastidious than their superiors in their treatment of blacks, so those who strayed too far from the settlement were attacked and eventually a man was killed. Philip responded with a punitive expedition he instructed to take or slay no more than six Aboriginal men, while leaving the women and children strictly alone. Whether the Aborigines would have appreciated this sense of proportion was never put to the test, because they evaded the marines altogether. Nor did Philip understand their structures of government. Though he noticed that the old men held authority, he thought it must mean that the most venerable elder was a kind of monarch. Nevertheless, in the early years, and especially before Philip's departure in 1792, conflict remained at a low level and there seemed to be a basis for mutual acceptance and cooperation.

This semi-amicable relationship was doomed by the settlement's need to feed itself. The soil around Sydney was thin and sandy, and the fleet had arrived well into the southern growing season. The first crops failed and the promised follow-up supply convoy failed to materialise. When a second fleet arrived with stores, it also brought more mouths to feed. The settlement was temporarily saved by the circumnavigation of John Hunter's *Sirius* to buy stores at the Cape, but the settlement took more and more aboriginal land for crops and livestock. Farms established at the head of the harbour at Rose Hill and around Parramatta struggled. Only the settlement from 1794 of the rich alluvial flats of the Hawkesbury River by freed convict families allowed the colony to be self-sustaining in food, but the Hawkesbury was too distant to be under the watchful and generally humane eyes of the Sydney authorities, so violence by whites usually went unpunished while Aborigines followed their custom of revenge killing.

As the pressure of white expansion increased, they seem to have adapted their political structures accordingly. By the early 1790s, men from the Dharawal (or Tharawal) and Dharag language groups were waging a guerrilla war of resistance from Jervis Bay in the south to the Hawkesbury

River in the north. Their raids were co-ordinated by Pemulwuy of the Dharawal-speaking Bediagal clan from Botany Bay. Pemulwuy became an heroic figure, especially after his wounding and capture near Parramatta in 1797, followed by his apparently miraculous escape with an iron shackle still fastened to his leg. Not all blacks followed him; when he was finally shot dead in 1802, some Aborigines insisted that his head be cut off and sent to the Governor in Sydney. By then, however, violence had become the dominant theme of inter-racial relations. Where collaboration did take place, the whites were now inevitably the masters.[17]

Securing Bass Strait

In 1797, the accidental discovery of Preservation Island north-east of Van Diemen's Land revealed not only huge exploitable populations of seals but a strong south-westerly swell indicating an open passage between Tasmania and the mainland. This convinced Governor King and at the end of the year a young naval surgeon, George Bass, penetrated into the strait with a twenty-eight-foot whaleboat. Next summer, Lieutenant Matthew Flinders sailed a sloop right through the strait, which he named after his friend Bass. Sealers and whalers – mostly New Englanders - moved into Bass Strait straightaway, and further investigations identified the main hazards, particularly King Island at its eastern end, and safest passages. By 1802, Bass Strait was the normal route for ships bound for New South Wales, lopping 700 miles off their voyages.[18]

Clearly the strait had considerable strategic value, and there was alarm in London when in 1800 it was reported that a French expedition had set out to examine the Australian coasts, including Bass Strait and Van Diemen's Land. The government immediately commissioned Flinders to carry out a counter-examination and charting of the entire coastline. Sailing in July 1801 in HMS *Investigator*, he was a long way behind the French commander, Commodore Baudin, who was already on the Australian coast. In March 1802, Baudin carefully surveyed Bass Strait before moving westwards along the mainland's southern coast. In April he met Flinders, who had taken the counter-clockwise route around the continent in Encounter Bay. Shortly afterwards scurvy forced Baudin to turn back for Sydney, where he was welcomed in June.

News of the Peace of Amiens did not allay the suspicions of King, who had already written home recommending a pre-emptive settlement be founded at Port Philip on the northern coast of Bass Strait. Some of Baudin's officers let slip that they were looking for a settlement site, a rumour that reached King soon after the French sailed south again in November. He sent an officer to survey Port Philip, take formal possession of King Island, and to warn the Frenchmen off. Baudin's polite rejection of the British claim only increased King's alarm. By the end of 1803, King had established a tiny settlement on the Derwent estuary in south-eastern Tasmania and an expedition from Britain had landed at Sorrento, just inside Port Philip Bay on Bass Strait itself.

Its commander, Lieutenant Colonel David Collins, did not like the place: fast tides in the narrow entrance and the danger of contrary winds meant that ships could be embayed there for days or weeks. The soil was poor and more fertile sites further north were too far from the strait. The Tamar River, on the Tasmanian side of the strait, proved difficult of access and offered a very narrow anchorage, so Collins finally decamped to Hobart, where the original Derwent settlers joined him. But while Collins had abandoned his original objective, London had not. In 1804 King received orders to form a base on Bass Strait, and by November one was established at the Tamar mouth. Lack of suitable soil forced a move upriver in the early months of 1806.

For the time being, environment had defeated strategic need, but the strategic need remained, amply demonstrated by the passage of the outward-bound East India convoy in 1805.[19] Privateers, pirates and the occasional British warship operating against the Dutch in the East Indies and the Spanish colonies in South America used Sydney as a base and as a place to sell their prizes. Even many ordinary whalers and other merchant vessels carried letters of marque, and in 1807 the 57-gun HMS *Cornwallis* became the first man o' war to arrive via Bass Strait.[20] Had the British not taken Mauritius (and the attack very nearly failed) and had not Napoleon rashly driven Spain into the arms of the British in 1808, the Bass Strait–New South Wales corridor might have become vital to the survival of Britain's China trade and to her bridgeheads in India.

Parochialism and Frontierism
The marine garrison was replaced by a specially raised regiment, the New South Wales Corps. In October 1792, eleven officers collectively chartered a ship to import a cargo of Cape food and livestock. Thereafter, drawing on their own pay and the regiment's collective credit, they were also able to buy up and resell goods brought in by calling ships, and to dominate local whaling and sealing, the sandalwood trade with the Pacific islands and China, and timber from New Zealand. For many years these 'Pacific frontier' enterprises were the economic mainstays of the colony. After Philip's departure, his temporary successor, Major Grose, allowed the officers and men to apply for land grants and assigned convict labour to work it. Rum, imported by the officers and their associates, became the local currency. In this way the regiment acquired deeply divided loyalties: isolation and their burgeoning economic interests led them to increasingly identify with the colony, so coming into conflict with metropolitan authority as represented by governors Hunter and King, the very authority they were meant to uphold.

The most articulate and politically active of the officers was one Lieutenant John Macarthur, promoted Captain in 1795, who acquired extensive sheep-grazing interests and opposed the governors' preference for agriculture as the essential basis of an ordered society. A clever, slippery, litigious and quarrelsome figure, Macarthur was sent home in 1801 to face a court martial for wounding his commanding officer in a duel. While fighting a senior officer was frowned upon, convictions for duelling were rare; and Macarthur – exploiting the war with Spain, the principal supplier of fine wool to British mills – used his English connections to obtain government support for his wool production project, including merino sheep from the King's flock at Kew and a conditional 10,000-acre land grant in New South Wales. When in 1804 it was at last decided that his crime should be tried in New South Wales, he resigned his commission and returned to the colony, where he had the backing of the brotherhood of the Corps, rank and file as well as officers.[21]

Rum Rebellion

As an élite, the officers were joined by pardoned convicts ('emancipists') such as Simeon Lord, who successfully evaded the law against ex-convicts owing vessels to become the colony's great shipping magnate; a trickle of substantial free settlers, such as the merchant Robert Campbell; and in 1804, gentry in the persons of the brothers John and Gregory Blaxland who sold their Kentish estates in order to emigrate. If there was a rift in this élite, it was between those who, like Macarthur, wanted to keep ex-prisoners in their place, and the 'emancipists' who naturally favoured greater equality. They were, however, united in their determination to protect their economic activities and property from government interference; and on this point they could appeal to moderately prosperous citizens, many of them rankers in the Corps.

King's failure to check the soldiers' commercial activities, not to mention the insurrectionary efforts of an influx of Irish convicts, caused the British government to look for a replacement who could impose discipline. Their choice, and that of Banks, was William Bligh, a naval officer who had made two voyages to the Pacific in search of breadfruit. The embarrassment to his career of the famous *Bounty* mutiny was offset by an extraordinary feat of navigation and leadership, in taking an open boat 3,000 miles to Batavia. More recently, he had protected his men from retribution after the mutinies at the Nore and Spithead and displayed great courage at the later battles of Camperdown and Copenhagen. Bligh clashed with Macarthur over his land grants and with the Corps over the rum trade, particularly officers who paid their men in spirits. Macarthur used legal technicalities to evade the confiscation of two imported stills and won over small Sydney property owners by defying Bligh's plans to re-design the town by expelling leaseholders from two small areas. When Macarthur was finally arrested for refusing to pay a bail bond (when a convict escaped on one of his ships) he was able to represent Bligh as behaving illegally and arbitrarily; a tactic which seems to have secured some popular support. On 26 January the Corps marched on Government House with fifes and drums playing and bayonets fixed and arrested the Governor.[22]

On condition of returning immediately to Britain, Bligh was allowed to board HMS *Porpoise* and in her he hovered off the coasts of New South Wales and Van Diemen's Land, vainly awaiting an opportunity to reimpose his authority. The rebels dismissed his officials, installed creatures of their own, set about prosecuting his supporters, and distributed land to their own followers. His official replacement, Lieutenant Colonel Lachlan Macquarie, arrived in 1809 with his own regiment, the 73rd, to replace the Corps as the governor's right arm. The Corps was withdrawn to Britain. Macquarie quickly learned to dislike Bligh and began healing rifts by courting both sides. Imperious and socially awkward, Macquarie set about transforming the colony morally, by overriding the objections of 'exclusives', who thought ex-convicts ('emancipists') and their children should forever be second-class citizens, and by the free use of his power of pardon. At the same time, probably wisely in view of the recent rebellion, he opposed the setting up of a nominated executive council, and even more vehemently the idea of an elected legislative body. The physical and visible aspect of his top-down reformation was the redesigning of Sydney and Parramatta, with grand public buildings and large open spaces, and the laying out of new towns as the frontier advanced and the density of settlement grew.[23]

Invasion into the hinterland

Settlers had by now spread out over the Cumberland Plain to the foothills of the Blue Mountains fifty miles distant from Sydney. Here the ranges were straddled by the territories of the Dhurag people to the east and the Gundungurra to the west, and between them was a zone shared by both language groups. Over a hundred and seventy mountain sites produced fine-edged stone axe-heads, knives, choppers and scrapers, which were traded into the Cumberland and western plains. From the time of Philip, official white attempts to penetrate this native industrial heartland were frustrated by valleys that ended in blank cliffs and ridges cut by impassable ravines. The aborigines had their own networks of paths, but none were anxious to guide the intruders, and perhaps the explorers did not think to ask. Significantly, the only black known to have offered his services was an outcast, a renegade. Thus the guarding of secrets, rather than fierce armed resistance, kept the invaders at bay for over two decades. Not until 1813 did three settlers find interconnecting ridges leading them far enough into the tangled ranges to glimpse the plains beyond. Within a year, Macquarie had surveyors marking out a rough and ready road and in 1815 the town of Bathurst was founded on the Macquarie River.[24] In traditional Australian historiography, the constricted settlement had triumphantly broken its bonds. From the Aboriginal perspective the mountain gates had been burst, allowing the invaders to swarm into the interior.

31

The Atlantic Empire Reconstructed

May you live in interesting times. The years between 1783 and 1815 were dominated by the impact of the American Revolution, the wars against the French Revolution and Napoleon and by the ending of the slave trade in 1807. Britain's Atlantic empire was now very much reduced but Canada and the West Indies, especially the latter, were still thought important for British trade and security. The Pitt ministry and its successors were keen to prevent the mainland colonies from being overrun by American arms and there were vigorous attempts to deprive the United States of its trade with the British Caribbean. At the same time, while the abolition of the British slave trade in 1807 threatened to reduce the West African enclaves to insignificance, the creation of Sierra Leone colony as a refuge for freed slaves, not to mention the activities of the anti-slavery naval squadron, pointed to a new kind of West African empire.

British North America
The Treaty of Versailles had specified that the United States should compensate Loyalists for property lost or seized. The USA, however, left it to individual states and the states declined to provide anything. It fell to the British government to provide for the 40-50,000 émigrés, about half of whom fled to the remaining North American colonies. About 35,000, perhaps a tenth of them black, went to the mainland part of Nova Scotia to find themselves handed clothing, rations, lands and tools and expected to get on with the business of carving farms out of an inhospitable landscape.

They also expected to live under similar constitutional arrangements to those they had left behind: a government restrained by an elected legislative assembly and by habeas corpus. As they outnumbered the existing white inhabitants, they had a case. Moreover, the more genteel among them expected employment suitable to their status. The solution adopted in 1784 was to form the mainland region into the new colony of New Brunswick. New Brunswick did not become an entirely an English-speaking region, however; the south became dominated by exiled Nova Scotians and their descendants returning from Louisiana. What held the two communities together was the threatening proximity of an expansionist United States of America.

Fewer Loyalists, somewhere between 6,000 and 10,000, arrived in Canada itself. Many of these were rural New Yorkers who settled on promising land west of Montreal along the St. Lawrence, around Lake Ontario and on the Niagara River. They, too, expected a representative assembly and English law, a demand which cut across the specifically French elements of the 1774 Quebec Act. As in Nova Scotia, the solution was to create a new colony. The Canada Act of 1791 elevated the Lake Ontario region into the colony of Upper Canada, with its own legislature of lieutenant governor and elected assembly. French Canadians also benefitted, in that they could dominate the new created assembly of the old province of Quebec, now Lower Canada. The Governor of Lower Canada was to be the governor-in-chief of both Canadas, creating a quasi-federal arrangement. It was an imperfect, almost ad hoc solution, which worked partly because of the unifying American threat.

Another internal conflict was handled less amicably. Far to the west of the Great Lakes, the Hudson Bay Company, under pressure from the rival Montreal-based North-West Company, was expanding its inland activities throughout the Hudson Bay drainage system, dangerously close to American Louisiana. When the Earl of Selkirk, anxious to find a communal home for his clansmen, bought a dominating share in the HBC and obtained a grant of 116,000 square miles within the limits of the Company's 1670 charter, some of it south of the Hudson watershed, the peril became acute. His 1811 Red River settlement lay squarely across the North-West Company's route from Montreal to the northern fur-bearing regions. Backwoods fighting broke out between the two companies, producing something akin to civil war at the very moment of imminent foreign invasion.

Anglo-American tensions
One cause of American hostility was the economic boost given to Canada, especially from 1793, by the Royal Navy's almost insatiable demand for mast timber, pitch and tar. Recapturing that traffic by conquest may have been one reason behind President James Madison's determination to go to war in 1812. In addition, the United States' refusal to compensate the Loyalist emigrants had prompted the British to delay their evacuation of the forts north-west of the Ohio and tempted them to intrigue with settlers in Vermont with a view to drawing them into the British sphere. In 1787 Vermont firmly plumped for America statehood, but the continued occupation of the north-west territories was a constant irritant.

The Atlantic Empire Reconstructed

Alongside this was a straightforward expansionism on the part of some Senators and Congressmen, often called the 'War Hawk' party. Modern American historians have tended to downplay this territorial explanation in favour of theories involving British interference with neutral American shipping during the wars against Napoleon, the pressing of American seamen who might plausibly be regarded as British subjects, an attempt to acquire a formal British recognition of neutral rights, and even a party move to neutralise New England secessionism. There was also an ideological factor: American republican purity was under threat from its proximity to the British empire.[25] All these elements were in the mix, but American territorial ambitions, already manifested in 1775 and which surfaced from time to time over the next century, should not be discounted.

In 1787, Congress passed a Northwest Ordinance asserting its sovereignty over the zone north of the Ohio, where it had already obtained land cessions from the Amerindians with a view to settlement. Until Jay's treaty of 1794, the British maintained important garrisons in the region and intrigued with Joseph Brandt's attempts to construct a Western Confederacy to block American expansion. Even then, however, Canadian officials and British officers continued to encourage Native resistance, provoking the western regions of the United States to demand the conquest of Canada. The purchase of Louisiana from France in 1803 gave the Americans a claim to territories stretching north-west of the Great Lakes as well as bringing them into competition with British traders on the Mississippi and their Fox and Salk allies. Everywhere, threatened Amerindian nations drew closer to the British, and in 1811 Senator Henry Clay of Kentucky claimed that the British were behind an indecisive clash with the Shawnees.

Clay was the most prominent of the 'War Hawks', strong in the western regions, expansionists who wanted to destroy the British-Amerindian alliance by conquering Canada. Such demands played into fears that the proximity of a still-powerful Britain would corrupt Americans' republican virtue. Clay also played on the effects of the British Orders-in-Council imposing an economic counter-blockade on Napoleon's France, but this was probably a pretext to justify his expansionist demands. The same is probably true of Madison's justification of his decision to go to war in 1812. It is indicative that the New England states who suffered most from British ship seizures and impressment of seamen were not enthusiastic and took little part in the fighting in 1812-1814.

The Anglo-American War of 1812-1814

When war broke out in 1812 it took the form of a series of American thrusts into Upper Canada at both ends of Lake Erie, around Detroit and along the Niagara River, and from Sackets Harbour at the eastern end of Lake Ontario. The Americans tried to concentrate overwhelming numbers in the Hudson-Lake Champlain corridor for an advance on Montreal. In the event, the offensives were uncoordinated and ill-supplied: all four were checked by determined British, Canadian and Native resistance. In the west the British took Fort Detroit and won a dramatic victory at Queenstown near Niagara. But In 1813 an American force penetrated Upper Canada by way of the Detroit River and won a battle at Moraviantown, when the charismatic Shawnee leader Tecumseh was killed. Further east they burned Niagara and crossed Lake Ontario to burn York, the Upper Canadian capital.

A British attack on Sackets Harbour failed and the Americans were poised to penetrate the upper St. Lawrence towards Montreal and join the Lake Champlain advance. That junction was prevented by Anglo-Canadian successes at the battles of Châteauguay (26 October) south-west of Montreal and Crysler's Farm (11 November) on the St. Lawrence. In 1814 a British counter-offensive on Lake Champlain was halted by an American naval success at Plattsburg. Canada had been successfully defended and meanwhile the United States' vulnerability to seaborne attack was demonstrated by the capture and sacking of Washington and an assault on Baltimore. Even Madison was now ready to negotiate. The parties met in neutral Ghent in August 1814.

Astonishingly, the Americans began by demanding both Canadas, an end to impressment on the high seas and an end to British-Native American alliances. The British countered by proposing the confirmation of Jay's treaty and boundary adjustments – including the acquisition of northern Maine and all American territory they then occupied. Above all, they wished to compensate for their abandonment of the Amerindians in 1783 with the creation of a separate Native buffer state. In the end, the Indians were sacrificed in the interests of compromise. Britain kept the Canadas, no guarantees were given to the Indians, occupied territories were restored, and the question of American access to Newfoundland fisheries was shelved. The Americans had achieved a diplomatic success in the wake of a military failure, and the British had once again sacrificed their Native allies.

The war was a major contribution to a Canadian sense of identity. British regulars, militia and French Canadian units had fought stoutly together against an enemy intent upon once again dispossessing Loyalist refugees and ending the special position of French Catholics in Lower Canada. The French Canadian performance at Châteauguay and Crysler's Farm demonstrated their confidence in the constitution of 1791. In Upper Canada there emerged a myth that Upper Canadian citizen soldiers had defeated the invasion on their own. The boundary issue was not settled even in theory until 1818, when the 49th parallel of latitude was adopted as a border effectively separating the Mississippi and Hudson Bay drainage systems. Although Canadian provinces could be wary of the erosion of civil government in the cause of military security,[26] although French Canadians might struggle to retain a distinct culture – and although the two fur-trading companies continued to fight each other until 1821 – the shadow of their powerful neighbour ushered their identities under the imperial umbrella.

The Caribbean 1783-1815: resistance, revolt and abolition
There was considerable tension between the planter societies of the British Caribbean and the home government. Pitt's attempt to exclude the United States from their trade drove up the prices of victuals, timber and other goods, which would now have to come from more distant colonies or from the British Isles. Worse still, the rise of the anti-slavery movement stirred resentment and deep anxiety in a society and economy deeply dependent upon coerced labour. While West Indian assemblies were increasingly inclined to regulate slave conditions, they strongly objected to metropolitan interference. Rumours of emancipation might stir up slave revolts at a time when the ratio of whites to blacks was steadily shrinking. The Maroons of Jamaica and Grenada – where there was a short war in 1785 – and the Black Caribs of St Vincent came under increasing suspicion, especially after the successful slave revolt in St. Domingue in 1791. Missionaries were restricted by law and harassed by the populace, and colonial assemblies continually asserted their rights against those of Crown and parliament.

What triggered widespread black rebellion and resistance was, however, the outbreak of war with France in 1793. Open conflict tempted the British to attack Caribbean islands where French royalists might be willing to assist them. A British task force captured Tobago before descending on St. Domingue, the richest French colony in the Caribbean. Early in 1794 Martinique, St Lucia and Guadeloupe were captured. Then it all went wrong. What was intended to be a swift conquest of St. Domingue turned into a long slogging match between the invaders and rebel and French troops. Significant British forces were tied down there, reinforced in 1795 by almost the whole of the regular garrison of Jamaica. Guadeloupe was counter-invaded by a French force under an able Jacobin commander, Victor Hugues, where on 10 December the British evacuated their last toehold. It now seemed more than likely that slave rebellion and French intervention would spread revolt throughout the British islands.

From Guadeloupe, Hugues struck at St Lucia and Dominica, aiming to combine with the Maroons there, triumphantly in the first case, unsuccessfully in the second. On St Vincent in March 1795 the

Black Caribs again went to war in defence of their lands, this time in collaboration with resident French planters who hoped to drive the British from the island, and with military assistance from Hugues. For some months the British were hard pressed, until reinforcements arrived and turned the tide. The French force surrendered in June 1796 but most of the Black Caribs fought a bitter guerrilla campaign almost until the end of the year. They were then deported to a nearby island where most of them died, the survivors being moved on to Roatán, off the coast of Honduras. This turmoil was the background to the outbreak of a new Maroon war.[27]

The Second Maroon War 1795-1796

Ever since about 1781, Maroon-planter disputes over land and boundaries had been frequent. These do not seem to have arisen from settler land hunger – there was still plenty of land more suitable for sugar than that of the Maroons' mountain fastnesses – but from the vagueness of the 1739-1740 treaty stipulations and from tardy surveying. By around 1790 the ratio of slaves to whites had grown to sixteen to one, engendering greater fear of a slave revolt and dividing planter society as to the reliability of the Maroons. Those living close to their towns tended to be more sympathetic and appreciated the Maroons' value as a police and defence force. The majority, especially those in less regular contact, became ever more suspicious and hostile, especially when the successful slave revolution in St. Domingue raised the spectre of a similar upheaval in Jamaica. In 1791 the assembly passed laws restricting the Maroons' freedom of movement. By 1793, when war broke out with France, fear turned to panic and paranoia. Rumours of French and Maroon attempts to stir up Jamaican slave revolts abounded and the arrival of a new governor, Alexander Lindsay, Earl of Balcarres, brought fear to the point of armed conflict.

Governors were always liable to identify with their colonies, and Balcarres seems to have swallowed planter conspiracy theories whole. He regarded John James, former superintendent at Trelawny Town as a potential rebel, plotting with the Maroons to seize the island for his own ends. Balcarres and the planter majority now aimed to expel the Maroons from Jamaica altogether.

The immediate cause of war was the arrest and flogging of two young Maroon men accused of stealing hogs. The sentence was particularly humiliating, being carried out by a black prison overseer in front of black slaves recently returned by the Maroons. When a deputation came from Trelawny Town to protest, demanding that their unpopular superintendent be replaced with his predecessor John James, they were arrested for plotting rebellion, and Balcarres turned out the militia. Remarkably, a group of local planters repeatedly tried to reopen negotiations, though they could not sway the governor and the Maroons understandably refused to back down.

As soon as the last regular garrison regiment was embarked for St. Domingue, the Trelawney Maroons went to war. At the eleventh hour Balcarres diverted the regiment to Montego Bay and demanded that the Maroons surrender to him there. A few complied but the majority went to war, attacking army outposts and raiding plantations. On 12 August 1795 they ambushed an army column, burned Trelawney Town and retired into the Cockpit Country. On 12 September they ambushed a second column. The British were committing the basic counter-insurgency blunder of sending large formations into enemy country, along narrow paths and across difficult fords. It is not surprising that Maroon success inspired desperate counter-measures.

The planter-dominated assembly now agreed that Balcarres should send to Cuba for a hundred hunting dogs, a move opposed by the peace party and which later provoked criticism in parliament and from George III himself. In fact, although the dogs arrived they were never used. Instead, Major General George Walpole, the commanding officer on the island, set about separating the Maroon guerrillas from their food supplies. On 21 December Maroon delegates attended a peace conference, at which they were told that everyone who laid down his arms by 1 January 1796 would be neither executed nor deported. About twenty-one came in by that date, by which time Walpole, who thought more time was needed, had halted his troops. Almost a hundred Maroons came in by the end of January, all expecting to qualify for the September terms. Though some held out in the mountains well into March, the revolt was as good as over, and on terms that might restore the hitherto reasonably harmonious relations achieved since 1739.

At this point Balcarres, no doubt aware of what an assembly of frightened planters would recommend, asked the assembly whether the September terms should apply to those who surrendered after 1 January. Predictably, the majority voted for expulsion from the island. Yet it is significant that the assembly voted 27 to 13: a large minority deplored the breach of faith and saw that they were about to destroy the very security system that had worked so well since 1739. Walpole, too, was disgusted. While Balcarres blandly accepted the assembly's gift of £700 for this piece of treachery, the military commander refused 500 guineas and a sword of honour, resigned his commission and turned to the abolitionist cause. His gesture was, of course in vain: in June 556 Trelawney Town people were embarked for the unwelcoming climate of Nova Scotia, whence in 1800 they were sent on to Sierra Leone.[28]

However, the Jamaican Maroon communities which had remained neutral or sided with the British were untouched. It is true that they were economically damaged by laws restricting their use as police – so-called party-service – and the ethnic distinctions between Maroons, free blacks and slaves were being eroded, but they retained their firearms and communal identities. They were more fortunate that the Maroons of Dominica, crushed in a vicious campaign in 1812-1814.

Victory and abolitionist stirrings
Despite being obliged to withdraw from St. Domingue in 1798, British forces defeated a Spanish attack on Belize and conquered a number of colonies of France's allies: Spanish Trinidad; Dutch Demerara, Esiquibo, Berbice, Surinam, Curaçao and St Eustatius; Swedish St Bartholomew; and Danish St Thomas and St Croix. Yet events in Europe were the ones that counted: at Amiens only Trinidad could be retained. Britain's position in the Caribbean, indeed her very presence, were far from guaranteed.[29] When war resumed in 1803, however, all the earlier conquests were swept up again, while St. Domingue was now the republic of Haiti. The mainland Dutch settlements of Berbice, Esiquibo and Demerara were reconquered by the British for the last time, retained in 1814 and in 1831 combined as British Guiana. By 1815 it was evident that Britain could not again be challenged in the Caribbean.

From the point of view of most West Indian planters, absentee or resident, and their agents and creditors, these campaigns were a period of remission from the threat of slave trade abolition. The narrow defeat of Wilberforce's Bill of 1803, which passed the Commons but failed in the Lords, was particularly frightening. That is what lay behind colonial assemblies' anxiety to pass laws protecting slaves from particularly brutal treatment. As early as 1788 Jamaica mutilation was made punishable by a year's imprisonment and a £100 fine, and murder of a slave was to carry the death penalty. The Leewards made similar arrangements in 1798. In 1810 a planter, Edward Huggins, was censured by Nevis Assembly for a 'barbaric' mass flogging (which resulted in the death of a female slave) but acquitted by a jury of his peers. 'The first negro had received three hundred and sixty-five lashes: deponent saith that Mr. Huggins, senior, gave another negro-man one hundred and fifteen lashes; to another negro-man sixty-five lashes ... and that the woman who received two hundred and ninety-one lashes appeared young...' In the following year one Arthur Hodge was convicted of the murder of one of his slaves and was hanged on 8 May.[30] The sadistic Hodge had in fact murdered as many as sixty.

Rumours about the abolition movement reach the slaves and gave rise to rumours that their masters were frustrating their emancipation. Plots were uncovered in Jamaica in 1803 and Trinidad in 1805. Actual short-lived revolts broke out Jamaica in 1807 and in Trinidad in 1808. By 1811 there was talk among planters of independence, but while slavery lasted and the Jamaican Maroons remained formidable, separation was a fantasy. Their internal threats locked the West Indian islands into the imperial network as surely as the American threat constrained Canadians.

West Africa in the age of abolition 1783-1815[31]

In 1806, using the excuse of the Fante sheltering some refugees, the Asantehene Osei Bonsu invaded the Fante Confederation. Though victorious at the battle of Abura Dunkwa, the Asante were finally defeated at Tantumkweri and withdrew in 1807. The Fante confederation survived but the British – like the Danes and Dutch – found themselves confronted by a power against whom their forts were useless and whose offensive had interrupted trade. From then on there was continual friction, as whenever the Fante states offended Asante, the Europeans were held responsible. Worse, from 1808 the forts were unable to check illegal traffic in slaves. In 1819 the British government bypassed the Company and began to negotiate directly with the Asante and in 1821 took over all the Company's establishments in the Gold Coast and Gambia, placing them under the expansionist governor of Sierra Leone, Sir Charles Macarthy, soon to die in a new Asante war.

What was to be done with the black ex-slaves who had fought on the British side in the War of American Independence? Nova Scotia, as we have seen, and the Bahamas were tried and both were found wanting. Granville Sharp and his friends fixed on Africa as the right continent for displaced Africans and Sierra Leone as the most convenient region. In May 1778, a few hundred ex-slaves and a handful of white prostitutes were set down with six months' food on a tiny enclave purchased from a local ruler. It was the wet season, the place was unhealthy, the work hard and unrewarding, and for ex-slaves from Virginia and the Carolinas the environment was challenging. Settlers gradually moved away, some finding employment with slave traders, until in 1790 the last few inhabitants were scattered by a Temne attack.

That failure did not deter Sharp, who concluded that adequate finance and a strong administration were needed to make such a colony work. The Sierra Leone Company, licensed by Parliament inn 1791, was given a British governor, a council and a team of craftsmen and traders. Forbidden to trade in slaves or to seek to monopolise trade locally, the Company was to support itself through legitimate trades with the interior. A new site was found and named Freetown. Sixty-four of the first settlers were relocated there and 1,200 black Loyalists were brought in from Nova Scotia. The new venture seemed to be off to a promising start.[32]

However, the governor and council were soon at odds with the settlers and with each other. The Nova Scotians preferred trade to coffee, sugar, cotton and food production – or at least to their role as wage labourers under white supervision. In any case, the soil was poor and its management not understood. Cash crops were quickly devoured by pests and food was already easily available in local markets. Production within the colony soon gave way to the purchase and export of local products: gold, rice, palm oil, hardwood and ivory. The problem here was that those very items were the results of slave labour, and trading in them encouraged local producers to acquire more slaves, so compromising the colony's core purpose. Those who held the plots parcelled out by the Company resented the payment of quit rents, and those 'apprenticed' as workers resented what looked like a new kind of slavery.

Many settlers wanted a representative assembly on the American model. Zachary Macaulay, governor from 1794 to 1799, tactfully allowed some popular participation in law making but residual resentment boiled over into rebellion in 1800, after Macaulay's departure. The arrival that year of 500 exiled Maroons from Jamaica via Nova Scotia gave the government a force anxious to prove its loyalty, and a tendency towards authoritarianism was confirmed by a royal charter clarifying the dominion of governor and courts.

The settlement was also alarmingly vulnerable to external attack. Freetown was sacked by the French in 1794 and had to be rebuilt from scratch, and Temne resentment of the growing enclave produced a frontier problem. In many 'palavers' (conferences) the Temne asserted their sovereignty over the Freetown peninsula and requested that their sacred sites be protected. The Company's officials brushed these requests aside, resulting in repeated armed attacks upon Freetown between 1801 and 1804.

From 1800 an annual British government subsidy enabled the colony to carry on despite its defence problem and a faltering economy. The company, however, had been set up in expectation of profit and was soon keen to shed its burden altogether. The British government, which saw Freetown as a potential base to protect the West African enclaves and to intercept slavers, was willing to take over, and in 1808 Sierra Leone became a royal colony. By 1815 its population had grown significantly, the legitimate trade was becoming sustainable, and it was proven that a black colony organised on European lines could thrive in West Africa. Against this must be set questions of representative government, the 'apprenticeship' of slaves freed by the Royal Navy, and the stimulus that its economy gave to local slavery. Sierra Leone was founded upon high-minded principles, but not necessarily upon intimate knowledge of the region or upon the aspirations of its setters.

This much reduced Atlantic world was still part of Britain's security system and a support to its world power status. While danger to the British Isles were now minimal, local threats kept both regions within the imperial orbit, and their products still supported British power. Sugar, the shipping it produced and the seamen it trained were still seen

The Atlantic Empire Reconstructed

as vital. In an age when steam was in its infancy and iron hulls almost unheard of, the forests of British North America were an important strategic resource. While the slave trade had gone, slavery itself survived, at least for the time being. Industrialisation had not yet displaced the old imperial imperatives.

EPILOGUE

A New British Empire?

A history book must end somewhere and there are some sound reasons for choosing the year of Waterloo and the final collapse of the Napoleonic empire. Britain and her empire, so vulnerable for the past two centuries, was now permanently among the great European powers and, through her naval might, a world power as well. The slave trade had been abolished and arguably the writing was on the wall for slavery itself. Britain was well into the process known as the world's first industrial revolution which, it has been suggested, required cheaper raw materials and food (and thus lower wages) through free trade. The Atlantic empire had been dramatically reduced and the Asian one greatly expanded, so arguably the whole process of imperial endeavour had shifted eastwards. In many ways a new empire was emerging my 1815. Yet much of the mercantilist world remained intact and changes were continuing processes, not finite events. The world did not suddenly renew itself on 18 June 1815.

A *'swing to the east'?*
The idea of a 'swing to the east', was first proposed in 1952 by Professor Vincent T. Harlow in the first part of his two-volume *The Founding of the Second British Empire, 1763-1793*. Harlow argued that in economic terms, and in terms of imperial effort, the shift to an Asia-centred empire had begun as early as 1763. For him, by 1793 there had been a decisive rejection of settlement colonies in favour of commercial penetration of Asia, and particularly of China. While it is certainly true that by 1815 the imperial centre of gravity had moved decisively eastwards, most historians would place it much later, and would challenge Harlow's analysis of its nature.

In 1791 the Pitt government did indeed try to gain greater access to Chinese markets through a mission led by Lord Macartney. The base established on Penang island in 1786 was partly intended to protect both

A New British Empire?

the Straits of Malacca, one of the key bottlenecks on the routes of the China convoys, and to tap the Malay state of Kedah's export trade in tin, pepper, elephants, ivory and rattans. Alan Frost has shown how even the new colony in New South Wales fitted into a broader plan to keep the China trade open. However, Penang's main purpose was to provide an alternative to Bombay in the hurricane season of October and November for British warships operating in the Bay of Bengal. Moreover, as Britain could offer little that the Chinese market badly needed, the Manchu government was determined to keep the foreign barbarians confined to the port of Canton. Thus, the peacetime foundation of Singapore in 1819 and the acquisition of Malacca in 1824 should be seen as steps to expand and secure Britain's Indonesian commerce at the expense of the Dutch.

The real heart of British enterprise in Asia was India. Whereas India's main export to Britain had been cotton cloth, it was now a supplier of raw materials to feed growing British industrial demand and a larger and larger consumer of British textiles. The EIC gave employment and very comfortable salaries to about 6,000 British people, half of whom were army officers. Indian exports paid for much of the tea and porcelain purchased in China, purchases of Indian goods were used by private individuals to send savings home, and the EIC used them to pay its dues to the British Crown. As contemporaries realised, Britain could not now afford to lose India – if they lost it to another European power the British Isles themselves would be in danger.

By Harlow's terminal date of 1793 the EIC was no more powerful in India than a decade earlier but by 1815 it had replaced the Mogul emperors in all but name. It is true that even by 1815 the British had barely established their dominance over the subcontinent, the last Maratha War was yet to be fought and north-western regions were outside its treaty system altogether. Within the system, many of the states later to be annexed into British India – Oudh, for example – were still autonomous. Moreover, British power, like Mughal power before it, was heavily dependent upon native collaborators – *zamindars* responsible for tax collection, three very large and mostly Indian armies, junior civil servants, policemen – and as the Mutiny demonstrated so tragically, the paramount power interfered with their religion and cultures at its peril. Yet enormous manpower and the revenues of India made Britain an Asian power, capable of intervening throughout the region, including Burma and India. Those resources could be brought to bear as far away as the Mediterranean and eventually in Europe itself.

At the same time, the remaining reconstructed Atlantic empire was still economically and strategically valuable and governments were prepared to go to great lengths to preserve and expand it. After the Peace of Versailles, the British still seemed to have a chance of exploiting the trades of the Mississippi basin. Indeed, the new United States was weak

The First British Empire

and might not survive intact. If that happened Britain might be able to extend her influence across the continent and acquire bases in Florida or New Orleans – her aims in the war of 1812-1814. That ambition was not entirely displaced by the survival of the Union or even by the Treaty of Ghent. Cargo for cargo, it is true, East India imports were more valuable than transatlantic exports, but the volume of trade across the Atlantic more than made up for that difference. While after 1783 a great deal of this commerce ran in channels outside the empire – as if Britain was already swinging towards a free trade economy – even in 1815 there was still valuable traffic with the West Indies and the remaining colonies of British North America.

Mercantilism or free trade?

The myth that by 1815 the empire was swinging towards an ideology of free trade arose from serious overestimation, made in hindsight, of the influence of Adam Smith's *Wealth of Nations*. Smith's work, it was assumed, was vindicated by the loss of America and influenced the post-war Pitt administration's economic reforms: slashing customs duties, and the Eden and Jay treaties. His ideas coincided with the dramatic expansion of British textile and metallurgical industry, which led manufacturers to demand access to the cheapest global sources of raw materials and the widest possible markets. The post-1783 measures put in place to exclude American shipping from the West Indies were modified in the Jay treaty of 1794 and in the long run according to the tenets of *The Wealth of Nations* it was impossible to limit American commerce with the British Caribbean.

In fact, the empire was still strongly mercantilist. The Navigation System was still considered essential to British security and prosperity and the Navigation Act of 1786 tightened up the legal definition of a British ship entitled to trade within the empire. Protectionism was given a further boost by the Corn Laws of 1804 and 1815, designed to shelter British agriculture, and the modifications made to the system in the late 1820s may have been meant to improve efficiency rather than to introduce free trade. The Corn Laws were not repealed until 1846, the Navigation Acts not until 1849, and the last protective duties went in 1860.

Antislavery and abolition

The abolition of the slave trade was certainly a major transformation and, undertaken at the height of its prosperity, well deserves Drescher's appellation of 'econocide'. Driven through by evangelicals still determined to be rid of slavery itself, enforced by a dedicated naval squadron and accompanied by the rise of missionary societies, it might seem to foreshadow a new approach to empire. The antislavery campaigns acquired a huge following, far greater than that generated by late eighteenth-century indignation over alleged offences in India. Disciples of the Williams thesis still insist that anti-slavery was inextricably linked to the development of capitalism, and indeed that slavery was abandoned only when it had paid for British industrialisation. One historian of Sierras Leone indicts the antislavery movement for 'its acquisitiveness, its gradualism and its militarism', which transformed it into 'an imperial project of expansion and colonialism'.[33] One might add that the very expansionism required by abolitionist crusading would lead to a sharper, often equally violent, form of racial exclusiveness, later characterised by the pseudo-scientific social Darwinism of the late nineteenth century.

However, while the logic of anti-slavery did indeed require expansion into inland Africa, such theories probably undervalue the genuine idealistic commitment of antislavery enthusiasts. Moreover, by 1815 the British still lacked the military and medical technology for significant expansion and the near-redundant chain of Gold Coast forts was at the mercy of local powers.

An autocratic empire?
In some ways, as C. A. Bayley argued in *Imperial Meridian: The British Empire and the World 1780-1830*, the empire was becoming more authoritarian than ever before. The vastly expanded Asian empire was, of course, run in an absolutist style, while Sierra Leone, Cape Colony and New South Wales were under the arbitrary rule of naval and military governors. However, all the North American settlement colonies, with the exception of bleak, underpopulated Newfoundland, had elected legislatures, and in New South Wales the growing free population demanded some movement towards civil government. In 1812 a Select Committee on transportation recognised the growing free settler element and in 1814 a new system of civil law courts was established. The Cape was like mid-eighteenth-century Canada in that contained a resentful non-British white population as well as a non-white majority and faced a turbulent frontier with the Xhosa peoples. Even here, however, British immigration was becoming an engine for change. Thus, we see a dichotomy: in new non-white colonies government was autocratic while the settlement colonies would by mid-century achieve full internal 'responsible government', with ministries answerable to their legislatures.

Direct control by the Crown was now replacing proprietors and chartered companies, partly because so many seventeenth-century foundations were lost in 1783, but even here there were continuities. The East India Company's India dominion did not end until 1858, and then only in the wake of the massive and tragic uprising that came close to ending British dominion in North India. It is also worth noting that chartered companies – the South Australia Company, the New Zealand

Company, the Royal Niger Company – were created for imperial purposes well into the nineteenth century.

Strategic considerations
Above all, the empire was still seen as essential to Britain's security and Great Power status. Britain unquestionably had the world's most powerful navy, but she still had powerful and populous land-power neighbours. In the immediate post-war period, the advancing power and ambitions of Russia were the main concern, but there was always the possibility of a French revival. The dangerous fragility of the seventeenth and eighteenth centuries had gone, but in what was still an age of wooden sailing ships, Canadian timber was an essential resource. And if Britain had been weakened in the Atlantic, India's manpower made her a major force in Asia and the world, able to deploy troops from Burma (now Myanmar) to China and to the Mediterranean, and ultimately into Europe itself.

Evidently it would be wrong to deny that the loss of the thirteen colonies and the conquest of India brought about a fundamental change in the British empire. For that reason, the concept of two British empires is a useful analytical tool. Nevertheless, it would be a greater error to ignore the continuities and to assume that 'the' British empire began in 1783, 1815, or – most misleadingly and like many a current syllabus or television programme – somewhere around 1870. 'The' British empire was in the end a single but complex organism, one that evolved, endured revolution, adapted and finally declined over three and a half centuries.

Endnotes

Introduction & Part I: Origins
1. J. H. Parry, *The Age of Reconnaissance: Exploration, discovery and Settlement, 1450-1650* (Phoenix Press, London, 1962).
2. Jane H. Ohlmeyer, '"Civilizinge of those Rude Partes"; Colonization within Britain and Ireland, 1580s-1640s', in Nicholas Canny (ed.) *The Oxford History of the British Empire Vol I: The Origins of Empire* (Oxford University Press, Oxford, 1998) 124-130.
3. David Grummitt, *The Calais Garrison: War and Military Service in England, 1436-1558* (Boydell Press, Woodbridge, 2008) 165-186; David Loades, *Mary Tudor* (Amberley, Stroud, 2011) 219-222; John Edwards, Mary I: *England's Catholic Queen* (Yale University Press, New Haven and London, 2011) 309-311.
4. John Guy, *Tudor England* (Oxford University Press, Oxford, 1990) 249, 264-265.
5. John Guy, *'My Heart is My Own': The Life of Mary Queen of Scots* (Fourth Estate, London and New York, 2004) 53-55, 83, 85-97.
6. Mack P. Holt, *The French Wars of Religion, 1562-1629* (Cambridge University Press, Cambridge, 1995) 53-56; John Guy, *Tudor England* (Oxford University Press, Oxford, 1988) 267-268.
7. Guy, *Tudor England*, 268-282.
8. Nicholas Canny, *The Elizabethan Conquest of Ireland: A Pattern Established 1565-1576* (Harvester Press, Hassocks, Sussex, 1976).
9. John Sugden, *Sir Francis Drake* (Kindle edition, Pimlico, London, 2006), locations 2381-2388.
10. Canny, *Elizabethan Conquest*, 79-81.
11. James O'Neill, *The Nine Years War, 1593-1603: O'Neill, Mountjoy and the Military Revolution* (Four Courts Press, Dublin, 2017).
12. Guy, *Tudor England*, 258-254.
13. Guy, *Tudor England*, 290-293, 306-307.

14. David Loades, *England's Maritime Empire: Seapower, Commerce and Policy, 1490-1690* (Longman, London, 2000) 88-93.
15. Loades, *England's Maritime Empire*, 93-94.
16. Loades, *England's Maritime Empire*, 94-97.
17. N. A. M. Rodger, *The Safeguard of the Sea: A Naval History of Britain 660-1649* (Kindle edition, Penguin, London, 2004) 242-243
18. Sugden, *Drake*, locations 1970-2131
19. James McDermott, 'Oxenham, John, (c. 1536–1580) ', *Oxford Dictionary of National Biography (ODNB)*, 23 September 2004, https://doi-org.lonlib.idm.oclc.org/10.1093/ref:odnb/21057; K. R. Andrews, *Elizabethan Privateering: English Privateering During the Spanish War 1585-1603* (Cambridge University Press, Cambridge, 1966) 178-180.
20. Sugden, *Drake*, Ch 9-11, locations 2766-3947. Parry, *Age of Reconnaissance*, locations 4075-4082 provides a short summary.
21. Loades, *England's Maritime Empire*, 115-116; Harry Kelsey, 'Drake, Sir Francis (1540–1596)', *ODNB*, 23 September 2004, https://doi-org.lonlib.idm.oclc.org/10.1093/ref:odnb/8022. For a more optimistic assessment see Sugden, *Drake*, Ch 10 *passim*, locations 3145-3588.
22. Rodger, *The Safeguard of the Sea*, 248-250.
23. David Beers Quinn, *Set Fair for Roanoke: Voyages and Colonies, 1584-1606* (University of North Carolina Press, Chapel Hill, 1985) is a detailed and comprehensive study of these enterprises.
24. James McDermott, *Martin Frobisher: Elizabethan Privateer* (Yale University Press, New York and London, 2001). For a shorter account, see the author's article on Frobisher in the *ODNB I* at https://doi-org.lonlib.idm.oclc.org/10.1093/ref:odnb/10191.

Part II: Toeholds 1603-1651
1. Barry Coward, *The Stuart Age* (Longman, London, 1994) 126-127; Ohlmeyer, 'Colonisation', 138-140.
2. Karen Ordahl Kupperman, 'Providence Island Company', in *Oxford Dictionary of National Biography*, published online 4 October 2007, https://doi.org/10.1093/ref:odnb/95346.
3. Loades, *England's Maritime Empire*, 145.
4. Coward, *Stuart Age*, 171-172.
5. Coward, *Stuart Age*, 199-200.
6. A vivid and detailed, if Anglo-centric, military history of the mainland campaigns is Peter Young and Richard Holmes's *The English Civil War: A Military History of the Three Civil Wars 1642-1652* (Wordsworth Editions, Ware, 2000).
7. Quoted in Ian K. Steele, *Warpaths: Invasions of North America* (Oxford University Press, New York, 1994) 39.
8. Loades, *England's Maritime Empire*, 141; Steele, *Warpath* 37-41.

9. A convenient and scholarly outline of Powhatan political structure and external relations can be found in Helen C. Rountree, *The Powhatan Indians of Virginia: Their traditional Culture* (Kindle edition, University of Oklahoma Press, Norman, 1989) Ch 10, locations 140-152. See also James Horn, 'Tobacco Colonies: The Shaping of English Society in the Seventeenth Century Chesapeake', *OHBE, I,* 170-192, esp. 174-175.
10. Steele, *Warpaths,* 44-45.
11. Proclamation forbidding the planting of tobacco in England and Wales, as being more unwholesome than that imported, and as causing the use of it to spread into the country parts of the kingdom. Calendar of State Papers, James 1, volume 111: page 101, 30 December 1619 Printed [Proc. Coll., No. 74.] British History Online https://www.british-history.ac.uk/cal-state-papers/domestic/jas1/1619-23/pp100-111#high.
12. Steele, *Warpaths,* 45-46.
13. R. C. Simmons, *The American Colonies; From Settlement to Independence* (Norton, New York, 1981) 43; Steele, *Warpath,* 47-48.
14. Simmons, *American Colonies,* 24
15. Alfred A. Cave, *The Pequot War* (University of Massachusetts Press, Amherst, 1996) 49-51.
16. Steele, *Warpaths,* 89-91; Cave, *Pequot War,* 57-61.
17. Cave, *Pequot War,* 144-151.
18. Cave, *Pequot War,* 151-163.
19. Cave, *Pequot War,* 163-167.
20. Simmons, *American Colonies,* 48.
21. Beckles, 'The Caribbean and Britain', 222. Karen Ordhal Kupperman, *Providence Island, 1630-1641: The Other Puritan Colony* (Cambridge University Press, Cambridge and New York, 1993) is a detailed history of this ill-starred enterprise.
22. W. Frank Craven, 'The Earl of Warwick, a Speculator in Piracy', *The Hispanic American Historical Review,* Vol. 10, No. 4 (Nov. 1930), pp. 457-479. Stable URL: https://www.jstor.org/stable/2518450 Accessed: 19-07-2019 22:35 UTC.
23. Hilary McD. Beckles, 'Kalinago (Carib) Resistance to European Colonisation of the Caribbean', Caribbean Quarterly, Vol. 38, No. 2/3 (June-September 1992, 1-3; Alan Burns, *History of the British West Indies* (Allen and Unwin, London, 1965) 35-47; J. H. Parry and P. M. Sherlock, *A Short History of the West Indies* (Macmillan, London, 1956) 48-53.
24. Beckles, 'Kalinago Resistance', 5-6; Burns, *West Indies,* 191-193, 195-196.
25. C. R. Boxer, *The Portuguese Seaborne Empire 1415-1825* (Hutchinson, London, 1969) 112-113.
26. A. R. Disney, *A History of Portugal and the Portuguese Empire: From the Beginnings to 1807: Volume 2 The Portuguese Empire* (Cambridge, Cambridge University Press, 2009) 221-223, 226-231.

The First British Empire

27. Beckles, 'The Caribbean and Britain', 227-231
28. Burns, *British West Indies*, 235-236.
29. Burns, *British West Indies*, 238-243.
30. Burns, *British West Indies*, 243-245. 5847
31. Philip J. Stern, *The Company-State: Corporate Sovereignty and the Early Modern Foundations of the British Empire in India* (Oxford University Press, New York, 2011). The argument is summarised in the Introduction, 5-16.
32. P. J. Marshall, 'The English in Asia', Canny (ed.), *Origins of Empire*, 269-272, 274.
33. John F. Richards, *The Mughal Empire* (Cambridge University Press, Cambridge and New York, 1993) esp. chapters 5 and 6, 94-150.
34. Colin Paul Mitchell, *Sir Thomas Roe and the Mughal Empire* (Area Study Centre For Europe, Karachi, 2000) 146-153.

Part III: Expansion 1651-1713
1. "April 1652: An Act prohibiting. the planting of Tobacco in England", in Acts and Ordinances of the Interregnum, 1642-1660, ed. C. H. Firth and R. S. Rait (London: His Majesty's Stationery Office, 1911), 580. British History Online, accessed July 28, 2019, http://www.british-history.ac.uk/no-series/acts-ordinances-interregnum/p580a.
2. J. R. Jones, *The Anglo-Dutch Wars of the Seventeenth Century* (Longman, London, 1996) 107-144.
3. "Charles II, 1660: An Act for the Encouraging and increasing of Shipping and Navigation", in Statutes of the Realm: Volume 5, 1628-80, ed. John Raithby (s.l: Great Britain Record Commission, 1819), 246-250. British History Online, accessed July 27, 2019, http://www.british-history.ac.uk/statutes-realm/vol5/pp246-250.
4. "Charles II, 1662: An Act for preventing Frauds and regulating Abuses in His Majesties Customes", in Statutes of the Realm: Volume 5, 1628-80, ed. John Raithby (s.l: Great Britain Record Commission, 1819), 393-400. British History Online, accessed July 28, 2019, http://www.british-history.ac.uk/statutes-realm/vol5/pp393-400.
5. "Charles II, 1663: An Act for the Encouragement of Trade", in Statutes of the Realm: Volume 5, 1628-80, ed. John Raithby (s.l: Great Britain Record Commission, 1819), 449-452. British History Online, accessed July 27, 2019, http://www.british-history.ac.uk/statutes-realm/vol5/pp449-452.
6. Rodger, *Command of the Ocean*, 21.
7. Roger, *Command of the Ocean*, 89-90.
8. Michael, J. Braddick, 'The English Government, War, Trade and Settlement', in Canny (ed.) *Origins of Empire*, 298-299. David Loades describes a much more fragmentary development. Loades, *Maritime Empire*, 220-221.

Endnotes

9. John Brewer, *The Sinews of Power: War, Money and the English State, 1688-1783* (Unwin Hyman, London, 1989).
10. The origins, course and results of these campaigns are examined in John Childs, *The Williamite Wars in Ireland* (Hambledon Continuum, London, 2007).
11. Simmons, *American Colonies*, 56-57.
12. Richard L. Haan, 'The "Trade Do's Not Flourish as Formerly": The Ecological Origins of the Yamassee War of 1715', *Ethnohistory*, Volume 28, No 4 (Autumn, 1981) 341-358.
13. Steele, *Warpaths*, 53-58; Warren M. Billings, 'The Causes of Bacon's Rebellion: Some Suggestions', *The Virginia Magazine of History and Biography*, Volume 78, No. 4 (October 1970), 409-435; Matthew Kruer 'Bloody Minds and Peoples Undone: Emotion, Family, and Political Order in the Susquehannock-Virginia War', *The William and Mary Quarterly*, Volume 74, No. 3 (July 2017), pp. 401-436.
14. Steele, *Warpaths*, 120-121.
15. Calder, *Revolutionary Empire*, 332.
16. Steele, *Warpaths*, 89, 96-97; Anderson, 'New England in the Seventeenth Century', 212-213.
17. Steele, *Warpaths*, 97-99; Anderson, 'New England in the Seventeenth Century', 214; Douglas Edward Leach, *Tomahawk and Musket: New England in King Philip's War* (Macmillan, New York, 1958) 4-29; Armstrong Starkey, *European and Native American Warfare, 1675-1815* (UCL Press, London, 1998) 57-67.
18. Steel, *Warpaths*, 108-109; Anderson, 'New England in the Seventeenth Century', 214.
19. Steele, *Warpaths*, 108
20. Arthur J. Ray, *Indians in the Fur Trade; their role as trappers, hunters and middlemen in the lands southwest of Hudson Bay 1660-1870* (University of Toronto Press, Toronto, 1974) 3-7, 27-50; Frank D. Lewis, *Commerce by a Frozen Sea: Native Americans and the European Fur Trade* (University of Pennsylvania Press, Philadelphia, 2010) 69-72.
21. Carlos, Ann M., and Stephen Nicholas. 'Agency Problems in Early Chartered Companies: The Case of the Hudson's Bay Company'. *The Journal of Economic History* 50, no. 4 (1990): 860. http://www.jstor.org.ezproxy2.londonlibrary.co.uk/stable/2122458.
22. Howard H. Peckham, *The Colonial Wars, 1689-1763* (University of Chicago Press, Chicago, 1964) 27-38.
23. Pestana, *Conquest*, Ch3, 65-92.
24. Beckles, 'The Caribbean and Britain', 229.
25. Beckles, The Caribbean and Britain', 233.
26. Dunn, *Sugar and Slaves*, 256-258.
27. Silvia de Groot, Catherine A. Christen and Franklin W. Knight, 'Maroon communities in the circum-Caribbean', in Frank W. Knight

(ed.), *General History of the Caribbean: Vol 3: The Slave Societies of the Caribbean* (UNESCO Publishing and Macmillan, London and Basingstoke, 1997) 174; Beckles, 'Kalinago (Carib) resistance', 5-7.
28. Dunn, *Sugar and Slaves*, 259-262.
29. Burns, *West Indies*, 270.
30. Burns, *West Indies*, 277-279.
31. Richard B. Sheridan, 'The Formation of Caribbean Plantation Society', in Canny (ed.) *Origins of Empire*, 394.
32. Sheridan, 'Caribbean Plantation Society', 397-398
33. P. E. H. Hair and Robin Law, 'The English in Western Africa to 1700', in Canny (ed.) *Origins of Empire*, 249-252.
34. Hair and Law, 'Western Africa', 252-255.
35. https://www.slavevoyages.org/assessment/estimates.
36. Hugh Thomas, *The Slave Trade: The History of the Atlantic Slave Trade 1440-1870* (Weidenfeld and Nicholson, London) 258; Hair and Law, 'Western Africa', 255-257.
37. Alfred Crosby, *Ecological Imperialism: The Biological Expansion of Europe, 900-1900* (Cambridge University Press, 2nd edition, 2004) 136-140, Kindle locations 2183-2208.
38. David Eltis, *The Rise of African Slavery in the Americas* (Cambridge University Press, Cambridge, 2000) 149.
39. Toby Green, *A Fistful of Shells: West Africa From the Rise of the Slave Trade to the Age of Revolution* (Penguin, London, 2020) 175-177.
40. J. D. Fage, *An Introduction to the History of West Africa* (3rd edition, Cambridge University Press, London, 1962) 55, 97-98.
41. Marshall, 'The English in Asia', 277-278.
42. Richards, *Mughal Empire*, 205-208.
43. Richards, *Mughal Empire*, 208-212.
44. James H. Vaughn, 'John Company Armed: The English East India Company, the Anglo-Mughal War and Absolutist Imperialism, c. 1675–1690', *Britain and the World*, Vol 1 (2018), No 1, 101, DOI: 10.3366/brw.2017.0283.
45. Vaughn,' John Company Armed'; Margaret Hunt, 'The 1689 Mughal Siege of East India Company Bombay: Crisis and Historical Erasure', *History Workshop Journal*, Vol 84, Autumn issue, 2017, 149-169.
46. Richards, Mughal *Empire*, 220-224.
47. Stern, *The Company-State*,134-141.
48. Richards, *Mughal Empire*, 196-204.
49. Stern, *The Company-State*, 156-163.

Part IV: Global Power? 1713-1763
1. Brendan Simms, *Three Victories and a Defeat: The Rise and Fall of the First British Empire, 1714-1783* (Allen London, London, 2007).
2. Simms, *Three Victories and a Defeat*, 184-203.

Endnotes

3. Rodger, *Command of the Ocean*, 232; James A. Henretta, *'Salutary Neglect': Colonial Administration under the Duke of Newcastle* (Princeton, 1972) 33-34.
4. The case was made long ago by Oliver M. Dickerson in *The Navigation Acts and the American Revolution* (University of Pennsylvania Press, Philadelphia, first published 1951, paperback edition, 1974) 45-48.
5. Frank O'Gorman, *The Long Eighteenth Century: British Political and Social History 1688-1832* (Bloomsbury, London, 2016) 80-92.
6. Glyn Williams, *The Prize of all the Oceans: The Triumph and Tragedy of Anson's Voyage Round the World* (HarperCollins, London, 1999) is the best modern account of this expedition.
7. O'Gorman, *Long Eighteenth Century*, 92-93.
8. Rodger, *Command of the Ocean*, 266.
9. Rodger, *Command of the Ocean*, 267.
10. Steele, *Warpaths*, 159-16. A recent and very thorough study is David La Vere, *The Tuscarora War: Indians, Settlers and the Fight for the Carolina Colonies* (University of North Carolina Press, Chapel Hill, 2013).
11. Haan, 'The "Trade Do's Not Flourish as Formerly"', 341-358; Steele, *Warpaths*, 165-166.
12. Geoffrey Plank, *An Unsettled Conquest: The British Campaign Against the Peoples of Acadia* (University of Pennsylvania Press, Philadelphia, 2004) 126-130.
13. Fred Anderson, *Crucible of War: The Seven Years' War and the Fate of Empire in British North America 1754-1766* (Faber and Faber, London, 2000) 17-21.
14. Anderson, *Crucible of War*, 17-18
15. Anderson, *Crucible of War*, 11-21.
16. Anderson, *Crucible of War*, 22-24; Simmons, *American Colonies*, 191.
17. For a detailed study of the Albany conference see Timothy. J Shannon, *Indians and Colonists at the Crossroads of Empire: The Albany Congress of 1754* (Cornell University Press, Ithaca, 2000).
18. Stephen Brumwell, *Redcoats: The British Soldier and the War in the Americas, 1755-1763* (Cambridge University Press, Cambridge, 2002) 12-14.
19. For an early balanced assessment of Braddock see Lee Cardell, *Ill-Starred General: Braddock of the Coldstream Guards* (University of Pittsburgh Press, Pittsburgh, 1958, paperback edition 1986) esp. Ch. IX -XIII, 135-265.
20. Anderson, *Crucible of War*, 144-149.
21. Anderson, *Crucible of War*, 225-231.
22. Forbes to Abercromby, [Philadelphia, 15 June 1758], Abercromby Papers, Huntington Library, San Marino, California, AB 356.

23. John Oliphant, *John Forbes: Scotland, Flanders and the Seven Years' War, 1707-1759* (Bloomsbury, London, 2015), esp. Ch. 9-13, pages 97-139.
24. Groot et al, 'Maroon communities', 182; Kenneth M. Bilby, *True-Born Maroons* (University Press of Florida, Gainesville, 2005) 162-174, 261-273; George Metcalf, *Royal Government and Political Conflict in Jamaica 1729-1783* (Longman, London, 1965) 39-63; Brown, *Tacky's Revolt*.
25. Groot *et al*, 'Maroon communities', 182-183.
26. Helen Mckee, 'From violence to alliance: Maroons and white settlers in Jamaica, 1739–1795', *Slavery and Abolition*, Volume 39 (2018), no 1, 27-30.
27. Richard Harding, 'The War in the West Indies', in Mark H. Danley and Patrick J. Speelman (eds.), *The Seven Years' War: Global Perspectives* (Brill, Leiden and Boston, 2012) 297-301; Black, *British Seaborne Empire*, 103; Rodger, *Command of the Ocean*, 232-233.
28. Rodger, *Command of the Ocean*, 236-238.
29. Harding, 'The War in the West Indies', 303-308.
30. Harding, 'The War in the West Indies', 308-310.
31. Harding, 'The War in the West Indies', 310-311.
32. Harding, 'The War in the West Indies', 311-313.
33. Harding, 'The War in the West Indies', 313-316.
34. Harding, 'The War in the West Indies', 316-318; Rodger, *Command of the Ocean*, 285-286; Rodger, *Wooden World*, 50-51.
35. Harding, 'The War in the West Indies'; Rodger, *Command of the Ocean*; Rodger, *Wooden World*, 156.
36. Rodger, *The Command of the Ocean*.
37. G. B. Malleson, *Lord Clive and the Establishment of the English in India* (Clarendon Press, Oxford, 1907) 44-45.
38. Malleson, *Lord Clive*, 45
39. Marshall, 'The British in India', 502.
40. Bryant, 'War in the Carnatic', 96.
41. Bryant, 'War in the Carnatic', 99-102.
42. Marshall, 'The British in India', 501-502.
43. Lloyd, *British Empire*, 76-77.
44. Lloyd, *British Empire*, 90.
45. Robin Law, *The Oyo Empire c. 1600-c. 1836: A West African Imperialism in the Era of the Atlantic Slave Trade* (Oxford University Press, Oxford, 1977) 188-189.
46. I. A. Akinjogbin, *Dahomey and its Neighbours 1708-1818* (Cambridge University Press, Cambridge, 1967).
47. Law, *Oyo Empire*, 225-241.
48. Margaret Priestly, 'The Ashanti Question and the British: Eighteenth Century Origins', *Journal of African History*, Vol 2, No 1, 1961), 35-48; Thornton, *Warfare in Atlantic Africa*, 71.

Endnotes

49. Warren Whatley, 'The Gun-Slave Cycle in the 18th century British slave trade in Africa', *Explorations in Economic History* (MPRA Paper No. 44492, 2013) 1-40: https://mpra.ub.uni-muenchen.de/44492/.
50. P. J. Marshal, *Edmund Burke and the British Empire in the West Indies* (Oxford University Press, Oxford, 2019) 161-164.
51. Joshua D. Newton, 'Slavery, Sea Power and the State: the Royal Navy and the British West African Settlements, 1748-1756', *Journal of Imperial and Commonwealth History*, Vol 41, No 2 (2013), 171-183: https://doi.org/10.1080/03086534.2013.779098.
52. Newton, Slavery, Sea Power and the State', 183-191,
53. James F. Searing, 'The Seven Years' War in West Africa: The End of Company Rule and the Emergence of the *Habitants*', in Danley and Speelman (eds), *The Seven Years' War: Global Views*, 263-291.

Part V: Crisis 1756-1783
1. Paul Kléber Monod, *Imperial Island: A History of Britain and its Empire, 1660-1837* (Wiley-Blackwell, Chichester, 2009) 210.
2. Monod, *Imperial Island*, 212-217.
3. L. Namier and J. Brooke (eds.) *The History of Parliament: The House of Commons 1754-1790* (London, 1964) www.historyofparliamentonline.org/volume/1754-1790/ member/wilkes-john-1725-97.
4. For his life story, see Olaudah Equiano, *The Interesting Life of Olaudah Equiano, or Gustavus Vassa, the African, Written by Himself* (Kindle edition, Modern Library, New York).
5. Alexander Jackman, 'Judging a Judge: A Reappraisal of Lord Mansfield and Somerset's Case', *Journal of Legal History*, Vol 39, No 2 (2018), 140-156; Prest, *Albion Ascendant*, 186.
6. O'Gorman, *Long Eighteenth Century*, 327-328; Thomas Bartlett, '"This famous island set in a Virginian sea": Ireland in the British Empire, 1690-1801', OHBE 2 264-268.
7. I. R. Christie, *Wars and Revolutions: Britain 1760-1815* (Arnold, London, 1982) 100.
8. John Oliphant, *Peace and War on the Anglo-Cherokee Frontier 1756-1763* (Palgrave, Basingstoke, 2001) esp. Chs 5 and 6, 140-190
9. Anderson, *Crucible of War.*
10. John Oliphant, 'The Cherokee embassy to London, 1762', *Journal of Imperial and Commonwealth History*, Vol. 27, No. 1 (January 1999) 1-26.
11. A lively and scholarly account of this conflict, and none too flattering to the British, is Gregory Evans Dowd's *War Under Heaven: Pontiac, The Indian Nations and the British Empire* (John Hopkins University Press, Baltimore and London, 2002).
12. Anderson, *Crucible of War*, 574-579.
13. Anderson, *Crucible of War*, 585-587.

14. Anderson, *Crucible of War*, 647-651.
15. Griffith, *War for American Independence*, 267-268, 297-300.
16. Rodger, *Command of the Ocean*, 335-342, insists that the correct strategic choice would have been to temporarily abandon America to deal with the Bourbons first. Yet with possession of America being regarded as the root of Britain's naval power, that could not have been an obvious option.
17. Simms, *Three Victories and a Defeat*, 612-614.
18. Here Rodger, *Command of the Ocean*, 341-342, argues that by sending Byron at all the government threw away the numerical superiority In home waters achieved by Sandwich's mobilisation. However, ministers' choices were never that simple.
19. William B. Willcox, 'The British Road to Yorktown: A Study in Divided Command', *American Historical Review*, Vol. 52, No. 1 (Oct.1946) 1-35 is still a balanced and perceptive assessment.
20. Captain John Hamilton to the Admiralty [10] November 1775, quoted in Griffith, *War of Independence*, 249.
21. Mike Bunn, *Fourteenth Colony: The Forgotten Story of the Gulf South During America's Revolutionary Era* (NewSouth Books, Montgomery, 2000) esp. Ch 2, pp. 22-43; Paul David Nelson, *General James Grant: Scottish Soldier and Governor of East Florida* (University Press of Florida, Gainesville, 1993) Ch. 4, pp. 45-58.
22. Bunn, *Fourteenth Colony*, Ch. 4, pp. 62-83; Nelson, *James Grant*, Ch 5, pp. 59-72.
23. Bunn, *Fourteenth Colony*, 15-22, 35-37, 45-71; Nelson, *James Grant*, 55-58.
24. Susan Schwartz, 'James Grant, British East Florida, and the Impending Imperial Crisis, 1764-1771', *Florida Historical Quarterly*, Vol. 93, No. 3, (Winter 2015), pp. 327-353.
25. Burnard, *Jamaica*, 121-123.
26. P. J. Marshal, *Edmund Burke and the British Empire in the West Indies* (Oxford University Press, Oxford, 2019) 49-52.
27. Rodger, *Command of the Ocean*, 338-339; Mackesy, *War for America*, 344-347.
28. Mackesy, *War for America*, 389-390, 405-406.
29. Mackesy, *War for America*, 407-408, 414n, 449-463, 473-484.
30. Mackesy, 483-484, 486.
31. Mackesy, *War for America*, 598-604.
32. Compare Rodger, *Command of the Ocean*, 353-354 with Kenneth Breen, 'Rodney, George Bridges, first Baron Rodney', *ODNB*, September 2004, https://doi-org.lonlib.idm.oclc.org/10.1093/ref:odnb/23936.
33. Philip Macdougall, 'British Seapower and the Mysore Wars of the Eighteenth Century', *Mariner's Mirror*, Vol 97, No. 4, 299-314. DOI: 10.1080/00253359.2011.10708961

34. 194 Bryant, *British Power in India*, 192-194.
35. Lloyd, *British Empire*, 90-91.
36. Bryant, *British Power in India*, 186-189.
37. Rodger, *Command of the Ocean*, 356-357.
38. Dalrymple, *Anarchy*, 257.
39. Matthew P. Dziennik, 'Till these Experiments be Made', *The English Historical Review*, Vol. 130, No. 546 (September 2015) pp. 1132-1161; Thornton, *Warfare in Atlantic Africa*, 49.
40. Priestly, 'The Ashanti Question', 48-59.
41. Akinjogbin, *Dahomey and its Neighbours*, 148-156.
42. https://www.slavevoyages.org/assessment/estimates.
43. Philip Edwards (ed.), *James Cook: the Journals. Prepared from the Original Manuscripts by J. C. Beaglehole for the Hakluyt Society, 1955-67* (Penguin, London, 2003) 122-130.
44. Edwards, *Cook*, 130-142.
45. Edwards, *Cook*, 142-156
46. Stephen H. Roberts, *History of Australian Land Settlement 1788-1920* (Macmillan, Sydney, 1968).
47. Glyndwr Williams, 'The Pacific: Exploration and Exploitation', *OHBE I*, 562-563.

Part VI: Recovery and Survival 1783-1815 & Epilogue
1. Christie, *Wars and Revolutions*, 184-185; O'Gorman, *Long Eighteenth Century*, 218.
2. John Coffey, '"Tremble, Britannia!": Fear, Providence and the Abolition of the Slave Trade, 1758-1807', *English Historical Review*, Vol 127, No. 527 (August 2012), pp. 844-881.
3. Eltis, *Rise of African Slavery*, 124.
4. Stanley L. Engerman, 'The Slave Trade and British Capital Formation in the Eighteenth Century: A Comment on the Williams Thesis', *Business History Review*, Vol. 46, No. 4 (Winter, 1972) 430-443; Robert Paul Thomas and Richard Nelson Bean, 'Fishers of Men: The Profits of the Slave Trade', *Journal of Economic History*, Vol 34, No 4 (December 1974) 885-914; David Eltis and Stanley L. Engerman, 'The Importance of Slavery and the Slave Trade to Industrialising Britain', *Journal of Economic History*, Vol 60, No 1 (March 2000), 123-144; J. E. Inikori. *Africans and the Industrial Revolution in England: A Study in International Trade and Economic Development* (Cambridge University Press, Cambridge, 2002); Seymour Drescher, *Econocide: British Slavery in the Era of Abolition* (2nd edition, University of North Carolina Press, Chapel Hill, 2010).
5. O'Gorman, *Long Eighteenth Century*, 328-329.
6. O'Gorman, *Long Eighteenth Century*, 329-330; Christie, *Wars and Revolutions*, 243-244.

7. O'Gorman, *Long Eighteenth Century*, 330-331.
8. Rodger, *Command of the Ocean*, 528-544.
9. Rodger, *Command of the Ocean*, 554-555; O'Gorman, *Long Eighteenth Century*, 250.
10. Vinay Krishin Gidwani, '"Waste" and the Permanent Settlement in Bengal', *Economic and Political Weekly* Vol. 27, No. 4 (Jan. 25, 1992), pp. PE39-PE46
11. Meredith Martin, 'Tipu Sultan's Ambassadors at Saint-Cloud: Indomania and Anglophobia in Pre-Revolutionary Paris', *West 86th: A Journal of Decorative Arts, Design History, and Material Culture*, Vol. 21, No. 1 (Spring-Summer 2014), pp. 37-68. Stable URL: https://www.jstor.org/stable/10.1086/677868
12. Randolph G. S. Cooper, *The Anglo-Maratha Campaigns* (Cambridge University Press, Cambridge, 2004) Chapters 3 and 4, 82-212; Roy, 'Military Synthesis in South Asia: Armies, Warfare, and Indian Society, c. 1740-1849', *Journal of Military History*, Vol. 69, No. 3, 669-674.
13. Henry Reynolds, *The Other Side of the Frontier: Aboriginal Resistance to the European Invasions of Australia* (3rd edition, University of New South Wales Press, 2006).
14. The outlines of this academic set-to can be traced in Geoffrey Blainey, *The Tyranny of Distance: How Distance Shaped Australia's History* (Sun Books, Melbourne, 1966) 1-37; Alan Frost, *Convicts and Empire: A Naval Question* (Oxford University Press, Oxford, 1980; Mollie Gillen, 'The Botany Bay Decision, 1786: Convicts, Not Empire', *English Historical Review*, Vol. 97, No. 385 (Oct. 1982), 740-766; Robert Hughes, *The Fatal Shore: the Epic of Australia's Founding* (Vintage, New York, 1988) 56-67; Alan Atkinson, *The Europeans in Australia: Vol 1: The Beginning* (Oxford University Press, Melbourne, 1997) xv, 58; Alan Frost, *The First Fleet: The Real Story* and *Botany Bay: The Real Story* (Black Inc, Collingwood, Melbourne, 2012).
15. Blainey, *Tyranny of Distance*, 37.
16. Atkinson, *Europeans in Australia*, 147-155
17. Atkinson, *Europeans in Australia*, 165-167; Willey, *When the Sky Fell Down*, 156-182.
18. Blainey, *Tyranny of Distance*, 73-75; Frost, *Convicts and Empire*, 162.
19. Blainey, *Tyranny of Distance*, 75-81.
20. Colin Jones, 'Echoes of a Distant War', *Mariner's Mirror*, Vol 105, No 3 (2019), 331-335 https://doi.org/10.1080/00253359.2019.1613096
21. Gavin Kennedy, *Captain Bligh: the Man and his Mutinies* (Duckworth, London, 1989).

Endnotes

22. Kennedy, *Captain Bligh*, 287-294; Margaret Steven, 'Macarthur, John, 1766-1834', in *ODNB,* https://doi-org.ezproxy2.londonlibrary.co.uk/10.1093/ref:odnb/17337; Alan Atkinson, 'The Little Revolution in New South Wales', *International History Review*, Vol 12, No 1 (February 1990) 65-75.
23. Verena Mauldon, 'Shaping the Domain: The Macquaries, Prestige and Parklands in Colonial Parramatta', *Garden History*, Vol 4, Supplement 1, Autumn 2016, 191-203; Atkinson, *Europeans in Australia*,333-342.
24. Trevor J. Daly, 'Elements of the Past: An Environmental History of the Blue Mountains, Australia', Vol. 1 (PDF, 21.49MB), unpublished PhD thesis, University of Sydney, 2000, http://hdl.handle.net/2123/3650, 48-66.
25. J. C. A. Stagg, *The War of 1812: Conflict for a Continent* (Cambridge University Press, New York, 2012) 1-17. For a British summary of the expansionist case see Lloyd, *British Empire*, 123-125. A more modern British interpretation from an international perspective is Jeremy Black, *The War of 1812 in the Age of Napoleon* (Continuum, London, 2009) 3-43. For a very detailed account of land operations see George F. G. Stanley, *The War of 1812: Land Operations* (Macmillan of Canada, 1983).
26. Elizabeth Mancke, David Bent, and Mark J. McLaughlin, '"their unalienable right and privilege": New Brunswick's Challenge to the Militarization of the British Empire, 1807-1814', Acadiensis, Winter/Spring 2017, Vol. 46, No. 1, 49-72.
27. Burns, *British West Indies*, 564-572; Kim, 'Caribs of St. Vincent', 127-132.
28. Campbell, *Maroons of Jamaica*, Ch. 7, 209-249.
29. Burns, *British West Indies*, 573-579.
30. Burns, *British West Indies*, 557-558, 602-604
31. A useful study of this anti-slavery experiment is Padraic X. Scanlan, *Freedom's Debtors: British Antislavery in Sierra Leone in the Age of Revolution* (Yale University Press, New Haven and London, 2017).
32. Scanlan, *Freedom's Debtors*, 11-12.
33. Scanlan, *Freedom's Debtors*, 24.

Suggested Further Reading

A full bibliography for over two hundred years of empire would go on for ever. This is a select bibliography of secondary works to provide access to more specialist works and academic debates.

General Works and the British Isles
General histories of the British Empire, from foundation to dissolution, include T. O. Lloyd's worthy but unexciting *The British Empire 1558-1995* (Oxford University Press, Oxford, 1996). More dynamic, and with a deliberate maritime focus, is Jeremy Black's *The British Seaborne Empire* (Yale University Press, London and New Haven and London, 2004). *The Oxford History of the British Empire* is a massive multi-volume collection of incisive essays, the first two volumes of which Nicholas Canny (ed.) *The Origins of Empire* and P. J. Marshall (ed.) *The Eighteenth Century* (Oxford University Press, Oxford, 1998) cover the period 1558-c.1815.

David Loades' *England's Maritime Empire: Seapower, Commerce and Policy, 1490-1690* (Longman, 2000) is an attempt to fuse economic, naval and political history to uncover the roots of English maritime expansion. Paul Kléber Monod, *Imperial Island: A History of Britain and Its Empire, 1660-1837* (Wiley-Blackwell, Chichester, 2009) fuses domestic and imperial developments. Frank O'Gorman's *The Long Eighteenth Century: British Social and Political History 1688-1832* (2nd edition, Bloomsbury Academic, 2016) has a mainly domestic focus but offers some useful insights.

There are a number of exciting works putting British imperial growth into the context of European oceanic expansion from the early fifteenth century. J. H. Parry's *The Age of Reconnaissance* (1963) is still a thrilling read, especially for his emphasis upon maritime and navigational technology. G. V. Scammell, *The First Imperial Age: European Overseas Expansion c. 1400-1715* (Routledge, London and New York, 1989) is a little more recent and provides a gripping analysis.

Suggested Further Reading

The subjugation and planting of Ireland to 1660 can be traced in two works by Nicholas Canny:

The Elizabethan Conquest of Ireland: A Pattern Established 1565-1576 (Harvester Press, Hassocks, Sussex, 1976).
From Reformation to Restoration: Ireland, 1534-1660 (Helicon, Dublin, 1987)

The conquests under Elizabeth I and William III are examined in

James O'Neill, *The Nine Years War, 1593-1603: O'Neill, Mountjoy and the Military Revolution* (Four Courts Press, Dublin, 2017).
John Childs, *The Williamite Wars in Ireland, 1688-91* (Hambledon Continuum, London, 2007).

Scotland's role in the English and then the British empire in the seventeenth and eighteenth centuries is discussed by T. M. Devine in *Scotland's Empire 1600-1815* (Allen Lane, London, 2003) and *Recovering Scotland's Slavery Past: The Caribbean Connection* (Edinburgh University Press, Edinburgh, 2015).

For a naval perspective, one can do little better than N. A. M. Rodger's two-volume opus, *The Safeguard of the Sea: A Naval History of Britain 660-1649* Penguin, London, 2004) and *The Command of the Ocean: A Naval History of Britain, 1649-1815* (Allen Lane, London, 2004). John McAleer and Christer Petley, *The Royal Navy and the British Atlantic World, c. 1750-1820* (Palgrave Macmillan, 2016) is a collection of perceptive essays on the Navy's relationship with the North Atlantic empire in the later eighteenth century. For the navy during the Interregnum, see Bernard Kapp, *Cromwell's Navy: The Fleet and the English Revolution, 1648-1660* (Clarendon Press, Oxford, 1989).

The Atlantic world approach, which stresses the interconnectedness of polities and peoples bordering and using the Atlantic Ocean, can be useful for students of imperial history. David Armitage, *Greater Britain: Essays in Atlantic History* (Ashgate, Aldershot, 2004) and David Armitage and Michael Braddick (eds) *The British Atlantic World 1500-1800* (Palgrave, Basingstoke, 2002) are rewarding. J. H. Elliot's *Empires of the Atlantic World: Britain and Spain in America 1492-1830* (Yale University Press, New Haven and London, 2006) provides an enlightening comparison.

Works linking the internal history of the three British kingdoms with foreign policy include J. R. Jones, *Britain and the World 1649-1815* (Fontana, London, 1980), which is still a stimulating synthesis. Brendan Simms, *Three Victories and a Defeat: The Rise and Fall of the First British Empire, 1714-1783* (Allen Lane, London, 2007) makes an important, if rather strident, case for the primacy of foreign policy in all domestic and imperial decision-making.

For the Elizabethan period, see Kenneth R. Andrews, *Elizabethan Privateering: English Privateering During the Spanish War 1585-1603* (Cambridge University Press, Cambridge, 1964) and David Beers Quinn, *Set Fair for Roanoke: Voyages and Colonies, 1584-1606* (University of North Carolina Press, Chapel Hill, 1985). James McDermott, *Martin Frobisher: Elizabethan Privateer* (Yale University Press, New York and London, 2001) depicts failed attempts to open a north-west passage and to colonise Baffin Island.

North America

The most complete and useful general history is still R. C. Simmons, *The American Colonies: From Settlement to Independence*, originally published in 1976 and still going strong in a paperback edition (Norton, New York and London, 1981).

Perhaps the best introduction to Native America in the context of empire is Ian K. Steele's *Warpaths: Invasions of North America* (Oxford, New York, 1994), while Armstrong Starkey's *European and Native American Warfare, 1675-1815* (UCL Press, London, 1998), compares military cultures. Patrick M. Malone's *The Skulking Way of War: Technology and Tactics Among the New England Indians* (Johns Hopkins University Press, Baltimore and London, 1993) examines Native adaptations to the settler military challenge.

Seventeenth-century conflicts between Native Americans and settlers are the subjects of Ethan A. Schmidt, 'Cockacoeske, Weroansqua of the Pamunkeys, and Indian Resistance in Seventeenth-century Virginia', *American Indian Quarterly*, Vol. 6, No. 1 (Summer 2012) 288-317. Matthew Kruer, 'Bloody Minds and Peoples Undone: Emotion, Family, and Political Order in the Susquehannock-Virginia War', *William and Mary Quarterly*, Vol 76, No 3 (July 2007) deals with the conflict often overshadowed by its result: Bacon's Rebellion. Metacom's War is examined in James D. Drake, *King Philip's War: Civil War in New England 1675-1676* (University of Massachusetts Press, Amherst, 1999), and Lisa Brooks, *Our Beloved Kin: A New History of King Philip's War* (Yale University Press, New Haven and London, 2018). A respected but older account of King Philip's War is D. E. Leach, *Flintlock and Tomahawk: New England in King Philip's War* (Macmillan, New York, 1958).

David La Vere, *The Tuscarora War: Indians, Settlers, and the Fight for the Carolina Colonies* (University of North Carolina Press, Chapel Hill, 2013) examines the complex threads of that conflict. Richard L. Haan's 'The "Trade Do's Not Flourish as Formerly": The Ecological Origins of the Yamasee War of 1715', *Ethnohistory*, Vol 28, No 4 (1981), 341-358, rightly emphasises the intrusions of hunters, settlers and their livestock in provoking frontier conflict. J. Russell Snapp, *John Stuart and the Struggle for Empire on the Southern Frontier* (Louisiana State University Press, Baton Rouge and London, 1996) and John Oliphant, *Peace and War on the Anglo Cherokee*

Suggested Further Reading

Frontier, 1756-1763 (Palgrave, Basingstoke, 2001) point to the centralisation of Indian policy during and after the Seven Years' War. Stephen Brumwell's *Redcoats: The British Soldier and the War in the Americas, 1755-1763* (Cambridge University Press, Cambridge, 2002) explains how the British army adapted to wilderness warfare. Eighteenth-century frontier issues are also discussed in Fred Anderson's *Crucible of War: The Seven Years' War and the Fate of Empire in British North America* (Faber and Faber, London, 2001), which also locates the Revolution in the experience of the war.

Richard White's *The Middle Ground: Indians, Empires and Republics in the Great Lakes Region, 1650-1815* (Cambridge University Press, Cambridge, 1991) is important for an understanding of the workings of Native societies of the Great Lakes region, and particularly for the way they understood relations with the French and British. The tragic outcome of early British mismanagement in that region is discussed by Gregory Evans Dowd in *War under Heaven: Pontiac's War, the Indian Nations and the British Empire* (John Hopkins University Press, Baltimore and London, 2002). Colin Calloway's *Crown and Calumet: British-Indian Relations 1783-1815* (University of Oklahoma Press, Norman, 1987) takes the theme up to and beyond the Treaty of Ghent.

Around Hudson's Bay, where there were traders and no settlers, relations tended to be more business-like than violent. Arthur J. Ray's *Indians in the Fur Trade; their role as trappers, hunters and middlemen in the lands southwest of Hudson Bay 1660-1870* (University of Toronto Press, Toronto, 1974) is comprehensive, while Ann M. Carlos and Frank D. Lewis, *Commerce by a Frozen Sea: Native Americans and the European Fur Trade* (University of Pennsylvania Press, Philadelphia, 2010) examines the behaviour of Indians as producers and consumers and uses statistical methods to calculate the fur trade's ecological impact.

The American Revolution is the subject of innumerable volumes, scholarly and popular. For origins, perhaps the most convenient starting point is Colin Bonwick, *The American Revolution* (Palgrave, Basingstoke, 2005). For British and American perspectives, compare Piers Mackesy, *The War for America, 1775-1783* (first published 1964, Bison edition, University of Nebraska Press, Lincoln and London, 1993) with Samuel B. Griffith, *The War for American Independence: From 1760 to the Surrender at Yorktown in 1781* (University of Illinois Press, Urbana and Chicago, 2002). The later has in-depth coverage of causes as well as of the war. The argument that the conflict arose originally out of imperial centralisation during the Seven Years' War is strongly made in Anderson, *Crucible of War*.

The Anglo-American War of 1812-1814 is conveniently covered by Jeremy Black in *The War of 1812 in the Age of Napoleon* (Continuum, London and New York, 2009). There is a wealth of military detail and analysis in George F. G. Stanley, *The War of 1812: Land Operations* (Macmillan of Canada, 1983) J. C. A. Stagg's *The War of 1812: Conflict for a Continent* (Cambridge

University Press, New York, 2012) is thorough but perhaps gives insufficient weight to the aggressive expansionism of the American 'War Hawks'.

The West Indies and Bermuda

J. H. Parry and P. M. Sherlock, *A Short History of the West Indies* (Macmillan, London, 1956) is dated but provides a good overview, while Richard S. Dunn's *Sugar and Slaves: The Rise of the Planter Class in the English West Indies, 1624-1713* (Jonathan Cape, London, 1973) explores the development of plantation societies. George Metcalf in *Royal Government and Political Government in Jamaica 1729-1783* (Longman, London, 1965) examines factional rivalries and tensions between royal government and assemblies in the eighteenth century. Sir Alan Burns's *History of the British West Indies* (Allen and Unwin, London, 1965), though tending in places towards a chronicle of governorships, adds a huge amount of detail. In *Providence Island 1630-1641: The Other Puritan Colony* (Cambridge University Press, Cambridge, 1993) Karen Ordahl Kupperman examines the rise and fall of the short-lived privateering base.

More exciting is modern scholarship on slavery and the resistance of slaves, Maroons and Caribs. The third volume in UNESCO's General history of the Caribbean, Frank W. Knight's *Slave Societies of the Caribbean* (UNESCO Publishing and Macmillan, London and Basingstoke, 1997) is strong on social structures. Carla Gardina Prestana's *The English Conquest of Jamaica: Oliver Cromwell's Bid for Empire* (The Belknap Press, Cambridge Massachusetts and London, 2017) explores not only the planning and execution of the invasion, but also the dogged guerrilla resistance of former slaves, the predecessors of the Maroons. Maroon history is covered meticulously in Mavis C. Campbell, *The Maroons of Jamaica: A History of Resistance, Collaboration and Betrayal, 1655-1796* (Africa World Press, Trenton, 1990). Trevor Burnard, *Jamaica in the Age of Revolution* (University of Pennsylvania Press, Philadelphia, 2020) is strong on Tacky's Revolt, the Second Maroon War and their contexts. The work overlaps to some extent with Vincent Brown's *Tacky's Revolt: The Story of an Atlantic Slave War* (The Belknap Press, Cambridge Massachusetts and London, 2020) which examines earlier slave revolts from the late seventeenth century, the growth and nature of Maroon societies, and argues that all these, including the 1760 upheaval, drew on African military experience.

A venerable work providing a sound, readable account of developments in Bermuda is Henry C. Wilkinson, *The Adventurers of Bermuda: a history of the island from its discovery until the dissolution of the Somers Island Company in 1684* (Oxford University Press, London, 1958).

The Slave Trade and Slavery

A handy short introduction to this complex and contentious subject is Jeremy Black's *The Slave Trade* (Social Affairs Unit, London, 2005).

Suggested Further Reading

More challenging is the most famous work on the subject, Eric Williams's *Capitalism and Slavery* (University of North Carolina Press, Chapel Hill, 1943). Williams argued that the trade was fundamental to the whole economy of eighteenth-century Britain, and that it was abolished only because it became economically redundant. The argument has been refined by Joseph Inikori in *Africa and the Industrial Revolution in England: A Study in International Trade and Economic Development* (Cambridge University Press, New York, 2002). It has been strongly challenged by those who argue that abolition was economically damaging, including Seymour Drescher in *Econocide: British Slavery in the Era of Abolition* (2nd edition, University of North Carolina Press, Chapel Hill, 2010).

Professor Philip Curtin was the first to attempt an objective estimate of the scale of the slave trade in *The Atlantic Slave Trade: A Census* (University of Wisconsin Press, 1969). Curtin has been challenged by those, including Inikori, who find his numbers far too low. Two leading scholars, David Eltis and David Richardson, have produced a magnificent *Atlas of the Transatlantic Slave Trade* (Yale University Press, New Haven and London, 2010), using maps and statistical tables to demonstrate the scale of the trade, the African origins of the slaves and their destinations. Their up-to-date estimates can be most conveniently consulted on the Slave Trade Data Base at https://www.slavevoyages.org/.

Africa

Many scholars view West African societies through the lens of the slave trade, including David Eltis in *The Rise of African Slavery in the Americas* (Cambridge University Press, Cambridge, 2000). However, other works look at African economies, polities and societies as entities in their own right. The clearest succinct survey is still probably J. D. Fage, *An Introduction to the History of West Africa* (4th edition, Cambridge University Press, Cambridge, 1969). while A. G. Hopkins, *An Economic History of West Africa* (2nd edition, Routledge, Abingdon, 2019) is more sophisticated and up-to-date. Toby Green's *A Fistful of Shells: West Africa from the Rise of the Slave Trade to the Age of Revolution* (Penguin, London, 2017) stresses the significance of cowrie shell currency. Studies of individual West African states include I. A. Akinjogbin, *Dahomey and its Neighbours 1708-1818* (Cambridge University Press, Cambridge, 1967) and Robin Law, *The Oyo Empire c. 1600-c. 1836: A West African Imperialism in the Era of the Atlantic Slave Trade* (Oxford University Press, Oxford, 1967).

Asia

Any reader new (or even not-so-new) to the vast complexities of the subcontinent's history could do much worse than to begin with Douglas Peer's little book in the Seminar Studies Series, *India Under Colonial Rule, 1700-1885* (Routledge, Abingdon, 2013). John F. Richards, *The Mughal*

Empire (Cambridge University Press, Cambridge, 1993) offers a more detailed account of government from the sixteenth century. For initial English contacts, see Colin Paul Mitchell, *Sir Thomas Roe and the Mughal Empire* (Area Study Centre For Europe, Karachi, 2000).

The East India Company's rise from vulnerable client to major Indian power is discussed by G. J. Bryant in *The Emergence of British Power in India 1600-1784: A Grand Strategic Interpretation* (Boydel Press, Woodbridge, Suffolk, 2013). Randolf G. S. Cooper, *The Anglo-Maratha Campaigns and the Contest for India: The Struggle for Control of the South Asian Military Economy* (Cambridge University Press, Cambridge, 2003) homes in on the campaigns of 1803. William Dalrymple's *The Anarchy: The Relentless Rise of the East India Company* (Bloomsbury, London, 2019) is thoroughly researched and well-written, though his attempt to liken the EIC to a modern multinational company is rather strained.

Two collections of essays by Indian and British scholars provide a deeper insight into the complex issues and debates confronting historians of the sub-continent:

Seema Alavi (ed.), *The Eighteenth Century in India* (Oxford University Press, New Delhi, 2002).
P. J. Marshall (ed.), *The Eighteenth Century in Indian History* (Oxford University Press, New Delhi, 2003).

Australasia and the Pacific
Eighteenth-century British penetration of the Pacific is the subject of a series of essays edited by Glyndwr Williams and Alan Frost, *Terra Australis to Australia* (Oxford University Press, Oxford, 1988).

The first part of Geoffrey Blainey's ground-breaking *The Tyranny of Distance: How Distance Shaped Australia's History* (Sun books, Melbourne, 1966), which challenged the traditional convict-dumping interpretation of the founding of New South Wales, attracted an almost universal storm of protest from established historians. Since then, Alan Frost has uncovered a mountain of evidence to demonstrate that Blainey was not only right, but that his claims for a strategic factor were too modest. His most important academic work was *Convicts and Colonies: A Naval Question, 1776-1811* (Oxford University Press, Oxford, 1980) but his material is more easily approached through *The First Fleet: The Real Story* and *Botany Bay: The Real Story* (both published by Black Inc., Collingwood, Melbourne, 2012). Ripostes to his arguments, whether academic or popular and exceptionalist, tend to brush his evidence aside rather than to grapple with it.

Index

Abenaki, 53, 101, 137, 140
Abercromby, Ralph, 149–150, 295
Aborigines, 240–242, 264, 266–268, 272
Acadians, 137–138, 140
Accra, 175
Act of Union 1800, 253–255
Adams, Samuel, 197, 199, 201, 203
Addington, Henry, 255
Afghan, 71, 164, 230
Afghanistan, 71, 118
Agra, 72, 262
Aix-La-Chapelle, Peace of 1748, 129–130, 167, 177
Akyem, 175
Albany, 92, 95, 99–100, 130, 137, 141, 143, 146–149, 207, 295
Albany conference, 130
Algiers, 79, 82–83
Allada, 112, 114–116, 174
Allahabad, 171
Allegheny River, 143
Amboina, 70
America, 11, 13, 26–27, 30, 34, 39, 45, 47, 49, 51, 54–55, 58, 63, 66, 77, 79, 81, 83, 85, 88–89, 91–93, 96, 113, 125, 128, 130, 132–135, 137, 139, 141, 143, 145, 147, 149, 151, 160–163, 169, 177, 181–182, 184, 188, 190, 193, 196–200, 202–203, 210, 213, 221–224, 229, 270, 273–274, 283, 286, 290, 295, 298, 303–305

Amerindians, 46, 51, 94, 97, 116, 135, 222, 267, 275–276
Amherst, Jeffrey, 150, 152, 161, 194
Amiens, Peace of 1802, 255, 269, 280
an accompanying Declaratory Act / Declaratory Act 1766, 199
Anderson, Fred, 140–141, 295
Andros, Edmund, 92, 97
Anglo-American War 1812-1814, 256, 274–277, 286, 301, 306
Anglo-Dutch Wars, 78, 83, 91, 105, 111, 292
Angola, 110
Annapolis Royal, 101, 137–138
Anson, George, 128, 132, 160, 162, 238, 295
Antigua, 62, 64, 67, 106, 108–109, 223–224, 226
Appalachian Mountains, 134, 193–194, 214
Arcot, 164, 167–168, 170
Argaum, 262
Arnold, Benedict, 207, 209, 216
Asante (Ashanti), 116, 173, 175, 235–236, 281, 296, 299
Asia, 10–11, 13, 20, 34–36, 46, 69, 71, 73, 77, 82, 99, 117, 133, 209, 250, 284–285, 288, 292, 294, 300, 308
Assam, 117–118
Assaye, 261–263
Assiniboin, 97
Attingal, 121
Aurangzeb, 117–119, 121, 164–165
Axim, 113

Bacon's Rebellion, 90, 96, 145, 293, 304
Bahadur Shah, 165
Bahamas, 62–63, 81, 281
Balcarres, Alexander Lindsay, Earl of, 278–279
Baltic, 81, 98, 111–112, 250, 267
Bank of England, 85
Banks, Joseph, 239–240, 266, 271
Bantam, 70, 72–73
Barbados, 44, 62–67, 88, 102–103, 106–107, 109, 153, 160, 223–224, 226
Barbary pirates, 79, 82
Barbuda, 64
Bass Strait, 268–270
Bass, George, 268–269
Batavia, 121, 238, 266, 271
Bathurst, 272
Bay of Bengal, 232, 285
Bayley, C. A., 287
Bence Island, 173, 235
Bengal, 73, 117–118, 120–122, 132–133, 164–166, 169–171, 185–186, 228–232, 262, 285, 300
Benin, 110–111, 114–116, 173, 175, 236
Bennelong, 267
Bennington, 209
Bermuda, 40, 50, 63, 306–307
Bhonsola, 119
Bihar, 118, 171
Bijapur, 119–120
biological factors, 114
Black Carib War, 222, 224
Black Carib War, 222–224
Blainey, Geoffrey, 265, 267, 300
Blake, Robert, 79
Bligh, William, 271–272, 300
Blue Mountains, 272, 301
Board of Control, 249, 263
Board of Trade, 84–85, 96, 127, 130, 140, 142–143, 154, 177, 190, 194, 236, 248
Bombay, 73, 82, 84, 117, 119–121, 166, 230–233, 249, 262, 285, 294

Bonny, port of, 115
Boston, 56–57, 95, 101, 137, 140, 157, 183, 186, 197, 199–201, 203–205, 211, 296
Boston Massacre, 200
Boston Port Act, 201
Boston Tea Party, 201
Botany Bay, 240–241, 250, 265–266, 268, 300, 309
Bouquet, Henry, 193–194
Braddock, Edward, 130, 146–148, 295
Bradstreet, John, 138
Brahmaputra River, 118
Brandt, Joseph, 211, 275
Brandywine Creek, 208
Brazil, 10, 63, 65–66, 156
Brest, 130, 132, 151, 188, 209–210
Brooklyn Heights, 206
Buccaneering, 104–106
Bunker Hill, 204–205
Burgoyne, John, 204, 207–209, 212, 217
Bussy, Comte de, 167–168
Bute, Earl of, 182–183
Butler, Walter, 211
Buxar, 171, 229, 232
Byng, John, 131
Byron, John, 188, 210, 224

Cadigal, 241
Calabar, 112
Calcutta, 121, 169–170, 229, 231, 258, 260
Calvert family, 51
Camden, 211
Canada, 94–95, 97–101, 129–130, 132–134, 138–139, 141, 143, 146, 150–152, 163, 196, 201, 204–205, 207, 209–210, 214–215, 217–219, 249, 256, 273–276, 287, 301, 306
Canada Act, 249, 274
Cape Breton Island, 11, 101, 133–134, 138
Cape Coast, 112–115, 175, 177, 236
Cape Colony, 255, 287
Cape Fear, 89, 205–206

Index

Caravel, 12
Caribbean, 10, 28, 31, 36, 39, 41, 44, 49, 61–63, 65–67, 77, 79, 81, 83, 91, 102–103, 105–107, 109, 111–112, 114, 122, 128, 132–133, 136–137, 139, 153–155, 157–163, 188, 190, 196, 202, 209–213, 217, 220–227, 236, 249, 251, 256, 273, 277, 280, 286, 291–294, 296, 298, 301, 303, 306
Carleton, Guy, 205, 207, 209, 213, 215–216
Carnatic, 133, 164, 167–171, 228, 231–232, 259, 261, 296
Carolina, 31–32, 81, 88–89, 91–92, 127, 134–136, 141–142, 146, 193, 195, 205–206, 211–212, 290, 295, 299, 304, 307
Carteret, Lord, 128
Cartwright, John, 189
cattle, 14, 24, 61, 66, 89–90, 94, 104, 109
Cayman Islands, 81
Cayuga, 141
Ceded Islands, 220–222
Ceylon (Sri Lanka), 190, 232
Chanda Sahib, 167–168
Chandanagore, 169–170
Charleston, 135–136, 189, 200, 206, 211, 213
Cherokee, 146, 152, 194, 204, 297
Cherry Valley, 211
Chickasaws, 218
China, 231, 256, 266, 270, 284–285, 288
Chittagong, 120–121
Choctaws, 218
Clarkson, Thomas, 250
Clay, Henry, 274–275
Clinton, Henry, 204–207, 209–213, 223
Clive, Robert, 132, 166–171, 228–229, 231, 233, 296
Coercive Acts, 200
Collaborators, 25, 29, 154, 229, 240, 285

Company of Merchants Trading to Africa, 110, 176
Concord, 203
Congregationalists, 60–61, 135, 138
Congress of Augusta, 218
Connecticut, 53, 57–61, 95–96, 100, 138–139, 205, 209
Continental Army, 204, 208, 210–211
Convicts, 265, 268, 271–272, 300, 309
Cook, James, 233, 239–242, 250, 264, 266, 299
Coote, Sir Eyre, 170
Coramantees, 108
Corn Laws, 286
Cornwallis, Charles, 1st Marquess Cornwallis, 190, 205–208, 211–213, 226, 249, 254, 257–260
Cornwallis, HMS, 270
Coromandel Coast, 73–74, 122, 166–167, 232–233
Corsica, 187
cotton, 63, 66, 73, 81, 108, 113, 235, 248, 251, 281, 285
Cowpens, 212
Cree, 97
Creek, 46, 136, 205–206, 208, 218
Creeks, 135–136, 194, 218
Cromwelll, Oliver, 44, 57, 67, 78–80, 128, 303, 306
Crosby, Alfred, 114, 294
Crown Point, 146–150, 207, 216
Cuba, 79, 103–104, 155, 158, 161, 217, 225, 279
Cuddalore, 167, 233
Cudjoe, 108, 155–157
Cumberland, Duke of, 129, 132, 145
Curaçao, 280
Currency Act, 197

D'Estaing, Admiral, 211, 223–224
Dahomey, 115–116, 173–175, 236, 296, 299, 308
Dallas, K. M., 265
Darien, 113
De Grasse, Admiral, 212, 226–227
Deane, Silas, 205

311

Declaratory Act 1720, 189
Declaratory Act 1765, 198–199, 201
deerskin trade, 218
Delaware, 53, 81, 93, 137, 141, 148, 207–208
Delaware River, 53, 93, 137, 141, 207–208
Delhi, 119, 165, 171, 228, 230, 261–263, 308
Demerara, 226, 280
Denkyira, 175
Dettingen, 129
Dhurag, 272
Dickinson, John, 199
Dinwiddie, Robert, 142–143
Diwani, 171
Dixcove, 112, 115, 175–176
Dominica, 133, 161, 163, 220–221, 223–224, 227, 277, 280
Dominion of New England, 85, 88, 145
Dorchester Company, 56
Drake, Francis, 23, 28–31, 33–34, 103, 289–290, 304
Drescher, Seymour, 251, 286, 299
Duke of York, 84, 89, 91–92, 98, 105, 112
Dunkirk, 80, 129
Dunmore, John Murray, Earl of, 195, 204
Dupleix, 130, 166–169

East Florida, 217–219, 298
East India Company, 36, 70, 73–74, 78, 84, 111, 117, 119–121, 125, 133, 164, 166, 170, 183–186, 189, 191, 200, 228, 230–231, 247, 250, 257, 287, 294, 308
Egremont, Charles Wyndham, Earl of, 194–195
Egypt, 253, 255, 260
Elizabeth I, 11, 15, 20–22, 24–28, 30–32, 35–36
Ellis, Henry, 194
Elmina, 112, 114
Eltis, David, 111, 113–115, 251, 294
emancipists, 271–272

Equiano, Olaudah, 186, 297
Essequibo, 226
'exclusives', 272

Falkland Islands, 187, 242
Family Compact, 127
Fante, 116, 177, 235–236, 281
First Anglo Dutch War, 78
First Anglo-Mughal War, 120
First Coalition, 252
First Maratha War, 231
First Maroon War, 155
Fiscal-military state, 85
fishing, 32, 36, 45, 54–56, 58, 61, 97, 117, 129, 138, 177, 190, 241, 267
flax, 77, 81, 98, 233, 250, 264–267
Flinders, Matthew, 269
Florida, 31–32, 51, 89, 125, 129, 133–134, 136, 162, 190, 196, 214–215, 217–219, 225, 286, 296, 298
Fontenoy, 129, 139
Forbes, John, 150, 193–194, 295–296
Fort Beauséjour, 140, 146–147
Fort Chartres, 134, 218
Fort Duquesne, 143, 146, 150, 193
Fort Edward, 147–148, 209
Fort Frontenac, 150
Fort James, 48, 113, 235
Fort Niagara, 146–147, 210–211, 274, 276
Fort Pitt, 150, 194
Fort Severn, 99
Fort St David, 121, 166–168
Fort St George, 74, 117, 228
Fort St Louis, 113, 234
Fort Stanwix, Treaty of 1768, 195
Fort Toulouse, 218
Fort William, 121–122, 148–149
Fort William Henry, 148–149
Fox, Charles James, 191, 247
Fox, Henry, 145
France, 12–15, 19–22, 26, 40–41, 44, 63, 77, 79–80, 84–85, 87, 94–95, 97–101, 111, 125–130, 132–134, 138–143, 145–146, 150–153,

Index

158, 161, 178, 182, 187–188, 190, 205–206, 213, 219, 224, 226, 234, 239, 248, 250–257, 259–260, 275, 277–278, 280
Francis, Phillip, 230–231
Franklin, Benjamin, 139, 144, 195
Frederick II, 128–130, 132
Freeman's Farm, 209
Free Ports Act, 220
Freetown, 281–282
Free trade, 108, 234, 247–248, 251, 255
Frobisher, Martin, 35, 290, 304
Frost, Alan, 265–266, 285, 300
fur trade, 11, 36, 53, 55, 57, 59, 61, 83, 88, 91–92, 94–95, 97–99, 101, 214, 293, 305

Gage, Thomas, 79, 147, 198, 201, 203–204
Gambia, 110–114, 234, 281
Gambia Adventurers, 112
Gambia River, 110
Ganges River, 117, 120, 122, 171, 230, 262
Gaspée, revenue cutter, 200
Gates, Horatio, 209–211
George III, 181–183, 190, 202, 213, 242, 254, 279
Georgia, 127, 136, 194, 198, 201
Germain, Lord George, 187, 190, 205, 207, 209
Germantown, 208
Ghent, Treaty of, 276, 286
Gibraltar, 80, 82–83, 86, 125, 127, 131, 188, 190, 213, 224–225, 227
Ginger, 81, 113, 221
Glen, James, 146
Glorious Revolution, 85, 96, 120, 252
Glorious Revolution in America, 96
Goa, 69, 72, 119, 121
Golconda, 73, 119–120
gold, 10, 28–30, 32–33, 35, 40, 45–46, 66, 108, 110–116, 142, 173, 175–177, 235–236, 281–282, 287

Gold Coast, 108, 110–112, 114–116, 175–177, 235–236, 281, 287
Gordon riots, 189
Gorée, 112–113, 133, 160, 176–178, 234–235
Grand Ohio Company, 195
Grant, James, 193, 217, 223–224, 298
Grattan's parliament, 189, 253
Graves, Samuel, 212, 226
Great Barrier Reef, 241
Green, Toby, 115, 294
Grenada, 64, 161, 163, 221–222, 224, 227, 277
Grenville, George, 182–183, 196–198
Guadeloupe, 64, 133, 153, 155, 160–163, 177, 220, 225, 277
Guiana, 62–63, 67, 256, 280
Guilford Court House, 212
Guinea, 28, 110–111
Guinea Company, 110
Gujurat, 117, 262
Gulf of St. Lawrence, 147, 151
gum arabic, 66, 110, 114, 177
Gundungurra, 272
Gwiyagal, 241

Haarlem Heights, 207
Haidar Ali, 228
Halifax, George Montagu Dunk, Earl of, 140, 145, 197, 234
Halifax, Nova Scotia, 140, 149, 204, 210
Hancock, John, 197
Hard Labor, Treaty of 1768, 195
Harlow, Vincent T., 284–285
Hastings, Warren, 186, 228–233, 249
Havana, 31, 79, 125, 133, 157–158, 161, 163, 220, 225
Hawkesbury River, 268
Headright system, 217
Henry, Patrick, 198, 201
Hessian, 207
Hillsborough, Earl of, 195, 199
Hindu, 73–74, 118, 165, 167, 169
Hispaniola, 65–66, 79, 102–104
Hobart, 269

Holdernesse, Robert D'Arcy, Earl of, 145
Holkar, 261–262
Holmes, Robert, 112
Honduras, 106, 162, 278
Hood, Admiral Samuel, 212, 226–227
Howe, Richard, 205–206, 210–211
Howe, Lord William, 204–211
Hudson Bay Company, 84, 88, 98, 274
Hudson River, 53, 91–92, 129, 134, 137, 139–140, 146, 148–150, 205, 207–209, 216–217, 276
Hudson-Lake Champlain corridor, 129, 134, 216, 276
Hughes, Edward, 232–233, 250, 265
Hughes, Lotte, 113–114
Hunter, John, 268, 270
Hyderabad, 164–165, 167–168, 170, 231–232, 259–260

Illinois, 134, 141, 194–195, 305
Illinois Company, 195
indentured servants, 51, 64–66, 106–107, 217
Indigo, 66, 72, 80–81, 108, 113, 217–218, 235, 248
Indonesia (East Indies), 30, 70, 74, 78, 121, 239, 256, 270
Inikori, J. E., 251, 299, 307
Ionian Islands, 256
Irish reform and the Act of Union, 253
Iroquois (Haudenosaunee), 90–93, 100, 135, 137, 140–142, 152, 195, 204, 211
ivory, 10, 72, 74, 111–112, 114, 282, 285

Jacobites, 85–87, 126, 129, 139
Jaghirdars, 165
Jaghirs, 165
Jahangir, 72–73
Jamaica, 79, 102–109, 153–159, 186, 220, 223, 225–226, 277–278, 280, 282, 296, 298, 301, 306
James Bay, 98–99
James Island, 112

James River, 46, 48, 212
Jamestown, 46–48, 91
Java, 121, 256
Jay treaty, 252, 286
Johnson, William, 137, 147–148, 195
Johnstone, George, 218

Kalinago (Carib), 64, 106, 108, 222–224, 291, 294
Kentucky, 195–196, 275
King Philip's War, 94, 96–97, 137, 293, 304
King's Mountain, 212
Kingston, 154, 159
Kormantin, 111–112
Kuku-yalanji, 241

Lafayette, Comte de, 212
Lagos, 115, 132, 151
Lake Champlain, 129, 134, 146, 152, 205, 207–208, 216, 276
Lake Erie, 47, 142–143, 275
Lake George, 148–150, 208
Lake Oneida, 207
Lake Ontario, 141, 146–147, 150, 207, 249, 274, 276
Lake, Gerard, Viscount Lake, 261–262
Lally, Comte de, 170
language groups, 264, 268, 272
Leeward Islands, 62–64, 66, 107–108, 153, 157, 220, 223–226, 280
Lenape (Delawares), 53, 93, 137, 141–142, 146, 150
Lexington, 203
Ligonier, Field Marshal John, Earl Ligonier, 132, 160
Lisbon, 69, 80, 86
Lochaber, Treaty of 1770, 195
Logwood, 106, 133
Long Island, 54, 58, 96, 206
Loudoun, John Campbell, Earl of, 148–150
Louis XIV, 85–87, 121, 126, 130, 137
Louisbourg, 129, 132, 134, 138–140, 149–150, 160–161

Index

Louisiana, 125, 133, 146, 162, 217, 219, 255, 274–275, 305
Lower Canada, 249, 274, 276
Loyalists, 190, 203–208, 210–213, 219, 226, 247, 249, 273–274, 276, 281

Macarthur, John, 271, 301
Macassar, 70
Macaulay, Zachary, 282
Macquarie, Lachlan, 271–272, 301
Madison, James, 274–276
Madras, 74, 117, 121, 129, 164, 166–170, 184, 228, 230–233, 249, 259
Maine, 45, 53–54, 92, 100, 137, 216, 276
maize, 32, 53, 61
Malabar coast, 84, 121, 259
Malta, 83, 253, 255–256
Mangalore, 232–233, 260
Mangalore, Treaty of 1784, 233
Manhattan Island, 206
Mansfield judgement, 186
Mansfield, John Murray, Earl Mansfield, 186, 297
Maoris, 240, 265
Marathas, 119, 121–122, 164–166, 168, 171, 228, 230–233, 259–263, 285, 300, 308
Marlborough, John Churchill, Duke of, 86–87
Martinique, 64, 109, 133, 153, 155, 160–162, 177, 220, 223, 225–226, 256, 277
Marwar, 118
Maryland, 41–42, 51, 88–89, 137, 139, 148, 193
Massachusetts, 42, 53–61, 84, 88–89, 95–97, 100, 137–140, 147, 149, 197, 199–201, 215, 291, 304, 306–307
Massachusetts Bay, 42, 53–56
Massachusetts Bay Company, 42, 56
Massachusetts Government Act, 201
Masuliputam, 73, 170

Mauritius, 184, 231–232, 250, 256, 260, 266, 270
Mayflower, 55
McCardell, Lee, 146
McKee, Helen, 156, 296
Mercantilism (see also Navigation System), 286
Metacom (King Philip), 92, 95, 304
Mewar, 119
Mexico, 10, 28–29, 217
Mi'kmaq, 137–138, 140
Miami, 142–143
Mingos, 143
Minorca, 83, 87, 125, 130–133, 160, 187–188, 190, 224, 253, 256
Mir Jafir, 170–171
Mir Qasim, 171
Mississippi, 125, 133–134, 141–142, 152, 196, 215, 217–219, 275, 277, 285
Mobile, 217, 219, 224, 232
Mohammed Ali Khan, 168
Mohawk, 94–95, 100, 137, 148, 150, 207, 211
Mohawk Valley, 137, 148, 150
Mohegan, 53, 59–60
Molasses Act, 127, 137, 154, 163, 182, 196–197
Moluccas, 30, 70
Monmouth Court House, 210
Monongahela River, 146
Montcalm, Marquis de, 148–151
Montgomery, Richard, 216
Montreal, 100, 132, 134, 139, 146, 150–152, 161, 204, 214–216, 274, 276
Montserrat, 62, 67, 106–107, 109, 226
Moore's Creek Bridge, 205–206
Moose Factory, 99
Morgan, Henry, 105
Moroccan/Morocco, 10, 12, 82
Mosquito coast, 162
Mourning war, 90
Mughal army, 71
Mughal Empire, 45, 70–71, 117–118, 120–122, 166, 292, 294, 308

315

Murray, James, 151–152, 215
Muslim/Islam, 10, 16, 71, 74, 117–118, 164–165, 169, 171, 228
Mysore, 74, 168, 171, 184, 228, 231–233, 259–261, 298

Nanny, 155–156
Nanny Town, 155
Napoleon, 251–252, 254–256, 260, 270, 273, 275, 301, 306
Narragansett, 53, 59–60
Natchez, 218
National Debt, 122, 181–182, 196, 247–248, 257
Naval stores, 82, 89, 98, 221, 233, 250, 265–267
Navigation Ordinance, 44, 67, 77–78, 81
Navigation System, 78, 80–81, 83, 91, 108, 125, 127, 153, 183, 192, 221, 225, 247–248, 286, 295
Negapatam, 232
Nelson, Horatio, 253, 255, 260
Nevis, 62–63, 67, 109, 226, 280
New Brunswick, 249, 274, 301
New Caledonia, 264
New England, 36, 39, 42, 44, 53–62, 65, 81, 85, 88, 91–92, 94–97, 99–101, 129, 135, 137–140, 145, 147–148, 153, 196–197, 199, 201, 204–205, 207, 211, 275, 293, 304
New Hampshire, 57–58, 88, 96, 100–101, 137–138, 143
New Haven, 57–58, 61, 289, 301–304, 307
New Holland, 240, 242
New Jersey, 88, 91, 93, 96, 137, 139, 143, 203, 207–208, 211
New Netherland, 51, 53, 58, 83–84, 88, 91
New Orleans, 133–134, 141, 152, 218–219, 286
New South Wales, 242, 265–266, 269–271, 285, 287, 300–301, 309
New South Wales Corps, 270

New York, 81, 84–85, 88, 91–93, 96, 99–101, 129, 137–139, 143, 147–150, 157, 188, 197–201, 203–207, 209–213, 226, 289–293, 297, 300–301, 303–304, 306–307
New Zealand, 238–240, 242, 264–265, 270, 287
Newcastle, Thomas Pelham-Holles, Duke of, 127–128, 131–132, 138, 145, 182
Newfoundland, 11, 32, 36, 54–55, 87, 101, 125, 190, 239, 249, 276, 287
Newport, Rhode Island, 211–212
Newton, John, 250
Niagara, 146–147, 210–211, 274, 276
Nicaragua, 63, 225
Niger Delta, 112, 115
Nikmucks, 95
Nizam of Hyderabad, 164–165, 167–168, 170, 228, 231, 259–261
Nobte de Dios, 29
Nootka Sound, 250
Norfolk Island, 264–267
North America, 11, 26–27, 39, 45, 47, 49, 51, 63, 66, 81, 83, 85, 88–89, 91–93, 125, 130, 133–135, 137, 139, 141, 143, 145, 147, 149, 151, 160–161, 163, 169, 188, 193, 196–197, 203, 210, 221–224, 229, 273, 283, 286, 290, 295, 304–305
North Briton, 182
North Carolina, 31–32, 89, 135, 141–142, 205–206, 212, 290, 295, 299, 304, 307
North ministry, 185, 188–189, 195, 200–201, 219
North, Frederick, Lord North, 195, 200, 212, 220, 236
North-West Company, 274
North-west passage, 31, 34–36, 46, 238, 242, 304
Northern Circars, 168, 170
Nova Scotia, 53, 87, 101, 125, 129, 134, 137–140, 214, 216, 219, 249, 273–274, 279, 281–282

Index

Ohio, 130, 134, 140–143, 150, 193–196, 201, 215, 252, 274–275
Olgethorpe, James, 136
Oneida, 207
Onondaga, 93, 100, 140–142
Opechancanough, 49–50
Oriskany, 209
Orissa, 118, 165, 171
Oswego, 147–148, 152, 209
Otis, James, 197
Ottoman Empire, 10, 15, 82, 187, 255
Oudh (Awadh), 165, 171, 230, 285
Oxenham, John, 29, 290
Oyo, 116, 173–175, 296, 308

Panama, 29–31, 105, 154
Panipat, 228
Paoli, 208
Paris, Peace of 1763, 125, 133, 152, 162–163, 178, 182
Paris, Treaty of 1783, 190, 213
Parramatta, 268, 272, 301
Parry, J. H., 10, 289, 306
Pemulwuy, 268
Penang, 284–285
Pennsylvania, 88, 92–93, 135, 137–139, 141–144, 148, 150, 193, 199, 203, 293, 295, 305–306
Pensacola, 190, 217–219
Pequot, 53, 59–60, 94, 291
Pequot War, 59–60, 94, 291
Persian, 69, 71–73, 164–165
Peshwa of Poona, 231, 261
Philadelphia, 93, 137, 139, 148–150, 194, 200–201, 205, 207–208, 210, 293, 295, 305–306
Philadelphia Campaign 1777, 208
Philip, Arthur, 266–268
pirates and privateers, 16, 25, 29, 31, 34, 41, 45, 59, 63, 109, 113, 138, 161, 238, 290, 304, 306
Pitt's India Acts, 1784 and 1786, 249
Pitt, William (the Elder), 128, 132–133, 149, 160, 183–184, 199

Pitt, William, the younger, 247–256, 258, 265–266, 273, 277, 284, 286
Plassey, 132, 169–170, 171
Plymouth Colony, 54
Pocahontas, 48–49
Poland, 128, 132, 187
Pollilur, 232
Pondicherry, 166–167, 170, 231
Pontiac (Obwandiyagtiac), 194
Pontiac's War, 218, 305
Poona (Pune), 231–232
population, 46–47, 49–51, 57–58, 60, 64, 67, 89–94, 103, 106, 108, 119, 131, 134–135, 137, 140–141, 186, 198, 214, 217–218, 222, 229, 251, 282, 287
Port Jackson, 241, 266
Port Philip, 269
Porto Bello, 29, 79, 105, 128, 154, 158
Portugal, 10, 16, 30, 80, 82, 86, 111, 256, 292
Portuguese, 10, 12–13, 15, 27–28, 61, 65–66, 69–73, 80–82, 84, 110, 115, 119, 121, 156, 196, 236, 238, 291–292
Powhatan (Wahunsenacawh, 46–50, 53, 291
Powhatan confederacy, 46, 48–49
Pragmatic Sanction, 129
Presbyterianism, 42, 44, 85
Princeton, 207, 295
Privy Council, 21, 27–28, 35, 39, 42, 49, 85, 194, 221
Protectorate, 80, 82–83, 106
Prussia, 127–128, 130, 133, 187, 252
Puritan, 40–41, 54–55, 58–59, 63, 88, 94, 97, 291, 306

Quaker, 92–93, 97, 141
Quartering Acts, 1765 and 1774, 198–199, 201
Quebec, 87, 92, 100–101, 132, 139–140, 149–151, 196, 201, 204, 210, 214–216, 221–222, 239, 249, 274
Quebec Act, 196, 201, 215, 274

Quiberon Bay, 132, 151
Quinn, David, 33, 290

Ragunath Rao, 231–232
Rajput, 71, 118, 164
Redwood, 66, 110–112
Regulating Act, 185, 229
Reinart, William, 113–114
Restoration, 77–81, 83–85, 87, 89, 92, 96, 98, 233, 303
Rhode Island, 57–58, 60, 96, 101, 138, 211–212
rice, 90, 122, 135, 228, 235, 282
Richardson, David, 111, 307
Richelieu River, 152, 216
Roberts, Stephen, 242
Rochambeau, Comte de, 212
Rockingham, Marquis of, 183, 185, 189–190, 198–199, 227
Rodney, George, 188, 213, 225–227, 298
Roe, Sir Thomas, 45, 73, 292, 308
Roger, N. A. M., 31, 82, 131, 290
Rohilla War, 230
Rohillas, 230
Royal African Company, 84, 89, 106, 112–113, 173
Royal Proclamation 1763, 49, 214, 217, 221, 291
Royalists, 44, 66–67, 78–79, 83, 88, 111
Rum Rebellion, 271
Rump Parliament, 44, 67, 74, 77
Rupert House, 99
Rupert's Land, 87, 97–98, 125
Rupert, Prince of the Rhine, 67, 87–89, 97–99, 111, 125
Russia, 98, 127, 132–133, 187, 255–256, 288
Ryswick, Treaty of 1697, 113

Sagadahoc, 45, 53
Saints, Battle of the, 227
Saxe, 129
Schuyler expedition, 216
Scindia, 233, 261–262

St Augustine, 217–218
St. Domingue, 109, 155, 220, 277–280
St. Eustatius, 63, 109, 220, 225, 280
St Kitts, 62–64, 67, 87, 109, 125, 224, 226
St. Lawrence River, 53, 100–101, 134, 138, 150–152, 216, 239, 274, 276
St. Leger, Brigadier General Barry, 207, 209
St Lucia, 62, 64, 161, 210, 223–227, 256, 277
St Vincent, 301
Salem, 56–57, 97
Salstee, 121
Sandwich, John Montagu, Earl of, 184, 187–188, 209
Santiago, 103, 158
Saratoga, 139, 208–209
Savannah, 103, 116, 136, 176, 211, 213, 224
Scottish Company Trading to Africa and the Indies, 113
Second Coalition, 253
Second Maroon War 1795-1796, 278
Sekondi, 115
Seneca, 141
Senegal, 113–114, 133, 160, 177, 190, 234–235
Senegal River, 113
Senegambia, 110, 176, 234–235
Separatists, 42, 54–56, 58
Shah Alam II, 171, 259, 261–262
Sharp, Granville, 186, 250, 281, 287
Shawnee, 137, 195, 211, 276
Shelburne, William Petty, Earl of, 183, 190–191, 213, 248
Sherbro, 110–111
Sherbro River, 110
Sheridan, Richard, 189
Shirley, William, 138–140, 147–149
Shivaji, 119, 164
Shore, John, 250, 260
Sierra Leone, 110, 173, 273, 279, 281–282, 287, 301
Sierra Leone Company, 281
Sikh, 118, 164–165

Index

silver, 28–30, 32–33, 41, 45, 69, 71, 74, 80, 132
Singapore, 285
Siouan language group, 47, 97
Siraj-ad-Daula, 169–170
Slave Coast, 112, 114, 173–175
slave resistance, 107
slave trade and slavery, 10, 27–29, 51, 64–67, 82–83, 90, 95, 102–116, 133, 135–137, 148, 153–159, 161, 163, 173–177, 181, 186–187, 204, 217–218, 220–222, 234, 236–237, 247–248, 250–252, 273, 277–278, 280–284, 286–287, 293–294, 296–297, 299, 301, 303, 306–308
Smith, John, 23, 46, 48, 203, 286
Solander, David, 239
Somerset, James, 186
Sons of Liberty, 198, 200
South Carolina, 127, 134–136, 146, 193, 195, 206, 211–212
South Sea Company, 128, 154, 173
Spain, 10–13, 16, 19, 25–28, 30, 36, 39–41, 44–45, 54, 63, 69, 71, 77, 79–80, 86–87, 105, 111, 125–128, 132–133, 136, 157–158, 161–162, 187–188, 190, 209, 213, 219, 250, 252, 256, 270, 303
spices, 10, 69–70, 112, 173, 285
Stamp Act, 183, 198, 218, 220
Stamp Act Congress, 198
Stamp Act crisis, 183, 198
Staten Island, 206
Steel, Ian K., 91, 290
Steelboys, 189
Straits of Gibraltar, 82
Straits of Malacca, 69, 285
Strategic outlier theory, 266
Stringer Lawrence, Major, 167–168
Suffren, Pierre André de, 232, 250, 265
sugar, 45, 61, 64–66, 77, 80–81, 88, 102–103, 105–109, 111, 113, 127, 133, 137, 153–154, 159–160, 163, 196–197, 220–222, 235, 278, 281–282, 293–294, 306
Sugar (American Duties) Act, 196

Sugar Revolution, 65–66, 77, 88, 111
Surat, 71–73, 117–122, 231–232
Surat, 71–73, 117–122, 231–232
Surinam, 67, 84, 280
Suspending Act, 199
Susquehannah Valley, 141
Susquehannock War, 90
Sydney, 266–272, 299, 301

Tacky's Rebellion, 154
Tahiti, 239–240
Tamar River, 269
Tanaghrisson, 143
Tangier, 80, 82–83
Tanjor, 167–168
Tea Act, 186, 200, 229
Tecumseh, 276
Temne, 281–282
terra nullius, 242
Thornton, Henry, 250
Ticonderoga, 148, 150, 204, 207–208, 216
Tipu Sultan, 233, 258, 300
Tobacco, 45, 49–51, 61, 63–66, 78, 81, 88–89, 91, 108, 142, 221, 236, 248, 291–292
Tobacco Ordinances, 78
Tobago, 133, 161, 163, 190, 221, 226, 255–256, 277
Tone, Theobald Wolfe, 253–254
Tories, 83, 87, 93, 101, 125, 181–182, 205
Tortuga, 41, 63
Toulon, 86–87, 125, 130–132, 151, 188, 209–210, 252, 266
Townshend legislation, 198–199
Townshend, Charles, 183–184, 198–200
Trafalgar, Battle of, 255
Travancore, 259
Trelawny Town, 157, 278
Trenton, 207, 306
Trinchinopoly, 168
Trincomalee, 190, 232–233
Trinidad, 46, 255, 280
Tunis, 79, 82
Tupia, 240

Tuscarora, 135, 295, 304
Tuscarora War, 135, 295, 304

United Colonies of New England, 60, 94
United Irishmen, 253–254
United States of America, 190, 192, 213, 227, 248–249, 252, 256, 273–277, 285
Upper Canada, 274–276
Ushant, 188, 209–210, 225
Utrecht, 87, 100–101, 109, 125–129, 131, 133–134, 137, 154, 173
Utrecht, Peace of 1713, 87, 100–101, 109, 125–129, 131, 133–134, 137, 154, 173

Van Diemen's Land (Tasmania), 238, 265, 268–269, 271
Vandalia, 195
Vera Cruz, 217
Vermont, 139, 274
Vernon, Edward, 158, 160
Vienna, 126–127, 256
Vijayanagar empire, 74
Vinegar Hill, 254
Virgin Islands, 62, 67, 81
Virginia, 29, 32, 35, 40, 42, 44–45, 49–51, 54–55, 63, 65–66, 78, 88, 90, 96, 130, 135–136, 139, 142–143, 148, 150, 195, 197, 204, 212, 281, 291, 293, 304
Virginia Capes, 212
Volunteer movement, 189

Wabash Company, 195
Wadgaon, 232
Walking Purchase, 141
Walpole, Robert, 126, 128, 158
Wandiwash, 170
War of American Independence, 186–188, 202–203, 205, 207, 209, 211, 213, 215, 220, 223, 236, 281
War of the League of Augsburg, 86, 100, 109

War of the Polish Succession, 128
War of the Spanish Succession, 86, 100, 109, 113–114, 122
Warren, Peter, 139
Washington, George, 142–143, 146, 150, 195, 202, 204, 206–208, 210–213
Wedgwood, Josiah, 250
Wellesley, Arthur (later Duke of Wellington), 261–262
Wellesley, Richard, Lord Mornington, 260
Wesley, John, 186
West Africa, 10, 27, 66, 84, 110–111, 113–115, 133, 173, 175, 177, 190, 209, 234–237, 251, 281–282, 294, 297, 307
West Florida, 214, 217–218, 225
West India interest, 163
Western Design, 67, 79, 102, 128
Whigs, 83, 120, 125–126, 181–183, 185, 188, 191, 252
Whiteboys, 189
Whitetail deer, 89–90
Whydah, 114, 116, 174, 236
Wilberforce, William, 250–251, 280
Wilkes, John, 182–183
Williams, Eric, 251, 287, 307
Williams, Glyndwr, 243, 295, 299, 308
Williams thesis, 251, 287, 299
Windward Islands, 64
Winneba, 115
Wolfe, James, 150–151, 253–254
Woollen Act, 85, 127
Wyoming Valley, 142, 211
Wyvill, Christopher, 188–189, 247

Yamasee, 90, 135, 305
York Fort, 99–100
Yorktown, 189–190, 202, 212–213, 219, 226, 257, 298, 305

Zamindar, 121, 258